The Principles of New Ethics II

From Descartes to Spinoza, Western philosophers have attempted to propose an axiomatic systemization of ethics. However, without consensus on the contents and objects of ethics, the system remains incomplete. This four-volume set presents a model that highlights a Chinese philosopher's insights on ethics after a 22-year study. Three essential components of ethics are examined: metaethics, normative ethics, and virtue ethics.

This volume is the first part of the discussion on normative ethics. The author sets out to discuss morality, and shows how the reasoning behind it can be both good and bad for human society from various perspectives. A system of an ultimate standard of morality is introduced and it is shown that where there are conflicts between different moral norms that cannot be compromised, people undoubtedly sacrifice less important moral norms to follow more fundamental and important moral norms or principles. The ultimate standard of morality is also the ultimate value standard for the evaluation of the goodness or badness of state institutions. Justice is the fundamental value standard to measure state institutions. Equality is the most important justice.

The Chinese version of this set sold more than 60,000 copies and has exerted tremendous influence on the academic scene in the People's Republic. The English version will be an essential read for students and scholars of ethics and philosophy in general.

Wang Haiming is a professor at the Department at Philosophy at Peking University, China, and a specially appointed professor at Sanya University, China, mainly studying ethics and political philosophy. He has written ten academic monographs, including *Stateology; A Theory of Justice;* and *The Economic Characteristics of China.* Email: wanghaimingw@sina.cn

China Perspectives

The *China Perspectives* series focuses on translating and publishing works by leading Chinese scholars, writing about both global topics and China-related themes. It covers Humanities & Social Sciences, Education, Media and Psychology, as well as many interdisciplinary themes.

This is the first time any of these books have been published in English for international readers. The series aims to put forward a Chinese perspective, give insights into cutting-edge academic thinking in China, and inspire researchers globally.

Titles in philosophy currently include:

Leaping Over the Caudine Forks of Capitalism
Zhao Jiaxiang

Theories and Practices of Scientific Socialism
Zhao Jiaxiang

The Principles of New Ethics III
Normative Ethics II
Wang Haiming

The Principles of New Ethics I
Meta-ethics
Wang Haiming

The Principles of New Ethics II
Normative Ethics I
Wang Haiming

The Metaphysics of Philosophical Daoism
Kai ZHENG

For more information, please visit www.routledge.com/series/CPH

The Principles of New Ethics II
Normative Ethics I

Wang Haiming

LONDON AND NEW YORK

This book is published with financial support from the Chinese Fund for the Humanities and Social Sciences.

First published in English 2021
by Routledge
2 Park Square, Milton Park, Abingdon, Oxon OX14 4RN

and by Routledge
52 Vanderbilt Avenue, New York, NY 10017

Routledge is an imprint of the Taylor & Francis Group, an informa business

© 2021 Wang Haiming

Translated by Yamin Wu, translation polished by Matthew Hood and proofread by Yang Aihua.

The right of Wang Haiming to be identified as author of this work has been asserted by him in accordance with sections 77 and 78 of the Copyright, Designs and Patents Act 1988.

All rights reserved. No part of this book may be reprinted or reproduced or utilised in any form or by any electronic, mechanical, or other means, now known or hereafter invented, including photocopying and recording, or in any information storage or retrieval system, without permission in writing from the publishers.

Trademark notice: Product or corporate names may be trademarks or registered trademarks, and are used only for identification and explanation without intent to infringe.

English Version by permission of The Commercial Press.

British Library Cataloguing-in-Publication Data
A catalogue record for this book is available from the British Library

Library of Congress Cataloging-in-Publication Data
A catalog record has been requested for this book

ISBN: 978-1-138-33162-4 (hbk)
ISBN: 978-0-429-44720-4 (ebk)

Typeset in Times New Roman
by Newgen Publishing UK

 Printed in the United Kingdom by Henry Ling Limited

Contents

List of figures   vi

PART I
The standard of moral value: The goal of morality   1

1 The concept of morality   3
2 The origin and goal of morality   29
3 The ultimate standard of morality: The ultimate value standards of the state institutions   61

PART II
The substance of moral value: Fact of ethical behavior   81

4 Human nature   83

PART III
Moral value and moral norms: Excellent morality is the moral norms that conform to moral value   135

5 Good: General principles of morality   137
6 Justice and equality: Fundamental value standard of state institutions   175

Index   267

Figures

1.1	The structure of morality	11
1.2	The categories of morality	15
2.1	The dynamic structure of society	40
4.1	The law of *degrees of love*	112
5.1	The six principles of good and evil	145
6.1	The principle of contribution	213
6.2	The proof of the justness of the principle of justice	237

Part I
The standard of moral value
The goal of morality

1 The concept of morality

1.1 Definition of morality

What is morality? Actually, it is the most difficult problem in modern ethics. The term morality, as Pojman points out, quoting Whiteley, "Cannot be given any single exhaustive definition of analysis in the terms of marks of the moral."[1] But the scientific ethics can never be established without solving this problem. When examined carefully, however, one will find that the key to solving it rests on understanding the following three relationships: morality and ethics, morality and "ought," morality and law.

1.1.1 Morality and ethics

Most scholars believe that morality and ethics share the same concepts. Judging from the etymological meanings of morality and ethics in western languages, this is true: both "mos," which is Latin for "morality," and "ethos," which is Greek for "ethics," mean moral "character, spirit, mores, customs, etc." In the final analysis, both terms refer to the norm that ought to be for people's actions: they are externalized as the social mores and customs, and internalized as each individual's virtue and moral traits.

However, in China the etymological meaning of morality and ethics are somewhat different. The original meaning of the Chinese character "伦" (pronounced "lun") is "the generations in family." The first Chinese dictionary, the *Analytical Dictionary of Characters (ShuoWenJieZi)*, annotates that: "ethics is the generations in family." It is extended to mean "interpersonal relationships." For instance, the "Five ethics" are five different interpersonal relationships: the monarch and his subjects, father and son, husband and wife, elderly and young, and friends. The original meaning of the Chinese character "理" (pronounced "li") is to carve jade stone. The *ShuoWenJieZi* annotates it as "Carving jade stone ... the un-carved jade is called unprocessed jade stone ("璞" pronounced "pu")," and it is also extended to mean renovation and the veins of matters, such as repair and the veins of wood, the veins of skin, etc., and is then further extended to mean laws and rules. It is the natural law of facts: "It is nothing else but necessity ... it is the never changing law of the nature of heaven, earth, human beings and all matters."[2] It also means the rules for human action that ought to be: "Only the rules for human action that ought to be, are law."[3] Therefore, in China, the so-called ethics, in terms of its etymological meaning, is the laws of human behavioral facts and the norms for human action that ought to be.

The original meaning of the Chinese character "道"(pronounced "dao") is road. The *ShuoWenJieZie* annotates it as the "road, on which people walk." Then it is extended as both a law and rule. The original meaning of the Chinese character "德" (virtue) is to obtain, to get. That is why Zhu Xi (朱熹) said: "'德' (virtue) is something to be obtained; when you follow morality, you will obtain virtue in your mind."[4] The Chinese character "道" (road, law, rule, etc.) in "道德 (morality)" obviously only refers to the norms of action that ought to be, not to the laws of the facts of matters, because virtue cannot be obtained through a person who acts in accordance with the laws of facts, but only obtained by acting according to the norms that ought to be.

Thus, both the Chinese etymological meanings of "道 (road, law, rule, etc.)" and "德 (virtue)" in "道德(morality)," refer to the norms of action that ought to be. The difference is that, as the external norm, "道 (law and rule)" is the social norm which still has not transformed into the stable internal mental state of each individual, and that, as the internal norm, "德(virtue)" is the social norm that has already transformed into the stable internal mental state of each individual. Consequently, the etymological meaning of morality is nothing more than the norms of action that ought to be.

Ethics and morality, judging from their etymons in the West, have the same meaning in that both refer the norms of action that ought to be. While, in China, ethics and morality have different meanings in that ethics is related to morality as a whole to a part. Ethics, which is understood as the whole, has two meanings in that it is concerned with both the law of behavioral facts and the norms of *behavioral oughts*, while morality, which is understood as the part, has only one meaning in that it is concerned the norms of *behavioral oughts*. However, what are the connotations of morality and ethics from the point of view of each concept?

Obviously the connotations of morality and ethics conform to their Chinese etymological meanings: ethics is the law of behavioral facts and the norms of *behavioral oughts*, while morality is just the norms of *behavioral oughts*. For instance, in terms of the concept of the "Five Ethics" in ancient China**,** we can only say that the relationships between the monarch and his subjects, father and son, husband and wife, elderly and young, and between friends are five kinds of ethical relationships, but cannot assert that they are five different kinds of moralities. We can assert that the relationship between the monarch and his subjects comes under the category of ethics, but not that of morality. Morality is different in that it is only the "righteousness" that exist between the monarch and his subjects. Ethics, then, is both the relationship of the monarch and his subjects, as well as the righteousness of monarch and his subjects. This is because the relationship between the monarch and his subjects is the fact of the interpersonal relationship, while the righteousness that exists between monarch and his subjects is the norm of the interpersonal relationship that ought to be. Morality, then, is only the interpersonal relationship that ought to be, while ethics includes both the interpersonal relationship that ought to be and the facts of the interpersonal relationships.

1.1.2 Morality and ought

Are "the laws of human behavioral facts and the norms of human behavioral oughts" a definition of the concept of ethics? The answer is in the affirmative, but it is a little too broad and not exact enough. Not all the laws of human behavioral facts and the norms of human behavioral oughts are ethics. It is obvious that some behavioral norms, such as that one ought to eat solid food with chopsticks or a knife and fork, does not belong to the category of ethics. Ethics only refers to the laws of human behavioral facts and the norms of human behavioral oughts which have social utility. This definition of the ethics is exact, in the same sense, "the norms of human behavioral oughts" does not make for an exact definition of the morality. This is because not all norms of human behavioral oughts are morality. In discussing the distinction between morality and cultural customs Swann gives the example that westerners are used to eating with knives and forks, while many cultivated Indians are used to eating with fingers. These two different kinds of habits undoubtedly are in the ambit of the norms of behaviors that ought to be, but not the ambit of morality.[5]

Then, what is the distinction between morality and these norms of behaviors that ought to be? As Swann states, the distinction is whether there is social importance.[6] In other words, the distinction is whether the behavior has the utility of advantage or disadvantage to others, oneself and society: morality is the norm of behavioral oughts which have social utility insofar as the norm is an advantage or disadvantage to each individual and society. Imagine, Why does morality have nothing to do with our choice to use chopsticks, knives and forks, or fingers to eat? Isn't it because eating these three different ways does not factually have an advantage or disadvantage to the existence and development of society—that it has no social utility? Then, why are honesty and cheating, justice and injustice, humanity and inhumanity, etc., in the ambit of moral norms? Is it not because these norms do have the utility of advantage or disadvantage to each individual and to society?

However, is "having the social utility of advantage or disadvantage" the only distinction between *morality* and *ought*? The answer is no. Because whether a kind of norm of behavioral oughts is the moral norm, not only depends on whether it has the social utility of advantage or disadvantage, it also depends on who makes the norms and who recognizes them. If a certain behavioral norm has a social utility that is made or recognized by society, then, no matter how absurd and wrong the norm is, it is morality; if it is not made or recognized by society but only by one person, then, no matter how excellent the norm is, it is not morality but only the maker's own *ought*.

For instance, if a society makes or recognizes the behavioral norm that "females ought to bind their feet," then, no matter how absurd it is, it is morality. Thus, if a female binds her feet, she follow the morality and thus is moral. On the contrary, if she makes the opposite behavioral norm that "females ought not bind their feet" which has not been recognized by society, it is only her own behavioral norm. No matter how right and good it is, it is not morality. If she does not bind her feet, it is a breach of the morality and she might be judged as unprincipled.

So it is very obvious that another fundamental feature distinguishing *morality* from *ought* is that *morality* certainly is made or recognized by society, while *ought* is not necessarily made or recognized by society: morality is the norm made or recognized by society concerning human actions with social utility that ought to be. In view of this feature, morality is surely social: a social contract (an instrument of society) made by at least two or more persons that ought to be observed by everyone. Conversely, the behavioral norms that ought to be are not necessarily social. They can completely be daily rules made for oneself such as by an individual who has isolated himself or herself in one way or other from society.

In a similar fashion, William K. Frankena emphasizes that "morality is sometimes defined as an instrument of society as a whole, as if an individual, family, or social class cannot have a morality or moral action-guide of its own that is different from that of its society."[7] Morality is a social contract (an instrument of society) that everyone ought to be observed, which is the fundamental characteristic that *morality* is different from *ought*. The earliest philosopher to discover this feature was Epicurus, who said that "Justice is the expedient contract to prevent mankind from doing harm to one another."[8] Hume was another who wrote that justice originates from the human contract,[9] as had Gilbert Harman, who, in advocated the theory of "Moral Bargaining," stating that "My thesis is that morality arises when a group of people reach an implicit agreement or come to an tacit understanding about their relations with one another."[10]

1.1.3 Morality and law

Is the proposition that "morality is the norm made or recognized by society concerning human behavioral oughts with social utility" a correct definition of morality? It is still not the case. That is because, as the jurists have declared, laws are also the behavioral norms that *ought to be:* "Laws are the norms, rules and standards that determine how people ought to behave in the society."[11] Paulsen has noticed this common ground shared by both morality and law: "What the moral law declares is ought to be ... undoubtedly [is] also what the law ought to express."[12] What then is it that differentiates morality from law?

The concept of morality 7

In the final analysis, the difference between morality and law is that whether there is any kind of compulsion, namely *power*. This is because, the so-called power, as is generally known, is a coercive force possessed only by rulers and recognized by society to force the ruled to obey. In this way, on the one hand, from the point of view that power is the coercive force possessed only by the ruler which compel people to follow, power has the necessity and is the force that people must follow; on the other hand, from the point of view that power is recognized by society and agreed by people, power has the so-called "legitimacy," power is the force that people ought to follow. In short, power is a force that people must and ought to follow. Given this definition, laws are the norms of power; they are the behavioral norms that ought to be followed and must be followed. On the contrary, morality is a non-power norm that merely ought to be followed.

This is determined by the nature of behaviors that are regulated by morality and law. Morality regulates all human actions with social utility while law only regulates parts of them, namely those actions with important social utility. Just think, why is it categorically a law that "one ought not to commit murder and arson," but more a question of morality rather than an enforced law that "one ought to give one's seat to those who are old, weak, ill or disabled"? Isn't because murder and arson have important social utility, but giving one's seat is not an important social utility? Therefore, Henry Sidgwick said:

> in a well-organized society, the most important and indispensable rules for social action will have the compulsion of law while the actions that are less important are maintained by the morality with factual basis. Law seems to give to some extent the skeleton or frame-work, which Morality clothes or fills it.[13]

What law regulates is the behavior with important social utility, which determines that law have various compulsions: these vary from weakest compulsions (i.e., compulsions on public opinion), to the most powerful compulsions (i.e., compulsions on human action); and that the compulsion of law is the compulsion of the compulsory organization, is the compulsion only owned by the rulers and leaders of society, in the final analysis, is the compulsions of power and the compulsions that *ought to be and must be*. As Ou Yanggu (欧阳谷) states: "Law is the norms of social life and enforced by social force (power)."[14] On the contrary, what morality regulates is all actions with social utility, which determines that morality only has the weakest compulsions (i.e., compulsions on public opinion). Obviously, it is a kind of compulsion without compulsory organization, which is owned by all members of the whole society; in the final analysis, it is non-power compulsion, and the compulsion that *merely ought to be*.

By making a comprehensive survey on the similarities and differences of *morality*, *law*, and *ought*, we are able to draw the conclusion that morality is the behavioral norm with social utility that *ought to be* followed, but *not*

8   The standard of moral value

necessarily be followed, and is therefore a non-power behavioral norm. This is the definition of morality. If we start with this definition, it will be easier to solve the core problems of normative ethics, that is, the structure of morality, and the basis, ways, and postulations for making excellent morality.

1.2 The structure of morality

1.2.1 The basic structure of morality: Moral norm and moral value

The definition of morality—as a non-power norm for human actions with social utility that *ought to be*—indicates that morality falls into the normative category: that *morality, moral norm, and moral contract* are all the same concept. Therefore, the so-called structure of morality is also the structure of a moral norm. How, then, is a moral norm constituted? A moral norm is man-made, it is a contract made or recognized by people. Consequently, to know how a moral norm is constituted, we should know first how and on what basis people make a moral norm or a moral contract.

It is self-evident that people make moral norms for human actions that *ought to be* according to certain utilities of behavioral facts (i.e., the utility of the behavioral facts to the goal of morality). Let's take "one ought to be honest" and "one ought not to cheat" for examples. How are these two moral norms or moral contracts made? They are surely made based on certain utilities of honesty and cheating. For instance, honesty is the basic bond for social cooperation, conforming to the goal of morality which is to safeguard the existence and development of society as well as promote everyone's interests. On the contrary, cheating undermines social cooperation and does not conform to the goal of morality. Realizing these utilities of honesty and cheating, people take honesty as the moral norm or the moral contract to regulate actions that *ought to be*, but regard cheating as the moral norm or the moral contract to regulate actions that *ought not to be*.

Thus, it is very clear that people make or recognize morality, moral norms, or moral contracts according to the utilities of the behavioral facts to the goal of morality. As we discussed before, the utilities of the behavioral facts to the goal of morality are the behavioral oughts, in the final analysis, are the moral value. Thus, in the final analysis, morality, moral norms, or moral contracts are made or recognized according to moral value, which means that morality consists of two elements: moral value and moral norm (or moral contract). But people usually think that "morality," "moral value," and "moral norm" are the same thing, not knowing the important difference between them. While a moral norm or morality is made or recognized by people moral value is not. Obviously, any value—whether a moral value or a non-moral value—is not made or recognized by people. Just think, how can the nutritional value of corn, wheat, soybean be made or recognized by people? What, then, is the relationship between moral values and moral norms?

Morality or a moral norm is made or recognized according to moral value, which means that morality or a moral norm is simply a form of expression

The concept of morality 9

of the moral value, and the moral value is the content. This is easy to understand. What, one might ask, is the moral norm that "one ought to be honest"? It is simply both an expression and a response to the utility and value of honesty: honesty is the bond for social cohesion, conforming to the goal of morality, so it is *ought to be*.

Thus, morality, a moral norm or a moral contract itself is only the form or expression of the moral value it contains. In other words, morality is structured by form (moral norm) and content (the moral value): its form is the moral norm or moral contract, and that its content is the moral value.

1.2.2 The complete structure of morality: Moral value, moral value judgment and moral norm

On closer inspection, the moral structure of the "content of moral value and the form of moral norm" is only the basic structure of morality. By no means is it the complete structure of morality. As we shall see, it is not possible to combine moral norms and moral values without a certain intermediary, namely moral value *judgment*. Although a moral norm (or a moral contract) is certainly made in accordance with moral value, people cannot make the moral norm (or moral contract) if there is only the moral value. Before making a moral norm (or moral contract) people should first know the moral value of the various actions and then form their moral value *judgment*. Only under the guidance of the moral value judgment can the moral norm (or moral contract) conforming to the moral value be made. For example:

Before making the moral norm (or moral contract) that "one ought to benefit others for one's self-interest" or "one ought not benefit others for one's self-interest," we should first understand the moral value of *benefiting others for self-interest* and form our moral value judgment: is *benefiting others for self-interest* beneficial to the existence and development of society, does it conform to the goal of morality and have positive moral value? Then, only under the guidance of the moral value judgment of *benefiting others for self-interest* can we make the moral norm that conforms to the moral value of *benefiting others for self-interest*. If *benefiting others for self-interest* has negative moral value, we would make the moral norm (or moral contract) that one "ought not benefit others for self-interest"; if *benefiting others for self-interest* has positive moral value, we would make the moral norm (or moral contract) that one "ought to benefit others for self-interest."

Thus the complete structure of morality actually consists of the following three elements: *moral value, moral value judgment*, and *moral norm*. The moral norm (or moral contract) is the expression and the form of the moral value judgment, and the moral value judgment is the expression and the form of the moral value. Therefore, like the moral value judgment, the moral norm is also the expression and the form of moral value; both take the moral value as their content, object, and copies. However the moral value judgment is the direct form of the moral value. As a reflection of the moral value in the human mind

10   *The standard of moral value*

it is the "thought form" of the moral value, while the moral norm (or moral contract) as the indirect form of moral value, is the reflection of "the action" taken in regard to the moral value—through the intermediary of the moral value judgment—and is therefore the normative form of moral value.

Thence the moral value judgment has the distinction of truth and fallacy: the judgment that conforms to the moral value is a truth; the judgment that does not conform to the moral value is a fallacy. On the contrary, the moral norm (or moral contract) has no such distinction. The distinction is rather a matter of rightness and wrongness, good and bad (excellence and inferiority): the moral norm (or moral contract) that conforms to the moral value is not a truth, but is good, excellent, and correct; the moral norm (or moral contract) that does not conform to the moral value is not a fallacy, but is bad, inferior, and incorrect. Let's take the following example:

If "one ought not to benefit others out of one's self-interest" (which is a moral value), the judgment that "one ought to benefit others out of one's self-interest" would not conform to its moral value, thus it would be a false judgment. Therefore, if we take "benefiting others out of one's self-interest" as the moral norm it also does not conform to its moral value. Thus it is a bad moral norm or moral contract. But we can only say this kind of moral norm (or moral contract) is bad or good, not a truth or a fallacy.

1.2.3 The deep structure of morality: Behavioral fact and the goal of morality

It is obvious to see that a moral value also consists of two elements, which are the goal of morality and the behavioral fact. This is because the so-called moral value (or the behavioral *ought*) is the utility of the behavioral fact conforms to or violates the goal of morality: if the behavioral fact conforms to the goal of morality, the utility is a behavioral *ought* or positive moral value; if the behavioral fact violates the goal of morality, the utility is a behavioral *ought not* or negative moral value. Let's ask: what is the moral value of the statement "one ought to benefit others"? It is simply that the utility of "the fact of benefiting others" to the goal of morality—to safeguard the existence and development of society as well as promote everyone's interests, which is equal to "the utility of the fact of benefiting others conforms to the goal of morality." Then, what is the moral value of the statement "one ought not to harm others"? It is simply that the utility of "the fact of harming others" to the goal of morality, which is equal to "the utility of the fact of benefiting others violates the goal of morality." This is the reasoning of the moral value:

> Premise 1: The behavioral fact (benefiting others or harming others)
> Premise 2: The goal of morality (safeguarding the existence and development of society as well as promoting everyone's interests)

The concept of morality 11

The relationship between these two premises: the relationship between the behavioral fact and goal of morality (benefiting others conforms to the goal of morality, harming others violates the goal of morality)
Conclusion: *The behavioral ought* (ought to benefit not harm others)

The reasoning shows that, firstly, "the behavioral fact" is the property of the behavior which exists independently of the goal of morality, and is the property of the action regardless of whether it is related to the goal of morality. It is, therefore, an inherent property of action, and is called as the "substance of moral value" since it is the source or the base from which the moral value (or *the behavioral ought*) is made and deduced. Secondly, "the goal of morality" is the condition under which *the behavioral ought* is derived from the behavioral fact, and is called "the standard of the moral value" since it is the standard for the judgment of the behavioral fact that ought or ought not to be. Finally, the combination of both the behavioral fact and the goal of morality constitutes "*the behavioral ought*." It does not exist independently as a property in action. Rather it comes into being as a property when the behavioral fact is related to goal of morality. It is then the utility of the behavioral fact to the goal of morality, and is relational property of behavior, and is termed as "the moral value."

Thus, it is very clear that moral value is the utility of actions to the goal of morality. It is composed of two elements: the "behavioral fact" and "goal of morality." The former is the source and the substance in which the moral value is constituted, and the latter is the condition and standard for the constitution of the moral value. This is, in short, the structure of moral value and the structure of moral content, thus also the deep structure of morality.

After making this comprehensive survey of the structure of morality, we better understand its complexity. In Figure 1.1, we can see that both its content and form are twofold, and together consist of four elements: the moral norm, moral value judgment, goal of morality, and behavioral fact.

Clearly, the structure of morality is of great importance, which is much more important than the definition of morality, for what it reveals is the overall structure of ethics:

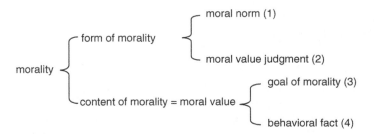

Figure 1.1 The structure of morality

The object of ethics, directly speaking, is an excellent moral norm; fundamentally speaking, it is a moral value; ultimately speaking, it is the goal of morality and behavior fact. Moral norm, moral value judgment, moral value, goal of morality, and behavioral fact thus have the relationship between the form and the content, and from the outside to inside with layers in depth: the moral norm is the form of moral value judgment, the moral value judgment is the form of moral value, and both together are forms of the goal of morality and behavioral fact.

Proceeding further, we find that an excellent "moral norm" is a moral norm that conforms to the "moral value" of behaviors, and that an inferiority "moral norm" is a moral norm that does not conform to the "moral value" of behaviors. Therefore, an excellent moral norm by no means can be made arbitrary; it can only be made based on "the moral value of behavioral ought"—namely the utility of "behavioral fact" to the "goal of morality." In the final analysis, it can only be deduced from "behavioral fact" through the "goal of morality." Thus, the excellence or inferiority of the moral norm directly depends on the truth or falsehood of the moral value judgment. Basically, on the one hand, the excellence or inferiority of the moral norm depends on the truth or falsehood of the fact judgment of the "behavioral fact," and, on the other hand, on the truth or falsehood of the subject judgment of the "goal of morality."

This is the process of making and deducing excellent moral norms directly based on the truth of the moral value judgment, and ultimately based on the truth of the judgment of the behavioral fact and the subjective judgment of the goal of morality, the way of deducing and making excellent moral norms, the "deductive postulate of the excellent moral norm of ethics" which can deduce all propositions of ethics. It can be shown in the following formula, termed as either the "deductive formula of moral value" or the "deductive formula of excellent moral norm":

> Premise 1: The behavioral fact (substance of moral value)
> Premise 2: The goal of morality (standard of moral value)
> Conclusion 1: The behavioral ought (moral value)
> Conclusion 2: The moral norm is good or bad (whether the moral norm conforms to the moral value)

1.3 Types of morality

1.3.1 The universality and particularity of morality: Universal morality and particular morality

At different times, different peoples, have had different or even opposite moral norms. For instance, the primitive societies advocate "eating the aged" while the present societies advocate "providing for the aged parents and attending upon their funerals." American condemn the act of suicide and accept the moral norm that "one ought not to commit suicide when one faces failure," while Japanese respect the acts of suicide and approve the moral norm that "one ought to commit suicide when one fails." In many countries women can show their faces but should cover their breasts and buttocks while in many areas in Africa women should expose their breasts and buttocks. Women in Tierra del Fuego are not allowed to expose their backs while it is normal for Tasaday women in the Philippines to be naked in their daily life. And, in the traditional Arabian society women should cover all parts of their bodies, etc.

However, these different moral norms only indicate the diversity and particularity of morality, they are not to deny the universality and generality of morality, for goodness, justice, happiness, honesty, self-respect, modesty, wisdom, continence, courage, etc., undoubtedly are the universal moral norms of every society or social class through time. It may well be asked: what society has not advocated honesty, self-respect, loyalty, diligence, generosity, courage, justice, probity, goodness, pleasure, modesty, wisdom, continence as moral norms? Who would venture to say that such norms have only ever belonged to certain societies or to a certain social class?

In recognizing that morality has both the properties of particularity and universality, we can assert that the nature of morality is the unity of universality and diversity. This is the principle of the particularity and universality of morality. Based on the universality and particularity of morality all moralities obviously can be divided into two types: universal morality and particular morality. China's autocratic feudal society, for instance, falls into the latter category. For example, the "Three Obediences" (in which a daughter at home was to obey her father, then after marriage was to obey her husband, and after the death of her husband was to obey her son) and the "Four Virtues" (fidelity, physical charm, propriety in speech and efficiency in housework), as well as the "Three Cardinal Guides (in which a monarch guides his subjects, a father guides his son and a husband guides his wife)" etc., were, as a particular type of morality, only applicable to a certain society (the autocratic feudal society in which the monarch rule the country like a family) and its people (the Chinese who lived in the autocratic feudal society). On the contrary, universal morality such as honesty, continence, modesty, justice, courage, the doctrine of the mean and wisdom etc., undoubtedly are and have been throughout time applicable to all societies as principles that ought to be followed by people.

In the final analysis, the relationship between the universality and the particularity of morality, is a relationship between what is fundamental and non-fundamental morality: universal morality can be understood as fundamental moral norms which determine and derive other norms, while particular morality can be understood as non-fundamental moral norms that are determined by universal norms, and are derived from universal norms. And, judging from this, morality also can be divided into the two large types of moral principle and a moral rule. The so-called moral principle is the fundamental moral norm in a certain field; it is the moral norm that determines

14 *The standard of moral value*

and derives, other moral norms in that field, and, in the end, is the universal, general and abstract moral norm in a certain field. On the contrary, the moral rule is the non-fundamental moral norm in a certain field that is determined and derived from the moral principle, and is, therefore, after all, the specific, individual, and particular moral norm in a certain field.

For instance, in China's feudal society in which the monarch rule the country like a family, the "Three Cardinal Guides" were fundamental moral norms determining other general and universal moral norms of the feudal morality in China, and therefore were the moral principles of the feudal morality in ancient China. On the contrary, the "Three Obedience and Four Virtues" were non-fundamental moral norms determined by the "Three Cardinal Guides," and therefore were specific, individual and particular moral rules in the feudal society of ancient China. To take another example, "to love others" and "to benefit others" are the fundamental, universal and general moral norms of any society which determine other moral norms, and are therefore moral principles for all societies. On the contrary, "wisdom, courage and faith" etc., which are each determined by the principles of "to love others" and "to benefit others," can also be universally applied to any society, but each is also more particular, specific and individual than the principles "to love others" and "to benefit others," and are therefore the moral rules for all societies.

Obviously, the relationship between moral principle and moral rule is also the relationship between universality and particularity. However, the moral principle is not necessarily the universal morality of society, and moral rule is also not necessarily the particular morality of society. To be more precise, moral principles are divided into two types: universal moral principles and particular moral principles. The universal moral principles, such as "benevolence" and "benefiting others," are common moral principles of all societies; the particular moral principles, such as the "Three Cardinal Guides," are the particular moral principles of a certain society. The moral rules are also divided into universal moral rules and particular moral rules. The universal moral rules such as "wisdom," "courage," and "faith" are common moral rules of all societies, while the particular moral rules such as "Three Obedience and Four Virtues" are the particular moral rules of a certain society. In short, based on the universality and the particularity, and on the above examples, morality can be divided into the categories shown in Figure 1.2.

1.3.2 *The relativity and absoluteness of morality: The absolute morality and relative morality*

By making a comparison of the relationship between universal morality and particular morality, and the relationship between moral principles and moral rules, one can see that the fundamental ordinary relationships among moralities are the causal relationships: on the one hand, all moral rules are derived from moral principles. On the other hand, all particular moralities

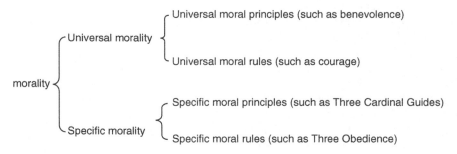

Figure 1.2 The categories of morality

are derived from universal moralities. In short, all particular moral rules and principles and all universal moral rules are derived from universal moral principles: universal moral principles are the morality that deduces all other moralities.

According to this, when different moralities conflict with one another, universal moral principles ought to be followed and other moralities sacrificed. Let's take the example Kant gave: when a person sees an innocent person who was pursued by a murderer hide somewhere, and when the murderer asks him the whereabouts of the innocent person, the person is then confronted by a moral conflict: if he follows the moral rule of being honest and tells the murderer the truth, he risks violating the universal moral principles of saving others' life and of benefiting others (in the case the innocent person), by putting him in the position of being killed; if he follows the universal moral principle of saving others' life and of benefiting others, and save innocent from death, he risks violating the moral rule of being honest by telling a lie to the murderer. Then, what should he do? Surely he ought to follow the universal moral principles of saving others' life and of benefiting others, and sacrifice the moral rule of being honest.

However, what is the thing one ought to do when universal moral principles conflict with one another? For instance, the principle "he who murders pays the forfeit of his life" embodies the principle of justice. However, it conflicts with the abolition of the death penalty which embodies the principle of humanity and benevolence: both come under the category of universal moral principles. Thus, if a country follows the principles of humanity and benevolence by abolishing the death penalty, it will violate the principle of justice that "he who murders pays the forfeit of his life"; but if the country complies with the principle of justice, and the murderer receives a death sentence, it will violate the principles of humanity and benevolence. Then, what should a country do when facing this dilemma? Undoubtedly, it ought to obey the more fundamental moral principle, namely justice. As Adam Smith stated: "Beneficence, therefore, is less essential to the existence than justice. Society may subsist,

16 *The standard of moral value*

though not in the most comfortable state, without beneficence; but the prevalence of injustice must utterly destroy it."[15]

To discuss these sorts of conflicts further, when the *fundamental* universal moral principle conflicts with the *more fundamental* universal moral principle, the latter ought to be followed. Thus, the most fundamental universal moral principle, namely, the ultimate principle of morality, ought to be followed. It is the principle that produces, determines, deduces all other moral principles; it is the principle which all moral norms should obey rather than violate when conflicts occurs; in short, it is the moral principle which each individual should follow not violate under any circumstance because it is the ultimate morality. As George Sher asserts, "to say that moral norms are 'absolute' is to say that they *have no exceptions.*"[16] Mill held a similar view when wrote: "there ought either to be some one fundamental principle or law, at the root of all morality ... the one principle, or the rule for determining between the various principles when they conflict."[17] Mill very much follows in the past traditions and termed this one principle the "ultimate standard" of morality, or the "first principle" of morality.[18]

Surely, there can only exist one ultimate morality or ultimate standard, otherwise, if there are two or more, then, when they conflict with one another one is surely followed and the other surely violated. Then, what is this ultimate morality or ultimate standard of morality? It undoubtedly is the ultimate goal of morality: promoting everyone's interests. As it has been argued, excellent morality cannot made arbitrarily, it can only be made in accordance with "the moral value of behavioral ought"—namely, the utility of the "behavioral fact" to the "goal of morality," since, after all, it can only be derived from the behavioral fact with *the ultimate goal of morality*: that is, the behavioral ought is the utility of the behavioral fact conforming to the ultimate goal of morality, while the behavioral ought-not is the utility of the behavioral fact violating the ultimate goal of morality. The process of deducing and making excellent morality can be concluded in the following formula:

Premise 1: The behavioral fact (substance of moral value)
Premise 2: The ultimate goal of morality (ultimate standard of moral value)
Conclusion 1: The behavioral ought (moral value)
Conclusion 2: Moral principle is good or bad (whether moral principle conforms to the moral value)

This formula indicates that the ultimate goal of morality—promoting everyone's interests—is the ultimate standard of moral value that produces, determines, and deduces all other moral principles, which ought to be obeyed, not violated when other moral norms conflict with it. Everyone, then, ought to follow the ultimate standard of morality under any condition. Therefore, it is the absolute moral principle or absolute morality.

The concept of morality 17

Obviously, morality has the property of relativity as well as the property of absoluteness. Thus, it can be divided into relative morality and absolute morality. There is only one absolute morality, namely the ultimate goal of morality (to promote everyone's interests), which is the ultimate standard of morality that ought to be followed under any condition. Except for the sole absolute morality, all moralities are relative moralities which only ought to be followed in certain conditions. It is clear then that relative morality should be followed only when it is consistent with absolute morality—and thus under general and normal conditions—while it should not be followed when it conflicts with absolute morality—and therefore under exceptional and extraordinary conditions.

1.3.3 The subjectivity and objectivity of morality, as well as the excellence and inferiority of morality: Excellent morality and inferior morality

Since morality is a kind of contract, agreement, and convention, it exists dependent on human will so it is subjective and can be chosen freely. The problem is, is morality completely subjective and arbitrary? No, it's not. This is because morality itself is the norm made or recognized by people, namely moral norm or moral contract, thus is completely subjective and arbitrary. However, morality itself, or the moral norm (or moral contract), as we have mentioned above, is only a form, its content is moral value. Morality is a unity the form of which is moral norm and the content of which is moral value. Moral values and moral norms are completely different because moral values obviously are not made, agreed upon or accepted by people. Who can say that value is a contract and an agreement? Who can say that the nutrition of an apple is a contract and an agreement? Is moral value objective?

The answer is yes because moral value, as mentioned above, is the utility of behavioral fact to the goal of morality. As a fact, the behavioral fact is undoubtedly objective. While it seems that the goal of morality is subjective, it is not, because the origins and purposes of individual behaviors can be subjective and arbitrary; however, the universal origins and the goals of the organizations established by people are objective and inevitable. For instance, are not the universal origins and goals of family, society and state objective and inevitable, independent of human will? are not the universal origins and goals of economy, politics, and law objective, inevitable, and independent of human will? Therefore, no wonder the universal origin and goal of morality are objective and inevitable, and independently of human will, certainly in that they are to safeguard the existence and development of society, as well as to promote everyone's interests.

Since universal goal of morality and behavioral facts are objective, the utility of behavioral fact to the goal of morality (i.e., the moral value) is certainly also objective: on the one hand, it is determined by the universal goal of morality that is objective and independent of human will, on the other

18 *The standard of moral value*

hand, it is determined by the behavioral fact that is objective and independent of human will, and is therefore itself also objective and independent of human will.

Let's take the moral value of *"benefiting others for self-interest"* as an example. If the behavioral fact of *benefiting others for self-interest* factually benefits both oneself and others, and if the universal goal of morality is to safeguard the existence and development of society as well as promote everyone's interests, then, no matter how Confucians and Kant had tried to deny the act of *benefiting others for self-interest,* and no matter how many people consider it a negative moral value, it still necessarily has a positive moral value, for it conforms to the universal goal of morality which is necessarily determined by the nature of the behavioral fact of *benefiting others for self-interest,* as well as the nature of the universal goal of morality, which is objective and independent of human will.

On the contrary, if *benefiting others for self-interest* necessarily leads to *harming others for self-interest,* or, if the universal goal of morality is to perfect everyone's virtue not to promote everyone's interest, then, no matter how rational egoists advocate the act of *benefiting others for self-interest,* and no matter how many people consider it a positive moral value, it still has a negative moral value, for it does not conform to the universal goal of morality. Therefore, that *benefiting others for self-interest* has a negative moral value is necessarily determined by the nature of the behavioral fact of *benefiting others for self-interest* and the nature of the universal goal of morality, and thus is objective and independent of human will.

Therefore, the thing that is subjective is not the moral value of "benefiting others for self-interest," but people's judgment of the moral value of "benefiting others for self-interest" and the moral norm or moral contract people made in accordance to the judgment: altruists believe that *benefiting others for self-interest* has a negative moral value, hence make the moral norms that one "ought not to benefit others for self-interest," while rational egoists consider that benefiting others for self-interest has a positive moral value, and therefore make the moral norm that one "ought to benefit others for self-interest."

Obviously, morality possesses both subjectivity and objectivity: its contents (the moral value, the goal of morality and the behavioral fact) are objective and independent of human will; its forms (the moral value judgment and the moral norm or moral contract) are subjective, dependent on human will. Based on the nature of the subjectivity and objectivity of morality, all moralities can be divided into two types: excellent morality and inferior morality or good morality and bad morality. Firstly, the subjectivity of the moral norm is the premise of the distinction between excellent morality and inferior morality, for only in the condition that the moral norm is subjective and arbitrary do moralities have the distinction of excellence and inferiority; on the contrary, if the moral norm is necessarily objective and cannot be chosen freely, how can it have the distinction of excellence and inferiority? Secondly, the objectivity of the moral value is the basis for distinguishing the morality from excellent morality and inferior morality. Suppose, if moral norms can be distinguished as good and bad, then, with what standards are they distinguished? It should be based on whether they conform to the objectivity of the moral value. The moral norm that conforms to the moral value is an excellent (i.e., right, good) moral norm; the moral norm that does not conform to the moral value is a bad (i.e., wrong, inferior) moral norm.

For instance, if *benefiting others for self-interest* does not conform to the goal of morality and has therefore a negative moral value, then the moral norm that one "ought to benefit others for self-interest" made by the rational egoists will not conform to the moral value of *benefiting others for self-interest*, and is therefore a bad moral norm; on the contrary, if the moral norm that one "ought not to benefit others for self-interest" made by the egoists conforms to the moral value of *benefiting others for self-interest*, then it is an excellent moral norm. But, if *benefiting others for self-interest* conforms to the goal of morality and has therefore a positive moral value, then, if the moral norm that one "ought to benefit others for self-interest" made by rational egoists conforms to the moral value of *benefiting others for self-interest*, it is an excellent moral norm. On the contrary, the moral norm of one "ought not to benefit others for self-interest" made by altruists does not conform to the moral value of *benefiting others for self-interest* then it is a bad moral norm.

The excellent moral norm is bound to be consistent with the moral value—the utility of behavioral fact to the goal of morality—then, clearly, it is bound to be consistent with the objective nature of human behavioral fact in addition to the goal of morality. Thus, on the one hand, judging from the position that excellent morality conforms to the objective nature of human behavioral fact—namely the so-called human nature—excellent morality certainly is the morality that everyone can and ought to follow; while bad morality which violates human nature cannot and ought not to be followed.

On the other hand, judging from the position that excellent morality conforms to the universal goal of morality—promoting everyone's interests—obviously, the excellent morality is the morality that everyone can and ought to follow; on the contrary, the bad morality which violates the universal goal of morality, that is, the goal of which is not to promote everyone's interests, cannot and ought not to be followed by everyone.

Since excellent morality certainly is the morality that everyone can and ought to follow, then it is bound to be the type of morality that can be universalized; the morality that cannot be universalized, that is, the morality not all can and ought to follow, is bound to be the bad morality. This is the nature of the universalizability of excellent morality. As Hare states, "Universality means that when a person says 'I should', he makes himself agree that anyone in his situation should."[19]

Thus, by making a comprehensive survey of morality it can be known that morality is the unity of subjectivity and objectivity: its contents (the moral value, the goal of morality and the behavioral fact) mainly are objective and exist independently of human will; and its forms (the moral value judgment, the moral norm or the moral contract) are subjective and exist dependently of human will. Thus, no matter what the human will and desire are, only the morality that conforms to the moral value and thus can be universalized is excellent and right; while the morality that does not conform to moral value and cannot be universalized is certainly bad and wrong.

1.4 Theories on concepts of morality

The nature of morality is extremely abstruse and complicated. Consequently, for more than two thousand years philosophers and ethicists have kept arguing the nature of morality. These arguments can be encapsulated as six main different schools of thought: ethical relativism, ethical absolutism, moral subjectivism, moral skepticism, moral objectivism, and moral realism.

1.4.1 Ethical relativism

Despite it being the main focus of the ethics field in the western world, the important figures of ethical relativism have not been ethicists and philosophers, but rather mostly anthropologists and sociologists such as W. G. Sumner, Edward Westermarck, Emil Durkheim, William Graham Sumner, and Carl Manheim. Under the banner of ethical relativism it seems that the only modern philosopher who is worth mentioning is Gilbert Harman whose theory is perhaps more moral subjectivism than ethical relativism. As Beauchamp has commented: "Although it has at times been fashionable in social sciences to view relativism as a correct and highly significant doctrine, moral philosophers have generally tended to discount the evaluation."[20]

Ethical relativism includes "cultural ethical relativism" and "normative ethical relativism." Cultural ethical relativism usually is simplified as "cultural relativism" or "descriptive relativism," and normative ethical relativism is usually simplified as "ethical relativism" or "normative relativism."[21] Descriptive relativism believes that morality is in fact completely relative, all morality exists relative to certain cultures and society, varying with different cultures and societies. There is no universal, absolute morality applicable to all cultures and societies. As Paul Taylor also holds: "According to descriptive relativism there is no common moral code applicable to all cultures."[22]

Ethical relativism starts from cultural relativism, and further holds that the validity of the moral norm people pursue is completely relative: any morality is correct only to the specific society that complies with it; there is no morality that is universally correct or absolutely correct to all societies. H. Gene Blocker writes:

> Ethical relativism, in short, is the view that the correctness of different moral standards is relative to different individuals and societies. It is correct to one person or society, but not to another person or society. Polygamy was correct in some countries, but wrong in the United States.[23]

The different or even opposite moral customs followed by different nations or the same nation in different times, which are described by ethical relativism, is specific or particular moral norms. The differences of these moral norms indicate the relativity of morality, but do not deny its absoluteness. The ultimate goal of morality, which is the premise from which these moral norms are deduced, is completely the same for all societies in that it is the promotion of the interests for everyone in a whole society: the ultimate moral standard is absolute, meaning that all members of every society should comply with it under any circumstance. Based on the same absolute ultimate moral standard, people formed the opposite moral customs and mores, this is simply because the expressions of the ultimate moral standard is different in different times and different regions.

In primitive society, there was a morality that "one ought to eat the elderly." why? This was because the social productivity in such primitive societies was extremely low, meaning that people would starve to death if they did not eat the elderly. Therefore, the purpose of "eating the elderly" in the primitive society was to guarantee the existence and development of society as well as to promote everyone's interest, just like the purpose of "providing for the elderly" in modern society. Then, these two opposite moralities that "ought to eat the elderly" in the primitive society and "ought to provide for the elderly" in modern society is simply two opposite expressions of the same ultimate goal of morality of "promoting the interests of everyone in the whole society" because of the fundamental difference in productivity between the two societies. Thus, the view hold by ethical relativism that all morals differ from society to society, and therefore there exists no universal and absolute morality applicable to all societies, mistakes the part for the whole: ethical relativism only sees the specific and particular moral norms, but neither see the absolute morality of "promoting the interests of everyone in the whole society" are the premise from which the particular moral norms are deduced, nor see the universal morality which are applicable to all societies, such as justice, honesty, continence, modesty, courage, the doctrine of the mean, self-respect, and wisdom.

Therefore, the ethical relativist view that any morality is right only in a particular society is untenable. It is because, the rightness or wrongness of a particular morality is tenable only in a certain society: a particular morality is right in one kind of society, while it is possibly wrong in another kind of society. For instance, the moral norm of cannibalism is correct, only for the primitive society: since in the primitive society it conformed to the moral value of the action of cannibalism, therefore it was a correct moral norm; in modern society, it is not consistent with the moral value of the action of cannibalism, and therefore it is an incorrect moral norm. Conversely, the rightness and the wrongness of the universal or absolute morality is the same in all societies: if a universal or absolute morality is right, then it would be right in all societies. The universal moralities of justice, honesty, continence, modesty, courage, the doctrine of the mean, self-respect, wisdom, etc., as they

22 The standard of moral value

are generally known, are the good and right moral norms that are universally applicable and can be applied to societies generation after generation: they are the right and excellent moral norms for any society.

It is thus clear that the rightness or wrongness of morality has both relativity and the absoluteness: the rightness or wrongness of the particular and relative morality is particular and relative, the rightness or wrongness of the universal and absolute morality is universal and absolute. The fallacy of the ethical relativism position that rightness certainly is tenable only in a particular society, obviously denies absolute morality: if all moralities are particular and relative because of the differences of societies, then their rightness certainly is tenable only in a particular society. If we look further we can see that ethical relativism is established by double elements in that the descriptive or cultural relativism (which holds that all moralities are particular and relative, and all are different because of the difference of the societies) is the premise of normative or ethical relativism (which holds that the rightness of all moralities are tenable only when they apply to the particular society). The key to refuting ethical relativism is to overturn its premise and to prove that there exist the universal or absolute moralities that are applicable to all societies.

1.4.2 Ethical absolutism: Situation ethics

Different from ethical relativism, the representative figures of ethical absolutism or moral absolutism are not anthropologists and sociologists but ethicists and philosophers such as Kant and Flatcher. As Pojman points out, ethical absolutism or moral absolutism is the opposite to ethical relativism: ethical relativism denies the existence of the absolute morality, arguing that all moralities are relative, while moral absolutism denies the relative morality in that it considers that all real moralities are absolute.[24] More exactly speaking, ethical absolutism or moral absolutism denies that relative morality can be true morality; that the true and excellent morality is absolute.

However, as mentioned above, there is only one absolute morality or ultimate moral standard, namely the ultimate goal of morality and all other moralities are relative. The error of ethical absolutism obviously lies in that it exaggerates this point. It mistakenly holds that, in terms of its true nature, morality is absolute. And it further mistakenly regards absolute morality as the moral principle system constituted by other moral principles or a serial of moral principles such as ought to love, ought not to tell lies, ought to fulfill one's obligation for obligation, not as merely the ultimate goal of morality. Thus, ethical absolutism on the one hand mistakenly overstates some of the relative moralities such as love and honesty as absolute morality, on the other hand mistakenly expels many relative moralities out of the field of morality, denying that these relative moralities are morality.

This denial of relative morality came to a climax in Fletcher's *Situation Ethics*. Fletcher's situation ethics is a typical moral absolutism, or to be more exact, it is a new Kant's moral absolutism, because like Kant, he holds that in terms of its true nature, morality is absolute, and that those moralities without absoluteness are not true moralities, thus there is no need for them to exist. Where Kant has at least considered that absolute morality, as the true morality, is a series of moral principles (such as responsibility and honesty etc.), situation ethics only considers one absolute morality, namely "love": "Only the commandment to love is categorically good."[25] Thus, only love is the true morality since it is absolute, and other moralities are not true moralities since they are relative, thus there is no need for them to exist. "Love is the only norm."[26] Thus, all behaviors that ought or ought not to be completely depend on the situation of the behaviors and on if the behaviors conform to the calculation of "love." Therefore, Fletcher asserts that there are two elements in the situation ethics: one is the absolute norm and the other is the calculating method in the specific situation.[27] However, if all moralities only have a norm of "love," aren't moralities equal to zero? Therefore, Binkley comments that, although Fletcher and other scholars of situation ethics do not mean to argue in favor of irresponsibility or non-moralism, their arguments are not much different from non-moralism.[28] Then, what is exactly the error of situation ethics?

This denial of relative morality came to a climax in Fletcher's *Situation Ethics*. Fletcher's situation ethics is a typical moral absolutism, or to be more exact, it is a new Kant's moral absolutism, because like Kant, he holds that in terms of its true nature, morality is absolute, and that those moralities without absoluteness are not true moralities, thus there is no need for them to exist. Where Kant has at least considered that absolute morality, as the true morality, is a series of moral principles (such as responsibility and honesty, etc.), situation ethics only considers one absolute morality, namely "love": "Only the commandment to love is categorically good."[29] Thus, only love is the true morality since it is absolute, and other moralities are not true moralities since they are relative, thus there is no need for them to exist. "Love is the only norm."[30] Thus, all behaviors that ought or ought not to be completely depend on the situation of the behaviors and on if the behaviors conform to the calculation of "love." Therefore, Fletcher asserts that there are two elements in the situation ethics: one is the absolute norm and the other is the calculating method in the specific situation.[31] However, if all moralities only have a norm of "love," aren't moralities equal to zero? Therefore, Binkley comments that, although Fletcher and other scholars of situation ethics do not mean to argue in favor of irresponsibility or non-moralism, their arguments are not much different from non-moralism.[32] Then, what is exactly the error of situation ethics?

As had been shown earlier, absolute morality is the morality that everyone under any condition ought to follow since there is only one ultimate goal of morality and that is *to promote the interests of all the members of a whole society*. Except this absolute morality, all moralities are relative and ought to be followed only in ordinary, normal or typical conditions—that is, ought not be followed in exceptional, extraordinary, or extreme conditions. Obviously, the necessary condition for the existence of relative morality is that the amount of normal behavior is far more than the amount of abnormal behavior. Thus, because relative moralities regulate the normal behaviors, the amount of time they ought to be followed is far more than the amount of time they ought not to be followed, which is the reason that it is necessary for them to exist. If, however, the relative moralities regulate the abnormal behaviors, then the amount of time it ought to be followed is far lesser than the amount of time it ought not to be followed, then their existence is unnecessary.

However, situation ethics gives both normal and abnormal behaviors the same importance: "the situation variables are to be weighted as heavily as the normative or 'general' constants."[33] This is the fundamental error of situation ethics. It denies the distinction between normal behaviors and abnormal behaviors, equating the situation that a relative moral ought to be followed to the situation that it ought not to be followed, then further equating the amount of time the relative moral that ought to be followed to the amount of time it ought not to be followed. Consequently, it is not essential for relative morality to exist because if the amount of time the relative morality ought to be followed equals the amount of time it ought not to be followed, then, is not the reason that it ought to exist equal to the reason that it ought not to exist? Since it is not essential for the existence of relative morality, then only absolute morality can be the true morality: thus, in this way the situation ethics denies relative morality and advocates moral absolutism.

1.4.3 Moral subjectivism and moral nihilism/skepticism

The so-called moral subjectivism, as is generally known, is the theory that denies the objectivity of morality, holding that morality is completely subjective and arbitrary. Therefore there are many scholars in the camp of moral subjectivism including emotionalist ethicists such as Hume, Russell, Wittgenstein, Ayer, and Stevenson, as well as ethical relativists such as W. G. Sumner, Edwards Westermarck, Emil Durkheim, William Graeme Sumner, and Carl Manheim—all of them are moral subjectivists. However, the main proponents of typical moral subjectivism surely is the ancient philosopher Epicurus, Hume, in the eighteenth century, and the modern American philosopher Gilbert Harman.

The most powerful argument the moral subjectivists elicit to declare that morality is completely subjective is undoubtedly the theory of "moral bargaining." The viewpoint of moral subjectivists is that all moralities or moral norms are human made, and can therefore be considered as the result of a certain contract or agreement. Epicurus stated that "Justice is the expedient contract to prevent mankind from harming one another"[34] and Hume had similarly stated that justice originates from human contract.[35] It was, however,

Gilbert Harman who further advocated the theory of "Moral Bargaining," writing that: "My thesis is that morality arises when a group of people reach an implicit agreement or come to a tacit understanding about their relations with one another."[36]

It is true that all moral principles and moral norms are human made and all are certain agreements, contracts, and conventions, therefore they unquestionably exist depending of human will and are subjective, arbitrary, free, and can be chosen as moral subjectivists assert. However, the moral subjectivists then further completely deny the objectivity of morality, holding that morality is not an objective fact but wholly subjective and wholly dependent on human will:

> Morality is only a function of people's moral beliefs, besides that it has nothing. In particular, there is no objective field of moral fact or something real which equivalent to what we have discovered in nature and studied by science.[37]

If it is true that morality is subjective, and not in any way objective, as moral subjectivists assert, then the judgment of morality has no matter of truth or falsehood, and the morality made in accordance with this kind of judgment obviously also has no question of excellence or inferiority, rightness or wrongness. Therefore Ayer repeatedly says: "In emphasizing the noncognitive aspects of ethical judgments my analysis does not cause the terms 'true' and 'false'."[38] This is the so-called moral nihilism/skepticism which is the theory holding that the moral judgment has no issue of truth or falsehood and the moral norm has no matter of rightness or wrongness. In summarizing the fundamental traits of moral nihilism/skepticism Pojman writes: "Moral skepticism is the view that we cannot know whether there are moral truths."[39]

The theories of moral subjectivism and moral skepticism are untenable. As mentioned above, on the one hand, morality is the unity of subjectivity and objectivity. Its forms (the moral value judgment and the moral norm or moral contract) are subjective and exist dependently of human will, while its contents (the moral value, the goal of morality, and the behavioral facts) are objective and exist independently of human will. On the other hand, the excellence and inferiority of the moral norms and their standards of evaluation are completely objective and are independent of human will. No matter what the human will or desire are, only the morality that conforms to the moral value is excellent and right, while the morality that does not conform to the moral value is bad and wrong. Moral subjectivism and moral skepticism only see the subjectivity of the morality itself, but not the objectivity of the content of morality, and consequently derive the conclusion that morality is completely subjective: that there are not so-called moral truths, and that morality has no question of rightness or wrongness.

1.4.4 Moral objectivism and moral realism

Moral objectivism holds that morality has an objective nature independently of human will, and that the rightness of behavior and the correctness of moral norms are objective and independently of human will. The representative figures of moral objectivism mostly are the great masters in the field of ethics, such as Plato, Aristotle, Thomas Aquinas, Hutcheson, Kant, Ross, Mill, Henry Sidgwick, and Moore.

Moral objectivism undoubtedly is a truth. As mentioned above, on the one hand, only the forms of morality (the moral value judgment and the moral norms) are subjective and arbitrary, while its contents (the moral value or the rightness of behaviors, the goal of morality, as well as the behavioral facts) are objective and exist independently of human will. On the other hand, the correctness of moral norms is completely objective and exists independently of whether we believe it. No matter what the human will or desire are, only the morality that conforms to the moral value is excellent and correct, and vice versa.

However, things develop in the opposite direction when they tend to the extreme. The extreme moral objectivism, namely moral realism, is a fallacy. The representative figures of moral realism are E. J. Bond and David O. Brink, to name just two. Moral realism holds that morality itself is a fact similar to colors that exist independently of the needs and will of the subject: the basic feature of moral realism is that it acknowledges the existence of so-called "moral facts." Pojman says: "Moral realism claims that there are moral facts in ethics."[40] The so-called "there are moral facts," as R. M. Hare explains, mean that moral good and evil are similar to colors existing independently of the needs, desires, and purposes of the subject, they are a kind of fact, belonging to the category of facts: "So far we have been talking about the property of wrongness, and the fact that an act was wrong, in just the same terms as the property of redness, and the fact that a thing is red."[41]

It is obvious that moral realism is untenable. Its error lies in that it equates the property of the factual relationship of object with the property of the value relationship. They correctly perceive that the moral good is similar to the red color, that both have the properties of the relationship that the object exists dependently on subject, but not the inherent properties. However, what they do not see is, on the one hand, that the red color is the property of object that exists independently of the needs, desires and ends of the subject, and that it is therefore the factual property of object, the property of the factual relationship, and the "second property" of the object, falling into the category of facts. On the other hand, the moral good is the property of object that exists dependently on the needs, desires, and purposes of subject, and is the utility of the factual property of object to the needs, desires, and purposes of the subject—namely the utility of "behavioral facts" conforms to "the goal of morality"—and is also the property of the value relation of the object and the "third property" of the object, falling into the category of value but not the facts. The error of moral realism is that it equates the existing nature of morality with the existing nature of color, and then from the viewpoint that color is a fact, draw the wrong conclusion that morality is also the fact and that there are moral facts.

Notes

1. Tom L. Beauchamp: *Philosophical Ethics*, McGraw-Hill, New York, 1982, p. 15.
2. Huang Jianzhong: *Comparative Ethics*, National Academic Press Inc., 1974, p. 28.
3. Ibid., p. 27.
4. Zhu Xi: *The Notes on the Four Books*, Chapter of Learning.
5. John Hartland-Swann: *An Analysis of Morals*, London, George Allen & Unwin Ltd, 1960, p. 57.
6. Ibid., p. 62.
7. William K. Frankena: *Ethics*, Prentice-Hall, Englewood Cliff, NJ, 1973, p. 6.
8. Mortimer J. Adler: *Treasures of Western Thought*, Jilin People's Publishing House, 1988, p. 944.
9. David Hume: *A Treatise of Human Nature*, Clarendon Press, Oxford, 1949, p. 494.
10. Louis P. Pojman: *Ethical Theory: Classical and Contemporary Readings*, Wadsworth, Belmont, CA, 1995, p. 38.
11. *Blackwell Encyclopedia of Political Science*, translated by Deng Zhenglai etc. China University of Political Science and Law Press, 1992, p. 393.
12. Friedrich Paulsen: *A System of Ethics*, China Social Sciences Press, 1988, p. 18.
13. Henry Sidgwick: *The Methods of Ethics*, Thoemmes Press, 1996, p. 17.
14. Ouyang Gu: *A General Theory of Jurisprudence*, The Shanghai Law Compiler Society, 1946.
15. Adam Smith: *The Theory of Moral Sentiments*, Clarendon Press, Oxford, 1979, p. 86.
16. George Sher: *Moral Philosophy: Selected Readings*, Harcourt Brace Jovanovich, New York, 1987, p. 158.
17. John Stuart Mill: *Utilitarianism*, China Social Sciences Publishing House, Chengcheng Books Ltd, 1999, p. 4.
18. Ibid.
19. Richard Mervyn Hare: *Essays in Ethical Theory*, Clarendon Press, Oxford, 1989, p. 179.
20. Tom L. Beauchamp: *Philosophical Ethics*, McGraw-Hill, New York, 1982, p. 34.
21. Louis P. Pojman: *Ethical Theory: Classical and Contemporary Readings*, Wadsworth, Belmont, CA, 1995, p. 16.
22. George Sher: *Moral Philosophy: Selected Readings*, Harcourt Brace Jovanovich, New York, 1987, p. 147.
23. H. Gene Blocker: *Ethics: An Introduction*, Haven Publications, Oxford, 1988, p. 38.
24. Louis P. Pojman: *Ethical Theory: Classical and Contemporary Readings*, Wadsworth, Belmont, CA, 1995, p. 16.
25. Joseph Fletcher: *Situation Ethics*, The Westminster Press, Philadelphia, 1966, p. 26.
26. Ibid., p. 80.
27. Ibid., p. 27.
28. Luther J. Binkley: *Conflict of Ideals*, Commercial Press, Beijing, 1983, p. 356.
29. Joseph Fletcher: *Situation Ethics*, The Westminster Press, Philadelphia, 1966, p. 26.

28 The standard of moral value

30 Ibid., p. 80.
31 Ibid., p. 27.
32 Luther J. Binkley: *Conflict of Ideals*, Commercial Press, Beijing, 1983, p. 356.
33 Joseph Fletcher: *Situation Ethics*, The Westminster Press, Philadelphia, 1966, p. 29.
34 Mortimer J. Adler: *Treasures of Western Thought*, Jilin People's Publishing House, 1988, p. 944.
35 David Hume: *A Treatise of Human Nature*, Clarendon Press, Oxford, 1949, p. 494.
36 Louis P. Pojman: *Ethical Theory: Classical and Contemporary Readings*, Wadsworth, Belmont, CA, 1995, p. 38.
37 Barbara Mackinnon: *Ethics: Theory and Contemporary Issues*, Wadsworth, Belmont, CA, 1995.
38 Charles L. Stervenson: *Facts and Values: Studies in Ethical Analysis*, Yale University Press, New Haven and London, 1963, p. 219.
39 Louis P. Pojman: *Ethical Theory: Classical and Contemporary Readings*, Wadsworth, Belmont, CA, 1995, p. 17.
40 Ibid., p. 469.
41 Ted Honderich: *Morality and Objectivity*, Routledge & Kegan Paul, London, 1985, p. 45.

2 The origin and goal of morality

Kropotkin said: "the fundamental problem of modern ethical realism is (as Wilhelm Wundt pointed out in his *Ethics*) to solve the problem of the goal of moral."[1] He is absolutely right! The origin and goal of morality are not only the fundamental problems of ethics but also the problems of extreme complexity with various different points of views enwrapped in the triple relationships which should be solved for understanding the origin and goal of morality: firstly, the moral needs of the moral community, secondly, the moral needs of human society, and, thirdly, personal moral needs.

2.1 The origin and goal of morality: From the point of view of moral community

2.1.1 The concept of moral community: Moral agent and moral patient

If the first problem of normative ethics is to analyze the concept of morality and to understand what morality is, then its second problem obviously is to whom or what the morality ought to or ought not to be applied? i.e., who or what is the object that ought to be treated with morality? This is the so-called problem of the moral community. As Belles says, it is the totality of the objects that ought to be treated morally or that ought to be moral concerns: "What I refer to with the 'moral community' is the scope of substance which we can appropriately express our moral concerns."[2]

For instance, the violence of one group against the other group is based on the so-called enemy not being members of the moral community on one group. The members of one moral community do not share the same moral norms with the enemy. Killing the enemy is therefore not an immoral act because the morality of the community does not apply to the morality of the enemy. By this reasoning, the more one member of the community kills the enemy the more virtuous that member is.

Thus, no matter what a thing it is, even a dog, if it becomes one of the members in the moral community, it possesses the so-called "moral standing." If, in the case of humans, one member is ejected from the moral community, then the ejected member no longer has moral standing. The moral standing is the qualification for the members to be a part of the moral community. Members have the benefit of being treated morally by others in the group. Members of a moral community enjoy the moral concerns of the group.

However, on a closer analysis, the moral standing the members possess in the moral community is not completely the same, but can be divided into the following two types: the "moral agent" and the "moral patient." What is a moral agent? Taylor gives the answer:

> A moral agent, for both types of ethics, is any being that possesses those capacities by virtue of which it can act morally or immorally, can have duties and responsibilities, and can be held accountable for what it does. Among these capacities, the most important are the ability to form judgments about right and wrong; the ability to engage in moral deliberation, that is, to consider and weigh moral reasons for and against various courses of conduct open to choice; the ability to make decisions on the basis of those reasons; the ability to exercise the necessary resolve and willpower to carry out those decisions; and the capacity to hold one self answerable to others for failing to carry them out.[3]

This means that moral agent is the subject of the moral behaviors and the one who has moral consciousness and is capable to carry on the moral or immoral behaviors, and thus can take moral responsibility for his own actions. But, why do we call the subject of the moral behavior the moral agent?

It turns out that the subject of moral behavior is a member of the moral community that is capable of acting in accordance with the moral norms. And under the constitutions of the moral norms, it can restrain itself and treat other members with respect, so that the moral norm can be realized: the moral agent is the agent of moral norms, which is the subject of moral behavior that can apply and realize moral norms. Therefore, Taylor continues:

> Why is it that valid moral rules apply only to beings having the capacity of moral agents? The reason is that, if a moral rule does apply to an agent (one who intentionally acts or refrains from acting), the agent must be able to use the rule as a normative guide to its own choice and conduct. This requires having the capacity to make moral judgments on the basis of the rule, as well as the capacity to consider it a reason-for-action that an action open to choice is in accordance with the rule.[4]

Of course, the reason why the subject of moral behavior is the moral agent is because there are some members in the moral community, such as babies, the mentally ill, or dementia patients, who do not have moral consciousness and so are not capable of possessing moral behaviors or assuming moral responsibility. Consequently, they can only be the object, not the subject, of moral behavior. Thus, the interests, or the rights and obligations of these members must be deputized by those who are capable of being the subject of moral behavior. Therefore, those members who are capable of being the subject of moral behaviors are the moral agents for those who are not capable being the subject. Hence, the subject of moral behaviors are moral agents both for moral norms and for those who are not capable of being the subject, such as madmen and dogs.

Those who do not have moral consciousness, are incapable of having moral behavior and cannot be the subject of the moral behaviors. As the members of the object of moral behaviors they are of course incapable of self-restraint and of treating other members of the community in accordance with the moral norms. They can only be treated by other members in accordance to the moral norms, and for this reason are called the moral patient. As the objects of the moral behaviors of the moral agents and in this sense existing for the moral agents who can assume their moral obligations and take actions on their behalf that are morally right or wrong. As Taylor writes: "we may define a moral subject as any being that can be treated rightly or wrongly and toward whom moral agents can have duties and responsibilities."[5]

The moral patient includes not only those members of the moral community who cannot act but can only be treated in accordance to the moral norm, but also all the members who are capable of behaving in accordance to the moral norms. It includes all moral agents: the moral agents undoubtedly ought to be treated more in accordance to the moral norms and deserve more moral concern. In fact, the moral patients are all members of the moral community, that is, those who possess moral standing. Thence, as Taylor also says, "The class of moral subjects, however, is broader than the class of moral agent. All moral agents are moral subjects, but not all moral subjects are moral agents."[6]

Then, what existing beings ought to be included as all the members of the moral community? Or, in the other words, what is the boundary of a moral community? Ought it to be anthropocentrically limited to human beings as traditional ethics holds, or ought it to follow the proposal of modern anti-anthropocentric ecological ethics that all living beings such animals and plants, and inanimate things, such as rocks, lands, and rivers, be included?

2.1.2 Boundary of moral community: The living beings that are beneficial to human beings

In summarizing the traits of the members of moral community Taylor writes: "in the role of moral *agents* they can treat others rightly or wrongly."[7] He is absolutely right! Only the things that possess interests (namely, possess *the abilities of distinguishing goodness from badness, and the capacity of choice to make use of advantage and avoid disadvantage), can be treated morally or deserve moral concern, and become the members of the* moral community. Thus, only the living being can be *the members of the* moral community and it is not possible for non-living beings to be a part of the moral community. Rock and iron simply do not possess the abilities of distinguishing goodness from badness, nor do they have the capacity to make a choice. In other words, they do not have interest.

Every living being, even a living being such as an insect or plant possesses the ability to distinguish and choose between goodness and badness, advantage, and disadvantage. For instance, in the Carboniferous the wings of dragonflies proved to be "'spectacular examples of microengineering' giving them 'the agile, versatile flight necessary to catch prey in flight.'" And, as has been well documented:

> Plants need to photosynthesize to gain energy from the sun, which requires access to carbon dioxide in the atmosphere. They also need to conserve water, vital to their metabolism, and to have access to atmospheres which evaporate water ... The problem is solved by stomata on the undersides of leaves, which can open and close, letting in or shutting out the air.[8]

These two kind of responses show that, animals and plants have the abilities of distinguishing goodness and badness, advantages and disadvantages as well as the capacity of choice which makes them capable of making good use of advantages and carefully avoiding disadvantages.

Then, can we draw the conclusion that all living beings ought to be of moral concern so are all members of the moral community? Most answers from western ecological ethicists are definite:

> If we are ever to do justice to the lower races (i.e., animals), we must get rid of the antiquated notion of a "great gulf" fixed between them and the mankind, and must recognize the common bond of humanity that unites all living beings in one universal brotherhood.[9]

But, as it is generally known, having interest is a necessary but not a sufficient condition for receiving moral concern. The condition under which non-human beings receive moral concern as members of the moral community is not just that they have interest, but also are beneficial to human beings. In this way, non-human beings constitute an "interest community" which can be regarded as kind of general reciprocal relationship, since not even a human being ought to necessarily be a member of a moral community. An evil person who kills and does everything evil ought to be executed but not to be a member of moral community. If even a human being be treated this way, let alone the non-human beings.

Therefore, being beneficial to human beings is the more fundamentally necessary condition for non-human beings to receive moral concern to become members of moral community; having interest is the premise, and being beneficial to human beings is the basis. Then, is the combination of these two conditions a sufficient condition for getting moral concerns? The answer is yes. Having interest and being beneficial to human beings are a sufficient condition for non-human beings to receive our moral concern.

If any kind of living being is capable of making good use of advantage, or avoiding disadvantage, and if it is beneficial to our interest, then we ought not to harm them but ought to benefit them. This is only insofar as our actions upon them are equal to the principle of justice: it being an *exchange of equal interests* which is just and moral. Otherwise, if we do not benefit them but harm them instead, we violate the principle of justice of the exchange of equal interests, which is unjust and immoral. Let's consider the following example:

Plants greatly benefit us. They also have *the evaluative competence to distinguish goodness or badness and advantage or disadvantage and the abilities to choose advantage and avoid disadvantage*, so that they also have certain interests. Hence, in accordance of principle of justice, we ought to be grateful to plants and benefit them, not to harm them. If we harm plants by cutting trees' branches arbitrarily, or trample heedlessly on flowers and grasses, we violate the principle of justice of the exchange of equal interests. Our actions are then immoral. Uprooting a plant arbitrarily, like killing a person, is a moral error, as Taylor repeatedly says: "the killing of a wildflower ... is just as much a wrong ... as the killing of a human"[10] and Edward Abbey writes: "I could no more sink the blade of an ax into the tissue of a living tree than I could drive it into the flesh of a fellow human."[11]

2.1.3 The origin and goal of morality: Safeguarding the interest community and promoting human interests

As mentioned above, having interest (seeking interests and avoiding harms) and being beneficial to human beings are sufficient conditions under which nonhuman ought to receive moral concern as members of the moral community. The boundary of a moral community is all living beings that are beneficial to humans. This means that the so-called moral community is the interest community, the members of which are beneficial to each other: the members of a moral community are the members of an interest community. They are just different names for the same community. Thus, obviously, the origin and goal of any morality is to safeguard the existence and development of the interest community.

Nothing can be accomplished without norms or standards and any interest community, even if it has only two members, cannot exist and develop without moral norms. To exist and develop, an interest community must become a moral community to make its members behave in accordance to the moral norms. If the members of the interest community violate the morality and harm one another, then this interest community will collapse, disintegrate, and no longer exist. Therefore, generally speaking, the reason why human beings create morality is to make the interest community of human beings and non-human beings become a moral community to safeguard the existence and development of this interest community. Morality itself then can be said to have originated from the needs of the existence and development of interest community, where the general goal of morality has been to safeguard the existence and development of the interest community.

Then, what is the goal of morality in safeguarding the existence and development of the interest community? Or, in this respect, what is the purpose of the general goal of morality? Is it for promoting the interest of all members in the moral community? Or, in the final analysis, what is the ultimate goal of morality? Promoting the interests of human beings as well as that of all non-human beings? Undoubtedly, if non-human animals and plants are common creators of morality and the common creators of the moral contract, then it certainly can be said that the ultimate goal of morality is to promote both the interests of the non-human members of the interest community and the interests of the human members of the moral community because the ultimate goal of any kind of contract is to promote the interests of each contracting party.

However, morality is not jointly created by human beings and non-human beings. It is created by human beings. In other words, the moral contract can only be made by humans, among humans. It is not possible to make a contract with non-human living beings such as animals and plants. If morality is jointly created by human beings and non-human beings, morality would restrict and regulate the actions of both humans and non-humans. However, as it is generally understood, morality is only used to restrict and regulate human actions. It is not used in an absolute sense to restrict and regulate the actions of non-human beings. Although morality encompasses how people ought to attend to the very different kinds of actions of non-humans, it does not include how non-humans ought to attend to the very different kinds of actions of human beings.

The actions of non-human beings are the objects of study for zoology, botany, and other sciences but not ethics: ethics only studies the interactions of people, and how people interact with non-human beings, not how non-human beings interact with human beings. For instance, the problem of how humans treat tigers, whether to kill them or to protect them, is a matter of being moral or immoral. But the problem of how tigers treat humans, even if they kill and eat humans, has no issue of being moral or immoral. Since morality only restricts the actions of human beings, not that of non-human beings, then, how can non-human beings be those who make the moral contract? How can there be a contract that cannot restricted those who make it?

Then, can it be said that human being is the agent of the moral contract made with animals and plants? The answer is no. It is true that humans can be the agent of the interests of animals and plants, but humans cannot make a moral contract with animals and plants and then be the agent of that moral contract because the fundamental problem of the so-called moral contract, undoubtedly, concerns how human ought to treat interrelate with animals and plants: it is a moral question, under many different circumstances, as to whether or not human beings ought to kill animals (such as to eat them), cut down trees, or uproot vegetation. Can human beings act as the agent for animals and plants and make such a contract? It is obviously impossible! Animals and plants clearly cannot make a contract with human that they ought to be killed, cut down or uprooted by humans. Consequently, can it be said that the ultimate goal of the moral contract is for promoting the human interests but not that of non-human beings?

The answer is yes. Since there is no compromise when the interests of humans conflict with that of non-human animals and plants, surely the lesser moral value ought to be sacrificed for safeguarding the greater moral value. Only with this net balance can there be a positive moral value: a value that ought to be and is therefore moral. However, how do we judge which moral value is greater? The moral value only is the utility of behavioral facts on the goal of morality, therefore, if the ultimate goal of morality is to promote human interests, then the moral value of human interests is undoubtedly greater than that of non-human beings. Since there can be no compromise when the human interests conflict with that of non-human interests, we ought to safeguard the interests of human beings and sacrifice that of non-human beings.

However, if the ultimate goal of morality is for promoting both the interests of human beings and non-human beings, then the moral value of human interests can be seen as lesser than the moral value of non-human beings, for human beings are only one species, we are only a small part of a colossal ecosystem. Therefore, when there is no compromise when the interests of humans conflict with that of non-human beings, we ought to sacrifice the interests of human beings and safeguard that of non-human beings. Thus, the theory of biocentrism that "the ultimate goal of morality is to promote both the interests of human beings and non-human beings" cannot extricate itself from the conclusion of anti-humanism. Analyzing Callicott's biocentrism Roderick Frazier Nash has his most incisive comments that:

> Callicott's "ethical holism" calculated right and wrong in reference of not to individuals but to the biotic community. The whole, in other words, carried more ethical weight than any of its component parts, "oceans and lakes, mountains, forests, and wetlands are assigned a greater value than individual animals," Callicott explained, and he certainly included humans in the latter category. It followed that from the standpoint of the integrity of the ecosystem, the life of a single organism of an endangered species would be more valuable, more worthy of ethical respect of people, than the life of a person or even a substantial part of the large *Home sapiens* population. He agreed with Edward Abbey's well-known opinion that he would rather kill a man than a snake. From Callicott's ecocentric perspective even soil bacteria and oxygen-generating oceanic plankton carried more ethical weight than beings at the top of the food chains such as humans.[12]

36 The standard of moral value

Any conclusion that leads to violence against humanity drawn from the theories that hold that the ultimate goal of morality is to promote the interests of both human and non-human beings is obviously wrong. This is because, regardless of any other considerations, morality is created only by human beings. Is the ultimate goal of humans to create morality for or against itself? Surely it is not for destroying itself? For this reason, it is not imaginable to promote both the interests of human and non-human beings as the ultimate goal morality, since it would not be possible to promote of the interests of human beings in sacrificing ourselves for non-human interests.

It is true that the direct goal of some particular moral norms made by human beings is to promote non-human beings. For instance, people used to make or agree with moral norms such as: "When an old dog that has faithfully served the master and is too old to serve any more, the master ought not to kill it but ought to provide for its needs until it dies." "When a horse has served outstanding military exploits dies it ought not to be eaten but ought to be properly buried." The direct origin and goals of these particular and specific moral norms are intended to protect the interest of old dogs and meritorious horses, and not made for the interests of the masters. However, this is merely a particular and direct origin and goal of morality, but not the universal origin and goal of morality, much less the ultimate origin and goal of morality.

Each specific moral norm has a direct origin and goal that is different from other moral norms. But the origins and goals of all specific moral norms do contain a universal and ultimate origin and goal that is common to all moral norms. For instance, the origin and goal of the particular moral norm that one "ought not let animals suffer unnecessarily" is to promote the animals' interests, and the origin and goal of the particular moral norm that one "ought not destroy flowers or plants" is to promote the interests of flowers or plants. The universal origin and goal of morality contained and expressed in these moral norms is to "safeguard the existence and development of the interest community of human and non-human beings" and to "ultimately promote the human interests": safeguarding the existence and development of the interest community of human and non-human beings is the direct and universal goal of morality; promoting human interest is the ultimate universal goal of morality, namely the ultimate goal of morality.

In short, the particular and direct origin and goal of morality can be for the promotion of the interests of non-human beings; however, the ultimate origin and goal of morality is only to promote the human interests. The goal of morality in this regard is the moral standard that evaluates the goodness and badness of every action. Thus, on the one hand, when the interests of human and non-human are in harmony, it ought to follow the particular goal and standard of morality, promoting the interests of human and non-human, or even to promote the interests of non-human merely for the interests of non-human, such as the master ought to provide for the old dog when it cannot serve anymore until it dies of old age.

On the other hand, when the interests of non-humans and humans are in conflict and no compromise can be made, the function of the particular goal and standard of morality stops. Under such circumstances the ultimate goal and standard of "promoting human interests" ought to be resorted to and this means sacrificing the interests of non-humans to safeguard the human interests. For example, if human beings refrain from eating both animals and plants (including seeds, fruit, etc.), they may well save the lives of both animals and plants, but, in doing so, sacrifice their own happiness or well-being in the short term and overtime are likely starve to death. No compromise can be had when the happiness and lives of human beings conflict with lives of both animal and plants. Eating animals and plants certainly violates the particular goal and standard of morality of "promoting the interests of both animals and plants," but, because it conforms to the ultimate goal and standard of "promoting human interests," it is moral and ought to be.

2.2 Origin and goal of morality: From the point of view of the social moral needs

2.2.1 The social moral needs: The origin and goal of morality

To survey the origin and goal of morality from the point of view of the social moral needs is to reveal that from the relationships between morality and other matters in human society, that is to say, we can reveal the origin and purpose of morality from the needs of various things in society for morality. Therefore, surveying the origin and goal of morality from point of view of the social moral needs is also the comparative survey of various components of the social structure.

Society, is just a "community" composed of at least two or more persons bonded together. Looking at society statically, as a so-called "group" of humans, we see that is also a system for different "groups" of human beings. In viewing society dynamically, as a totality of human "social activities," we see that it is an exchange of interests through human cooperation and the division of labor, which are systems of social activity for creating material wealth and spiritual value. Accordingly, society can be divided into a static structure and dynamic structure. But, in asking which of these social structures reveals the origin and goal or morality, it is undoubtedly the dynamic social structure, namely the structure of the sum of social activities. What then are the activities of human society?

Basic human activities can be divided into two categories: the activities creating material wealth and the activities creating spiritual values. The activities concerning the production, exchange, distribution, and consumption of material wealth, are generally termed as "economy" or as "economic activities." The activities concerning spiritual values are the creation, publication, circulation, performance, study, and appreciation of matters such as writing books, setting up theories, drama, dancing, drawing, sculpturing, teaching, and attending lectures, etc. These activities relate to the human spirit but are neither spiritual nor simply incorporeal reflections of brain activities but are material activities or matters for the purpose of creating spiritual values, more generally referred to as so-called "culture" and "cultural activities."

So-called culture is the valuable things created by human thought: in a narrow sense, culture is the direct creation of thinking through human language, that is, thought, psychology or concept, such as cognition, emotion, will, knowledge, experience, and science, etc.; in a broad sense, culture is everything that human thought can create to meet needs by using the body (such as hands and feet) and tools, everything that is useful and valuable created by the human thought, such as houses, clothes, vessels, and social organizations, etc.

Both economy and culture are activities of creating wealth, which are inevitably and indivisibly related to wealth. On the contrary, those activities which have no necessary and inseparable relationship with wealth, that is, the activities that do not create wealth at all, can be termed as "interpersonal" activities, such as the contacts among friends or colleagues or schoolfellows, kinship, love, marriage, cheating, burglary, fray, and killing. Economic, cultural and interpersonal activities are all social activities. Therefore, to make society exist and develop, we must make them have a certain order to follow and do not conflict with each other. There is a need to manage these activities. Thus the management activities came into being. However, some management activities create wealth, some do not. Wealth-creating management activities, such as production scheduling and Orchestra conducting, undoubtedly belong to economic and cultural activities respectively: production scheduling belongs to economic activities; orchestra conducting belongs to cultural activities.

Other forms of management that do not create wealth are further divided into two categories: politics and the *ruling of virtue*. Sun Yat-sen (孙中山), stated that politics is a kind of management by explaining the combination of two Chinese characters that form the meaning of politics: " '政' is public affairs, and '治' is administration, and managing public affairs is politics (政治)." However, as Ma Qihua says, not all the management of public affairs is politics; politics is only a kind of power management: "it can be said that power is the symbol of politics." Politics is the power management of human actions by society, therefore it is the human action management that ought to be and must be because the so-called power, as mentioned above, is the coercive force owned only by rulers and recognized by society that ought to and must be obeyed. On the one hand, this power is expressed as restriction by force, such as court sentences, imprisonment, execution by shooting or some kind of physical punishment, etc.; on the other hand, it is expressed as administrative coercion, demotion, and reduction of payment, etc. On the contrary, the ruling of virtue is non-power management which is the social management upon human beings depending on non-power force. Such a force ought to be but not must be. Because the so-called non-power force, as we mentioned above, is also the force that people ought to but not necessarily must obey. On the one hand, it is the force that people voluntarily obey, namely so-called

The origin and goal of morality 39

education, indoctrination of thought, edification, and culturing, etc.; on the other hand, it is the non-power coercion, namely the coercion of public opinions such as public comments, denouncement, praise, criticism, etc.

The distinction between politics and the *ruling of virtue* is based on the different natures of the objects of the management. The objects of politics are only those social actions with important social utility such as conflicts between or among nations, class struggle, murder, arson, corruption, stealing, etc. What is regulated by politics are all the actions with *important social utility*, which determine that politics has a force—that power is the nature of politics and that politics is a form of power management—for determining what actions "ought to and must be obeyed." On the contrary, the object of ruling of virtue are all actions with *social utility*, which include both actions with and without important social utility, such as helping or misleading people, such as the elderly or children, or being polite or impolite. Consequently it determines that the ruling of virtue only possesses the force that "ought to be but not must be followed," such that education in this is the nature of ruling of virtue: it is non-power management of the actions of the ruled as to what ought to be, but not must be. Hence, the actions with important social utility are the object of politics and need to be managed by the power management of politics. At the same time they are also the object of the ruling of virtue and need to be managed by the non-power management of the ruling of virtue. Conversely, those actions with no important social utility are only the object of ruling of virtue, and only need to be managed by the non-power management of the ruling of virtue.

Thus, though both politics and the ruling of virtue originate from the needs out of the necessity of the management of economy, culture, and the interpersonal activities, they are not simply only the management of economy, culture and the interpersonal activities, for actualizing the management of these activities certain organizations and institutions are needed, and from this ensues the active management of the managing organizations or institutions as well as the management of the activities of management itself. Therefore, in politics and the ruling of virtue there is a double management of the activities of the people being managed and the managing itself, namely it is the management of all human actions with social utility. In short, politics is the power management—which does not create wealth—of actions with important social utility of "ought to be and must be"; the ruling of virtue is the non-power management—which does not create wealth—of actions with social utility that "ought to be but not must be."

However, as Mencius commented: "The forms of square and circle cannot be made without rules."[13] Only by resorting to behavior norms can the management of actions, the management of politics and the ruling of virtue be actualized to safeguard the existence and development of economic, cultural, interpersonal activities, and all other activities that have the social utility. It is generally known that there are two kinds of norms. One is political norms, namely *law*. It is the norms for political activities, which is the power norms

40 *The standard of moral value*

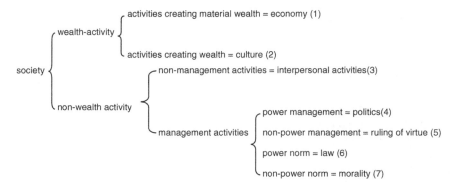

Figure 2.1 The dynamic structure of society

that regulate actions with important social utility that *ought to be and must be* complied with. The other is the norms of the ruling of virtue, namely *morality*. It is the norms for the activities of the ruling of virtue, which is the non-power norms for the actions with social utility that *ought to be but not must be* followed.

It is very clear that in so-called society, the dynamically social activities are the totality of wealth-activity and non-wealth activity. The wealth-activity is divided into two kinds: activities that create material wealth, namely the economy, and activities that create the spiritual wealth, namely culture. Non-wealth activity is also divided into two kinds: first, activities that are not necessarily related to wealth, and can be separated from wealth, or which completely have nothing to do with the creation of wealth, namely the interpersonal activities; second, activities that are necessarily related to wealth and are inseparable from it, namely the activities of management that do not directly but indirectly create wealth. Both these kind of activities of management are also divided into the norms of power management and norms of non-power management: The former is politics and law, and the latter is the ruling of virtue and morality. Therefore, the dynamical structure of society consists of seven activities—economic, cultural, interpersonal, political, and the ruling of virtue, law and morality which can be shown in Figure 2.1.

To sum up, the existence and development of economic, cultural, interpersonal activities—all activities with social utility—need the safeguard of morality: this is the so-called "the social moral needs," that is, the moral needs for the existence and development of society, and the moral needs for the existence and development of economic, cultural, interpersonal activities, and all activities with social utility. As we know, morality originates from the social moral needs, that is, from the needs for the existence and development of economic, cultural, interpersonal activities, and all activities with social utility: the goal of morality then is to satisfy the social moral needs and to safeguard the existence and development of economic, cultural, interpersonal activities, and all activities with social utility.

2.2.2 All sources and goal of morality

If morality originates from the social needs of morality and its goal is to safeguard the existence and development of economic, cultural, interpersonal activities, and all other activities with social utility, then, except for economic, cultural, and interpersonal activities, what else is included in this "all activities with social utility"? As shown above, it already includes law and politics as part of the seven kinds of activities that constitute the social structure—because both law and politics obviously fall into the category of "activities with social utility." Hence, judging from the social needs of morality, the origin and goal of morality, comprehensively speaking, are to safeguard the existence and development of five kinds of economic, cultural, interpersonal, political, and legal activities. In other words, the origin and goal of morality are not only the needs of the three large social activities of economy, culture, and interpersonal relationships, but also the needs of the two large social activities of law and politics. Because morality is not only the necessary condition and fundamental means for the existence and development of economic, cultural, and interpersonal activities, but also the necessary and fundamental means for making excellent laws and realizing good politics: without morality it is impossible to make excellent laws and realize excellent politics.

It turns out to be that, if we discuss the norm itself without discussing the force on which the norms depend, the extension of morality is broader than that of law. Generally speaking, morality and law are the relationship of universality and particularity, the whole and the part, because, on the one hand, *not all moralities are laws*, such as modesty, prudence, cherishing life, diligence, doctrine of the means, and things like continence, courage, benevolence, etc., *all are moralities but not laws*; on the other hand, *all laws are moralities*, such as "no abuse," "do not to kill people," "do not cause harm to others," "raise one's children well," "support elderly parents" etc., are they not rules of law as well as the moral norms? Therefore, before discussing the norm itself without discussing the force on which the norms depend, we can already see that law is one part of morality—that morality is the superior concept of law. Then, what part of morality is law? Law is both a specific kind of morality and the lowest kind of morality. Jelling concluded it with the famous words: "Law is the minimum of morality."

Therefore, laws are merely trivial rules given they are specific and particular, and have no principles in themselves, but are based on the principle of morality. As it is generally known, the so-called principles of law are justice, equality and liberty, etc., but, frankly speaking, these principles are not in the category of law or laws, but in the category of the principle of morality. This is self-evident, because who would say that justice is a piece of law? Who would say that equality is a piece of law? Who would say that freedom is a piece of law? Isn't that we say that justice is morality, equality is morality, and liberty is morality? Where the moral principles of justice, equality, and liberty, etc., are seen to be the principles of law, they should instead be political principles—since politics takes laws as its norm, politics is then the realization of law. That is why the core problems of jurisprudence and political philosophy all are justice, equality, and liberty; justice, equality, and liberty all are the principles of both law and politics.

The principles of laws and politics are inferior to the principle of morality. This obviously means that the laws and politics which do not follow the moral principles or follow the inferior moral principles are inferior, and that excellent laws and politics certainly follow excellent moral principles. The so-called excellent laws and politics mean the laws and politics that follow excellent moral principles; on the contrary, inferior laws and politics mean the laws and politics do not follow moral principles or follow inferior moral principles. This is to say that the making of excellent laws and politics needs morality: morality not only originates from the needs of the existence and development of economic, cultural, and interpersonal activities, but also from the needs of making excellent laws and politics. Therefore, the goal of morality is not only for promoting the development of economy, flourishing culture and safeguarding the freedom and safety of interpersonal activities, but also for the making of excellent laws and politics: promoting the development of economy, flourishing culture, and safeguarding freedom and safety of interpersonal activities are the common goal of morality, laws, and politics; and the making of excellent laws and politics is the particular goal of morality.

Therefore, the so-called moral needs of society can be concluded as five large moral needs: the moral needs of economic activities, the moral needs of the development of culture, the moral needs of interpersonal activities, the moral needs of making excellent laws and the moral needs of making excellent politics. Thus, judging from the moral needs of society, there are five large origins and goals of morality: economy, culture, interpersonal relations, law, and politics. These five activities—together with morality and the *ruling of virtue*—are the so-called "activities with social utility" and the so-called "social activities" as well as the so-called "society." Hence the five large origins and goals of morality can also be concluded as one: to safeguard the existence and development of society. Therefore, from the perspective of social moral needs, the general purpose of morality is to ensure the existence and development of society, and the five sub-goals of morality are to promote economic development, to promote the prosperity of culture, to guarantee the freedom and the safety of interpersonal activities, and to make excellent laws, and to make excellent politics.

These origins and goals of morality undoubtedly are the origins and goals of all moralities, hence they are the universal origins and goals of morality. Therefore, Richard Kraut says: "the general goal of morality is to establish the orders in the social connections,"[14] and Warnock puts it: "Morality has a content, the purpose of which is to ameliorate the human predicament, which has a tendency to worsen."[15] What is, then, the particular origin and goal of morality? It can be declared that every moral norm has its particular origin and goal. To take the example of "continence." It obviously originated from the conflict of reason and the passion in regard to excessive indulgences such as in drinking or sex. Its goal is to steer everyone in the direction of reason as means of control over passion so one clearly knows what one ought to do and ought not do, which is the special origin and purpose of "continence." Thus, if everyone in society is continent, in control of their passions through reason, then, will not the existence and development of society, which is the universal goal of morality, be safeguarded? It follows that the universal origins and goals of morality are contained in its particular origins and goals.

Every moral norm has its own particular origin and goal, but universal origins and goals are contained in them. If we make this observation from not just the perspective of the moral needs of human society, but also from the interest community that is made up of human and non-human beings, then morality has "one general goal and six sub-goals" rather than just the five sub-goals mentioned. The general goal is then to safeguard the existence and development of human society and the interest community, and six sub-goals, namely the development of "economy," the flourishing of "culture," the freedom of "interpersonal relationships," the excellence of "politics" and "laws," and the promotion of "the interests of non-human (animals, plants, etc.)."

Are they entirely the sources and goals of morality? No. Let's pursue this question further. What is the final goal of safeguarding human society—economy, culture, interpersonal relations, law, and politics—and the existence and development of interest community of human and non-human beings? Obviously it is to satisfy the needs of everyone, as well as to promote the interests and actualize the happiness of everyone. Thus, safeguarding the existence and development of society—economy, culture, interpersonal relations, laws and politics—and the community of interests of human and non-human beings is the direct universal goal of morality; and, satisfying the needs of everyone, promoting the interests of everyone, and actualizing the happiness of everyone are the final universal goal of morality, namely the ultimate goal of morality. Therefore, as Mill repeatedly says, "happiness is the end and aim of morality."[16]

In sum, all of the origins and goals of morality can be divided into two large types: the particular origins and goals and universal origins and goals. While each moral norm has its particular origin and goal. The universal origins and goals of morality can be divided into the direct origins and goals and the ultimate origin and goal. The ultimate origin and goal of morality is to promote everyone's interest, while the direct origins and goals of morality are "one general goal and six sub-goals": the general goal is to safeguard the existence and development of human society and the interest community, and six sub-goals, namely the development of "economy," the flourishing of

44 *The standard of moral value*

"culture," the freedom of "interpersonal activities," the excellence of "law" and "politics," and the promotion of "the interests of non-human beings."

2.2.3 *The social nature of the origin and goal of morality*

All origins and goals of morality indicate that the origins and goals of morality are entirely based on social needs but not on individual or self needs: social needs are the essence of morality and the ultimate nature of morality. It is true that the ultimate origin and goal of morality is to promote "everyone's interest" and satisfy "everyone's needs." However, "Everyone's interest" is different from "individual interest" or "self-interest." "Individual interest" or "self-interest" belong to the category of "the self," and thus can be in harmony with or in conflict with the interest of society. If the act of the self benefits society it might harm the self; if it benefits the self it might harm society. For instance, acting bravely for a just cause is beneficial to society but it might result in some sort of self-sacrifice. Or, doing nothing to save another from some kind of danger might be beneficial to the self but might result in greater harm to society.

Conversely, "everyone's interest" or "the interest of every self" falls into the category of society, thus it certainly conforms to the interest of society: whatever benefits (or harms) society obviously is certainly beneficial (or harmful) to every self, and whatever benefits (or harms) every self is certainly beneficial (or harmful) to society. Therefore, the ultimate origin and goal of morality is to promote "everyone's interest" and satisfy "everyone's needs," it also means that "social needs" are the ultimate origin and goal of morality; consequently, we can never draw the conclusion that ultimate origin and goal of morality is for individual or self needs or for promoting individual or self-interest.

Darwin concluded in his survey of the origin of morality that morality originates from social needs, the needs of social instincts:

> We have now seen that actions regarded by savages, and probably so regarded by primeval man, as good or bad, solely as they obviously affect the welfare of the tribe,—not that of the species, nor that of an individual member of the tribe. This conclusion agrees well with the belief that the so-called moral sense is originally derived from the social instincts, for both relate at first to the community.[17]

But, in opposition to this, in the point of view of individualists, the origin and goal of morality is to satisfy individual or the self's needs and interests. Russell wrote:

> The practical need of morals arises from the conflict of desires, whether of different people or of the same person at different times or even at one time. A man desires to drink, and also to be fit for his work next morning. We think him immoral if he adopts the course which gives him

the smaller total satisfaction of desire. We think ill of people who are extravagant or reckless, even if they injure no one but themselves ... Even Robinson Crusoe had occasion to practise industry, self-control and foresight which must be reckoned as moral qualities, since they increased his total satisfaction without counterbalancing injury to others.[18]

This is to say, morality has double origins and goals: on the one hand, morality originates from social needs and the conflicts of human desire; on the other hand, it originates from individual needs and the conflicts of desire of individual self. Therefore, even if one lives lonely in an uninhabited island he certainly has morality because there also exists the source of morality: he will surely have various desires which conflict with reason. If he is able to control his desires through reason, he would have the virtue of "abstemious," but if his desires are too strong, he would sink into a vicious cycle of "the self-indulgence." In sum, this is Russell's view.

Russell's account, however, is a kind of sophistry of morality. One who lives in an uninhabited island surely will not have morality and virtue. One can make some behavioral norms for oneself in relation to such things as one's continence, industriousness, or wisdom. However, they are only the behavioral norms for one's own use, not morality. As we discussed above, the so-called morality is a social contract, therefore, one of the standards for evaluating whether any behavioral norm is a moral norm is who make or agrees with them. If a behavioral norm is made or agreed upon by society it is a social contract, then, no matter how absurd and wrong it is, it is a morality; if a behavioral norm is not made or agreed upon by society but only made by oneself, then, no matter how excellent the norm is, it is not morality because it is not a social contract. It is just one's own behavioral norm.

For instance, if unfortunately, Yang Zhu's moral thought of hedonism were to dominate a society and society makes or agrees upon the behavioral norm that one "ought to be indulgent rather than abstemious," then, no matter how absurd it is, it is still a social contract and therefore is morality. Hence, if one is self-indolent, one conforms to morality and is moral and virtuous. If one makes or agrees with the opposite behavioral norm that one "ought to be abstemious rather than indulgent," which has not been agreed upon by society, and is only one's own behavioral norm, then, no matter how correct and excellent it is, it is not a social contract, thus by no means is morality. Hence, if one is abstemious, and not self-indulgent, one violates morality and is amoral and virtueless.

Even if Robinson Cruseo had remained alone on an uninhabited island and had made some behavioral norms for himself such as continence, industriousness, wisdom etc., the norms would not be morality simply because they were not agreed upon by another party. Even if he always behaved in accordance with these norms—upholding the characteristics of continence, industriousness, or wisdom—by no means are his characteristics moral characteristics. His characteristics are kinds of non-moral characteristics. We can liken non-moral characteristics to the utility of muscles. As we know, muscle strength is crucial for survival such as enabling prey to run at speed from predators, so muscles do have purpose, but not moral characteristics. Discussing Robinson Crusoe and the origin of morality, Liang Qichao (梁启超) wrote that "Morality originates from human conflicts ... as described in *Robinson Crusoe*, if one remains alone on an uninhabited island, then one is neither moral nor immoral."[19] Thus, morality has only one source: it originates from social needs and the conflict of human desire, not from the individual needs and the conflict of individual desire. It has only one goal, which is to solve the problems of interpersonal conflicts and to safeguard the existence and development of society. Its aims are not to solve the problem of conflicts arising from desires of the self and promote the interest of the self.

It is true that moralities can be divided into two types: moralities of other-regarding that solve the conflict of human desire, such as selfless, self-sacrifice, justice, compassion, honesty, generosity, and moralities of self-regarding that solve the conflicts of individual desire, such as continence, pleasure, prudence, open-mindedness, moderation, self-fulfillment. If, as discussed before, morality neither originates from the conflicts of individual desire, nor solves the conflicts of individual desire, why does society make or recognize the moral norms that solve the conflicts of desire of the individual self?

That's because actions done with self-regard have the utility of benefiting society and others, while actions done without self-regard have the utility of harming society and others. Let's consider self-regard in terms of self-fulfillment. What would be more beneficial to others than the realization of one's own potential or the creativity of the self? Would not the suppression of one's own potential or the creativity of the self be more harmful to others? As Darwin said, if a society does not realize the social utility of actions done with or without self-regard, then society would not make the moral norms of self-regard. In this respect, Darwin found differences between primitive society and civilized society in that civilized society takes the normative behaviors or actions of holding oneself in high regard, such as where continence is seen as a virtue, while primitive society disapproves of such behavior or action in that it only takes as virtue the behaviors or actions that hold others in high regard. This is because—as Darwin repeatedly said—civilized society is better at reasoning and recognizing the social utility of actions done with or without self-regard. In primitive society, writes Darwin:

> Powers of reasoning are insufficient to recognize the bearing of many virtues, especially of the self-regarding virtues, on the general welfare of the tribe. Savages, for instance, fail to trace the multiplied evils consequent on want of continence, chastity, &c.[20]

Hence, the origin and goal of moral norms that society makes or agrees upon for solving the conflicts of various desires of the self and for promoting self-regard are only for safeguarding the existence of society, not for promoting individual interest, and even not for promoting "everyone's interest," because, as we discussed above, promoting everyone's interest is not the origin and goal of morality, but the origin and goal of society. The origin and goal of morality is only for the existence and development of society; only the existence and development of society can promote everyone's interest. When morality might be seen to be promoting everyone's interest it only has this as an origin and goal through the intermediary of "society." In this respect, promoting everyone's interest is the goal of morality (only via society), and, in this sense, is also the (indirect) ultimate goal of morality.

However, as discussed, promoting "everyone's interest" is different from promoting "individual interest." The nature of the former is based on society, and thereby falls into the category of "society," and the nature of latter is based on the self or the individual, and thereby falls within the category of the "individual" or "the self." Thus, in whatever sense, the origin and goal of morality, the most profound nature of morality, is only contained in social needs. As Frankena states:

> Morality ... is a social enterprise, not just a discovery or invention of the individual for his own guidance ... it is also largely in its origin, sanctions, and functions ... it is an instrument of society as a whole for the guidance of individuals and smaller groups.[21]

2.3 The origin and goal of morality: From the point of view of personal moral needs

2.3.1 *Personal moral needs: The ways and means for the actualization of morality*

Undoubtedly human beings are the creatures of morality, since everyone more or less has moral needs of following morality, most obvious is that everyone desires to be a good or noble person with virtue, but even evil persons who perpetrate heinous crimes have the moral need to be good, although these kinds of moral needs are weaker in them where their evil desires are stronger, such as whenever circumstances allow their evil desires to prevail. Kant had termed good or noble kind of moral needs as "the reverence for the moral laws" as had the Confucian school similarly termed them as "the mind of being sacred and saints." More precisely speaking, these kinds of moral needs can also be termed as being as "the mind perfecting the moral character of oneself." Then, why does each of us more or less have the desire to perfect the moral character of ourselves and the need to be a good person?

That is because the human being is a social creature and each of our lives must totally depend on others. Since all one's interests is given by others, the most fundamental and the greatest interest in one's own interests is whether one is appreciated by others. And it is self-evident that the key to being appreciated by others largely rests entirely on one's moral character, namely whether one's behavior is beneficial or harmful to others: if one is of good moral character and is virtuous, and one's behavior is beneficial to others, then one will be appreciated in turn; if one is otherwise, then one will likely be denounced and one's life may be ruined. As Paulsen commented: "The first great and fundamental truth to which all peoples have been led in their reflections upon moral matters is the truth that the good man fares well and the wicked man badly."[22]

Everyone initially has the moral need to be a good person, since morality is the most fundamental and most important means for one's own interest. One's moral need in this sense is a kind of need of means. However, the means can be transferred to the goal. When one pursues money, one at first certainly takes money as the means of obtaining pleasure and happiness, and will nevertheless then come to deeply love money for it provides great interest and pleasure. Because the so-called love is merely the psychological reaction to the interests and pleasure, the deep love of money and fascination with making more of it result in money being no longer a means but a goal, and consequently that person becomes a miser and cheapskate: isn't a miser and cheapskate a person whose goal in life is money?

Morality is similar. If one at first takes morality and virtue as the means for self-interest, gradually one will fall in love with morality and virtue because morality and virtue constantly bring him great interest and pleasure. Then one will pursue morality and virtue for the sake of morality and virtue themselves, namely being moral for morality, being dutiful for duty, being virtuous for virtue, and turn morality and virtue from a means into a goal. Mill, in discussing such issues, arrived at a most perfect conclusion that "What is virtuous, they not only place virtue at the very head of the things which are good as means to the ultimate end, but they also recognize as a psychological fact the possibility of its being, to the individual, a good in itself."[23]

Therefore, everyone's moral needs are expressed in two ways: on the one hand, to benefit oneself, being a good person, following morality, and pursuing virtue, are to take morality and virtue as moral needs of means for self-interest; on the other hand, being a good person for being a good person, following morality for following morality and being virtuous for virtue, are to take morality and virtue as the goal of behaviors. Thus, it is obvious that taking virtue as the means is the lower and basic personal moral needs; taking virtue as the goal is the advanced personal moral needs: the latter is the result of continuous accumulation and growth of the former. For instance:

Let's suppose if one believes that honesty is the best strategy and deals honestly with every customer, then, what one possesses is taking the virtue of being honest as the personal moral needs for the means of obtaining one's own interest, therefore it is the lower and the basic of personal moral needs. Nevertheless, as the virtue accumulates day-by-day and year-by-year, gradually his being honest may no longer be for obtaining interest any more but for possessing the virtue of being honest itself, for being an honest and good person in stark opposition to one who is wicked and lies. By now, even if being honest harms his interests he will still be honest. Hence what he possesses is the goal of virtue of being honest as the personal moral needs, and thus the advanced personal moral needs.

However, needs are the sole motive of the actions. If one has the moral needs to follow morality and to be a good person, whether one takes virtue as a means or ends, he will voluntarily follow morality and be a good person, in order to satisfy one's moral needs: personal moral needs are then the ways and means to actualize morality. But if one takes virtue as a means, one will be happy with the interests that one's virtue brings not with the virtue one possess: virtue and happiness are not the same thing. It is conditional for him to follow morality and pursue virtue: only when virtue brings one interests will one follow morality and pursue virtue; otherwise, one will not follow morality and not pursue virtue.

On the contrary, if one's moral needs aims at virtue, one will be happy with virtue: virtue and happiness are the same thing. Hence, it is unconditional for him to follow morality and pursue virtue: one will follow morality and pursue virtue, whether virtue brings interests or not. Therefore, personal moral needs are the ways and means of the actualization of morality: personal moral needs, with virtue as its means, is a conditional way and means of actualizing morality; personal moral needs, with virtue as its end, is an unconditional way and means of actualizing morality.

Obviously, the personal moral need of perfecting the moral character of the self is the way and the means of actualizing morality, which implies that the personal moral need of perfecting the moral character of the self is not the origin and goal of morality. It is true that one's so-called moral character is merely the result of a long-term commitment to follow or violate morality: as Zhu Xi says, "Virtue is obtaining. If one act according to morality, one will obtain virtue."[24] Thus, morality is the cause, and virtue is the result of morality. It is the case that the personal moral need of perfecting one's moral character originates from morality, while it is not the case that morality originates from the personal moral need of perfecting one's moral character.

However, in the final analysis, whether morality originates from the personal moral need of perfecting everyone's moral character and whether the goal of morality is to perfect everyone's moral character, depends on whether morality and virtue are a kind of intrinsic good or a kind of necessary bad: if they are an intrinsic good, the answer may be positive; if they are a necessary bad, the answer is bound to be negative. Then, are morality and virtue a necessary bad or an intrinsic good?

2.3.2 Morality and virtue: A kind of necessary bad

Examining the benefits and harms each element of social dynamic structure brings to human, we can easily see that the three kinds of economic, cultural, and interpersonal activities are fundamentally different from the four kinds of activities of politics, the *ruling of virtue*, laws, and morality. Politics, the ruling of virtue, laws, and morality, in terms of themselves, not only do not create wealth, they constrain or violate certain human desires and freedom, so they themselves are "harmful" rather than "beneficial" to humans; what is beneficial to humans is not these management and regulations but the result or purpose of these management and regulations, namely the existence and development of economic, cultural, and interpersonal activities.

Hence, morality, laws, politics, and the ruling of virtue, are the means human beings create to harm themselves (limit some desires and freedom) in order to achieve the purpose of "benefiting" themselves (safeguarding the existence and development of economic, cultural, and interpersonal activities), and are therefore a "necessary bad." Because the so-called "necessary bad," as mentioned before, is a thing that is bad in itself with a good result, producing a net balance of good over bad consequences. Certainly, morality, laws, politics, and the ruling of virtue, in themselves, restrict, suppress, and impede everyone's needs and desires, and thus are kinds of bad. Nevertheless, this bad can prevent the greater bad (the collapse and disintegration of economic, cultural, and interpersonal activities) and pursue the greater good (safeguard the existence and development of economic, cultural, and interpersonal activities), and the net balance of the results is good, therefore it is called "necessary bad."

Conversely, economy and culture create both material and spiritual wealth and directly satisfy both the material and spiritual needs of human; though interpersonal activities do not create wealth, they satisfy the needs of interpersonal communication. Therefore, these three in themselves are desirable and are able to satisfy human needs, and are the goal humans pursue, which, in the final analysis, are the goal of politics, the ruling of virtue, laws, and morality: isn't the fundamental goal of politics, the ruling of virtue, laws, and morality to safeguard the development and the prosperity of culture, as well as the freedom of interpersonal activities? Thence, the economic, cultural and interpersonal activities are three kinds of "intrinsic good" or "good-as an-end," or "good-in-itself." As we have seen, the so-called "intrinsic good" also can be referred to as "good as an end" or "good-in-itself." It is a good that itself is desirable, and can satisfy human needs and is the end people pursue.

It is easily to understand that politics and laws are the necessary bad. The classic understanding of it is Bentham's dictum: "Every law violates freedom." "Every law," Bolin explained further,

> while it may be possible to promote one kind of freedom, it also abates certain freedom. Whether it enhances the total amount of freedom available depends, of course, on each particular case. A law that states that "no one can impose force on others within a given scope," although it clearly enhances the freedom of the majority, even such laws "violate" the freedom of lurking thugs and police. Under such circumstance, the violation may well be worth our pursuing, but it is still a "violation."[25]

But, is morality the same as law? Yes. Generally speaking, all legal norms are also the moral norms. Isn't what Bolin quoted that "no one can impose force on others within a given scope" a legal norm as well as a moral norm? Aren't universal legal norms "no violence," "do not kill people," or "do not harm others," or more specific legal norms, such as in China "to raise one's children well, to support one's parents" etc., all moral norms as well? If we say that "no violence" is a legal norm that restricts, constrains and violates the freedom of police, then, as a moral norm, does it not also restrict, constrain, and violate the freedom of police? Morality and laws all are regulations, restrictions, and constraints on the human behavior, therefore they all in some way suppress, check, or violate human desires and freedom (namely those with negative social utility).

However, in terms of the forces that law and morality depend on, morality limits, suppresses, and violates human freedom and desire lighter than law: law is a kind of violation with power in that its violations are in the form of violent coercion or administrative coercion, while morality is a kind of non-power violation in that its violations are in the form of ideological education or coercion by public opinion. However, as far as the actions that laws and morality violate are concerned, morality infringes more on people's freedom and desire than law: laws only constrain human desires and freedom with important social utility, while morality constrains all human desires and freedom with social utility; laws only require that one does not harm others, while morality demands that one make some kind of self-sacrifice for others. As Yelling had summed up, "law is the minimum of morality." Therefore, just as laws, morality, in terms of itself, is a kind of bad. We can also say: "Every rule of morality restricts and violates freedom" and "Every rule of morality restricts and suppresses desires."

Then, is virtue the same? Yes, because so-called virtue is a stable inner state formed by long-term behaviors that have conformed to morality. Thus "virtue" and "morality" are all the behavioral norms that ought to be; the distinction is that "morality" corresponds to an external norm which is a social norm that has not yet transformed into the stable psychology of individual, while "virtue" corresponds to an internal norm, a social norm that has transformed into the stable psychology of individual. Therefore, on the one hand, just as morality, virtue, in itself, is also a kind of harm or bad: "Every virtue restricts and suppresses desires" and "Every virtue restricts and violates freedom"; On the other hand, virtue and morality are the same, the higher the state virtue requires, the heavier the violation of freedom and desire, and the easier to suffer from self-torture over one's sense of guilt and cause neurosis—as Freud found.

It can be seen that morality, the ruling of virtue, laws, and politics are "four harms," or "four bads" created by humans to safeguard the existence and development of society and economic, cultural, and interpersonal activities. However, the damage they do to everyone is obviously far less than the benefits they give to everyone: only when there are morality, laws, politics, and the ruling of virtue, there are society and economic, cultural, and interpersonal activities, and what everyone loses are nothing but the desires and freedom that have negative social utility; conversely, without morality, laws, politics, and the ruling of virtue, society no longer exist, so are economic, cultural, and interpersonal activities, everyone will lose everything.

We can see that virtue is the same argument as morality in terms of benefit and harm because everyone is a social animal and everyone's life totally depends on other people and society: everyone's interest is provided by others, hence one's most important or fundamental interest is whether one is appreciated by others. The key to being appreciated obviously depends on one's moral character: those considered to have good moral character are appreciated, and those without good moral character are condemned. Whatever the harm of virtue might be, it is obviously lesser than the interest of virtue, since it brings the benefit of being praised by others and by society in which it obtains every interest one depends on to exists and develop. Without virtue, though one obtains the desires and freedom with the negative social utility, one is condemned and loses all the interests on which one need to exist and develop.

In short, on the one hand, morality itself, like law, is a kind of harm or bad, since it restricts, suppresses, and violates certain desires and freedoms of human; however, in terms of its results or purposes, it can prevent greater bad (the collapse of society and economic, cultural and interpersonal activities) and seeks greater advantages or good (the existence and development of society and economic, cultural and interpersonal activities), so it is a kind of *good over bad*, namely *necessary bad*. On the other hand, virtue itself, like morality, is a kind of bad, since it restricts, suppresses, and violates certain desires and freedoms of virtuous people, however, as far as its result or goal is concerned, it can prevent the greater harm or bad (the contempt from others) and pursue greater advantages or good (the praise from others), so it is a kind of *good over bad*, namely necessary bad.

However, most of the deontologists, such as Confucianist and Kantist, only see the advantage and good of the result of morality and virtue but not the harm and bad in themselves, and further confuse their results with themselves, so they come to the wrong conclusion that morality and virtue are a kind of good-in-itself, good-as-an-end or intrinsic good but not a necessary bad: morality or virtue "is not a necessary bad but a necessary good."[26] On the contrary, the Taoist school and anarchists do not see the advantage and good of the result of morality and virtue but the harm and bad in themselves, considering both morality and virtue themselves and their results as bad, and therefore draw the wrong conclusion that morality and virtue "both are unnecessary bad."[27]

2.3.3 The nature of heteronomy of the origin and goal of morality

Morality and virtue are *necessary bads*, which means that the origin and goal of morality is by no means autonomous: on the one hand, it is impossible for morality to originate from morality itself and the personal moral needs of perfecting the moral character of the self; on the other hand, it is impossible for the goal of morality to be a goal for itself and to satisfy the personal moral needs of perfecting the moral character of the self. This is because morality and virtue themselves are nothing but bads that restrict, suppress, and violate human desires and freedom. So, if the goal of morality is in morality itself and in the perfection of everyone's moral character, does it not mean that the goal of morality is to give harm and bad to everyone, that the goal of morality is to restrict, suppress, and violate human desires and freedom, that morality suppresses human desires for the sake of suppressing human desires, restricts human freedom for the sake of restricting human freedom, harms human beings for the sake of harming human beings?

Since any necessary bad itself is a kind of bad, it is obvious that it cannot be its own end: every "necessary bad" aims at something other than they themselves. Appendicitis is a kind of necessary bad, so its goal is not possibly for itself, that is, it is not possible for it to be the purpose to operate on one's belly. Its goal rather is for a matter other than for the appendicitis operation itself, namely avoiding death. Since morality is a necessary bad, the origin and goal of morality certainly are heteronomous. On the one hand, morality originates from matters other than morality, namely it originates from the needs of human society and the interest community: it directly originates from the needs for the existence and development of human society (economic, cultural and interpersonal activities) as well as from the interest community, and ultimately originates from the needs of promoting everyone's interests. On the other hand, the goal of morality is to safeguard matters other than morality, namely to satisfy the moral needs of human society and the interest community: the direct goal is to safeguard the existence and development of human society (economic, cultural, and interpersonal activities, laws, and politics) as well as the interest community, and the ultimate goal is the promotion of everyone's interest.

The origin and goal of laws are as the same as that of morality: law is a kind of necessary bad, thus the origin and goal of laws are heteronomous not autonomous. On the one hand, laws originate from matters other than laws, that is, they originate from the legal needs of human society and the interest community: it directly originates from the existence and development of the human society—economy, culture, interpersonal activities, and politics—and the interest community, and its ultimate goal is to promote everyone's interest. On the other hand, the purpose of laws is to protect the things other than laws, namely to satisfy the legal needs of human society and the interest community: the direct purpose is to safeguard the existence and development of human society—economy, culture, interpersonal activities, and politics—and the interest community, and its ultimate goal is to promote everyone's interest. Therefore, Marx wrote that:

> The relationship between laws, like the form of a state, cannot be understood either by itself or by the general development of the so-called

human spirit, on the contrary, they are rooted in the life relationship of material.[28]

As far as the origin and goal are concerned, all norms (not just the morality and laws) are heteronomous not autonomous, not for norms themselves but for matters other than norms. This is because, all norms themselves are certain restrictions, constraints and violations to human desires and freedom, they are harmful not beneficial to humans, thus are *bads*; what is beneficial can only be the other things that norms produce through the damage to human. For instance, learning to swim has certain norms or rules. If one does not follow these rules, though one is free to do as one please in the water, one will not learn well. If one learns to follow the rules, it would be monotonous, repetitive, boring, and not fun or free, but one learns quickly and swims well. Therefore, the rules for learning to swim, in themselves, are only the restrictions, constraints and violations of the freedom of swimming, and make the learner feel that it is monotonous, repetitive, boring, and not fun or free, it is harmful not beneficial and thus is a bad. However, this kind of bad can lead to greater good: that is leaning swimming and being able to save one's own life or that of another if such a circumstance were to arise. Thus the rules for learning to swim are a kind of bad, but the net balance of it is good, so it is a necessary bad. Therefore, the origin and goal of the rules for swimming is not autonomous but heteronomous, not for the rules itself but for matters other than the rules for learning to swim: that is, swimming well and health and longevity.

As we have discussed above, the origins and goals of morality and virtue only can be heteronomous, only for other matters other than morality and virtue, namely safeguarding the existence and development of society and promoting everyone's interest. Therefore they are not possible to be autonomous, impossible to be for the morality itself and for the perfection of everyone's moral characters. The personal needs of perfecting the moral character of the self completely originate from morality, and are completely the ways and means the morality is followed then actualized. This is the objective law of the origin and goal of morality which is determined by the most profound nature of morality—morality and virtue are kinds of bad.

2.4 Theories on origins and goals of morality

2.4.1 Anthropocentrism and anti-anthropocentrism

Traditional ethics, as generally known, is the ethics of anthropocentrism; not until the twentieth century, with the establishment and growth of the environmental ethics, did the controversies between anti-anthropocentrism and anthropocentrism emerge. The representative figures of the anthropocentrist school are the likes of John Passmore and Bryan Norto; however, its real masters still are the traditional ethics thinkers such as Plato, Aristotle,

Aquinas, Descartes, Locke, and Kant. The important proponents of anti-anthropocerntrism mainly are the scholars for animal liberation and animal rights such as Peter Singer and Tom Regan, the scholars of biocentric theory such as Paul W. Taylor, and scholars of ecocentrism such as Aldo Leopold and Holmes Rolston III. The works of these thinkers have shown that both anthropocentrism and anti-anthropocentrism are ethical theories concerning the relationship between human beings and non-human beings; in the final analysis, both are the ethical theories concerning how human beings ought to treat non-human beings. The distinctions between these two schools are summed up as follows:

Anthropocentrism holds that only human beings are the ends, and all non-human beings are merely the means for serving human interests. Therefore, the origin, goal and standard of morality should also be only for the human interest, and all moral good and evil should be measured by the standard of human interest. Thomas Aquinas wrote:

> We refute the error of those who claim that it is a sin for man to kill brute animals. For animals are ordered to man's use in the natural course of things, according to divine providence. Consequently, man uses them without any injustice, either by killing them or employing them in any other way.[29]

On the contrary, anti-anthropocerntrism holds that all creatures can distinguish between good and bad and have their own interests, and thence should be get moral concern as members of the moral community. The origin, goal, and standard of morality is the common interest of human beings and non-human beings and all moral good and evil should therefore be measured by the standard of the common interest of human beings and non-human beings. Albert Schweitzer writes:

> The man who has become a thinking being feels a compulsion to give to every will-to-live the same reverence for life that he gives to his own. He experiences that other life in his own. He agrees as being good: to preserve life, to promote life, to raise it to its highest value life which is capable of development; and as being evil: to destroy life, to injure life, to repress life which is capable of development. This is the absolute, fundamental principle of the moral.[30]

Both anthropocentrism and anti-anthropocentrism are one-sided truths! Because, as previously discussed in detail, promoting the common interests of human beings and non-human beings is only the particular origin, goal, and standard of morality, while the ultimate origin, goal, and standard of morality is completely for the promotion of human interests. Thence, on the one hand, when the interests of human beings and non-human beings are in harmony, the particular and direct standard of morality should be followed to promote the interest of both human and non-human beings, or even to promote the interest of animals and plants just for the promotion of the interest of animals and plants; on the other hand, when the interests of non-human animals and plants conflict with that of human beings, the function of the particular moral standard discontinues: under such circumstance it should resort to the ultimate standard of morality of "promoting human interest," sacrificing the interest of non-human animals and plants to protect that of humankind.

Judging from the ultimate origin, goal, and standard of morality, the anthropocentric view is correct since the ultimate origin, goal, and standard of morality is just for the promotion of human interest. However, this view is greatly exaggerated by anthropocentrism in that it mistakes that the entire origin, goal, and standard of morality is only for human beings, and therefore leads to the wrong conclusion that the human treatment of animals and plants under any condition has nothing to do with being moral or immoral. On the other hand, judging from the direct, particular origin, goal, and standard of morality, anti-anthropocentrism is correct since the direct, particular origin, goal, and standard of morality is for both the interest of human beings and non-human beings, not just for the promotion of human interest. However, this view is also greatly exaggerated by anti-anthropocentrism in that it mistakes that the ultimate origin and ultimate goal of morality is also for the promotion of the common interest of human beings and non-human beings, and therefore leads to the anti-humanist conclusion that "when their interests conflict the human interest should be sacrifice to protect that of non-human beings."

2.4.2 Theories of moral heteronomy and moral autonomy

The theory of moral heteronomy—namely the theory of heteronomy of the origin and goal of morality—is the theoretical premise of utilitarianism. Thus, its representative figures, like utilitarianism, are Bentham, Mill, and Sidgwick. The most fundamental view of the theory of moral heteronomy is that morality is a kind of necessary bad. It is true that Bentham, Mill, and Sidgwick did not find that morality is a kind of necessary bad but only stated that law is a kind of necessary bad: "Every coercive law creates an offence"[31] because

> all punishment is mischief: all punishment in itself is evil. Upon the principle of utility, if it ought at all to be admitted, it ought only to be admitted in as far as it promises to exclude some greater evil.[32]

However, that law is a kind of necessary bad implies that morality is a kind of necessary bad because all legal norms are also moral norms. If "no stealing" is a legal norm restricting and violating a thief's freedom and desires, then, as a moral norm, does it not also restrict and violate the thief's freedom and desires? As discussed, both morality and virtue are the same as law, which, in themselves, are the restriction of human behaviors and the suppression of certain human desires and freedom, thus they are also a kind of bad; nevertheless, judging from their results and goal, they prevent greater bad (the collapse of society) and pursue greater good (the existence and development of society), thus their net balance is good, which makes them necessary bads.

Thus, like law, the origin and goal of morality is by no means autonomous. It is neither for morality itself nor for the perfection of everyone's virtue. It is heteremonous and only for things other than morality, that is, everyone's interest and happiness. As Bentham wrote: "Ethics at large may be defined, the art of directing men's actions to the production of greatest possible quantity of happiness, on the part of those whose interest is in view."[33] Mill also repeatedly stated that "happiness is the end and aim of morality."[34]

On the contrary, moral autonomy theory—namely the autonomy theory of the origin and goal of morality—is the theoretical premise of deontology. Thus, its representative figures, like deontology, are the Confucian school, Kant, and Christian ethicists. The most fundamental point of view of moral autonomy theory is that laws and morality are not a necessary bad but a necessary good, a necessary intrinsic good, good-as-an-end and good-in-itself. Fung Yulan (冯友兰), the scholar of new Confucianism wrote: "The social organizations of the state, the legal and moral norms are necessary for the growth of human beings based on its nature. They are necessary for human beings, not the necessary bad but the necessary good."

The view that morality and virtue are kinds of a necessary good and kinds of necessary intrinsic good and good-in-itself had been systematically expounded by Kant who believed that the good of moral will and moral character are not only intrinsic good and good-in-itself, but also are unconditional or absolute good. He wrote that:

> In the world, or even outside the world, it is impossible to conceive of an unconditional good except good will ... Good will is goodness not by what it makes, nor by what it expects, nor because it is good at achieving its intended goal but it is good simply because of will, which is the intrinsic good.[35]

Since both morality and virtue in themselves are good and kinds of good-in-itself, then the origin and goal of morality are really autonomous: morality originates from morality itself, it originates from everyone's needs of perfecting the moral character of the self; the goal of morality is in morality itself and in the perfection of everyone's moral character. Francis Herbert Bradley, a believer of Kant's theory of moral autonomy, wrote it clearly as: "Morality says, she is sought as a goal for her own sake, not as a means of reaching something other than herself."[36]

The theory of moral autonomy and the theory of moral heteronomy, which is right and which is wrong? The analysis of the nature of morality and virtue indicates that, the same as law, morality, and virtue are kinds of necessary bad; that the origin and goal of morality cannot possibly be autonomous, that morality and virtue themselves can only be heteronomous, and are only for safeguarding matters other than morality: the existence and development of society and promoting everyone's interest. Therefore, the theory of moral heteronomy is a truth and the theory of moral autonomy is a fallacy.

The fundamental error of the theory of moral autonomy is its confusion of good-as-an-end with good-in-itself. On the one hand, things like cleverness, the ability to understand, reason, or judge things, or to have spiritual wealth, honor, health, happiness, etc., in themselves, are desirable and can satisfy human needs, and they are sorts of goals people pursue each is thus good-in-itself, good-as-an-end, and an intrinsic good; but that which is good-in-itself might lead to bad consequences if their possessors have no virtue. Therefore, judging from its results, it might be bad.

On the other hand, good will, good moral character or virtue, in themselves are each the suppression and violation of certain desires and freedom of those who are virtuous, thus they are kinds of bad; however, judging from their results, they are also kinds of a greater good because they can prevent those who are virtuous from greater bad, such as prevent cleverness leading to bad consequences (a wise man can be ruined by his own cleverness). Therefore virtue is a kind of good-as-an-end: but in itself is bad.

The fundamental error of Kant and other scholars' theories of moral autonomy is that, on the one hand, it mistakes good-as-an-end, such as morality and virtue, as good-in-itself; on the other hand, it mistakes good-in-itself, such as being happy or being wise, as good-as-an-end. Consequently, they derived from the theory of moral autonomy that "the goal of morality is in morality and virtue themselves"; on the contrary, if morality and virtue is not good-in-itself but a necessary bad, the goal of morality is not possible for morality and virtue themselves.

The error of the theory of moral autonomy also lies in confusing *the goal of morality* with *ends of actions* and the two meanings of *moral autonomy*. As previously discussed in detail, on the one hand, everyone's actions can originate from the personal moral need for the perfection of one's moral character, the goal of which is to perfect both the moral character of the self and morality itself, which is the moral autonomy in the cause and purpose of personal action, and is a truth. On the other hand, morality originates from everyone's moral needs for the perfection of moral character, the goal of which is to perfect everyone's moral character and morality itself, which is the moral autonomy in the origin and purpose of morality, and is a fallacy.

In other words, one's ends of action might be for morality itself, as well as for the perfection of the moral character of the self, but it is never possible for the goal of morality to be for morality itself, or for the perfection of human moral character. In this respect, morality here can be likened to money in that one's purpose can be for accumulating money itself, but it is never possible for the purpose of money to accumulate the money itself. The error of the theory of moral autonomy on the origin and goal of morality is that it equates the moral autonomy of the personal "cause and ends of action" with the moral autonomy of the social "origin and goal of morality," and thereby from the right premise that personal actions can be caused by the need to perfect one's moral character and the goal to perfect the moral character of the self, draws the wrong conclusion that morality originates from the human need to perfect their moral character, the goal of which is to perfect everyone's moral character.

Notes

1 Peter Kropotkin: *The Origin and Development of Ethics*, Pingming Bookstore, 1936, p. 17.
2 Joseph P. de Marco, ed.: *New Trends in Ethics in the Modern World*, China Youth Publishing House, 1990, p. 305.
3 Paul W. Taylor: *Respect for Nature: A Theory of Environmental Ethics*, Princeton University Press, Princeton, NJ, 1986, p. 14.
4 Ibid., pp. 15–16.
5 Ibid., p. 17.
6 Ibid., p. 16.
7 Ibid.
8 Holmes Rolston III: *Naturalizing Values: Organism and Species*, cited from Louis P. Pojman: *Environmental Ethics: Readings in Theory and Application*, Wadsworth, Belmont, CA, 2001, p. 77.
9 Roderick Frazier Nash: *The Rights of Nature: A History of Environmental Ethics*, The University of Wisconsin Press, London, 1989, p. 28.
10 Ibid., p. 155.
11 Ibid., p. 169.
12 Ibid., p. 153.
13 Mencius: *Li Lou.*
14 Hong Qian, ed.: *Logical Empiricism, Second Volume*, Commercial Press, Beijing, 1989, p. 643.
15 G. J. Warnock: *The Goal of Morality*, Methuen & Co Ltd, London, 1971, p. 26.
16 J. S. Mill: *Utilitarianism, On Liberty and Representative Government*, J. M. Dent & Sons Ltd, London, p. 22.
17 Charles Darwin: *Descent of Man and Selection in Relation to Sex*, John Murray, London, 1922, p. 182.
18 Bertrand Russell: *What I Believe*, E. P. Dutton, New York, 1925, pp. 17–18.
19 Liang Qichao: *The Theory of New People*, Zhongzhou Ancient Books Press, 1998, p. 197.
20 Charles Darwin: *Descent of Man and Selection in Relation to Sex*, John Murray, London, 1922, p. 183.
21 William K. Frankena: *Ethics*, Prentice-Hall, Englewood Cliffs, NJ, 1973, p. 6.
22 Friedrich Paulsen: *System of Ethics*, trans. Frank Thill. Charles Scribner's Sons, New York, 1908, p. 400.
23 J. S. Mill: *Utilitarianism, On Liberty and Representative Government*, J. M. Dent & Sons Ltd, London, p. 33.
24 Zhu Xi: *The Notes on the Four Books*, Chapter of Learning.

25 Isaiah Berlin: *Four Articles on Freedom*, Taibei Lianjing Publishing Company, 1986, p. 53.
26 Fung Yulan: *Complete Works of Sansong Tang, Vol. 4*. Henan People's Publishing House, 1986, p. 592.
27 Ibid., p. 603.
28 Karl Marx and Friedrich Engels: *Selected Works of Marx and Engels, Vol. 2*. People's Publishing House, 1972, p. 82.
29 Joseph R. Des Jardins (College of Saint Benedict): *Environmental Ethics: An Introduction to Environmental Philosophy*, Wadsworth, Belmont, CA, 1993, p. 111.
30 Ibid., p. 149.
31 Jeremy Bentham: *An Introduction to the Principles of Morals and Legislation*, Clarendon Press, Oxford, 1823, p. 330.
32 Ibid., p. 170.
33 Ibid., p. 310.
34 J. S. Mill: *Utilitarianism, On Liberty and Representative Government*, J. M. Dent & Sons Ltd, London, p. 22.
35 Immanuel Kant: *The Principle of Moral Metaphysics*, Shanghai People's Publishing House, 1986, pp. 42–43.
36 Francis Herbert Bradley: *Ethical Research, Vol. 1*. Commercial Press, Beijing, 1944, p. 76.

3 The ultimate standard of morality
The ultimate value standards of the state institutions

3.1 The system of ultimate standard of morality

3.1.1 Increasing or decreasing everyone's quantum of interests:
The ultimate general standard of morality and the ultimate general
value standard of the state institutions

The ultimate general standard of morality originates from the frequent conflicts among different moral norms. When the conflicts occur between different moral norms and cannot be compromised, it undoubtedly should sacrifice the less important moral norms to follow more important moral norms or moral principles. Taking the example Kant gave. When a bystander sees a target hide somewhere from a violent perpetrator in their pursuit and the perpetrator asks the bystander for the whereabouts of the potential victim the bystander is then confronted with a moral conflict: if he follows the moral rule of being honest and tells the perpetrator the truth, he violates the more important moral principle of saving people's life and benefiting others, and puts the potential victim in the position of being killed; if he follows the more important moral principle of benefiting others such as to save the life of the victim, he violates the moral rule of being honest by deceiving the murderer.[1] What one should do under such circumstance? It is obvious that one should follow more important moral principle of "saving a life" and sacrifice the moral norm of "honesty."

But, what should one do when conflicts occur between the moral principles? Undoubtedly one should obey more fundamental moral principle and violate the moral principle that is determined by the former. To explain further, when a comparatively fundamental moral principle conflicts with a more fundamental moral principle, one should obey the moral principle that is more fundamental. To obey the most fundamental moral principle, is to follow the ultimate moral standard: the most fundamental moral standard by which all moral standards are determined and deduced is the moral standard that should be obeyed when moral norms are conflict. In following the moral standard it should not be violated under any circumstance, it should be followed absolutely without exception, it is the ultimate moral standard, namely the absolute morality. With regard to the absolute moral standard Mill wrote: "There ought to be some one fundamental principle or law, at the root of all morality ... and the one principle, or the rule for deciding between the various principles when they conflict."[2] Mill followed the old tradition and called it the ultimate standard of morality, or the "first principle" of morality.[3]

Obviously, there can only be one ultimate moral standard. Two or more would conflict with each other. One would have to be violated and that would certainly mean that it could not be the ultimate moral standard. Then, what is this ultimate moral standard? Warnock gives the answer that it is the general goal of morality that to our knowledge is to be made advantageous use of, and be taken as, the behavioral norm: "the general object of morality, appreciation of which may enable us to understand the basis of moral evaluation."[4] Thilly makes it clearer: "Morality serves a purpose in the world, and that this purpose is its final ground."[5]

This is indeed true! As the study on meta-ethics indicates, the moral ought, the moral good and the moral values of behavioral oughts, are the utility of the behavioral facts to the goal of morality, and therefore consists of two aspects of "the behavioral facts" and "the goal of morality." The behavioral facts are the source or the substance of the behavioral oughts, and is thereby termed as "the substance of moral oughts" or "the substance of the moral good," which, in the final analysis, is the "substance of moral value"; the goal of morality is the condition for the emergence and existence of the behavioral oughts from the behavioral facts, and it is the standard to evaluate whether the behavioral facts have their moral values, and is thereby termed as "the standard of moral ought" or "the standard of the moral good," namely "the standard of moral value." Let's take Kant's example once more:

When a person sees a victim who is pursued by a murderer hide somewhere, and when the murderer asks about the whereabouts of the victim he confronts the following moral conflict: whether he ought to follow the moral rule of being honest and tell the murderer the truth? Kant thought he ought to be honest and tell the truth: "Truthness in statements which can not be avoided is the formal duty on an individual to everyone, however great may be the disadvantage accuring to himself or to another."[6] But he has not understood that under such a circumstance being honest would mean the victim would be killed and would then violate the goal of morality—safeguarding the existence and development of society. Thus the person ought not to be honest since this kind of honesty is immoral. Lying in this circumstance would save a life and conform to the goal of morality, therefore his behavior of lying is what ought to be and is moral. Kant's error is that he did not understand that the goal of morality is the standard of moral value for measuring whether the action of honest or lying is ought to be or not.

The goal of morality is the standard of moral value, which obviously means that the ultimate goal of morality is the ultimate standard of moral value, i.e., the standard which produce, determine, and deduce all other moral standards; the moral standard ought to be followed and not violated when moral norms conflict; the moral standard should be followed and absolutely should not violated under any circumstance; it is the so-called "ultimate moral standard." Therefore, the key for the establishment of the ultimate standard of morality is to understand the underlying question: what is the ultimate goal of morality?

As we discussed in the previous chapter, the goal of morality is to promote everyone's interests. Therefore, the ultimate standard of morality is to promote everyone's interests. Speaking more exactly, the goal of morality should be quantized as: increasing or decreasing everyone's quantum of interests because every standard as a standard should be something that can be quantized. Therefore the ultimate standard of morality is not entirely equal to the ultimate goal of morality, instead, it is the quantization of the ultimate goal of morality: increasing or decreasing everyone's quantum of interests.

"Increasing or decreasing everyone's quantum of interests" is the ultimate standard of morality, which contains two implications: it is not only the ultimate standard for goodness and evilness of all actions, but also the ultimate standard for the excellence and inferiority of all moralities. On the one hand, increasing or decreasing everyone's quantum of interests is the ultimate standard for goodness and evilness of all actions: the action that increases everyone's quantum of interests, no matter how unsatisfactory and imperfect its moral realm is, it is what ought to be and moral; the action that decreases everyone's quantum of interests, no matter how ideal and perfect its moral realm is, it is what ought not to be and immoral. On the other hand, increasing or decreasing everyone's quantum of interests is the ultimate standard for the excellence and inferiority of all moralities: whichever morality most effectively safeguards the economy, makes culture flourish, safeguards the freedom of interpersonal activities, makes the best laws and politics, increases everyone's interests to the utmost, it is according to these facts themselves the most excellent morality, no matter how it is termed or if it is demonized. The inverse would also holds true, factually speaking, of the most vicious or incorrect form of morality regardless of how it is termed or if it is sanctified.

It is obvious that morality, laws, state, and politics, can only have their distinctions in their direct and particular goals, but their ultimate goals are the same in that they are all for the promotion of everyone's interests. Because the state is a society which possesses the sovereign power, any power undoubtedly emerges, forms, and originates from the general agreements of the members of society, and any agreement by two or more persons for certain exchange of interests undoubtedly is a contract. Hence, the same as law, morality, and politics, the sovereign power or state, certainly directly emerges, forms, and originates from the contract. Consequently, the ultimate goal of state, politics, laws, and morality obviously aims at promoting the interests of the makers of the contract, namely everyone in the country. This is the reason why the ultimate goal of morality—promoting everyone's interests—is the ultimate goal of the state and laws and politics: These four ultimate goals share the same concepts.

64 The standard of moral value

Therefore, "increasing or decreasing everyone's quantum of interests" is not only the ultimate standard of moral value for the evaluation of the excellence and inferiority of morality as well as of the goodness and badness of actions, it is also the ultimate standard of legal value for the evaluation of the goodness or badness of laws, and the ultimate standard of political value for the evaluation of the goodness or badness of politics. After all, it is the ultimate value standard for the evaluation of the goodness or badness of state institutions. The first person who found this standard was Aristotle who repeatedly said that the ultimate goal of state is to seek the interests for everyone and satisfy the needs of everyone's existence and development to the fullest, actualizing everyone's "best life" or "self-sufficient and perfect life":

> The city-state is a union of several well-off families or tribes in pursuit of self-sufficiency and the best of life;[7]
> The goal of a city-state is to live the best life that man can achieve;[8]
> The polis grew out of the development of human life, and its actual existence was for the "good life";[9]
> The polis not only exists for the sake of life, but also for the good life.[10]

What he said is so true! However, speaking more exactly, "increasing or decreasing everyone's quantum of interests" is the ultimate general standard of morality, the ultimate general legal standard, the ultimate general political standard, and the ultimate general standard of state institutions. Because this standard has different expressions under different circumstances, we can derive from it three ultimate sub-standards, namely the standard of the net balance of maximum interest, the standard of the greatest interests for the greatest number, and the standard of increasing quantum of interests without negatively affecting anyone.

3.1.2 The net balance of maximum interests: The ultimate standard under the circumstances that the interests are in conflict

"Increasing everyone's quantum of interests" is the ultimate standard of morality, the ultimate legal standard, the ultimate standard of politics, and the ultimate value standard of state institutions. However, the problem is, when human interests conflict with one another and cannot be compromised it is impossible to increase everyone's interests. Under these circumstances, on the one hand, increasing some individuals' interests certainly has to decrease the interests of some other individuals so it is impossible to increase everyone's interests; on the other hand, avoiding harming some individuals' interests certainly will worsen the conditions of some others, so it is impossible to avoid everyone being unharmed.

Under these circumstances, it is only possible to increase or decrease "the net balance of interests." The so-called net balance of interests is, on the one hand, the balance of the increased and decreased interests; on the other hand, it is the balance of the harms avoided, and the harms inflicted. If "the increased interests are lesser than the decreased interests" or "the harms avoided are lesser than the harms inflicted," then the net balance is a disadvantage instead of an advantage, thus it decreases the net balance of interests; if "the increased interests are greater than the decreased interests" or "the harms avoided are greater than the harm suffered," then the net balance is an advantage, not a disadvantage; thus it increases the net balance of interests.

Under these circumstances, obviously one ought to "choose the greatest interests and sacrifice the least interests" and "choose the least harm to avoid the greater harm" to maximize the net balance of interests: this is the so-called "the standard of the net balance of maximum interests." In summarizing this standard Sidgwick wrote: "By Greatest Happiness is meant the greatest possible surplus of pleasure over pain."[11] Beauchamp also says:

(1) that an action or practice is right if it leads to the greatest possible balance of good consequences or to the least possible balance of bad consequences in the world as a whole; and
(2) that the concept of duty and right are subordinated to or determined by that which maximizes the good.[12]

Thus, the standard of the net balance of maximum interests has positive and negative implications. The positive aspect is the standard of the net balance of maximum interests that in the circumstance of "increasing some individuals' interests certainly has to decrease the interests of some other individuals," which can be concluded as "comparing two kinds of interests to take the greater one": that one ought to choose the greatest interests and sacrifice the least interests. This is because, under such a circumstance, the outcome of choosing the greatest interests and sacrificing the least interests is the net balance of maximum interests. For example, let's imagine a primitive type of society short of monetary wealth:

If the economic wealth in that society is distributed on the basis of labor, and the persons who work harder have more economic wealth and also have the non-basic economic rights (that is, the non-human-rights economic rights), then some people would starve to death without having the basic economic rights (that is, the economic human rights); if the wealth is evenly distributed and everyone equally enjoys the fundamental economic right (economic human rights), then those who work harder cannot get more and enjoy the non-fundamental economic rights (non-human-right economic rights). What should be done then? Should the primitive society choose the even distribution, this kind of distribution is completely correct because the economic human rights of all people undoubtedly is greater than the non-human economic rights of some people who work harder: choosing the economic human rights for all people and sacrificing the non-human-right economic rights of some people who work harder, is an outcome that is the net balance of maximum interests.

66 *The standard of moral value*

The opposite aspect, or the negative aspect of "the net balance of maximum interests," is the standard of the net balance of maximum interests under the circumstance where "avoiding harm to some people certainly will cause harm to some other people," which can be concluded as "comparing two kinds of harms to take the least one": choosing the smallest harm and avoiding the greater harm. Under such a circumstance the outcome of choosing the smallest harm and avoiding the greater harm is the net balance of maximum interests. Take the example of the crux of the problem of the classic thought experiment known as the trolley dilemma, which is very popular in the field of western ethics. Imagine a runaway trolley hurtling down the tracks toward five workers, if it is diverted down a second set of tracks it would lead to the death of one lone worker on the left, or, if not diverted, it would lead to the death of the five on the right, or three of the five workers could rush to make a middle track of sorts, but that would cause the death of these three workers. What track should the trolley be diverted to? It should be diverted to the left of the track to lead to the death of one worker. Because it chooses the least harm (the death of one person) and avoids the greater harm (the death of five or three persons), the outcome is the net balance of maximum interests.

Generally speaking, "the net balance of maximum interests" is to choose the least harm and avoid the greater harm, and is to choose the greatest interests and sacrifice the least interests, which is to minimize the interests that has to be decreased and to maximize the interests that can be increased, thus to maximize the net balance of the interests.

The net balance of maximum interests is not only the ultimate standard of morality, the ultimate legal standard, the ultimate standard of politics and the ultimate standard of state institutions for settling the interests conflicts that cannot be compromised, it is also the ultimate standard of self-regarding for settling the various interests conflicts of the self that cannot be compromised. For instance:

I want to enjoy in my own way everything that is pleasurable in life, the satisfaction of all things that I desire, and I also hope to enjoy a long and healthy life. But these two opposite desires conflict with one another and cannot both be actualized. What should I choose? Most would say that the better option would be to sacrifice an indulgent lifestyle and enjoy a long and healthy life. But, what is the reason for this? It is because the benefits of a long and healthy life exceed the benefits of whatever the indulgence might be: the net balance is advantage since it conforms to the standard of the net balance of maximum interests. Whereas the net balance would be a disadvantage if I was to sacrifice a long and healthy life for one of indulgence.

3.1.3 The greatest interests for the greatest number: Precedencing over the standard of the net balance of maximum interests

All human interest conflicts, in the final analysis, can be summed up as interest conflicts between the greater number and the smaller number of people. Generally speaking, if interest conflicts cannot be compromised, the greatest interests of the greatest number ought to be protected and the least interests of the least number sacrificed, the net balance of which is the maximum interests, conforms to the standard of the net balance of maximum interests and, therefore, it is ought to be, good, right, and has a positive value. On the contrary, protecting the least interests of the least number and sacrificing the greatest interests for the greatest number, the net balance will be the greatest disadvantage and violate the standard of net balance of maximum interest and, therefore, it is ought not to be, bad, wrong, and has a negative value. This is the so-called standard of "the greatest interests for the greatest number," or "the greatest happiness for the greatest number."

It is easy to see that this standard is not only directly deduced from the standard of "the net balance of maximum interests," which is the embodiment of the ultimate sub-standard (that is for settling the interest conflicts among human beings), but also directly deduced from the ultimate general standard of "increasing or decreasing everyone's quantum of interests," which is the embodiment of the ultimate general standard of "increasing or decreasing everyone's quantum of interests": "the greatest interests for the greatest number" is *the approximate ultimate general standard* for settling interest conflicts. It is because, when human interests conflict with one another and cannot be compromised, undoubtedly, only the protection of the greatest interests for the greatest number, and the sacrifice of the least interests of the smallest number, is closest to "preserving everyone's interests": preserving the interests of the greatest number then is much closer to preserving everyone's interests than preserving the interests of the smallest number, and sacrificing the interests of the greatest number is much closer to sacrificing everyone's interests than sacrificing the interests of the smallest number.

Since the standard of "the greatest interests for the greatest number" is directly deduced from both the standards of "the net balance of maximum interests" and "increasing or decreasing everyone's quantum of interests," it contains the possibility of conflicts between these two standards. This possibility might be expressed this way: the interests of the greatest number might not necessarily be the greatest interests; the greatest interests rather might be the interests of the smallest number. Consequently, only the interests of the smallest number are protected and only by sacrificing the interests of the greatest number can the net balance of maximum interests obtained; if this is reversed in terms of protecting the interests of the greatest number and sacrificing the interests of the smallest number, then the net balance is a negative value. Under such circumstances, ought we sacrifice the interests of the greatest number and protect the interests of the smallest number? If the answer is yes, then the terms of the standards of "the greatest interests for the greatest number" or "the greatest happiness for the greatest number" are not exact, and should be changed to the standard of "the greatest interests" or of "the greatest happiness," and this is the trap that coaxed Bentham to rename

Bercaria and Hutcheson's standard of the "greatest happiness for the greatest number" to the standard of "greatest happiness."[13]

Could it really be possible to change the standard of "the greatest happiness for the greatest number" into the standard of "the greatest happiness" as Bentham had done? The answer is no. When human interests conflict, only the act of protecting the interests of the greatest number, and of sacrificing the interests of the least number, most closely conform to the ultimate general standard of "increasing everyone's quantum of interests." Therefore, when the interests of the greater number conflict with that of the smaller number, even if the value of the interests of smaller number is greater than the value of the interests of greater number, we ought to protect the interests of the greater number and sacrifice that of smaller number. Though this practice violates "the net balance of maximum interests" it most closely conforms to "increasing everyone's quantum of interests": whenever any value standard such as "the net balance of maximum interests" conflicts with the ultimate general standards of "increasing everyone's quantum of interests," the ultimate general standard ought to be followed.

Hence, though "the standard of the greatest interests for the greatest number" is derived from "the standard of the net balance of maximum interests," it has absolute precedence over "the standard of the net balance of maximum interests" because it is the closest to "the standard of increasing everyone's quantum of interests." Let's go on with the trolley dilemma we mentioned above. If the person standing on the right of the track is Einstein, a great physicist with great value, and the total value of the five workers on the left is far less than the value of Einstein, hence if Einstein was killed, the net balance would be a negative value; and if the five workers were killed, the net balance would a positive value. Then, what should the driver do? The correct answer is that the driver ought to kill great Einstein to save the lives of the five ordinary workers! Although the death of Einstein violates the "standard of the net balance of maximum interests," it most closely conforms to the ultimate general standard of "increasing everyone's quantum of interests" for it conforms to "the greatest interests for the greatest number": "protecting the interests of greater number" is much closer to conforming with "protecting everyone's interests" than "protecting the interests of smaller number."

When human interests conflict, and no compromise can be found, "the standard of the greatest interests for the greatest number" has precedence over "the standard of the net balance of maximum interests," and therefore first ought to protect the interests of the greatest number and sacrifice the interests of the smallest number in accordance with "the standard of the greatest interests for the greatest number"; then protect the greatest interests and sacrifice the least interests to maximize the net balance of the interests in accordance with "the standard of the net balance of maximum interests." For instance, under the circumstance that interests conflict, and cannot be compromised, and the population of the greatest number is 90% of the total population, the interests of the 90% population ought to be protected and the interests of the 10% sacrificed, even if the opposite choice would obtain the greater interests or the maximum of the net balance of interests. If, however, both sides of the conflicts are each 50% of the population, the interests of which side ought to be protected (or sacrificed) depends on the net balance of maximum interests.

Undoubtedly, however, these situations barely exist, since in most cases, "the standard of the net balance of maximum interests" is usually totally in accordance with "the standard of the greatest interests for the greatest number." It is because, in most cases, the interests of the greatest number undoubtedly is the greatest interests, and the interests of the smallest number undoubtedly is the least interests. Therefore, protecting the interests of the greatest number and sacrificing the interests of the smallest number is the only way the net balance of maximum interests can be obtained.

In short, "the greatest interests for the greatest number" is the ultimate standard of morality, ultimate legal standard, ultimate standard of politics, and ultimate standard of the state institutions for settling human interest conflicts. According to this standard, under any circumstance when human interests conflict, we ought to protect the interests of the greatest number and sacrifice the interests of the smallest number, even if the greatest interests is the interests of the smallest number instead of the interests of the greatest number. Thence, the key wording of the dictum "The Greatest Happiness for the Greatest Number" is "the greatest number," not "the greatest happiness." The standard cannot be changed as Bentham had done by omitting "the greatest number" and changing it into "the greatest happiness." Because after all, the greatest happiness may be the happiness of the smallest number, not the happiness of the most people, no matter how small this possibility may be.

3.1.4 Increasing the quantum of interests without negatively affecting anyone: The ultimate standard under the circumstances that the interests are not in conflict

As discussed, the standard of "the net balance of maximum interests" and "the greatest interests for the greatest number" are only the ultimate standard in the circumstance of conflicting interests where no compromise is possible, and both are only the embodiment of the ultimate general standard of "increasing everyone's quantum of interests" in the circumstance of conflicting interests. But what is the ultimate standard if compromise is possible or indeed when human interests do not conflict but are in harmony with one another or, in other words, under such circumstances, what is the particular expression for the ultimate general standard of "increasing everyone's quantum of interests"?

Under the circumstances that the interests are not in conflict but in harmony with one another, the ultimate general standard of "increasing everyone's quantum of interests" is particularized as the standard of "increasing the quantum of interests without harming others" or as "increasing the quantum of interests without negatively affecting anyone." According to this standard, we should increase people's interests without harming any one, promote everyone's interests or some people's interests harmlessly, and make everyone's situation better or some people's situation better without making others' situation worse. This is because the ultimate general standard is to increase everyone's quantum of interests but not to increase the net balance of maximum interests or the greatest interests for the greatest number: the net balance of maximum interests or the greatest interests of the greatest number is the unwilling choice under the circumstance that the interest conflicts cannot be compromised so that everyone's interests cannot be increased.

Therefore, under the circumstance that interests conflicts do not occur or if there are conflicts and compromise is possible, only increasing the quantum of interests without negatively affecting anyone (namely the betterment of conditions for everyone or for some individuals without worsening others' conditions) can it conform to the ultimate general standard of "increasing everyone's quantum of interests," then it is good, ought to be, and has positive value; on the contrary, if sacrificing the least interests of the smallest number for the greatest interests for the greatest number, no matter how great it increases the net balance of maximum interests, no matter how great it increases the net balance of interests, such as the greatest happiness it brings for the greatest number, it violates the ultimate general standard of "increasing everyone's quantum of interests," and so it is bad, ought not to be, and has negative value. For instance:

Suppose a country harms the interests of the smallest number of the population as part of its rapid development program to bring about the greatest happiness for the greatest number and maximize the net balance of interests. Conversely, if the country does not harm the interests of the smallest number of the population the greatest number of the population will not be harmed, but development would slow or come to a halt, which means that greatest number of the population cannot obtain the greatest happiness and the net balance of interests cannot be maximized. In these circumstances what ought to be? Causing harm to smallest number to make the greatest happiness for the greatest number neither conforms to the ultimate general standard of "increasing everyone's quantum of interests" nor to the ultimate sub-standard of "increasing the quantum of interests without negatively affecting anyone," and thus it *ought not to be*. Not causing harm to anyone, even if the country does not develop because of that, conforms to the ultimate general standard of "increasing everyone's quantum of interests," and conforms to the ultimate sub-standard of "increasing the quantum of interests without negatively affecting anyone," and is then *what ought to be*.

Gilbert Harman once designed two famous dilemmas of a moral principle which not only baffled himself but also both the western and Chinese scholars. The first dilemma is when a doctor who has six patients who are all in danger of dying, but one is much worse than the others. If the doctor devotes all of his resources to that patient the others will die. The doctor obviously ought to save the other five and let the one who is much worse die. The second dilemma facing the doctor is that he has five patients who are each in need of a separate organ of kidney, a lung, a mind, and so forth, and patient whose vital organs are all healthy. If the perfectly healthy organs of the one patient are removed and transferred to the five other patients then their lives will be saved. What ought the doctor to do? Obviously he ought not to cut up that healthy person.[14] Why is it then, in the first case, that the doctor ought to sacrifice one person's life for saving the lives of five persons, while, in the second case, he ought not to sacrifice one person's life for saving the lives of five others?

There are two reasons. In the first case, because the interests of the five patients conflict with that of the one patient, protecting the interests of the five patients would harm the interests of just one other patient, meaning that the sacrifice of one patient would save the lives of other patients. This is what ought to be. When interests conflict in a circumstance such as this it ought to conform to the ultimate standard—the standard of the greatest interests for the greatest number and the net balance of maximum interests.

In the second case, because the interests of the five patients, each with an unhealthy organ, do not conflict with that of the patient with healthy organs, protecting the interests and life of this one patient does not harm the interests and lives of the other five patients, meaning that the interests and the life of this one relatively healthy patient is not in exchange with the interests and lives of the other five patients. It is not that the relatively healthy patient who wants to live causes the death of the other five patients and it is not that the death of all five other patients would save the life of the one relatively healthy patient. The death of all five patients is the result of their own diseases and not related in any way to the life of the relatively healthy patient. Without such a relation how can interest conflicts occur? Therefore, under the circumstance that no interests conflict occurs, the doctor ought not do the procedure. Although the doctor's removal and transferance of the healthy organs of relatively healthy patient would save the lives of the other five patients conforms to the ultimate standard (namely the standards of greatest interests of the greatest number and the net balance of maximum interests), it violates the ultimate standard of non-interests conflict (namely increasing the quantum of interests without negatively affecting anyone). This is why in the first case the doctor ought to save the five lives and sacrifice one life, and in the second case, he ought not to sacrifice one life to save five lives.

In short, "increasing the quantum of interests without negatively affecting anyone" is the embodiment of the ultimate general standard of "increasing everyone's quantum of interests" under the condition that the interests conflicts do not occur or if there are conflicts and compromise is possible. It is the ultimate standard of morality, the ultimate legal standard, the ultimate standard of politics, and ultimate standard of state institutions in the condition that the interests conflicts do not occur or if there are conflicts and compromise is possible. Mencius might have been the earliest philosopher who put forward this standard where he concluded that one "ought not to kill an innocent person for obtaining the world."[15] However, the first person to prove this standard was neither strictly speaking a political scientist nor an ethicist, but predominantly an economist, known as Pareto, thus it was termed the Pareto Criterion or Pareto Optimum. For this standard or state Pareto writes:

> We see that there are two problems to be solved to maximize a collective welfare. If certain criteria for allocation are established, we can use these criteria to determine which states will bring the greatest possible benefits to the individual members of the collective. Let us consider any particular state and envisage a minimal change that does not conflict with various relationships. If this were done, the welfare of all men would be increased, and it was clear that this new state of affairs would be more favorable to each of them; on the contrary, if everyone's welfare is reduced, this is a disadvantage. If the welfare of some people remains unchanged it does not affect these conclusions. But, on the other hand, if this small change increases the welfare of some people and reduces the welfare of others, it cannot be said to be beneficial to society as a whole. Therefore, we define the maximum utility state as that in which it is impossible to make any small change in the state of all men's utility, all of which, except those whose utility remains constant, increases or decreases.[16]

Obviously the so-called Pareto Optimum is a state of allocation of resources from which it is impossible to relocate so as to make any one individual better off without making one individual worse off. The reason that this state is the optimal state is because of the so-called Pareto Criterion, namely we "ought to improve everyone's or some individual's welfare without worsening others' conditions," in short, we "ought to increase the quantum of interests without negatively affecting anyone."

This is where Pareto, the master of new welfare economics, is wiser than Pigou, the master of the old welfare economics. Based on the Law of diminishing marginal utility (i.e., the more one's wealth the less its marginal utility) Pigou made the famous conclusion that "income ought to be equalized":

Let's suppose a scenario, for instance, where there is one rich man and ten poor men. By taking one pound from the rich man and giving it to the first poor man, the total quantity of satisfaction increases. But the rich man is still richer than the second poor man, so if we continue to transfer one pound from the rich man to the second poor man, the third poor man, etc., the total quantity of satisfaction increases until the rich man is no longer richer than anyone.[17]

Not knowing that "the standard of the net balance of maximum interests" is the ultimate standard only under the circumstance when conflicts occurs and no compromise can be reached, Pigou overstates "the standard of the net balance of maximum interests," mistakenly holding that it ought to be followed under any circumstance as long as it can increase the net balance of the interests of society. On the contrary, Pareto set the ultimate standard for circumstances when interest conflicts do not occur: increasing the quantum of interests without negatively affecting anyone. If it harms one individual's interests, no matter how great the net balance of interests increase, it ought not to be followed.

3.2 Theories on the ultimate standard of morality

3.2.1 Deontology and utilitarianism

Deontology, which is also called the theory of duty or non-teleology, is a theory on the ultimate standard of morality. It is opposite to utilitarianism with representative figures that include the Confucian school, Christian ethicist, Kant, Bradley, Pritchard, and Ross, as well as contemporary virtue ethicists of deontology such as Michael Slote and Gregory Velazco Y. Trianosky. The theory of deontology is so abstruse that it has not been clearly explained for two thousand years. Any examination of deontology therefore should be based on the original works, especially on that of the well-known exponents of deontology like the Confucian school and Kant.

All deontologists are exponents of the autonomy of the origin and goal of morality. They all hold that morality and virtue are not a necessary bad but a necessary good: a kind of intrinsic good and good-in-itself, even an unconditional and absolute good. Therefore, they all believe that the origin and goal of morality are autonomous; put it in another way, they all hold that morality originates from morality itself and from the needs of perfecting the moral character of the self, that is, the goal of morality lies in morality itself or perfecting everyone's moral character and actualizing human beings as human being.

Starting from this theory of moral autonomy, deontologists logically conclude that whether an action is moral can only be judged from its utility to the actor's moral character, but not from its utility to everyone's interests: the action that can perfect the actor's moral character actualizes human beings as human beings, no matter how much it decreases everyone's and society's quantum of interests. Because it conforms to the goal of morality, it ought to be and is therefore moral; the action that cannot perfect the actor's moral character, and cannot actualize human beings as human beings, no matter how much it increases everyone's and society's quantum of interests, does not conform to the goal of morality, and thus ought not to be and is immoral. Dong Zhongshu (董仲舒), the great scholar of Confucianism and deontology, famously concluded: "The purpose of an act is not to seek one's interests, but to express justice."

Therefore, only the action that is for the perfection of the moral character of the self, the action that perfects moral character for the purpose of perfecting of moral character—namely the action out of duty, acting dutifully for duty and acting morally for morality—is moral and ought to be for it actualizes human beings as human beings. Therefore, Kant claimed that "the perfection of morality is to fulfill duty for duty (i.e., law is not only the rules regulating one's action but also the motive of one's action)."[18] But, specifically speaking, what kind of action can perfect the moral character of the self, or fulfill duty for duty, or actualize human beings as human beings? It is the action of *selflessly benefiting others*, namely benefiting others for the purpose of benefiting others! Just as the scholar of new Confucianism Fung Yulan pointed out:

> It can be said that the pursuit of one's own interests is out of the animal traits of human beings, it has no connection with human beings as human beings. For the actualization of human beings as human beings, we cannot say that one should pursue one's own interests ... but the pursuit of interests of others does have a connection to human beings as human beings. For the actualization of human beings as human beings, we can say, human beings should pursue the interests of others.[19]

In short, deontology is a school that takes the duty (not interests) as the ultimate standard of morality, increasing or decreasing the degree of the perfection of everyone's moral character (not increasing or decreasing everyone's quantum of interests) as the ultimate standard of morality, and, in the end, the unselfishly benefiting others as the ultimate standard of morality.

Utilitarianism is also termed teleology. Its principal advocators are the great philosophers such as Socrates, Hume, Paley, Elvis, Holbach, Barley, Darwin, Spencer, Bentham, Mill, Paulsen, Sidgwick, Moore, and Tilly. Its modern representative figures are J. J. C. Smarter and the contemporary western virtue ethicist of utilitarianism Von Wright. Owing to its historic depth, as Rawls comments: "During much of modern philosophy the predominant systematic theory has been some form of utilitarianism."[20]

Advocates of utilitarianism are scholars of the theory of the heteronomy of the origin and goal of morality. They hold that, like law, morality and virtue are kinds of a necessary bad, and that it is not possible therefore for the origin and goal of morality to be autonomous, and not possible for morality to be for itself or for the perfection of everyone's moral character. It is only possible for morality and virtue to be heteronomous, that is, only for matters other than morality and virtue such as for everyone's interests and happiness. As Mill said: "Happiness is the ends and aim of morality."[21]

The goal of morality is the ultimate standard of morality for the evaluation of the goodness or evilness of all actions as well as for the excellence or inferiority of morality. Thence, in the view of utilitarianist, the ultimate standard of measuring the goodness or evilness of all actions and the excellence or inferiority of morality can only be interests and happiness, it cannot be morality and virtue themselves; it can only be *increasing or decreasing of everyone's quantum of interests*, not *increasing or decreasing the perfection of everyone's moral character*; it can only be interests, it cannot be duty.

Therefore, utilitarianism or teleology is the opposite of deontology: it is a school that regards interests (not duty) as the ultimate standard of morality, and it is a school that regards increasing or decreasing everyone's quantum of interests (rather than the perfection of everyone's morality) as the ultimate standard of morality. Beauchamp writes: "Utilitarians hold that the moral worth of actions is to be determined by our efforts to maximize the production of such *nonmoral* intrinsic values as pleasure and health."[22] Frankena, however, states it much more clearly: "A teleological theory says that the basic or ultimate criterion or standard of what is morally right, wrong, obligatory, etc., is the nonmoral value that is brought into being."[23]

3.2.2 The truth and fallacy of utilitarianism and deontology

Deontology is a fallacy and utilitarianism is a truth. This is because, On the one hand, judging from the premise of utilitarianism—the theory of the heteronomy of the origin and goal of morality—is a truth, and the premise of the theory of deontology—the theory of the autonomy of the origin and goal of morality—is a fallacy. On the other hand, judging from their conclusions, utilitarianism is a truth for it takes "increasing or decreasing everyone's quantum of interests" as the ultimate standard of morality, and deontology is a fallacy for it takes "increasing or decreasing everyone's perfection of moral characters" as the ultimate standard of morality.

As we discussed above, on the one hand, both morality and virtue are a kind of necessary bad, thus it is not possible for the origin and goal of morality to be autonomous, and it is not possible for the morality to be for itself or for the perfection of everyone's moral character; morality and virtue can only be heteronomous in that both are for matters exclusive of themselves, i.e., safeguarding the existence and development of society and finally increasing everyone's interests. On the other hand, the ultimate standard of morality, i.e., the quantization of the ultimate goal of morality can only be "increasing or decreasing everyone's quantum of interests," it cannot possibly be "increasing everyone's perfection of morality."

Furthermore, deontology, in taking the "increasing or decreasing of the perfection of moral character" as the ultimate standard of morality, on the one hand, most seriously restricts, suppresses, and violates everyone's desires and freedom: it denies all desires and freedom of everyone the end of which is beneficial to the self; on the other hand, because it denies self-interest and the pursuit of all personal interest it is an impediment to increasing everyone's interests and therefore the interests of society, thence obstructing the most powerful source for everyone to increase the interests of others and society. In conclusion, deontology is the morality that gives everyone the greatest ratio of disadvantage to advantage; it is the morality "most likely to decrease everyone's interests" and "least likely to increase everyone's interests," and therefore is the worst morality.

Utilitarianism, in taking the "increasing of everyone's quantum of interests" as the ultimate standard of morality, on the one hand, is the least restrictive, least suppressive and least likely to violate everyone's desires and freedom; it only denies everyone's purposive self-interest where there is harm to others; on the other hand, it is the most rapid means of increasing everyone's interests and that of society for it affirms all pursuits that are beneficial to personal and societal interests, thence is the most powerful source for increasing the interests of the whole society. In conclusion, the morality of utilitarianism is the morality that gives everyone the greatest ratio of advantages to disadvantages, it is the morality "least likely to decrease everyone's interests" and "most likely to increase everyone's interests," therefore it is the best morality.

Interestingly, however, though we can discern the truth of utilitarianism and the fallacy of deontology above, utilitarianism has received more critical scrutiny than deontology. Why is this? Even Rawls, a true utilitarian, unexpectedly went against it and considered himself an advocate of deontology. In answer to this, serious shortcomings in the accounts of utilitarianism invited much criticism.

3.2.3 The previous utilitarianism: The shortcomings and reproaches

Utilitarianism, like deontology, is probably the most abstruse, complicated, and mostly disputed theories. The presentations and explanations of the utilitarian doctrine, whether by Bentham, Mill, Sidgwick, or Moore, as well as other utilitarian thinkers, all therefore have their shortcomings. The most serious and general accusation is that utilitarians have not collectively understood that the standard of utilitarianism is actually a moral standard system consisting of a certain number of standards. Instead utilitarians hold that there is only one standard for utilitarianism, and equate it to the standard of "the net balance of maximum interests" or "the greatest happiness for the greatest number."

Bentham, for instance, wrote:

> The principle of utility was an appellative, at that time employed by me, as it had been by others, to designate that which in a more perspicuous and instructive manner, may, as above, be designated by the name of the greatest happiness principle.[24]

In defining utilitarianism, Sidgwick also wrote: "By Utilitarianism is here meant the ethical theory ... under any given circumstances, is externally or objectively right, which will produce the greatest amount of happiness to all whose interests are affected."[25] The contemporary ethicists in the West also generally equate utilitarianism to the principle of "the net balance of maximum interests." Pojman writes in *A Glossary of Ethics Terms* that utilitarianism is the theory that "the right action is that which maximizes utility."[26]

The ultimate standard of morality 77

These are really all a kind of parochial view of utilitarianism! They do not know that the standard of utilitarianism is not merely "the net balance of maximum interests" or "the greatest interests for the greatest number," but a moral ultimate standard system that consists of a general standard and two sub-standards: "increasing or decreasing everyone's quantum of interests" is the moral ultimate general standard that ought to be followed under any circumstance; "increasing the quantum of interests without negatively affecting anyone" is one ultimate sub-standard for the circumstance when the interests does not conflict or if there are conflicts and compromise is possible; "the net balance of maximum interests" and "the greatest interests for the greatest number" are the other ultimate sub-standard under the circumstance when there are conflicts and compromise is impossible. Therefore, the previous utilitarians equated the standard of utilitarianism to "the net balance of maximum interests" or "the greatest interests for the greatest number," mistaking the part for the whole, triggering the famous heckling that utilitarianism will certainly lead to injustice.

Of the different sorts of heckling the most important is undoubtedly the very famous experiment in which an innocent person is framed and convicted to placate a mob threatening to riot unless someone is caught. The experiment, referred to as "punishing the innocent," is summed up as follows:

The judge knows very clearly that the person is innocent, but if the innocent person is sentenced to death it would prevent a riot which would cost hundreds of lives. Then, punishing the innocent according to utilitarian principle—namely "the net balance of maximum interests" or the standard of "the greatest interests for the greatest number"—is ought to be and moral. It can be seen that utilitarian principles certainly lead to injustice: it is unjust to punish the innocent.[27]

However, if examined carefully, one can see that this experiment can have two possibilities. First, in the circumstance when the release of one innocent and the survival of hundreds of innocents conflict and no compromise can be reached, if one innocent person is not punished, hundreds of innocents would die, though it is an injustice to punish one innocent person, it avoids the greater injustice of losing hundreds of innocent lives—conforming to the standard of utilitarianism of "the net balance of maximum interests" and "the greatest interests for the greatest number"—and is therefore a so-called moral good, and by no means an injustice.

Second, in the circumstance when the release of one innocent does not conflict with the survival of hundreds of innocents or a compromise can be reached, if one innocent person is not punished, hundreds of other people would survive; if one innocent person is punished, the interests of hundreds of other people would increase greatly. Thus, in the circumstance that a compromise can be reached, the punishment of one innocent increases the net balance of interests by harming one individual's interests, it violates the standard of utilitarianism of "increasing the quantum of interests without

78 The standard of moral value

negatively affecting anyone," and therefore is an evil and an injustice, no matter how great the net balance of interests it obtains.

It is obvious that in both circumstances, though the punishment of the innocent increases the net balance of interests and obtains the net balance of maximum interests, the utilitarianism advocates only the former but not the latter possibility by which it can be declared that by no means does utilitarianism lead to injustice. The reason why numerous scholars such as Rawls hold that utilitarianism certainly lead to injustice is that they don't know the standard of "increasing everyone's quantum of interests" and "increasing the quantum of interests without negatively affecting anyone" of utilitarianism, equating utilitarianism with "the net balance of maximum interests" or "the greatest interests for the greatest number"; thus from that the standard of "the net balance of maximum interests" and "the greatest interests for the greatest number" certainly does lead to injustice in the cases that human interests do not conflict with one another, they derive the fallacious conclusion that "utilitarianism certainly leads to injustice." Rawls writes:

> The main idea is that society is rightly ordered, and therefore just, when its major institutions are arranged so as to achieve the greatest net balance of satisfaction summed over all the individuals belonging to it.[28]
>
> Thus there is no reason in principle why the greatest gains of some should not compensate for the lesser loses of others; or more importantly, why the violation of liberty of a few might not be made right by the greater good shared by many.[29]

The standard of "the net balance of maximum interests" or "the greatest interests for the greatest number" certainly leads to injustice in the cases that human interests do not conflict with one another, but it is the only moral standard in the cases that interests do conflict. When interests do conflict and no compromise can be reached, it is impossible to avoid harming anyone's interests. The only possibility is to choose between two options: either harm the interests of the smaller number to protect that of the greater number, or vice versa. Under the circumstance, is it not that one ought to sacrifice the interests of the smallest number to protect the greatest interests for the greatest number? Is it not that one ought to choose only the net balance of maximum interests? Are these not the better choices? Rawls admits that he does not know any moral standard for settling interest conflicts except utilitarianism:

> How are these duties to be balanced when they come into conflict, either with each other or with obligations, and with the good that can be achieved by supererogatory actions? There are not obvious rules for settling these questions. We cannot say, for example, that duties are lexically prior with respect to supererogatory actions, or to obligations. Nor can we simply evoke the utilitarian principle to set things straight. Requirements for

individuals so often oppose each other that this would come to the same thing as adopting the standard of utility for individuals; and, as we have seen, this is ruled out as leading to an incoherent conception of right. I do not know how this problem is to be settled, or even whether a systematic solution formulating useful and practicable rules is possible.[30]

Notes

1 Sissela Bok: *Lying: Moral Choice in Public and Private Life*, Vintage Books, New York, 1989, p. 268.
2 Louis P. Pojman: *Ethical Theory: Classical and Contemporary Readings*, 2nd edn. Wadsworth, Belmont, CA, 1995, p. 172.
3 Ibid., p. 173.
4 G. J. Warnock: *The Goal of Morality*, Methuen & Co Ltd, London, 1971, p. 26.
5 Frank Thilly: *Introduction to Ethics*, Charles Scribner's Sons, New York, 1900, p. 154.
6 Sissela Bok: *Lying: Moral Choice in Public and Private Life*, Vintage Books, New York, 1989, p. 268.
7 Aristotle: *Politics*, Commercial Press, 1965, p. 140.
8 Ibid., p. 364.
9 Ibid., p. 7.
10 Ibid.
11 Henry Sidgwick: *The Methods of Ethics*, Macmillan and Co., Ltd, London, 1922, p. 413.
12 Tom L. Beauchamp: *Philosophical Ethics*, McGraw-Hill, New York, 1982, p. 73.
13 Jeremy Bentham: *On the Government*, Commercial Press, Beijing, 1995, p. 36.
14 Louis P. Pojman: *Ethical Theory: Classical and Contemporary Readings*, 2nd edn, Wadsworth, Belmont, CA, 1995, pp. 478–479.
15 Mencius: *Gongsun Chou*.
16 Quoted from a secondary source from Hu Jichuang: *Western Economic Theory since 1870*, Economics and Science Press, 1988, p. 191.
17 Arthur Cecil Pigou: "Some Aspects of Welfare Economics," *American Economic Review*, June 1951, p. 299.
18 Immanuel Kant: *The Works of Kant*, Reform Press, 1997, p. 358.
19 Fung Yulan: *Complete Works of Sansong Tang, Vol. 4*. Henan People's Publishing House, 1986, p. 608.
20 John Rawls: *A Theory of Justice, Revised Edition*, The Belknap Press of Harvard University Press Cambridge, MA, 2000, p. xvii.
21 J. S. Mill: *Utilitarianism, On Liberty and Representative Government*, J. M. Dent & Sons Ltd, London, p. 22.
22 Tom L. Beauchamp: *Philosophical Ethics*, McGraw-Hill, New York, 1982, p. 81.
23 William K. Frankena: *Ethics*, Prentice-Hall, Englewood Cliffs, NJ, 1973, p. 14.
24 Jeremy Bentham: *An Introduction to the Principles of Morals and Legislation*, Clarendon Press, Oxford, 1823, p. 5.
25 Henry Sidgwick: *The Methods of Ethics*, Macmillan and Co., Ltd, London, 1922, p. 411.
26 Louis P. Pojman: *Ethical Theory: Classical and Contemporary Readings*, Wadsworth, Belmont, CA, 1995, p. 727.

80 *The standard of moral value*

27 Also see Tom L. Beauchamp: *Philosophical Ethics*, McGraw-Hill, New York, 1982, p. 99.
28 John Rawls: *A Theory of Justice, Revised Edition*, The Belknap Press of Harvard University Press, Cambridge, MA, 2000, p. 20.
29 Ibid., p. 23.
30 Ibid., pp. 298–299.

Part II
The substance of moral value
Fact of ethical behavior

4 Human nature

The object of study of this part is the substance of moral value, that is, human nature that is the object of ethical study: human nature is the nature of the facts of human ethical behavior. However, this definition we give to the concept of human nature in ethics might raise some objections. Is this definition the concept of human nature in ethics? Does this definition mistake the part for the whole? It is not possible to answer these in a few words. The issue of human nature has been the most difficult philosophical problem since ancient times in China. As Jiang Hengyuan (江恒源) claims, "The earliest and the most fiercely debated problem in our history of philosophy has been the issue of human nature."[1]

Since the establishment of new China in 1949, the issue of human nature has remained a major issue that has been heatedly debated for a long time in academia. The controversies, as generally known, experienced two stages: one is from the fifties to the period of Cultural Revolution, and the other stage is in the eighties and nineties after the downfall of the "Gang of Four." Even when we review these two stages, the ancient problem remains: what is human nature?

4.1 The concept of human nature

4.1.1 The definition of human nature: The universal nature that is inherent

In China, the noun human nature comprises two Chinese characters for "human" and "nature." "Human" is the general adjective or noun, and identifiable names such as Mary, John, and Peter are particular proper nouns. "Mary" and "human" for instance, can exist independently of each other as matter or as substance, "Mary" is the primary substance, and "human" is the secondary substance. "Nature," however, cannot exist independently of "Mary," since it exists dependent of and attaches to the substance, and thus is called "property." Consequently, the so-called human nature, judging from the words it implies, is the property of human, namely the property the human possesses. Because "human" is the overall name for every human being "human nature" is the property everyone possesses, namely it is the commonality and universality of all human beings. By this reasoning then, a particular property is not human nature since is that only possessed by certain people. In his well-known discourse in ancient China on the nature of two great men and two wicked men Xunzi (荀子) said: "The human nature of Yao (尧) and Shun (舜), Jie (桀), and Zhi (跖) is the same."[2] In Xunzi's account, we can discern that the mind of compassion is common to all mankind; it is a matter which everyone possesses, as the commonality and universality of all human beings. Thence when we feel compassion it is what everyone has felt at some point in time—such is the mind of compassion. The mind of compassion is a kind of human nature. But the mind of murder, robbery, blackmail, or exaction are not common or universal to all human beings; these are only the particular actions or nature of certain persons, thence they are not human nature.

Human nature is the property that everyone generally has. As long as one is human, no matter if they are a new born baby, they have the same human nature as any other person: human nature is the property commonly shared by a new born baby and an ageing senile person on the verge of death. Human nature is innate, not learned, since, if it was learned, a new born baby would not possess it. More so, if learned it certainly would not be a property that has been universally possessed since the time humans evolved. How could a learned behavior, for instance, the habit of playing cards, be a universal habit of all people, across all times? The definition of human nature as being inherently and innately universal was the commonly shared view of the different philosophers and authors in time of the Warring States in ancient China, despite great differences in their explanations.

Gao Zi (告子), the scholar who held that human nature is neither good nor bad, claimed our: "nature is inherent."[3] Dong Zhongshu (董仲舒), the scholar who held that human nature is both good and bad, declared: "The property that is inherent is called nature."[4] Han Yu (韩愈), the scholar who considered that human nature is threefold, said: "Nature is the inherent property when a person is born."[5] Xun Zi (荀子), the scholar who held that human nature is bad, stated: "The property that is inherent with birth is called nature."[6] Mencius, who has been well known for his view that human nature is good, also thought that human nature—namely what he termed as the mind of compassion, the mind of shame, the mind of modesty and yielding, the mind of rightness and wrongness—"is not what who teach me but my inherent nature."[7] In concluding the theories of western thinkers on human nature, Charles A. Ellwood also writes: "By human nature we mean the nature with which the individual *is* endowed *by* birth, and not that which he acquires through the influence of his environment *after birth*."[8] Fung Yulan (冯友兰) also noted that "both Mencius and Aristotle held that the human nature is the inherent nature of mankind."[9]

4.1.2 The structure of human nature: The substance and utility of human nature

Everything in the universe has its own structure and human nature is never an exception: human nature comprises two aspects, one is its quality and the other is its quantity. Judging from its quality, that is, "the existence or absence of human nature," human nature is completely inherent, cannot be created and destroyed, immutable, universal, inevitable, and cannot be chosen freely. However, judging from its quantity, that is, "the amount of human nature," human nature is acquired, changeable, particular, accidental, and chosen freely. Let's take loving-others and hating-others as example:

It is impossible for any person, no matter how selfish or cruel, not to at least love others: does not one at least have love for their parents, spouse, or children who may bring great pleasure and other benefits into one's life? It is impossible for any person, no matter how benevolent or kind, not to at least hate others: does not one at least hate the person who murders their parents, spouse, or children? Thus, judging from the existence or absence of loving-others and hating-others—the "quality" of loving-others and hating-others—both feelings are inherent; neither is created nor destroyed, they are both immutable, universal, inevitable, and cannot be chosen freely. Nevertheless, judging from the amount of loving-others and hating-others—the "quantity" of loving-others and hating-others, both undoubtedly can be learned, are more or less changeable, as well as particular, accidental, and chosen freely.

That is why, on the one hand, Mencius claimed that "everyone has compassion,"[10] which, as he explained, is the aspect of the quality of compassion. On the other hand, on the aspect of the quantity of compassion, he said: "If one pursues it one obtains it, abandon it one loses it. Or if one tries his best it will be returned innumerous times."[11] What he said here is the aspect of the quantity of compassion. In view of this, Su Dongpo (苏东坡) wrote:

> If a man of noble character diminishes his feelings of hatred then the quantity of hatred becomes less and less, but in quality it is the same. If a base man diminishes his feelings of love then the quantity of the feeling of love becomes less and less, even though in quality it is the same.[12]

Then, what is the relationship between the "quality" and the "quantity" of human nature? In answering this, we should make use of the classic Chinese philosophical tradition and term it as the relationship between "substance and utility": the "quality" of human nature is the "substance" of human nature, and the "quantity" of human nature is the "utility" of human nature. This so-called relationship between the "substance" and "utility" is the relationship between content and form in that "substance" cannot exist independently, it has to express itself through "utility." However, obviously, not all content and form is "substance" and "utility." Rather "substance" and "utility" are kinds of particular content and form: on the one hand, "substance" and "utility" are kinds of content and form in that they are a relationship between essence and phenomenon. On the other hand, "substance" and "utility" are kinds of content and form with relationships between "constance and change."

Thus, the relationship between the quality and quantity of human nature is a kind of relationship between "substance" and "utility." For example, compassion is human nature: "everyone has compassion." It is universal, immutable, and exists and is expressed, for instance, in Mary's or John's particular feelings of compassion with frequent changes.

Obviously, human nature consists of "substance" and "utility." The "substance" of human nature, the quality of human nature, namely the existence or absence of human nature such as existence or absence of the mind of compassion, is completely inherent, neither created nor destroyed, immutable, universal, inevitable, and not chosen freely. It is therefore totally the same for everyone. The "utility" of human nature, the quantity of human nature, namely the amount of human nature such as how much a person has the mind of compassion, is learned, frequently changes, particular, accidental, and is chosen freely, therefore it is different with every individual.

4.1.3 Types of human nature: Human characteristics and human animality

The inherent and universal nature of human beings obviously can be divided into two types considering the human relationship to animals: the first property is comparatively general, basic, and lower-level in that it belongs to the communality of both humans and animals such as the instinctual desire to be free, appetite for food, sexual drives, etc.; the second property is particular, advanced, and higher-level in that it belongs only to humans, and is what distinguishes humans from animals such as language, reason, and science, etc.

However, the traditional viewpoint represented by Mencius holds that the inherent animal nature of human beings is by no means human nature and that human nature only can be the feature of human beings as human beings. This point of view is based on the obvious fact that human nature is different from the nature of dogs, cattle, etc. In Mencius' *The Quotations from Gao Zhi*:

> Mencius asks: "The nature that is inherent is it not the same as white as white?" Answer: "Yes." He asks: "Is the whiteness of feather the same as the whiteness of snow, and is the whiteness of snow the same as the whiteness of white jade?" Answer: "Yes." He asks: "But, is the nature of a dog the same as the nature of cattle, and the nature of cattle the same as the nature of mankind?"

It is true that the *human* nature is different from *dog* nature and *cattle* nature. But, can we draw the conclusion that human nature is a feature that distinguishes human beings from dogs and cattle? We cannot because nothing is completely different. It is not possible for *human* nature to be completely different from *dog* nature or *cattle* nature, just as it is not possible for the nature of dogs or cattle to be completely different. While the nature of humans, dogs, and cattle differ significantly, they all share some same aspects. Though the features that distinguish humans from dogs and cattle, such as language, reason, sciences, etc., we share instinctual drives with dogs and cattle such as our appetite for food, reproductive drives, etc. Since animal instinctual drives exist in all human beings, how could they not be human properties, and how could they not be human nature?

In sum, it is very clear that human nature is an inherent universal property of all people: it includes Human Characteristics that distinguish humans from other animal and Human Animality that unites humans and animals as a communality of beings. Mencius' error is that he only considered the different aspects of *human* nature, *dog* nature, and *cattle* nature, and denied the sameness of *human* nature, *dog* nature, and *cattle* nature, equating human nature to only some parts of human nature (namely Human Characteristics, the higher-levels of human nature), and hence lopsidedly asserted that human nature is Human Characteristics that distinguishes human nature from *dog* nature and *cattle* nature, and therefore as that which makes human beings as human beings.

4.2 The concept of ethical behavior: The concept of human nature in ethics

Human nature, just as any other complex thing with multi-levels nature, is a research object for several different sciences, each one examining different aspects of human nature. Ethics is the science of morality, thus it is limited to studying human nature that can be expressed by good and evil or can be evaluated morally. The human nature that cannot be evaluated morally is the research object of other sciences such as psychology. For instance, cognition, emotion, will, and compassion are of a universal nature, thus all are human nature. However, cognition, emotion, and will do not express the good and bad of morality, hence they are not the objects of ethics but that of psychology. Only compassion is the human nature that can be expressed by good and evil or can be evaluated morally: "Compassion is the starting point of benevolence."[13] Thus compassion is the object of ethics, not the object of psychology.

The sufficient condition in which a matter can be expressed by good and evil is that it can be morally evaluated with moral norms. Any object that can be morally evaluated, as Huang Jianzhong said, is the domain of the ethical behavior of human beings: "The ethical behavior is the behavior that can be morally evaluated by the value judgement of good and evil." Hence the aspect of human nature that is able to be expressed by good and evil, that is, the human nature that ethics studies, is the nature of the facts of ethical behavior. Thus, there are two concepts of human nature in ethics: one is understood in a broad sense and one is understood in a narrow sense. The former refers

88 *The substance of moral value*

to the inherent universal nature of human beings, which is the concept of human nature as a general scientific term. The latter refers to the nature of the facts of ethical behavior of human beings, which is specifically the concept of human nature in ethics. Therefore, the starting point of the study of human nature in ethics is to analyze the concept of ethical behavior.

4.2.1 The definition of ethical behavior

The concept of ethical behavior, as generally known, is the same as the concept of moral behavior: the action regulated by moral norms, which can be morally evaluated and has moral value. But, what kind of action has moral value and can be morally evaluated? The so-called value, as we discussed before, is the utility of object to the purposes of the subject. Thus, the so-called action with moral value is the action that has utility to the goal of morality. The universal goal of morality, as we have also discussed, is to safeguard the existence and development of human society and the interest community of human beings and non-humans, and finally promote everyone's interests: safeguarding human society and the interest community is the direct universal goal of morality; promoting everyone's interests is the ultimate goal of morality. Thence the so-called action with moral value is the action that has utility to the existence and development of human society and the interest community and the promotion of everyone's interests, and also the action beneficial to or harmful to human society and the interest community, as well as everyone. In the final analysis, it is the action of advantage or disadvantage to oneself and others. John Hartland-Swann often emphasized:

> We see at once how it comes about that a personal type of conduct is called moral by a person community, since its performance is regarded as socially important and its neglect or violation socially disastrous; and how is it that the same type of conduct is not called either moral or immoral by another community, since neither its performance nor its neglect is regarded as socially important.[14]

However, anyone's action—more or less directly or indirectly—has the utility of advantage or disadvantage to oneself and others, with social importance. For instance, appreciating the beauty of flowers, watching fish swim in a pond, and taking a stroll in a park are not intended to benefit oneself, but actually are actions that do benefit oneself since are they not beneficial to one's health? But, can we say these actions are ethical behaviors? Obviously we cannot. Then, what is ethical behavior?

The basic feature of action, as we know, is controlled by consciousness. Then it is easy to understand that the basic feature of ethical behavior is controlled by consciousness with moral value; in the final analysis, action is controlled by the consciousness of advantage or disadvantage to oneself or others. We think that appreciating the beauty of flowers, watching fish swim, and taking strolls are generally not controlled by the consciousness of advantage or disadvantage to oneself or others, but are actions beyond any consciousness of advantage or disadvantage. However, if a person's appreciating the beauty of flowers, watching fish swim, and taking strolls is for the purpose of accompanying a friend or friends, that is, to make others happy through companionship, then it is controlled by the consciousness of benefiting others, and is thus ethical behavior. The core distinction between ethical behavior and non-ethical behavior then is whether it has *the consciousness* of advantage or disadvantage to oneself or others but not *the facts* of advantage or disadvantage to oneself or others. Thence Fung Yulan said:

> Whatever the action that can be named as moral behavior, certainly also is the action with consciousness. The action without consciousness, despite its conformity with the moral principle, exactly speaking, is not a moral behavior.[15]

4.2.2 The structure of ethical behavior

Action consists of ends and means: the ends is the result that is consciously obtained, i.e., the result of action expected by the subject of behavior; the means is the certain process for consciously obtaining a result, i.e., the behavioral process the subject of action consciously uses for obtaining the result of the action. However, judging from the scientific achievements of modern psychology, especially Freud's psychology, the ends and means are only the static and surface structure of behavior; the dynamic and deep structure of action consists of three elements: of ends, means, and ultimate motivation. The so-called ultimate motivation is the fundamental cause of instigating actions, and also the fundamental cause of instigating the ends and the means of action. The cause of means is the ends. Therefore, the ultimate motivation of action is the fundamental cause of instigating the ends of action, but the fundamental ends of action—the fundamental ends are the purpose of the ends—obviously are also the fundamental cause for the action. Then, what is the distinction between the fundamental ends of action and the ultimate motivation of action?

In Freud's point of view, ultimate motivation is the physical desire of the body, especially sexual desires. This view is in conformity with the pursuits of some ancient Chinese scholars: "The ends of seeking official rank and fame is to pursue love." Scholars sought fame as the ends for studying hard; the purpose of pursuing fame was to pursue love, which was the purpose of the ends of studying hard, that is, the fundamental purpose of studying hard. But the root cause of the purpose for pursuing love was no longer the ends, it was only the natural cause of "sexual desires"; sexual desire was the ultimate motivation of studying hard. It was the common view of different philosophers and authors in ancient China that desires are the ultimate motivation of behavior. The scholar of New Confucianism, Fung Yulan, wrote:

90 *The substance of moral value*

> The ultimate motivation of action is desires ... everyone has desires and wants to satisfy his own desires. All kinds of actions are caused by desires ... desire is a natural thing which is neither good nor evil, just like the mountains and rivers, which are neither good nor evil.[16]

It is thus clear that both ultimate motivation and the fundamental ends of action can be the root cause which instigate a certain ends. However, if the root cause instigating a certain ends is still the ends, such as pursuing love, then it is the fundamental ends; if the root cause itself is no longer the ends but the cause, it is no longer "for what," rather only "because of what"—such as sexual desires—that is the ultimate motivation.

Therefore, the distinction and similarity between the *ultimate motivation of action* and *fundamental ends of action* are that both are the fundamental cause of action; but, the fundamental ends of action are the fundamental "ends cause" of certain ends of action—such as pursuing love—it is the fundamental cause of the ends of action that still has not deepened to the degree of surpassing the ends-level; the ultimate motivation of action is the "non-ends causes" of the fundamental ends of action—such as sexual desires—which has deepened to the degree of surpassing the ends-level. Therefore, it can be said that the ultimate motivation of action is much more profound and more fundamental than the fundamental ends of action: the ultimate motivation of action is the "non-ends causes" that causes fundamental ends of action.

Through the deduction of the structure of behavior we can see clearly that the static and surface structure of ethical behavior consists of the *ends of ethical behavior* and *means of ethical behavior*; the dynamic and deep structure of ethical behavior consists of *ends of ethical behavior* and *means of ethical behavior* as well as the *ultimate motivation of ethical behavior*.

Firstly, the so-called ends of ethical behavior, in the final analysis, are the ends of actions that benefit or harm oneself and others, namely the ends of benefiting others, the ends of self-interest, the ends of harming others, and the ends of self-harming. Secondly, the so-called means of ethical behavior are the means of actions that benefit or harm oneself and others, namely the means of benefiting others, the means of self-interest, the means of harming others, and the means of self-harming. Finally, the so-called ultimate motivation of ethical behavior is the fundamental "non-ends cause" that causes the ends of ethical behavior. In the final analysis, it is the fundamental "non-ends cause" that causes the four ends of benefiting others, self-interest, harming others and self-harming.

4.2.3 Types of ethical behavior

The ends of the ethical behavior are divided into ends of benefiting others, ends of self-interest, ends of harming others, and ends of self-harming; the means of ethical behavior are divided into means of benefiting others, means of self-interest, means of harming others, and means of self-harming.

Table 4.1 Types of ethical behavior

Types of ends and means	Self-interest	Benefiting others	Self-harming	Harming others
Self-interest	1. completely self-interest	5. self-interest for benefiting others	9. self-interest for self-harming	13. self-interest for harming others
Benefiting others	2. benefiting others for self-interest	6. completely benefiting others	10. benefiting others for self-harming	14. benefiting others for harming others
Self-harming	3. self-harming for self-interest	7. self-sacrifice	11. completely self-harming	15. self-harming for harming others
Harming others	4. harming others for self-interest	8. harming others for benefiting others	12. harming others for self-harming	16. completely harming others

Therefore, in combining the ends of ethical behavior and means of ethical behavior there are in all 16 types of ethical behavior (see Table 4.1).

① "Complete self-interest" is the behavior with both ends and means that benefit only oneself, That is to say, the ends and means neither benefit others nor harm other but merely benefit oneself. This kind of behavior can be concluded with famous classic dictums by Yang Zhu (杨朱): "Never lose a piece of hair for the welfare of the world" and "Never change for the world with a hair in the leg." The protagonist Antoine Roquentin in Sartre's *La nausea* lives alone and is also such a kind of person who is completely lonely, he never talks with any others, receiving nothing and giving nothing.[17]

② "Benefiting others for self-interest" is the behavior in which the ends are self-interest, while the means benefits others. It is the behavior that pursues interest for oneself by benefiting society and others. Rational egoism actively advocates these kinds of behaviors. Holbach even said that "Virtue is but the art of making yourself happy with the welfare of others."[18]

③ "Self-harming for self-interest" is the behavior in which the ends are self-interest, while the means harms oneself. It is the pursuit of one's own interests by sacrificing some of one's other interests. It fits with the famous stories in ancient China of "sleeping on brushwood and tasting the gall to nurse vengeance" and "hanging a person's head on a beam and pricking the leg with an awl," as well as such things we might hear or see what people do in everyday life such as smoking or drinking, to more extreme actions such as undergoing amputation, masochism, etc.

④ "Harming others for self-interest" is the behavior in which the ends benefit oneself with the means of harming others, such as stealing, corruption, extortion, sadism, etc.
⑤ "Self-interest for benefiting others" is the behavior in which the ends benefit others and the means benefit oneself. Confucius claimed that "A man of noble character pursues morality but not food; if he studies hard then the foods are in that act itself." The ends of "study" and "pursuing morality" is to benefit others, while "the foods" is the means of benefiting oneself.[19]
⑥ "Completely benefiting others" is the behavior in which both the ends and means are beneficial to others, such as the famous story Mencius told of a person who saved a little child from a deep well out of compassion.
⑦ "Self-sacrifice" is the behavior in which the ends benefit others, while the means harms oneself. It is behavior that sacrifices one's own interests to protect the interests of society and that of others. Confucius highly praised this kind of behavior as "Those who live by high ideals do not seek their own survival to harm benevolence but sacrifice their own lives in order to be benevolent."[20]
⑧ "Harming others for benefiting others" is the behavior in which the ends benefit others, while the means harm others, such as a parent punishing a child to stop them from stealing again or a doctor giving a patient a very painful gastroscope in order to find a cure.
⑨ "Self-interest for self-harming" is the behavior in which the ends harm oneself but the means benefit oneself. It is also behavior done to realize the purpose of self- harming with a "more joyful" means or with a "less painful" means. In the ancient Rome Empire, Antony's wife, Egypt's beautiful queen Cleopatra, sought numerous secret recipes for an easy death by poison, and finally chose to take a bite out of a poisonous snake to end her life, using "self-interest for self-harming" with a "less painful" means to realize the purpose of committing suicide.
⑩ "Benefiting others for self-harming" is the behavior in which the ends harm oneself and the means benefits others. In Boccaccio's *10th Talk* there is a poor man who roamed the streets and slept in a mountain cavern. He wanted to commit suicide and, after meeting a murderer on the run from law, he decided to pretend that he was himself the murderer. He was imprisoned and put to death. Bringing harm to himself, as a way of actualizing his purpose of committing suicide this benefited others—the murder—while bringing harm to himself.
⑪ "Completely self-harming" is the behavior in which both the ends and means harm oneself. This kind of behavior, as Freud said, is usually because self-hatred results from feelings of guilt or evilness. An Indian once felt so guilty for killing his mother that one winter night he slept in the snow naked. Some mothers are said to have even pulled the hairs out of their scalp or to have slapped their own faces in incidences where

they felt they failed to discipline their badly misbehaved children. This is also triggered by self-hatred: they hate themselves for giving birth to such misbehaved children who are no better than animals.

⑫ "Harming others for self-harming" is the behavior in which the ends are self-harming and the means harming others. Such is the case when a person, driven by guilt, intends to go to prison to punish himself, and intentionally destroys public property and disturbs public order so that the police can catch him and put him to prison.

⑬ "Self-interest for harming others" is the behavior in which the ends harm others and the means is self-interest, such as one who does intensive physical exercises or practices martial arts for the sole purpose of killing the enemy.

⑭ "Benefiting others for harming others" is the behavior in which the ends harm others and the means benefit others. According to the legend, Liu Bang (who later became the first emperor of Han Dynasty) harbored deep hatred for the child who called him names, but he rewarded the child with some money, so as to nurture in the child a habit of calling names at others. Eventually, the child was killed for calling names at Xiang Yu, who was Liu Bang's opponent.

⑮ "Self-harming for harming others" is the behavior in which the ends harm others, while the means is self-harming. In Leo Tolstoy's *Anna Karenina* the heroine, Anna, had sought revenge on her love, Vronsky, by committing suicide on the railway tracks.

⑯ "Completely harming others" is the behavior in which both the ends and means harm others. Almost all traditional and modern martial arts fictions have such themes which are almost the same. In one fictional work, for instance, John's parents were killed by Peter; John had escaped to an old temple in a remote mountain, practicing martial arts and preparing for the revenge on Peter, and as soon as he had perfected his martial arts skills, over a period of many years, he came down from the mountain temple to kill Peter.

These 16 kinds of ethical behavior are the combination of all the *ends of ethical behavior* and the *means of ethical behavior* of human beings, which includes all the ethical behavior in all society and of everyone. One's ethical behavior, no matter which society one is in, no matter how strange, weird, or rare, are all included in the 16 kinds of ethical behaviors. However, the ethical behavior is not a single type but mostly a combination of several types. A scholar's life-long purpose for writing books, for instance, may not only for seeking renown or material benefits, but also for seeking the happiness of others. While the means to completing his lifelong work may benefit others in society, such that his scholarship in ways benefits people or society, or may harm the scholar's personal health because he neglected a good life balance. A scholar working hard toward completing a lifelong work, therefore, can be seen as a compound form of four different types of ethical behaviors: of "benefiting others for self-interest," "selflessly benefiting others," "self-harming for self-interest," and "self-sacrifice."

By making a comprehensive survey of the concept of ethical behavior we know that human nature studied in ethics, is the nature of the facts of the ethical behavior of humans; in terms of their structure, the ethical behavior consists of ends and the means and of ultimate motivation; in terms of their external types there are 16 types of ethical behavior. Examining carefully the nature of the facts of 16 kinds of ethical behavior we find that all of the ethical behavior develop and change along with the following four laws: the law of the ultimate motivation of ethical behavior, the law of the ends of ethical behavior, the law of the means of ethical behavior and the law of ethical behavior.

4.3 The law of the ultimate motivation of ethical behavior: Qualitative analysis of human nature

4.3.1 Introduction: The ultimate motivation of ethical behavior—love and hatred, personal pain and pleasure, as well as the desires of self-interest

In analyzing the ultimate motivation of ethical behavior it can only be found in desires and emotion, not in the reason. As Fung Yulan said: "Reason has no force and desire is blind."[21] And, according to Liang Qichao: "Reason only can let people know what they ought to do and how they ought to do it, but cannot force people to do it. Only emotion can lead people to do it."[22]

Psychology shows that so-called emotion is the psychological response of the subject to whether or not its needs are satisfied by the object. This kind of psychological response may point to the object, and thus is the subject's psychological response to the object as to whether the object satisfies its needs; it may also point to the subject itself, and thus is the psychological response of the subject as to whether or not its needs are satisfied. For example:

Pleasure and pain are the emotions directing the subject, and are the subject's psychological response to whether its needs are satisfied because pleasure is the subject's psychological response to the satisfaction of its needs, and pain is the subject's response to the dissatisfaction of its needs. On the contrary, love and hatred are the emotions directing the object, which is the subject's psychological response to the object which satisfies or impedes its needs, because so-called love, as many philosophers indicated, is the subject's psychological response to the cause of its pleasure, that is, the subject's psychological response to the object which satisfies its needs; hatred is the subject's psychological response to the cause of its pain, that is, the subject's psychological response to the object which impedes the satisfaction of its needs.

Emotion can be divided into basic emotions and non-basic emotions. Modern psychology identifies four kinds of basic emotions: pleasure, anger, sadness, and fear. It goes without saying that anger, sadness, and fear are the three main forms of pain, we can reduce the four to the two the basic emotions of pleasure and pain such that one is "the most basic positive emotion" and one is "the most basic negative emotion."[23] Furthermore, both pleasure and pain are the production of desires: pleasure is the psychological response when desires are satisfied; pain is the psychological response when desires are not satisfied. Therefore, desire is the most basic emotion, while pleasure and pain respectively are the most basic positive and negative emotions. More precisely, pain, and pleasure are the most basic positive and negative emotions that direct the subject; and since love and hate are derived from pleasure and pain they are the most positive and negative emotions directed to the object.

Almost all philosophers, psychologists, or any ordinary person would admit that "need" is the ultimate motivation of action—what we might otherwise term as a fundamental "non-ends cause of action." However, if we analyze "need" in depth, we find that it cannot directly cause an individual's actions. Only when the need is experienced and transformed into emotions—emotion is the psychological experience of whether need is satisfied—can it cause action: that is, need can only cause various psychological experiences concerning needs, i.e., emotions such as desire, pleasure, pain, love and hate etc., and only emotions can cause the ends of action, which are the cause of the means of the behavior that actualize it. In the overall process of behavior then, emotions such as desire, pain, pleasure, love, and hate, are the ultimate motivations that directly cause everyone's action, while need is the ultimate motivation that indirectly causes everyone's action.

This argument has been proved by the experiments of modern psychology. The research findings of Tomkins, a psychologist of ultimate motivational theory, indicate that the bare signal of the physical needs itself cannot cause action: "the first system of ultimate motivation is the system of emotion; the internal drive of a creature can only be motivated by the amplification of the emotional system."[24] For example, the signals of the physiological need to replenish water provided by cell dehydration and reduced blood volume do not trigger the act of drinking water. The physiological need to replenish water requires only the magnification of the thirst and urgency that it produces to trigger the act of drinking water:

The urgency of thirst is the fundamental non-purpose cause or ultimate motivation of the behavior of drinking water; while the physiological need to replenish water is the non-purpose cause or ultimate motivation that indirectly induce the actions of drinking water.

From above, we know, on the one hand, that emotion is the ultimate motivation of all kinds of actions; on the other hand, that desire is the most basic emotion, that pain and pleasure are the most basic positive and negative emotions directing the subject, and that love and hate, which are derived from pain and pleasure, are the most basic positive and negative emotions directing to the object. In combination: desire is the ultimate motivation behind all actions, and pain, pleasure, love, and hate are the positive and negative ultimate motivations that cause all actions. We also know that ethical

96 *The substance of moral value*

behavior belongs to the category of action, so desire is the ultimate motivation that causes all ethical behaviors, and pain, pleasure, love, and hate are the positive and negative ultimate motivations causing all ethical behaviors. As this is just the introduction to our research for the law of ethical behaviors, the research will further indicate that love and hate are the ultimate motivations of all ethical behaviors, and that personal pain and pleasure, as well as the desires of self-interest, are the deepest ultimate motivation that directly cause love and hate then indirectly cause all ethical behaviors.

4.3.2 Love and hatred: The ultimate motivation of ethical behaviors

Living in this world, a person knows more about love and hate than everything else. But what love and hate are, is difficult to be explain. Going through the classics that deliberate on human life, we can say that the interpretations by Locke, Hume, Feuerbach, and Freud are perhaps the most exact. Locke writes: "Our *love* and *hatred* of inanimate insensible Beings, is commonly founded on that Pleasure and Pain which we receive from their use and application any way to our Sense."[25] According to Hume:

> Whoever can find the means either by his services, his beauty, or his flattery, to render himself useful or agreeable to us, is sure of our affections: As on the other hand, whoever harms or displeases us never fails to excite our anger or hatred.[26]

Feuerbach says: "Love of things that are or will become the cause of pleasure is also human nature. In turn, the same is true of hatred for the causes of unpleasant feelings."[27] Love, claims Freud, is "the relation of the ego to its source of pleasure";[28] "Hate originally betokens the relation of the ego to the alien external world with its afflux of stimuli."[29]

In a word, love and hatred are kinds of psychological responses which have necessary connection to "pleasure and interests" as well as to "pain and harm": love is the self's psychological response to the cause of the pleasure the self experiences, the self's psychological response to the matter that is the source of the self's interests or pleasure; hate is the self's psychological response to the cause of the pain the self experiences, the self's psychological response to the matter that brings harm and pain to the self. Are these definitions tenable? The best way to affirm this obviously rests on examining the three types of the most universal, most complicated, and most important "love": maternal love, sexual love, and fraternal love.

Maternal love seems contradictive to this definition because, according to this definition, love, and hatred are conditional: the conditions of love are pleasure and interests, and the conditions of hatred are pain and harm. However, maternal love is an unconditional and inherent instinct. As both Fromm and Cai Yuanpei (蔡元培) have said: "Motherly love by its very nature is unconditional";[30] "Parental love to their children originates from the natural instincts, the depth of which cannot be surpassed by anything."[31]

But, what is the reason for the formation of this kind of unconditional instinct? Examined thoroughly, it might be, as many philosophers have declared, because the realization that we will die one day is the most fundamental and important sadness, while the most fundamental and important desire is the eternity of life. Is it that the love of parents "cannot be surpassed by anything" because children give parents the most fundamental and important interests and pleasure and satisfy the parent's desires of eternal life? Indeed, Plato said: "Don't be surprised that all people love their children, for this universal concern and love is for eternity."[32] What this means is that while parental love is unconditional, the cause for this kind of instinct is conditional: children give their parents' interests and pleasure. Therefore, the instinct of parental love is the psychological experience of the interest and pleasure they get from raising a child or children, this is a kind of psychological experience passes from generation to generation, and has evolved as a largely unconsciousness inherent trait.

A more comprehensive understanding of the nature of parental love, we know, is that it is also learned behavior. The inherent parental love is the unconscious psychological response to the interests and pleasure the children give their parents. On the contrary, the learned parental love is the conscious psychological response to the interests and pleasure the children give them. Talking about this kind of learn parental love Mao Dun (矛盾) wrote:

> The feelings of maternal love are always connected with the a strong sense of pleasure. When a mother hugs the soft body of her children, she forgets everything that makes her unhappy, she experiences only a sense of pleasure.[33]

If the children do not give their parents interests (pleasure) but cause them some sort of harm (pain) then the parent's love for them may turn into hatred instead. There are also many cases in which parents have sued in court the children they have raised. Why do parents who sue their children in court or even strangle their children hate their own children so much? It is because they have come to perceive their children as the source of harm (great pain).

Parental love, whether in terms of their innate instincts or in terms of the acquired parts, is a psychological response to the interests and pleasure their children provide. What, then, is sexual love? Why does one love his or her sex partner? Qualitatively, it is only because one's sex partner makes one happy, as Shapi pointed out: "Isn't love a kind of intoxication, and a kind of pleasure?"[34] Quantitatively, the reason why one's love to sex partner is the strongest, most beautiful, and most fascinating feeling of human beings is that sexual desire, the strongest desire of human beings, is the ultimate motivation and the deepest essence of love, the pleasure brought by the sexual partner therefore is the strongest, most beautiful, and entrancing pleasure. Sexual love originates from the pleasure brought by the sexual partner, which is a typical love interwoven with hatred, since, the sexual partner not only give pleasure, but also pain: "love is the synonym of pain."[35] If this kind of pain is caused by the actions of the sexual partner, such as some form of rejection, changing his or her mind, unfaithfulness, then the love one feels or expresses for the sexual partner can turn into hatred. As we all know, the kind of hatred that comes from some sort of rejection can be extremely overpowering, and often tragically leads to abuse, violence, murder, or suicide. But, why is the hatred directed toward the sexual partner so overpowering? It is because the heartache or pain brought by the sexual partner is an extremely strong emotion: the pain or the loss of sexual love (as it is for other types of love) is among the greatest types of human suffering.

If so-called sexual love, whether in terms of quality or quantity, is the psychological response to the pleasure and interests provided by the sexual partner, then, what is fraternal love? Fraternal love, we know is the love between or among friends, the love of friends: those whom we are socially close to, trust, and are able to offer help. The most essential nature of friendship is to share each other's interests and pleasure. According to Aristotle, "Any kind of fraternity can be regarded as pleasure."[36] The only difference is that the interests and pleasure exchanged are different because of different types of friends: friends wining and dining together exchange the interests and pleasure of drinking and eating; friends of writers and artists exchange the interests and pleasure of culture and knowledge; members of disreputable gangs exchange bawdy interests and types of pleasure; people involved in noble pursuits or endeavors exchange interests and pleasure in a simple and noble spirit. Regardless of the nature of the social activity, i.e., whether it's disreputable or noble, as Cai Yuanpei (蔡元培) said: "Friends are the persons who lessen one's pain and increase one's pleasure."[37]

Fraternal love is the psychological response to the interests and pleasure that friends provide. We might understand then the Chinese saying that "Men cannot be good for a thousand days and flowers cannot bloom for a hundred days." Because it is not easy to constantly exchange interests or pleasure with others, and it is difficult to continue fraternal love over a long period of time. It often fades because people do not always agree, fall out, feel alienated, and eventually become estranged from one another. Not only that. The closer the friends are, they are more inclined to have conflict over the interests that are important to them; consequently it is much more likely that these types of conflicts will cause more harm and suffering, and possibly a greater sense of hatred for one another, than similar conflicts among strangers. The same applies to national alliances. So, on a person-to-person level, when one turns his fraternal love for someone into hatred, it is simply the psychological response to the transformation of the pleasure the friend provides to suffering.

Obviously, though the maternal love, sexual love, and fraternal love are complicated and ambiguous, they clearly indicate the universal and necessary links among love—hatred, pain-pleasure, and advantage—disadvantage. These links are more apparent and simpler in other types of love and hatred. If asked why I love my country? It would answer, it is because I was born and raised in here, and I might mention additional ties or connections such

Human nature 99

as I educated here. After all, has not my country provided me the greatest interests? If, however, my country has oppressed, exploited, afflicted, or abused me, would I still love my country? As Mill had even once declared, under authoritarian rule there is only one patriot, and that is the autocrat himself.[38] Why is it that I love other people or indeed love everyone? Is it not because, as Spinoza says, "except for human beings nothing is more beneficial to human beings"?[39] Let's imagine someone called John wants to defame or harm me in some way, perhaps even wants to kill me for his own pleasure. Would I not dislike, even hate John? If my pet cat or dog, which both bring me pleasure, turned on me, and instead bit me every day, would I still love them? In other words, who loves the thing that makes him unhappy, and hates the thing that bring him pleasure? If you are a source of pleasure to others, they will likely love you. If you are a source of suffering to others, they will likely hate you.

Love and hatred are inevitable, not dissimilar to the phenomenon that occurs when iron reacts to oxygen—once the water or moistness the iron has been exposed to evaporate, it inevitably rusts. When one suffers some sort of harm from another, particularly one they love, emotional pain, or hatred is an inevitable psychological reaction existing independently of human will. So long as one obtains interests and pleasure, love is the inevitable psychological reaction to something that gives him interests and pleasure, also existing independently of human will. But, how love and hatred turn into the ultimate motivation of ethical behaviors?

Since pleasure and pain come not only from others but also from oneself, love and hate can be divided between loving others and self-love, and between hating others and self-hatred: to feel love for another person is a psychological response to that person being a cause of pleasure; to feel hate for another person is a psychological response to that person being a cause of pain; self-love is a psychological response to the self being a cause of pleasure; self-hatred is a psychological response to the self being the cause of pain. These four kinds of love and hatred are the fundamental "non-ends causes" or the ultimate motivations which trigger all four ethical behaviors—*benefiting others as an end, harming others as an end, self-interest as an end* and *self-harming as an end.*

4.3.3 Loving others, compassion and gratitude: The ultimate motivation of the behavior of benefiting others as an end

The so-called behavior of *benefiting others as an end*, i.e., the ends of the behavior is to benefit others but not the self, namely the behavior that *selflessly benefits others* and *self sacrifice*. Whether there is this kind of behavior is the fundamental issue that distinguishes altruism and egoism from one another, and has been debated since Confucius and Socrates' times to the present. However, it is obvious to see that, anyone, no matter however selfish they may be, more or less can selflessly benefit others. This is because they more or less obtain pleasure and interests from others, they will inevitably love others more or less. Loving-others, as a kind of psychological response to others who bring me pleasure, is what drives me to seek pleasure (or interests) for others: loving-others leads to the behavior of *selflessly benefiting others*.

According to a 1993 news report in *Hindustan Times*, in the State of Gujarāt in western Indian, a little child in a village was attacked by a lioness. On seeing the attack the mother ran to her child and yelled for help. Then the villagers arrived and scared away the lioness. Although the mother was seriously injured by the lioness, she was saved. Her son was not hurt. We might ask: what caused the mother to act selflessly and to make a self-sacrifice? It undoubtedly was her maternal love for her child. As Darwin said: "a young and timid mother urged by the maternal instinct will, without a moment's hesitation, run the greatest danger for her infant."[40] In most cases, a mother will sacrifice her own happiness, even her own life, to save her children from danger. To love, from the bottom of one's heart, is to understand what it means to selflessly benefit others and make self-sacrifices. On this, Confucius asked: "If one loves a person, will he not work hard for him?"[41] Mencius also said: "If you love a person then you hope him to be rich."[42] Hume believed that "Love is always followed by a desire of the happiness of the person beloved."[43] According to Fromm, "Love can be described by stating that love is primarily *giving*, not receiving."[44]

But, why does loving-others lead to the action of *selflessly benefiting others*? It turns out that, if one love a person, one would have compassion for that person, feeling the same emotions as that person. The more one loves, the stronger the compassion; the less one loves, the lesser the compassion. To the point that one has no love, only hatred instead, one does not have compassion any more. On the contrary, one is sad when a person one hates is happy, and is happy when the person one hates is sad. Therefore, compassion is derived from loving-others, and is the expression of loving-others. Thus, when one loves another person, one integrates with the person one loves; if the person one loves is happy, one is also happy; if the person one loves is sad, one is also sad, but will attempt to relieve the person their suffering. In relieving others of suffering one in a sense relieves oneself of suffering. Akin to obtaining pleasure for oneself, in fact, the ends of these kind of actions is usually not out of self-interest but out of making a self-sacrifice.

We all know that the maternal love is selfless. It is full of the spirit of self-sacrifice. But why do mothers pursue happiness and pleasure for their own children rather than for themselves? It is because they love their children and: they treat their children's pleasure and sadness as their own pleasure and sadness. One often sees, for instance, a mother giving something delicious from a plate of food to their infant child rather than eating it themselves. Why do mothers act this way? A mother's usual reply is that they sense the joy or pleasure of the child eating the delicious food, and this kind of pleasure is much stronger than what joy they would get if eating the food themselves.

If one loves others and treats others with compassion one achieves the lofty realm of selflessly benefiting others. Mencius said: "Compassion is the starting point of selflessly benefiting others"[45] Then, can loving-others, which lead to actions of selflessly benefiting others, only be achieved through compassion? The answer is no. As we have mentioned above, the reason why one love others is that others provided one with interests and pleasure: that loving-others is a psychological response to others who are the cause of one's pleasure. If these kinds of pleasure and interests are given by others unintentionally, such as the lovely behaviors of children or the beauty of lover, then such kinds of pleasure and interests are just pleasure and interests, that is, not some sort a favor extended to oneself from others. One only produce a psychological response of love to such kinds of pleasure and interests, which is not a mind of gratitude. Without doubt this kind of love can selflessly benefit others through compassion only.

On the contrary, if the pleasure and interests one obtains are given by others intentionally, such as parents rearing children, or help from friends, then these kinds of pleasure and interests are favors. One generates not only a psychological response of love to these kinds of pleasure and interests, but also the psychological reaction of intentionally giving others pleasure and interests. This so-called love is one of gratitude, of repaying the favor. Gratitude is the psychology that grows out of the intention of giving pleasure and interests to others who intentionally give one pleasure and interests. Therefore, gratitude is a kind of love in that it is an expression and a result of the basis of love. If parental love is typically love out of the mind of compassion, then the love of the children for their parents is typically the love of gratitude.

It is easy to see that the purpose of the action caused by gratitude is not necessarily "for," but "because" of the pleasure and interests obtained from the benefactor; the purpose resides in reciprocating the benefactor with pleasure and interests, and the cause resides in the benefactor having provided one with the pleasure and interests; but one repays or returns the pleasure and interests to the benefactor is not for obtaining the pleasure and interests from the benefactor again since one's purpose is to give, not to take, is for the benefactor, not for oneself. In short, gratitude is that which causes selfless actions that benefit others. When one loves others, if this kind of love is the psychological response to the pleasure and interests that others intentionally give one, then one will be grateful to others and grow in their general gratitude for life, and as well as seek pleasure and interests for their benefactors: through gratitude, love grows and leads to further actions of unselfishly benefiting others.

In sum, basically the reason why one's purpose of action benefits others selflessly is because one loves others with the mind of compassion and gratitude; after all, this is because one has received interests and pleasure from others: love is the psychological response to the interests and pleasure given or received. Therefore, the "non-ends cause" or ultimate motivation for the purpose of the action of *selflessly benefiting others* is loving-others, the mind of compassion and gratitude; the deepest ultimate motivation is the pleasure and interests one receives from others, thus is self-interest.

4.3.4 Hating others, envy, and vengeance: The ultimate motivation of harming others as an end

The so-called actions of *harming others as an end* are the actions that harm others rather than benefit the self as an end, and often in order to harm others through the means of self-harming. For instance, to harm others one may not hesitate to break the law to harm oneself such as the famous case in 1963, in the state of Georgia in the United States, when a black student shot one of his classmates to death because he was jealous that his classmate was elected as chairman of the class committee. The case demonstrates that *harming others as an end* is a kind of very unique action, it is similar to "harming others for self-interest" and "benefiting others as an end," but they are different in nature: on the one hand, both "harming others as an end" and "harming others for self-interest" are the actions of harming others, but, "harming others for self-interest" is the means of harming others, while "harming others as an end" is the ends of harming others; on the other hand, though the ends of "harming others as an end" and "harming others for self-interest" are opposite, the means are sometimes the same: harming the self.

Then, are these kinds of actions only done by those whose souls are extremely dark? This is not the case at all. Everyone, no matter how kind, more or less does the actions of harming others as an end. This is because everyone, no matter how kind, more or less, will suffer from pain and harms caused by others, which will inevitably lead to hating-others more or less. And hating-others, as a kind of psychological response to others who brings one pain, is what drives one to harm others: hating-others will lead to the behavior of *harming others as an end*. Throughout history, hatred has been the driver of harming others, to the extent that the one inflicting harm has no care in harming themselves, such as spending life in prison or even killing themselves. As Freud said, hatred "can then be intensified to the point of an aggressive tendency towards the object with intention to destroy it."[46] But why does hatred lead to actions of harming others as an end?

If one hates a person, one will develop antipathy for the person, one's feelings will be opposite to that of the person one hates. The typical antipathy is envy: envy is the psychology of being opposite to others because one feels they are in a position of disadvantage compared to the position of advantage of others; or it could be because an improvement in the inferiority of another's position threatens one's own advantage. Envy also stems from other people's harm and pain to oneself. However, these kinds of harm and pain are not intentionally given by others, but are the result of one's comparison with others: on the one hand, others are seen to have an advantage while one sees oneself at a disadvantage; on the other hand, others are seen to make improvements from disadvantage to advantage while seeing one's advantage as weakening to disadvantage. Others do not intend to harm me, but others' advantage puts me at a disadvantage, and others' improvement from disadvantage to advantage is a threat to my own advantage, so I grow envious with feelings of opposition to others: this is so-called envy.

Thus, if I hate others, this kind of hatred is my psychological response to other's advantage or to their improvement from a position of disadvantage, I am envious, I see other's pleasure and happiness only to feel the pain of my own misfortune; and am happy and pleased when I see other's pain and misfortune. So I try to make others feel unhappy and unfortunate, which is just like making myself feel happy and fortunate. If I can make others feel pain it's just like getting rid of my own pain. However, in fact, my purpose of action is purely harming others and not benefiting myself; my actions are not self-interested but usually are self-harming. As a real-life example of the above types of behaviors, for instance, in 1963, a casual worker drove his car on to the pavement after a baseball game in order to kill a champion and handsome baseballer. The murderer admitted that his motive was out of pure hatred and envy, noting especially that he envied the athlete's good looks: his envy drove him to violate the law to harm others rather than harm himself.

Then, does hating-others only comes through harboring feelings that are opposite to that of the person one hates—especially the envy—necessarily lead to harming others as an end? It is not the case. As we mentioned above, the reason one hates others is only because others give one pain and harm: hating-others is the psychological response to the person who is the cause of one's pain. If this pain and harm are given by others unintentionally—such as others' advantage or the improvement of their disadvantage—then my pain and harm are only pain and harm but not "enmity." I react to this kind of pain and harm it is both envy and hatred, but it is not out of the mind of vengeance. Yet, if my pain and harm are caused intentionally by another—such as making a false charge against me or persecution, then this kind of pain and harm is "enmity," and to this kind of pain and harm, I have not only the psychological response of hatred, but also the psychological response of intentionally returning the pain and harm, namely this kind of hatred is vengeance: vengeance is the psychology that wants intentionally to harm the person who has intentionally harmed oneself either directly or indirectly. Therefore, the mind of vengeance is a special kind of hating-others: it is the expression and result of the mind of hating-others.

Therefore, the ends of actions caused by vengeance also to harm others but not out of self-interest, and are usually with the means of self-harming: harming the enemy at the cost of one's own suffering. This kind of action of harming others as an end has been an intriguing social phenomenon dating back ancient times as important subjects or themes of dramas, novels, films, and so on—especially in the martial arts novels of China—both old and new—which are almost the same with their themes of vengeance such as the story of John mentioned earlier.

104 *The substance of moral value*

Therefore, the reason that one harms others as an end, basically speaking is because he hates others and then has the mind of jealousy and the mind of vengeance; one's being jealous and revenging to hate others, in the final analysis, is only because others inflict pains and harming on him: hatred is the psychological response to the pain and harms inflicted on oneself. Thence, the ultimate motivation of *harming others as an end*—namely the fundamental non-ends cause for *harming others as an end*—is the mind of hatred, mind of envy, and mind of vengeance; and the deepest ultimate motivation is the pain and harms others inflicted on him, is the pain, pleasure, advantage, and disadvantage, is the mind of self-interests for seeking pleasure and avoiding hardship, as well as seeking advantages to avoid disadvantages, it is self-interest.

4.3.5 Self-hatred, the sense of guilt and inferiority complex: The ultimate motivation of self-harming as an end

Self-harming as an end falls under the behaviors of self-harming, but not all behaviors of self-harming are *self-harming as an end*. This is because self-harming is not necessarily the ends but usually the means: if self-harming is to avoid greater pain and harm, it is not the ends but the means, since it is *self-harming for self-interest*, which belongs to the behavior of *self-interest as an end*. Self-interest has a double nature in that it seeks advantage for oneself and avoids disadvantage to oneself. For example, to avoid greater pain Freud harmed himself by killing himself with an injection of potassium cyanide after he suffered from nasopharyngeal cancer at the age of 83, thus his action is one of *self-interest as an end*.

However, suicide is not entirely a matter of *self-interest as an end* because some of the methods of committing suicide are extremely horrible: there are reports of people who have thrown themselves on to a whirling circular saw, ignited explosives in the mouth, inserted a red-heated iron bar into the throat, jumped into a burning furnace, jumped into a volcanic crater, nakedly frozen to death naked in the winter snow, etc. Why do people choose such painful ways to kill themselves? It is obviously not to escape pain and harm, but out of a strong desire to suffer, perhaps for the sake of suffering itself, harming themselves for the sake of being harmed, and therefore are the most extreme actions of self-harming as an end.

But why do people harm themselves? This is the core question of psychoanalysis. Studies by psychoanalysts such as Freud, Jung, Adler, Fromm, and Karen Horney show that one's purpose to self-harm is because one hates themselves, it is hatred turned onto oneself.

On the one hand, hatred is one's psychological response to something that gives him pain or some other harm. Although most of the pains or harms one suffered come from others, they are usually also caused by oneself. If one's pain or harm is caused by others, one would certainly hate others, and would certainly produce the mind of hating-others; if caused by oneself, one would certainly hate oneself and would certainly produce self-hatred: self-hatred is a psychological response to the self as the cause of one's own pain.

On the other hand, hatred is the cause of destructive and damaging behaviors:

> When the object is the source of the painful feelings, we feel a "repulsion" from the object and hate it; this hate can then be intensified to the point of an aggressive tendency towards the object with intention to destroy it.[47]

If the object of hatred is others, it would lead to the behavior of *harming others as an end*. If the object of hatred is oneself, it would lead to the behavior of *self-harming as an end*. Then, how does self-hatred actually trigger the behavior of *self-harming as an end*?

Actually, everyone has more or less the moral will to be a good person. In this way, if one harms others and does anything evil that violates morality, they will be in the pricks of conscience because the moral aspirations of being a good person are not realized, produce instead the sense of guilt, which is the psychological response to one's pain suffering pricks of conscience caused by harming others. Therefore both belongs to the category of self-hatred. This sense of self-hatred might be a kind of rather strong and persistent anxiety overtime, or an acute emotional disturbance that shocks the soul; if not neutralized and counteracted by self-love, one would self-punish with all the above injurious actions to get rid of the sense of sin and guilt, freeing oneself from anxiety to achieve the inner peace. In studying these facts psychoanalysts have further found that every type of neurosis has an unconscious need which is triggered by suffering from a sense of guilt. Freud cited a middle-aged woman as an example:

> She would fall down and sprain her foot, or injure her knee, or else hurt her hand while she was doing something or other. As soon as she saw how great a part she herself played in these apparently chance accidents, she altered her technique, as one might say. Instead of accidents she contracted on the same occasion slight illnesses, such as catarhs, sore throats, influenza conditions, or rheumatic swellings, until at last when she made up her mind to resign herself to inactivity ... As to the origin of this unconscious need for punishment, there can be, I think, no doubt. It behaves like a part of conscience, like the prolongation of conscience into the unconscious; and it must have the same origin as conscience, that is to say, it will correspond to a price of aggressiveness which has been internized and taken over by the super-ego. If only the words were less incongruous, we should be justified, for all practical purpose, in calling it *an unconscious sense of guilt*.[48]

Then, is the sense of guilt the entire motivation of *self-harming as an end*? No, because, as modern psychology has indicated, the main situational condition for pain is triggered when the behavior fails to achieve its ends. If one believes that a failure to achieve ends is caused by one's own incompetence, then the psychological response would be another type of self-hatred, which is different from the sense of guilt, namely inferiority complex. The sense of guilt is by contrast the hatred one has for one's own immorality, while one's inferiority complex is the hatred one has for one's own incompetence; it is a psychological response that attributes one's own pain to one's own incompetence. In a less severe, more everyday, sense the inferiority complex is akin to humility: "Humility is the pain caused by a man's examination of his own weakness."[49]

Rather, opposite to self-respect, an inferiority complex is the psychology of one who sees themselves incapable of being respected, of doing something good and being valuable. A fundamental feature of an inferiority complex is the lack self-confidence. The feeling that one is inferior does not readily lend itself to a sort of self-confession, but rather is a thinking of oneself as being incapable of changing one's sense of inferiority. The inferiority complex emerges, according to Adler, "when an individual ... faced with a problem he cannot properly cope with ... says he absolutely cannot solve the problem."[50] In this way, however, one only thinks of oneself as inferior, rather than as having inferiority—one is able to change the thinking of oneself as inferior into self-confidence or self-respect. People with severe physical defects, for instance, might develop over time a kind of inferiority complex because of not being able to easily change the severity of physical defect.

In the final analysis, self-hatred is at the mind of both psychological conditions of the inferiority complex and the sense of guilt even though they are different from each other. As psychological mechanisms of self-harming as an end, the sorts of self-punishment are therefore often the same. As mentioned previously, there are many reported cases in which the mothers of wayward children have self-harmed by slapping their own face with hands or even hitting their heads with sticks. These forms of self-punishment are triggered by the self-hatred that emerges from the feeling of being inferior: the mothers hate themselves for being so incompetent raising their own children as good citizens. Of course, an inferiority complex is different from the sense of guilt: the feeling of being inferior in a way is a form self-abandonment. If one feels incompetent at everything one does, they will likely give up everything, and hence also abandon themselves, thinking: what is the point fighting against the odds? Self-abandonment is entwined with one's sense inferiority, which, Karen Horney says, is essentially "about fighting against any struggle for improvement or achievement."[51]

In sum, the reason why one self-harms as an end is because one's hatred turns inward to oneself out of a sense of guilt or an inferiority complex or both psychological conditions; the reason one hates oneself after all is because the pain and harm one suffers are caused by either one's own immorality or incompetence or both: self-hatred is encompasses one or all of these conditions as part of a vicious cycle; it is the psychological response to a kind of self-perpetuating harm and pain. Therefore, the ultimate motivation of *self-harming as an end*—that is, the fundamental and "non-ends cause" of *self-harming as an end*—is self-hatred, encompassing either a sense of guilt or an inferiority complex or both conditions. Thence, the ultimate motivation of *self-harming as an end*—namely the fundamental non-ends cause for *self-harming as an end*—is the mind of self-hatred, a sense of guilt, and an inferiority complex; and the deepest ultimate motivation is still the pain, pleasure, advantage, and disadvantage, is the mind of self-interests for seeking pleasure and avoiding hardship, as well as seeking advantages to avoid disadvantages, it is self-interest.

4.3.6 Self-love, desires to live and self-respect: The ultimate motivation of self-interest as an end

It is self-evident that s*elf-interest as an end* is the behavior that seeks benefits for oneself—that seeks advantage and avoids disadvantage, pursues pleasure, and avoids hardship: pursuing pleasure and gain for oneself is positive self-interest; avoiding harm and hardship is negative self-interest. Nevertheless, most people would agree with Voltaire's words: "just as there is no need to prove that a person has a face, there is no need to prove why a person is self-interested, for everyone seeks advantage and avoids disadvantage, which is human instinct."[52] This is a superficial view because, as discussed previously, humans have not only self-interest as ends, but also self-harming as ends. If self-interest is human instinct, then why would one harm themselves? Obviously, one is self-interested only because one has self-love; if one hates oneself instead, one would not be self-interested, but would self-harm.

The desire to live is a basic expression for one's self-love. One's so-called desire to live is coexistent with a desire to love life, that is, to preserve one's existence. Just as everyone has an innate desire to live, everyone has a desire to love life—that is, simply a desire to be happy. Because the pleasure of life (being alive) is the most fundamental, most important, and the greatest pleasure of human. Pleasure and pain is a result of biological evolution. On the one hand, it stimulates a feeling of pleasure that is beneficial to life whereas stimuli that causes a feeling of pain is harmful to life. On the other hand, as part of our animal nature, pleasure, in terms of the feeling of pleasure it provides, as opposed to the feeling of pain, is more broadly speaking, that which drives us to seek kinds of pleasure and avoid kinds of hardship. In this way, animals—the material form of which is the most advanced and therefore the most difficult to maintain—can survive.

Since pleasure is the psychological response to what is beneficial in life, and pain is the psychological response to what is harmful in life, then the most fundamental, important, and greatest pleasure is the psychological response to life itself. With this, we can relate to Feuerbach's claim that "Life itself is pleasure"[53] or, even better, to Chuang-tzu's declaration: "Be alive and happy."[54] Life or being alive itself is the most fundamental, the most important and the greatest pleasure of everyone. Therefore, everyone's desire to live is the most fundamental, important, and greatest need. As Feuerbach went on to say:

> The wish of man, at least of those who do not limit their desire by the necessity of nature, is above all the desire to live forever. Yes, it is the last and highest desire of man, the desire of all desires.[55]

Then, considering everyone's desire to live, what will everyone's actions lead to? Obviously, they will lead to the existence and development of one's own life, of seeking advantage and avoiding disadvantage, pursuing pleasure and avoiding hardship. In the final analysis, the ends of the actions are self-interest.

Thus, we can draw the conclusion that the actions of *self-interest as an end* emerges not just directly from the desire to live, but, more fundamentally speaking, from the pleasure of life. While the desire to live triggers the basic and low-level action of self-interest or self-love (mere surviving or living), it cannot lead to the higher-level action of self-interest or self-love: such as living a life with a sense of achievement, merit and value. The cause of these actions is another kind of self-interest or self-love, namely self-respect.

One's self consists of his own life and personality. The desire to live is the expression of self-love in one's own life, which is the love of his own life. On the contrary, self-respect is the expression of self-love in one's own personality, which is the love of one's own personality.

The so-called personality is also one's behavioral ego. On the one hand, the formation of one's personality is a result of one's series of actions overtime: "what a man does, is what a man is."[56] If you steal frequently, this will come to define who you are, your personality, and you will likely be called or thought of as a thief or some other such name. If you do good things all the time, you will likely be called or thought of as a good person. In both circumstances, the principle is the same, and is accepted as the first principle of existentialism: "Man is nothing but his own creation."[57] On the other hand, one's personality (one's behavior overtime) in turn is what determines one's behavior. Alpert wrote: "Personality is the dynamic organization of an individual's internal psychophysical system, which determines the uniqueness of his behavior and thought."[58] Thus, in combination, one's personality is formed by and a self-expression of one's behavior: "One's personality is what a man is and does, it exists behind one's action, within the individual."[59]

But why would a person love his own personality? Modern psychology shows that the most important situational condition for pleasure is that a person pursues and achieves his ends. Everyone's behavior and purpose is to satisfy certain needs and desires. If one's actions are successful and thus satisfy his needs, fulfilling his desires and achieving his ends, then he is happy. Conversely, he suffers. It goes without saying that everyone, no matter how often they fail, has countless successes and untold pleasures (though these successes and pleasures may be so trivial, such as one is able to walk when one wants to, to go and see a movie when he wants to, etc.) These successes and pleasures are a result of one's own actions and personality. Therefore, the ultimate cause of everyone's pleasure is, specifically, people's own actions and, overall, people's own personalities. This is the answer why everyone loves his own personality.

It is self-evident that in loving one's self (i.e., in terms of one's own personality or conduct) also has the psychology behind it of making one's personality something to be respected, that is, by both others and oneself: to love one's self (one's own personality) is the same as having self-respect. Fung Yulan wrote: "Mencius said: 'who is Shun, who is me? But if I work hard I am the same as Shun.' A person with such aspiration and interests is said to have the mind of self-respect."[60] But, how can a person be respected by himself and others? There is no doubt that only by making a difference, achieving something, having made a contribution and to be of value can a person respect himself and gain it from others. In this sense, Mencius said: "If you are a chicken, a dog or a beast, it is impossible to be respected by others."[61] Therefore, self-respect certainly leads to the behavior of *self-interest as an end* and of making one successful, making a contribution and having value: one with self-respect then shall make an earnest effort to stand on one's own feet and be independent.

It can be seen that the reason why one is self-interested as an end is because one loves oneself, having the desire to live and self-respect. And the reason why one loves oneself and has the desire to live and self-respect is simply because one's own life and personality is the ultimate cause of one's pleasure: self-love is the psychological response to oneself being the cause of one's pleasure. Therefore, the ultimate motivation of self-interest as an end—the fundamental non-ends cause of self-interest as an end—is self-love, the desire to live, and self-respect, while the deepest ultimate motivation is still the pleasure and interest of the self, that is, self-interest.

4.3.7 Conclusion: The law of the ultimate motivation of ethical behavior

Examining ultimate motivations of *benefiting others as an end, harming others as an end, self-interest as an end*, and *self-harming as an end*, we can draw the conclusion that the ends of such actions are freely chosen since they are different for everyone: some actions may selflessly benefit others out of loving-others, compassion, or gratitude; some actions may be *self-interested* out of self-love, the desire to live, or self-respect; some actions may be purely intended to harm others out of hating-others, envy, or vengeance, just as they might be purely to self-harm out of self-hatred, a sense of guilt, or an inferiority complex. However, the ultimate cause of these actions—the ultimate motivation of all ethical behaviors—cannot be freely chosen, are inevitable, and exactly the same for everyone, it can only be one's self-interest, one's pain or pleasure, advantage, or disadvantage.

110   *The substance of moral value*

The ultimate motivation for ethical behavior reveals itself to be self-interest, such is the consensus among utilitarianism, egoism, deontology, and altruism. "There is a noble side to my behavior," said Chernyshevsky, the master of utilitarianism and egoism, "but it is motivated by the desire of self-interest in my own nature."[62]

> In general, with a little attention to the actions and emotions that appear to be selfless, we can see that they are still based on the idea of personal interests, personal happiness and personal welfare, the emotion that is still called egoism.[63]

Kant, the giant of deontology and altruism, also said: "All men have the greatest and deepest interest in their own happiness."[64]

> Though through the most ruthless self-examination, we cannot find anything but the moral basis of responsibility that forces us to do good things in one way or another, to endure great sacrifices, it is not certain that behind the apparent ideal there is no real selfish motive, which is an inherent and decisive cause of will.[65]

Confucianism, the representative of deontology and altruism in China, further finds that the moral realm of the gentleman and the villain is different only between the ends and means of their behavior, but does not relate to the ultimate motivation which triggers the ends and means because the ultimate motivation of action is inevitable, meaning that it cannot be freely chosen since it is exactly the same for everyone, it can only be one self's pain or pleasure, advantage, or disadvantage solely in regard to self-interest:

> All mankind is the same in one aspect: whether hungry, in search of food, or cold, in search of warmth, or laboring and then resting, seeks interests and avoids harm. This is the inherent nature of man, it makes no difference whether he is Yu (禹) or Jie (桀).[66]

The law of the ultimate motivation of ethical behavior undoubtedly is the most profound law of human nature. However, the study of this law is only a qualitative analysis of human nature in that it only analyzes why human beings can be selfless but not how much can one be selfless. To be more precise, it only reveals the ultimate motivation that leads to various ends of ethical behavior, with explanations as to why everyone has the four ends of self-interest, benefiting others, self-harming, and harming others, thus providing a basis for the existence of these ends—especially *the ends of benefiting others* that have been debated for more than two thousand years. But to what extent can people be selfless? Can a person, as Confucianism, Kant, and Christian ethicists say, be constantly or even completely selfless? The question as to how much can one be selfless and how long one can last being selfless, considering everyone's four ends of self-interest, benefiting others, self-harming, and harming others, leads to the further question of whether a relative quantity of selflessness has a law to follow.

4.4 Law of relative quantity of ends of ethical behavior: Quantitative analysis of human nature

4.4.1 Degrees of love: The most profound law of human nature

The so-called relative quantity of the ends of ethical behavior, of course, refers to the problem of the proportion of the number of the ends of everyone's various ethical behavior—ends of self-interest, ends of benefiting others, ends of self-harming, and ends of harming others—in the sum of one's actions in one's life. It goes without saying, however, that in terms of the sum of everyone's actions in life, the ends of self-harming and harming others are extremely rare and certainly are far less than the ends of self-interest and benefiting others. Therefore, what we really need to compare, confirm, and prove is the relative quantity, that is, the relative quantity of self-interest for self-love and selflessly benefiting others, and which is more and which is less. Thus, might an individual, as Confucianism, Kant, and Christian ethicists claim, after good moral education and moral cultivation, be constantly altruistic? And even reach a state of complete selflessness that, never out of self-interest, always unselfishly benefits others?

The answer is no. The ultimate motivation of ethical behavior shows that if I selflessly seek the interests of others, it is because I love others—loving-others leads to the behavior of *selflessly benefiting others*—and that I love others because others bring me interests and pleasure: love is the psychological response to something that gives one interests and pleasure. That is to say, whether I selflessly seek the interests of others depends on whether I love others, and whether I love others depends on whether others bring me interests and pleasure. Consequently, how much I selflessly seek the interests of others depends on how much I love others, and how much I love others depends on how much interests and pleasure others give me:

Those who give me less interests and pleasure certainly will be alienated from me and I will love them less, and less selflessly seek the interests of them; those who give me more interests and pleasure will be closer to me and I will love them more, and more selflessly seek the interests of them. After all, I certainly love myself the most and most of my actions in life certainly are to pursue my own interests, i.e., I love myself certainly more than loving others, and seek interests for myself more than interests of others; that is, self-love is greater than one's love for others, and self-interest is greater than that of benefiting others; everyone certainly constantly seeks their own interests and only occasionally that of others—by "constantly" I mean at least over half of the time, and by "occasionally" I mean less than half of the time. This is the law of *degrees of love*, which is illustrated by the use of concentric circles (see Figure 4.1).

112 *The substance of moral value*

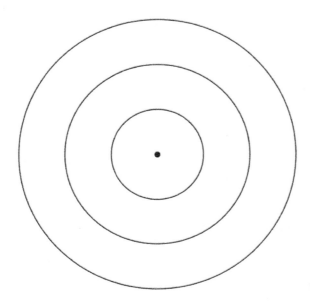

Figure 4.1 The law of *degrees of love*

The inner most center of the circle represents the self and the circles extending outwards represent others. The circle furthermost from the center, for instance, represents a person who gives me the least amount of interests and pleasure and thus is furthermost from me: I therefore love him or her the least and am less inclined to selflessly pursue his or her interests. On the contrary, the circle closer to the center represents a person who gives me the more interests and pleasure and is thus closer to me: I therefore love him or her more and am more inclined to selflessly seek his or her interests. Therefore, considering that inner most circle represents me, I love myself the most and am more inclined to seek my own interests, that is, my self-love is greater than my love for others, and my self-interest is greater than that of my benefiting others: everyone certainly constantly seeks their own interests and only occasionally the interest of others.

The *degrees of love* are undoubtedly the most profound laws of human nature. If the people I love the most are my parents or my children, is it not because they give me the most interests and pleasure? I may, by contrast, hate them the most if, for instance, my parents had abandoned me when I was young or my now grown-up children in some way mistreated me. A mother accused by her son of a serious crime such as attempted murder and found guilty may well have been the person her son loved the most. The son strangled by his mother was perhaps once the apple of his mother's eye. Why is it that a person one loves the most can become the person one hates the most? Is it not that that person who causes one the most harm and pain is the one who once gave the most interests and pleasure? No matter who it is, a parent, child, or lover, as long as he or she gives me the most interests and pleasure, I will love him or her the most; as long as he or she causes me the most harm and pain, I hate him the most. After all, do I not love myself the most?

The law of the degrees of love of human nature consist of "quality" and "quantity"—namely the "premise" and "conclusion." The "quality" or "premise" of the degrees of love, that is, "what is love?," originally belongs to the content of the law of ultimate motivation of ethical behavior, while the "quantity" or "conclusion" of the degrees of love, that is, "how much is the love?," is the core of the content of the law of the degrees of love. What is love? It is the psychological response to something that gives me interests and pleasure. How much is the love? Love is the psychological response to something that gives me interests and pleasure determines that whoever gives me the more interest and pleasure, I will certainly love him more; in the final analysis, I certainly love myself the most.

The law of the degrees of love of human nature consist of "quality" and "quantity"—namely the "premise" and "conclusion." The "quality" or "premise" of the degrees of love, that is, "what is love?," originally belongs to the content of the law of ultimate motivation of ethical behavior, while the "quantity" or "conclusion" of the degrees of love, that is, "how much is the love?," is the core of the content of the law of the degrees of love. What is love? It is the psychological response to something that gives me interests and pleasure. How much is the love? Love is the psychological response to something that gives me interests and pleasure determines that: who gives me the more interests and pleasure, I will certainly love him more, in the final analysis, I certainly love myself the most.

Interestingly, this law of human nature, as is well-known, was discovered by Confucius, who, against the act of "self-love," was the founder of altruism. According to Confucian classics such as *The Analects of Confucius*, the explanations of the *degrees of love* can be summed up as followings:

I love my parents because my most basic interests are given by my parents; I love others because my interests are also given by others. My parents give me more interests since they are in kind thick and big; others give me less interests since they are in kind thin and small. Therefore, the degrees of love between that given by parents and that by others are not the same since the interests differ in terms of being more and less, thick and thin: those who give me less interests, are people whom I love less; those who give me more interests, are people whom I love more.

From this, Mozi (墨子) expounded: I certainly love myself the most. A chapter in *Mozi* used the words of the Wu Mazi (巫马子) to outline Confucius' principle of the degrees of love:

> Wu Mazi told Mozi: "I am different from you, I cannot have universal love. I love people in Zou more than people in Yue, love people in Lu

more than people in Zou, love my village fellows more than people in Lu, love my family members more than my village fellows, love my parents more than my family members, and love myself more than my parents. This is because I am closest to myself."

Commenting on this, Fung Yulan remarked:

> Wu Mazi was a Confucian but he said "I love myself more than my parents," which might be exaggerated in the records in the Mohist School, which is obviously contradictory to Confucian's emphasis on filial piety. Except for this, Wu Mazi's words, generally speaking, are in accordance with the Confucian spirit.[67]

Fung Yulan is only half right. He neglected that "the degrees of love" implies two meanings: one is that "the degrees of love" is an objective law of behavioral fact; the other is that "the degrees of love" is a moral norm of behavioral oughts. From the point of view of the moral norm, "I love myself more than my parents" does not conform to Confucian filial piety, and it also contradicts the Confucian view that "it is immoral to benefit oneself as an end." Mozi's assertion that "I love myself more than my parents" is a Confucian proposition, which is undoubtedly exaggerated and distorted. Fung Yulan is right about this.

However, judging from the behavioral law, since those who give me more interests and pleasure, I will certainly love them more, then I certainly love myself the most: I love myself more than my parents. Therefore, although, saying "I love myself more than my parents" is opposed by the Confucian moral norm of "the degrees of love," it is an inevitable conclusion and the proper meaning of "the degrees of love" as the behavioral law, and in this sense is by no means Mozi's exaggeration. Confucianism avoids this conclusion, it is also one of the reasons that the system of altruism is unable to appropriately justify itself.

The law of the human nature of the *degrees of love* is an absolute objective law that can be applied all over the world and be followed from generation to generation! However, interestingly, the study of this law in the West belongs not to the science of ethics but to other sciences in the humanities such as psychology, social psychology, and sociobiology. Freud, and the social psychologists Wilson and Charles A. Ellwood, came to the conclusion that it is superficial to only see that everyone has ends of self-interest and ends of benefiting others; that the essence of the problem is that everyone's primary and regular ends of actions are mostly aimed at self-love and self-interest; that selflessly benefiting others is only a person's secondary and occasional ends of action:

> In the developmental process of the individual, the programme of [the] pleasure principle, which consists in finding the satisfaction of happiness, is retained as the main aim. Integration in, or adaption to, a human

community appears as a scarcely avoidable condition which must be fulfilled before this aim of happiness can be achieved ... the development of individual seems to us to be a product of the interaction between two urges, the urge towards happiness, which we usually called "egoistic," and the urge toward union with others in the community, which we called "altruistic." Neither of these descriptions goes much below the surface. In the process of individual development, as we have said, the main accent falls mostly on the egoistic urge; while the other urge, which may be described as a "cultural" one, is usually content with the role of imposing restrictions.[68]

Most altruistic actions, after all, are for themselves, both egoism and altruism may originate from human nature, although, like all other animals, the need for survival makes the tendency of one's egoism to be dominant and more powerful in nature.[69]

Of course, it cannot be said that Western ethicists did not study this law of human nature. But it was probably not until the nineteenth century that Bentham saw through this: "Every man is nearer to himself, and dearer to himself, than he can be to any other man."[70] Paulsen termed this law as "psychical mechanics":

It is evident that our conduct is actually guided by such considerations; every ego, we might say, arranges all other egos around it in [a] concentric circle; the farther away the interests from this center, the less weight and motive force they possess. That is a law of psychical mechanics.[71]

And the master of the theory of "Thick and black," Li Zongwu (李宗吾), thirty years or so younger than Paulsen, and seemingly inspired by his term for the law, wittily combines both Chinese and Western theories:

My thoughts at any moment are all centered on myself, determining my love of others as more or less in relation to the distance from me. When my little son compares his elder brother with our neighbor next door, he says that his elder brother is closer to him, and that he loves his brother more. When he compares his mother with his elder brother, he says that his mother is much closer to him, and that he loves his mother more. When he compares his mother with himself, he naturally says he loves himself more. Once when he saw his mother with some cake in her the mouth, he took it out to put into his own mouth ... therefore, we know it is human nature that those who are closer to me I love them more: that love and distance are in inverse proportion, similar to magnetoelectricity attraction.[72]

But Li Zongwu also declared that the theory of this law was his creation:

one day, walking in the street I suddenly felt that human nature is centered around the "I," as if there are many circles in front of the

"I" and surrounding the "I," layers of magnification just like a magnetic field; and that the changes of the human mind follow the laws of mechanics in every aspect ... at that time Einstein's theory of relativity had spread to China, so I applied both Einstein's theory and Newton's theory to psychology and created a theory: that "psychology varies according to the laws of mechanics."[73]

It turns out that he was unaware that Paulsen had already developed a theory of "concentric circles" and "law of psychological mechanics," and was also unaware that the Confucian school's "degrees of love" had been developed much earlier.

4.4.2 The law of relative quantity of the ends of ethical behavior: The deduction of the law of human nature of the degrees of love

By deducing the law of human nature of the *degrees of love* we can know that everyone's ends of action certainly constantly benefit oneself, and only occasionally benefit others, harm others or the self: in the sum of the actions in everyone's life, the ends of self-harming and harming others are certainly far less than that of the ends of self-interest and benefiting others. It is true that, on the one hand, everyone does quite a lot of actions that harm others, but it is almost always for the sake of self-interest: self-interest by harming. Harming others is however more often a means rather than ends, given that the actions of harming others as an end are by comparison extremely rare. On the other hand, everyone does quite a lot of actions that are self-harming, but mostly self-harming actions are for self-interest, such as the sacrifices one makes to study hard, which may lead to a good career or perhaps even to professional recognition. One may, for instance, sacrifice a healthy or balanced lifestyle—but this kind of self-harming is a means not an ends. No doubt, as an ends self-harming for the sake of self-harming is extremely rare.

Therefore, in terms of the sum of everyone's actions in his life, on the one hand, one certainly follow the law of *degrees of love*, thence does more actions as ends of self-interest than as ends of benefiting others; on the other hand, the actions of self-harm and of harming others as ends are extremely rare, undoubtedly far less than that of self-interest and benefiting others. Thus, in combination, everyone's ends of action are constantly out of self-interest, and only occasionally benefit or harm others, or are of a self-harming nature. This is the "law of the relative quantity of the ends of ethical behavior," of which the degree of love is the core.

Modern psychology confirms this law. For, on the one hand, Maslow proves that physical needs and desires are completely self-interested, while selflessly benefiting others is the attribute of higher needs and desires: "*The higher the need level the easier and more effective psychotherapy can be: at the lowest need levels it is of hardly any avail. Hunger cannot be stilled by psychotherapy.*" "Hunger is highly egocentric; the only way to satisfy it is to satisfy oneself. But the search for love and respect necessarily involves other people. Moreover, it involves satisfaction for these other people."[74]

Maslow, on the other hand, proved that on the whole it is not a free and arbitrary choice for everyone to satisfy or suppress their physical needs and desires; that one is destined to choose only satisfaction since it is not possible to constantly choose suppression: "In the long run, there can be no casual and arbitrary choice, except for non-basic needs."[75] This is because

> The stubbornness or intransigence of non-basic needs is inconceivable because they are resistant to all flattery, substitution, bribery, and choice. There is no way to deal with these needs except for appropriate and intrinsic satisfaction. Nevertheless, for a long time, people have always sought to meet them, consciously or unintentionally.[76]

To sum up, occasionally, everyone's ends of action are free and arbitrary: one can suppress or satisfy the physiological needs and desires (which are completely beneficial to oneself); one may or may not benefit oneself. But constantly, one is not free in that one is bound to obey the instructions from the physiological needs and desires, pursuing the satisfaction of the physical needs and desires (which are completely beneficial to oneself), one is bound to benefit oneself as an end.

This law was originally the most important discovery of Freudian psychology. On several occasions he explained this finding vividly in the analogy of a rider and a horse:

> In general, the self has to carry out its intention, which is accomplished by successfully creating the best conditions for the realization of its intention. This relationship between the self and the id can be explained by the relationship between the rider and the horse. The horse provides energy for movement, and the rider's prerogative is to determine the goal of the movement and guide the strong horse toward it. But we found that there is a very unsatisfactory situation between the self and id: in the long run, the rider has to lead the horse in the direction it wanted to go.[77]
>
> In general, the self has to carry out its intention, which is accomplished by successfully creating the best conditions for the realization of its intention. This relationship between the self and the id can be explained by the relationship between the rider and the horse. The horse provides energy for movement, and the rider's prerogative is to determine the goal of the movement and guide the strong horse toward it. But we found that there is a very unsatisfactory situation between the self and id: in the long run, the rider has to lead the horse in the direction it wanted to go.[78]

Freud's so-called "id" is the self-interested physical desire—it only seeks to satisfy its instinctive needs and is governed only by the principle of pleasure[79]—and is the psychological system of the ultimate motivation of

118 *The substance of moral value*

the ends of action; while the "ego" is the psychological system of the actual action caused by the "id," that is, the psychological system of the ends and means of action, which, in the final analysis, is the psychological system of action motives. Thence, what this metaphor of Freud reveals is the law that everyone's ends of action certainly constantly conform to and are only occasionally inconsistent with ultimate motivation, namely completely egoistic physical desire.

Freud attached great importance to this law. Because any action determined by the physiological desire is completely egoistic, that is, not free, he considered it as the third blow to human megalomania, alongside the discoveries of Copernicus and Darwin: "Human megalomania will have suffered its third and most wounding blow from the psychological research of the present time which seeks to prove to the ego that it is not even master in its own house."[80]

Modern psychology shows that, on the one hand, everyone's ends of action certainly constantly conform to and are only occasionally inconsistent with ultimate motivation; on the other hand, the ultimate motivation of everyone's actions can only be self-interest. Thus, taken together, it can be concluded that:

Everyone's ends of action, if it is self-interested and out of self-love, it is consistent with the ultimate motivation that ultimately makes it come into being, and therefore certainly is constant; on the contrary, if the ends are benefiting others or harming others or self-harming and out of loving-others, or hating-others, or self-hatred, they deviate from the ultimate motivation which ultimately makes them come into being, and are therefore only occasional. In short, everyone's ends of action are constantly self-interested, and only occasionally benefit or harm others, or are self-harming.

4.4.3 The significance of the law of human nature of the degrees of love

The Limit of Moral Perfection

If the law of the ultimate motivation of ethical behavior is the most profound law of human nature, then the law of the relative quantity of the ends of ethical behavior, that is, of the "degrees of love," is the most important law of human nature. For its importance, it is enough to point out that it tells us that it is impossible for one to be constantly and completely selfless. Therefore, no matter how hard a person tries to kill the instincts of self-interest he will never reach the state of constant selflessness, let alone the state of complete selflessness. So-called those who are constantly or completely selfless are just hypocrites. The great models of those who truly selflessly benefit others are not the ones who are constantly or completely selfless, but the ones who selflessly benefit others occasionally. It is impossible for those who are constantly or completely selfless to exist.

But, on the one hand, the amount of *selflessly benefiting others* of the great moral model far exceeds that of ordinary people. However, no matter how much the amount of action of *selflessly benefiting others*, it will never reach half the sum of their total actions. Even Confucius who strongly advocated selflessly benefiting others had to admit that even his disciple, Yan Hui (颜回), a person of extremely high moral character could only reach the realm of benevolence in three months a year without self-interest: "Confucius said: 'the mind of Hui conforms to benevolence for three months, but other people only can do that in much shorter time.'"[81]

On the other hand, from a qualitative point of view, the great moral models of selflessly benefiting others can make self-sacrifice when their interests conflict with that of others at the crucial moment. For example, in past wars, Joan of Arc, who led the French army against the British invasion, was always at the forefront of the battle. Once she was shot in the shoulder by an arrow and carried off the front line by the soldiers, but she quickly pulled the arrow out and returned to the battlefield. Finally, she failed and was arrested, but she would rather die than surrender and be burned alive. Dong Cunrui (董存瑞) is said to have sacrificed his life by smothering bomb in a bunker which exploded, Huang Jiguang (黄继光) had blocked a gun hole with his own body, Wang Jie (王杰) threw himself on to live grenades, Liu Yingjun (刘英俊) put himself in front of scared horse which killed him, and so on, all of which are heroic deeds beyond how people may normally act in such circumstances. In sum, the great moral models of *selflessly benefiting others* are those who are also constantly self-interested but whose occasional selfless actions are far more than that of ordinary people, and who make sacrifice in the decisive moments in life when their interests conflict with that of others. This is the limit of moral perfection!

However, altruists regard *selflessly benefiting others* as the sole standard for measuring whether a behavior is moral or not, and for guiding all actions of human, in doing so, they try to cultivate models that are constantly or even completely selfless in vain. By doing so, it destroyed everyone's human nature badly. In one sense, it is the antecedent of hypocrisy in that it facilitates the actions of hypocrites. In another sense, it is an obstruction to everyone's pursuit of personal interests, which is to say that it is also an obstruction to everyone's promotion of the interests of society or anything interests beyond that. Since everyone is mostly always self-interested, the altrusim model would result in the stagnation of society.

The Hypothesis of "Economic Man" in the Theory of Public Choice

The law of human nature, in terms of the *degrees of love*, can never be overestimated: it is not only an important discovery in ethics and in that of human nature, but also has great importance as both a social and state theoretical issue. Wilson, the contemporary sociobiologist, writes: "A key question of social theory, then, must be the relative amounts of hard-core as opposed to soft-core altruism."[82] This understanding reflects the views of author of this work in that hard-core altruism is namely *selflessly benefiting others* and soft-core altruism the *benefiting others for self-interest*. The law of human nature, in terms of the degrees of love, shows that the traditional assumptions of politics, namely the government represents the interests of citizens and that the goal of government officials is to maximize social interests, are unscientific. On the contrary, "economic man" in public choice theory and Hume's "rogue" are scientific hypotheses.

The basic feature of the theory of public choice, as is well known, is the hypothesis of economic man. According to this hypothesis, everyone in politics, like those in the economics, has ends of actions that are out of self-interest in that they seek the maximization of their own interests. This hypothesis, in the final analysis, is Hume's "rogue hypothesis":

> Many political commentators have made the following proposition a maxim: in designing any system of government and identifying certain constraints and supervisory institutions in that system, it is necessary to conceive of each member as a rogue since all of his actions aim at the pursuit of his own interests but not anything else. We must take advantage of this kind of personal interests to monitor him and make him accountable in the interest of public welfare despite his insatiable greed and ambition. Otherwise, they might say that bragging about the superiority of any particular system of government is futile talk, and that ultimately our freedom or property is insecure except for the benevolence of the rulers, that is to say, there is no guarantee at all. Therefore, the political maxim that everyone must be conceived as a rogue is correct.[83]

Roughly speaking, Hume's "rogue" and "economic man" hypothesis of public choice theory is not tenable. Clearly, the ends of economic man's behavior are self-interest. Not only are the ends not altruistic, they also compete for interests with others, competition being the law of market economy. But, in the case of the ends of action of a politician or a political official not all ends are for self-interest; the ends of actions may also reach the highest state of selflessly benefiting others: self-sacrifice. Not only Joan of Arc but also George Washington are great historic moral models who benefit others even to the extent of self-sacrifice. As commander-in-chief, Washington not only have no salary, but also give his own money away to supply the army. And he resigned and returned to his homeland on the day of his great success, it can be said to be a model of selflessness and altruism.

Roughly speaking, Hume's "rogue" and "economic man" hypothesis of public choice theory is not tenable. Clearly, the ends of economic man's behavior are self-interest. Not only are the ends not altruistic, they also compete for interests with others, competition being the law of market economy. But, in the case of the ends of action of a politician or a political official not all ends are for self-interest; the ends of actions may also reach the highest state of selflessly benefiting others: self-sacrifice. Not only Joan of Arc but also George Washington are great historic moral models who benefit others even to the extent of self-sacrifice. As commander-in-chief, Washington not only have no salary, but also give his own money away to supply the army. And he resigned and returned to his homeland on the day of his great success, it can be said to be a model of selflessness and altruism.

However, on closer examination, although the selfless actions of George Washington, as well as that of other noted officials in the history, was unique, it was nonetheless just as infrequent as any selfless action or behavior of say a common person. No doubt they lived out their lives with types of behavior that more frequently benefited themselves than others; it is just that they valued their own "reputation" more than their "interests." If they had constantly benefited others selflessly, not themselves, they would not have been human at all, but rather some kind of imagined legendary figures, since this would deviate from the law of the human nature of the degrees of love.

The crux of the problem is that the scientific design of the state institutions should be based on the purpose of each official's constant behavior, that is, the purpose of each official's behavior is for self-interest and for the maximization of his own interests, not on the occasional purpose behavior of every official, on the basis that every official's ends of action are for selflessly benefiting others and for the maximum interests of the country and society. Therefore, the law of the human nature of the degrees of love demonstrates that the traditional assumption of political science is unscientific in its basing the design of the state institutions on "the ends of officials to maximize the interests of society"; and that Hume's "rogue" and "economic man" hypothesis are scientific in its basing the design of state institutions on "the ends of actions of officials is self-interested."

Public Ownership Certainly Is Inefficient

The law of the human nature of the degrees of love means that whoever in whatever society—especially in a future ideal society—no matter how noble his or her moral character might be, certainly constantly seeks their own interests and only occasionally that of others. This law also applies to the concepts of private ownership and public ownership. Private ownership is an efficient system in any society. Where private ownership is prevalent in a society, because private assets are used only by the owner, any losses or gains are entirely borne by the owners; if assets cause a loss, the owners have to bear the loss completely, if assets create profits, the owners take full possession of the profits. Undoubtedly, since everyone certainly constantly seeks their own interests and only occasionally that of others, this is what inspires people to make maximum profit at minimum cost. Therefore, as an indicator of everyone's constant self-interest, a private-ownership economy is an efficient economy. This undoubtedly inspires people—everyone certainly constantly seeks their own interests and only occasionally that of others—to make the maximum profit at the minimum cost. Therefore, the private ownership economy is an efficient economy.

Conversely, public ownership does not have this efficiency mechanism. Because the public assets used by everyone, are not owned by everyone, one does not bear the losses, and one does not benefit from productivity gains by improving efficiency. Since the gains are shared with many people, one's gain is minimal. In short, when loss occurs, one need not bear the loss; when profit is created, one does not benefit from the profits. Since *everyone in every society certainly constantly seeks their own interests and only occasionally that of others*, a public-ownership economy is destined to be inefficient in any society.

Because it is an inefficient mechanism, public ownership violates the ultimate value standard of the state institutions of "increasing everyone's quantum of interests" and is therefore a bad state institution. As an efficient mechanism, private ownership conforms to the ultimate value standard of the state institutions of "increasing everyone's quantum of interests" and is therefore a good state institution. However, in any society, "private ownership" can fail. Where it tends to fail most is in the field of "providing public goods," which is, as Adam Smith called it, "the duty of erecting and maintaining those public institutions and those public works."[84]

Since the economy in a field such as this, which I refer to as the field of private ownership failure, can only be undertaken by the government, so it belongs to the category of the state or public ownership economy. Any public ownership economy—because its inefficiency violates the ultimate value standard of the state institutions of "increasing everyone's quantum of interests"—is originally a bad state institution. But, on the one hand, the public economy provides public goods, and only it can achieve the greater goodness—to meet the citizens' need for public goods—which therefore makes it a necessary bad. On the other hand, the advantage of the mass production of this kind of public-ownership economy can make up for the defects of the inherent inefficiency of public ownership. Adam Smith said:

> The duty of erecting and maintaining those public institutions and public works, which, though they may be in the highest degree advantageous to a great society, are, however, of such a nature, that the profit could never repay the expense to any individual or small number of individuals, and which it therefore cannot be expected that any individual or small number of individuals should erect or maintain.[85]

Therefore, in fact, in any country, at any time, there exists an economy of public ownership or state ownership. It is a helpless choice because of the failure of private ownership in the field of the provision of public goods, but it is also a form of ownership and an economic system of means of production which can be called "a necessary bad," meaning that it is a kind of goodness—a kind of good economic system. There is no doubt that in a country's economic activities, this kind of economic activity in the field of private ownership failure accounts only for a very small proportion and by no means even possibly occupies the dominant position. However, if a country's public ownership exceeds the field of private ownership failure and even dominates the entire national economy, then, public ownership—because of its inefficiency, which seriously violates the ultimate value standard of the state institutions of "increasing everyone's quantum of interests"—is therefore a vicious economic system of "pure bad."

4.5 Law of relative quantity of means of ethical behavior: quantitative analysis of human nature

The means of ethical behavior, as mentioned above, like the ends of ethical behavior, are divided into four categories: means of self-interest, means of benefiting others, means of harming others and means of self-harming. Then, do the relative quantity of these four means also have a law or laws to follow? Yes. However, the law of the relative quantity of the ends of ethical behavior, as mentioned above, is a completely non-statistical law. On the contrary, the law of the relative quantity of the means of ethical behavior has the distinction of statistical and non-statistical characteristics.

4.5.1 Non-statistical law of relative quantity of means of ethical behavior

It turns out that everyone's means of self-interest and self-harming obviously depends on oneself as the means. On the contrary, the means of benefiting others and harming others depends on others and society as the means. For example, long-distance running and sleeping on a bed of nails are two means to build one's will. Although they have the distinction of self-interest and self-harming, they are both depend on oneself as the means. On the contrary, making money and stealing money are two means of getting money. Although they have the distinction of benefiting others and harming others, the means of both depend on others and society as the means.

Suppose human beings are not social animals but live in isolation, then all the actions of everyone depend on oneself as the means, without any action which depends on others and society as the means. However, humans are social animals with a social life. It goes without saying that in social life, The most consistent behavior of everyone is certainly in the category of the division of labor and cooperation, which is more or less a social and collective activity related to others and society, while personal activities that are not a part of the division of labor and cooperation, are isolated and unrelated to others and society. These are extremely rare.

Therefore, in social life, everyone's behaviors that depends on oneself as the means might be very rare and occasional; as a means most of one's constant behavior certainly depends on others and society, which can easily be

124   *The substance of moral value*

understood. Not to mention how dependent everyone is on their parents or nurturers before they reach adulthood, even when one grows up, does what one does not depend on others and society for their food, clothing, housing, career, and love? Thinking carefully, we can see that the actions that only depend on oneself but not on others and society are really very rare, that is, of course, apart from activities one might undertake by themselves such as hiking, picking wild fruit, enjoying sightseeing, appreciating the beauty of flowers and the moon etc., what more activities can we cite?

Nevertheless, these sorts of activities which depend on oneself as the means are only occasional. Generally, everyone's behavior of depending on themselves as a means is extremely rare. This means that the sum of everyone's means of self-interest and self-harming, as two opposite expressions of depending on oneself, is very rare in terms of quantity or frequency since, in terms of individual actions, using oneself as the sole means is at most only occasional. On the contrary, the sum of the means of everyone's behavior of depending on others and society certainly is the most frequent or relatively constant behavior, which indicates that since the most constant means is benefiting others, the means of harming others are at most occasional but very rare; if the constant means is harming others, then the means of benefiting others would be at the most occasional but very rare.

It can be seen that everyone's means of behavior can only occasionally be self-interest and self-harming, but certainly constantly benefiting or harming others: if the means of benefiting others are constant, the means of harming others certainly is occasional; if the means of harming others are constant, the means of benefiting others certainly are occasional. This is the law of the relative quantity of means of ethical behavior determined by the social nature of human beings, or more exactly, the non-statistical law of the relative quantity of the means of ethical behavior. Therefore, does the total behavior of the whole society or that of most people follow another law of the means of ethical behavior? Yes, that is the statistical law of relative quantity of the means of ethical behavior.

4.5.2 *Statistical law of relative quantity of means of ethical behavior*

In terms of the sum of the actions of a society, is it possible that the constant means can harm others? No, it is not. This is because the so-called society, as we know, is a community formed by two or more people for certain interests, which is a system of cooperation in the interests of "I am for everyone, and everyone is for me." In this way, in terms of the aggregate behavior of a society, there certainly are more actions by means of benefiting others than by means of harming others, that is, the means of benefiting others certainly are constant, while means of harming others can only be occasional. Otherwise, almost everyone will suffer more harm from society than benefit from it. As a result, society, which is merely a system of cooperation for everyone's interests, will inevitably disintegrate and be non-existent.

Consider, for example, the activities of the medicine trade. We know that the sale of authentic medicine is a means of benefiting others, and that the sale of fake medicine is a means of harming others. In terms of the sum of this activity, if all drug stores sell more fake medicine than authentic medicine—that is, undertake the means of harming others more than that of benefiting others—the chance that customers will buy fake medicine is more than that of buying authentic medicine, and the chance of harm to customers is greater than their chance of interest. As a result, since the medicine trade is the cause of more harm than interest, more people will suffer. In this case, will people still buy medicine? Obviously not. Drug stores will close down, and the medicine trade will cease to exist.

It can be seen that the sum of actions of a society and the actions of a person follow different laws. As far as an individual is concerned, it is not certain whether his or her actions benefit others more or harm others more because the existence and development of society does not depend on a person's behavior. However, in any society, the means of benefiting others is greater than the means of harming others, and is the condition of its existence. Therefore, in terms of the sum of actions of a society, the means of benefiting others certainly exceeds that of harming others: the means of benefiting others certainly is constant, while the means of harming others only can be occasional. Thus, we can conclude that any means of ethical behavior in any society certainly changes according to the following statistical rules:

Law one: in any society, in terms of the sum of its actions, the means of benefiting others certainly is constant, while the sum of any other means—harming others, self-harming, and self-interest—can only be occasional. In other words, in terms of most actions in a society, the means certainly benefit others.

Law two: in any society, in terms of most people's actions, the means of benefiting others certainly is constant, while all other means—harming others, self-harming, and self-interest—can only be occasional. In other words, in terms of most actions in a society, the means certainly benefit others.

These two laws obviously are different expressions of the same law, and thus can be expressed in a unified way: any society, in terms of the sum of its actions, that is to say, its means of benefiting others, certainly is constant, and the sum of any other means—harming others, self-harming, and self-interest—can only be occasional. In other words, in terms of the most actions of a society, that is, the most actions of most people, the means certainly benefit others. This is the statistical law of the relative quantity of means of ethical behavior. The law might be said to have been discovered by Adam Smith, whose findings, though limited to the actions of economic man and inexactly expressed, were widely spread by the famous saying of "the invisible hand":

> Every individual is continually exerting himself to find out the most advantageous employment for whatever capital he can command. It is

126 *The substance of moral value*

his own advantage, indeed, and not that of the society, which he has in view. But the study of his own advantage naturally, or rather necessarily leads him to prefer that employment which is most advantageous to the society.[86]

As every individual, therefore, endeavours as much as he can both to employ his capital in the support of domestic industry, and so to direct that industry that its produce may be of the greatest value; every individual necessarily labours to render the annual revenue of the society as large as great as he can. He generally, indeed, neither intends to promote public interest, nor knows how much he is promoting it. By preferring the support domestic industry to that of foreign industry, he intends only his own security; and by directing that industry in such a manner as he produce may be of the greatest value, he intends only his own gain, and he is in this, as in many other cases, led by an invisible hand, to promote an end which is no part of his intention. Nor is it always the worse for the society, that is was no part of it. By pursuing his own interest he frequently promotes that of the society more effectively than when he really intends to promote it.[87]

Smith's immortal exposition can be summed up into two laws: (1) The purpose of economic man is only for self-interest; (2) economic man benefits himself certainly by benefiting others. However, the nature of these two laws is different. The first is a non-statistical law which is applicable to all actions of every economic man: all purposes of every economic man's actions certainly are for himself. The second is a statistical law, which is only applicable to the most actions of most economic men: there are always some economic men whose actions are harming others for self-interest instead of benefiting others for self-interest. Smith, however, equalized both of them as non-statistical laws applicable to every economic man's actions, which means that all actions of the economic man are benefiting others for self-interest and there are no actions of harming others for self-interest: is this not nonsense?

4.5.3 The significance of statistical law of relative quantity of means of ethical behavior

The statistical law of the relative quantity of the means of ethical behavior helps us understand why everyone's action certainly is out of constant self-interest, but what we see is the opposite: most people constantly work for the interests of others. This is because the end of action is invisible; what can only be seen is the means of action: the end of action is deduced by the means of action.

We can only see, for instance, teachers lecturing students, workers producing goods for others, or farmers farming for others. But who can see the purpose of a teacher's lecture? Who can see the purpose of labor? Who can see the purpose of farming? The statistical law of the relative quantity of the means of ethical behavior shows that, in any society, in terms of most people's actions, their means certainly benefit others. Therefore, what we see is that any society, in terms of its most constant actions, benefits others, and serves the people, and thus is expressly a phenomenon of "I am for all, and everyone is for me." However, this represents only external means of actions, not intrinsic ends of actions.

But, by the external phenomenon that people are serving the people, we often assert that their internal purpose is to serve the people, that their purpose is benefiting others, and then to assert that the purpose of people's behavior can reach the realm of constant altruism. This obviously takes the means of actions as ends of actions. It is right that people's constant actions are to serve the people; however, it is merely the means of actions. The means of most people's actions, generally speaking, is serving the people on a constant basis. However, it would be a great mistake to assert that serving the people can be the constant ends of people's actions. Because the law of the ends of ethical behavior tells us that serving the people can only be the occasional ends of people's actions but never as the constant ends. Therefore, serving the people has a distinction between ends and means: serving the people as a means can be constant, while serving the people as an ends can only be occasional. Distinguishing ends from means is the key to understanding the human nature.

4.6 Law of relative quantity of types of ethical behavior: Quantitative analysis of human nature

The law of relative quantity of the ends of ethical behavior concerns only the ends, and the law of relative quantity of means of ethical behavior involves only the means. In fact, however, ends and means are interdependent and cannot exist separately: everyone's behavior is a unity of ends and means. Therefore, the law of relative quantity of the ends of ethical behavior or the law of relative quantity of the means of ethical behavior is only one side of the law of ethical behavior. Only when the two are combined can it be the law of ethical behavior or the law of relative quantity of ethical behavior, namely, the law of relative quantity of the various types of ethical behavior. Since this law is the combination of the law of ends and means, there must be a distinction between statistical and non-statistical.

4.6.1 Non-statistical law of relative quantity of types of ethical behavior

According to the law of relative quantity of the ends of ethical behavior, everyone's ends of actions certainly are constantly self-interested and only occasionally benefit others or harm others or self-harm: only the ends of self-interest are constant. According to the non-statistical law of relative quantity of the means of ethical behavior, everyone's means of behavior certainly constantly benefit others or harm others, and are only occasionally self-interest and self-harm: only the means of benefiting or harming others can be constant. Therefore, the combination of these two laws constitutes the non-statistical law of relative quantity of types of ethical behavior

The constant action of everyone certainly is either *benefiting others for self-interest* or *harming others for self-interest* (if one benefits others for self-interest constantly, one would harm others for self-interest occasionally; if one harm others for self-interest constantly, one would benefit others for self-interest occasionally), while the occasional actions are *selflessly benefiting others*, *mere self-interest*, *purely harming others*, and *pure self-harming*. In other words, all of everyone's actions, only *benefiting others for self-interest* or *harming others for self-interest* can be constant, that is, can exceed half of the sum of one's behavior; and while the sum of the rest of other actions—namely *selflessly benefiting others*, *mere self-interest*, *purely harming others*, and *pure self-harming*—can only be occasional, that is, can only be less than the half of the sum of one's actions.

Those who constantly harm others for self-interest are so-called evil people such as those who live a life of crime, living off the proceeds of steeling, corruption, fraud, kidnapping for ransom, robbery, and other such means. But why do we often find it difficult to identify evil people? Isn't it because evil guys also have many actions of benefiting others for self-interest? But no matter how many actions of benefiting others for self—interests, they are certainly less than that of harming others for self-interest, otherwise they are not evil people. Most Chinese people know the Chinese saying that "even the evilest tiger never eats its cubs." But, it is impossible for evil people to completely lose the love for others. Do not evil people love their parents, children and lovers? Do they not seek interest for them? But evil people's actions of selflessly benefiting others is extremely rare and is mostly only for very few people.

Those who constantly *benefit others for self-interest*, such as the farmers who produce food for others, the workers who produce goods for others, the businessmen who trade the products to those who need them and the teachers who impart knowledge to students, as well as those ordinary people who live on their work so as to contribute to other, are all so-called good people. But it is impossible that good people never *harm others for self-interest*. Who has never harmed others for self-interest? Even the most virtuous among us such as old Tolstoy repented that he once deceived a horse buyer when he prepared for his daughter's dowry. But no matter how many behaviors good people do to harm others for self-interest, they are certainly lesser than that of benefiting others for self-interest, otherwise they are not good people. It is impossible for good people to be completely free from the intent purely harming others. Think: who has not experienced feelings of envy, vengeance, or hatred at one time or other? Who never has the intention of harming others? It's only just that it is extremely rare that good people have a pure intent to harm others.

Those who can selflessly benefit others when interests conflicts and can *benefit others for self-interest* when interests are in harmony, and thus almost have no actions of *harming others for self-interests, purely harming others*, and *purely self-harming*, are the so-called morally perfect people. However, though the morally perfect people's actions of *selflessly benefiting others* are far more than that of ordinary people, these actions are also only occasional. This is because the law of human nature of *the degrees of love* indicates that the ends of actions of everyone certainly is constantly self-interested and only occasionally benefits others. Even the most morally perfect person one can think of possesses the inherent nature of that all other human beings. His or her constant actions, which like anyone else, exceed half of the sum of his or her actions, are certainly benefiting others for self-interest. Otherwise, if he or she selflessly benefits others all or most of the time it is a violation of the law of human nature of "the degrees of love"—it follows that he or she cannot being human.

4.6.2 The statistical laws of relative quantity of types of ethical behavior

According to the law of relative quantity of the ends of ethical behavior, the ends of everyone's actions certainly is constant self-interested, while the ends of benefiting others, harming others and self-harming are only occasional: only the ends of self-interest are constant. According to the statistical law of relative quantity of the means of ethical behavior (1), any society, in terms of the sum of its actions, the means of benefiting other certainly is constant, while the sum of all other means—harming others, self-harming and self-interest—is only occasional. According to the statistical law of the relative quantity of the means of ethical behavior (2), any society, in terms of the actions of most people, the means of benefiting others certainly is constant, while the sum of all other means—harming others, self-harming, and self-interest—is only occasional. Therefore, the combination of these laws, as the statistical law of relative quantity of types of ethical behavior, constitute the following laws:

Law one: any society, in terms of the sum of its actions, *benefiting others for self-interest* certainly is constant, while the sum of all other actions—*harming others for self-interest, selflessly benefiting others, mere self-interest, purely harming others*, and *pure self-harming*—can only be occasional. In other words, in any society, the vast majority of actions certainly benefits others for self-interest, while all other actions can only be occasional and minor.

Law two: any society, in term of the actions of most people, *benefiting others for self-interest* certainly is constant, while the sum of all other actions—*harming others for self-interest, selflessly benefiting others, mere self-interest, purely harming others* and *pure self-harming*—can only be occasional. In other words, in any society, the vast majority of its people's constant behavior certainly benefits others for self-interest while all other actions can only be occasional and minor.

These two laws obviously are different expressions of the same law and can therefore be formulated in a unified manner as follows: any society, in term of the sum of actions, namely the actions of most people, *benefiting others for self-interest* is constant, while all other actions—*harming others for self-interest, selflessly benefiting others, mere self-interest, pure self-harming*—only can be occasional. In other words, any society, the vast majority of the actions of most people, certainly benefits others for self-interest, while the sum of all other actions only can be occasional and minor. This is the statistical law of relative quantity of the types of ethical behavior.

This law, like the statistical law of relative quantity of the means of ethical behavior, obviously originates from the most profound nature of society: that society is a community formed by two or more persons with a certain relation of interests, which is a system of the interest cooperation of each individual. This nature determines that any society, no matter how good or bad it is, certainly has more good people than bad people, and has more people who constantly benefit others for self-interest than the people who constantly harm others for self-interest. Only in this way, can the interest everyone obtains from others be more than the harm they get so that society can exist and develop. Otherwise, if bad people are more than good people, and the actions of harming others for self-interest are more than that of benefiting others for self-interest, then the harm everyone gets from others would be more than the interests they obtain, and society thus is destined to collapse.

However, the worse the moral character of a society is, the more bad people and less good people it will have, and the more the actions of harming others for self-interest will increase and the actions of benefiting others for a decrease in self-interest. On the contrary, the nobler the moral character of a society is, the more good people and the less bad people it has, and the actions of benefiting others for self-interest will increase and the actions of harming others for a decrease in self-interest. But even in the darkest, most corrupt, and ugly society, which, at its worst, is where *harming others for self-interest, pure harming others, mere self-interest* is prevalent, and the actions of selflessly benefiting others is extremely rare, nevertheless, no matter how common these evils may be, will, on the whole certainly be less than *benefiting others for self-interest*: even in the darkest, most corrupt and ugly society, *benefiting others for self-interest* certainly still is constant, while the sum of all other actions is also occasional and minor.

Is it possible, then, in the noblest and most perfect society, its constant actions will be *selflessly benefiting others* rather than *benefiting others for self-interest*? That's impossible. It is true that of the so-called most perfect society of mankind, on the one hand, the actions of *selflessly benefiting others* will be extremely prevalent and far more than that in present ordinary society, and much, much more than that in society with evil moral character; on the other hand, the vicious actions of *harming others for self-interest, purely harming others, pure self-harming*, mere *self-interest* will be extremely rare. However, in terms of the sum of its actions, no matter how many altruistic actions it has, it can only come close to the half of the sum of its actions but is never equal to the half of its total; it can only come close to but never reach the amount of the actions of benefiting others for self-interest, because, as the human nature of *degrees of love* indicates: everyone's ends certainly is constantly self-interested and occasionally benefits others. Therefore, a society, even an ideal society of the future, will benefit others for self-interest for these actions constantly exceed the half of its total actions, while *selflessly benefiting others* are only occasional and can never reach the half of the total actions. If a society, even an ideal society of the future, its constant actions will be *selflessly benefiting others* rather than *benefiting others for self-interest*, it could not be a human society for it does not conform to the laws of human nature.

Notes

1 Jiang Hengyuan: *The Ancient Chinese Philosophers on the Nature of Mankind*, Commercial Press, Beijing, the eleventh year of Republic of China, p. 4.
2 Xunzi: *The Evilness of Human Nature*.
3 Mencius: *The Quotations from Gao Zhi, the First Part*.
4 Extensions of Spring and Autumn Annal: *On Name and Human Nature*.
5 Han Yu: *Primordial Nature*.
6 Xunzi: *The Evilness of Human Nature*.
7 Mencius: *Gaozi*.
8 Charles A. Ellwood: *An Introduction to Social Psychology*, D. Appleton and Company, New York, 1920, p. 51.
9 Cited from Zhang Dainian: *Outline of Chinese Philosophy*, China Social Sciences Press, 1982, p. 197.
10 Mencius: *The Quotations from Gao Zhi, the First Part*.
11 Ibid.
12 Cited from Zhang Dainian: *Outline of Chinese Philosophy*, China Social Sciences Press, 1982, p. 7.
13 Mencius: *Gongsun Chou*.
14 Tom L. Beauchamp: *Philosophical Ethics*, McGraw-Hill, New York, 1982, p. 9.
15 Fung Yulan: *Complete Works of Sansong Tang, Vol. 1*. Henan People's Publishing House, 1985, p. 535.
16 Ibid., p. 556.
17 Jean-Paul Sartre: *Aversion and Others*, Shanghai Translation Publishing House, 1987, p. 13.
18 Paul Anly Holbach: *The System of Nature, Volume A*, Commercial Press, 1964, p. 247.
19 *The Analects of Confucius: Wei Linggong*.
20 Ibid.
21 Fung Yulan: *Complete Works of Sansong Tang, Vol. 1*. Henan People's Publishing House, 1985, p. 537.
22 Cited from Fung Yulan: *Complete Works of Sansong Tang, Vol. 1*. Henan People's Publishing House, 1985, p. 556.
23 Meng Zhaolan: *The Emotions of Human Beings*, Shanghai People's Publishing House, 1989, p. 289.
24 Wallace Craig: *An Outline of Psychology*, People's Education Press, 1989, p. 443.
25 John Locke: *An Essay Concerning Human Understanding*, Clarendon Press, Oxford, 1975, p. 230.

132 The substance of moral value

26 David Hume: *A Treatise of Human Nature*, Clarendon Press, Oxford, 1949, p. 348.
27 Ludwig Feuerbach: *Anthology of Feuerbach's Philosophical Works*, SXD Joint Publishing House, 1959, p. 430.
28 Sigmund Freud: *Collected Papers, Vol. 4*. Basic Books, New York, 1959, p. 78.
29 Ibid., p. 79.
30 Erich Fromm: *The Art of Love*, Harper Colophon Books, Harper & Row, New York and Evanston, 1962, p. 41.
31 Quoted from Cai Yuanpei: *The Treasure of Philosophy of Life*, China Radio and Television Press, 1992, p. 620.
32 Plato: *Plato's Dialogues*, Liaoning Education Publishing House, 1998, p. 198.
33 *Complete Works of Mao Dun, Vol. 14, On the Maternity of Ellen Kay*. Cited from *The Treasure of Philosophy of Life*, China Radio and Television Press, 1992, p. 598.
34 Cai Yuanpei: *The Treasure of Philosophy of Life*, China Radio and Television Press, 1992, p. 648.
35 Ibid., p. 650.
36 Aristotle: *Complete Works of Aristotle, Vol. 8*. Renmin University Press, 1992, p. 413.
37 *Complete Works of Cai Yuanpei, Vol. 2*. Zhonghua Book Company, 1984, p. 188.
38 *The Treasury of Western Thought*, China Radio and Television Press, 1991, p. 250.
39 Baruch de Spinoza: Ethics, Commercial Press 1st edition, p. 170.
40 Charles Darwin: *Descent of Man and Selection in Relation to Sex*, John Murray, London, 1922, p. 168.
41 *The Analects of Confucius*, Li Ren.
42 Mencius: *Gongsun Chou.*
43 David Hume: *A Treatise of Human Nature*, Clarendon Press, Oxford, 1949, p. 367.
44 Erich Fromm: *The Art of Love*, Harper Colophon Books, Harper & Row, New York and Evanston, 1962, p. 22.
45 Mencius: *Gongsun Chou.*
46 Sigmund Freud: *Collected Papers, Vol. 4*. Basic Books, New York, 1959, p. 80.
47 Ibid.
48 Sigmund Freud: *New Introductory Lectures on Psycho-Analysis*, trans. W. J. H. Sprott. W. W. Norton, New York, 1933, p. 149.
49 Baruch de Spinoza: *Ethics*, Commercial Press, Beijing, 1962, p. 195.
50 Alfred Adler: *Inferiority Complex and Transcendence*, Author Press, 1985, p. 42.
51 Karen Horney: *The Struggle of Self*, China Folk Art Press, 1986, p. 130.
52 François Voltaire: *The Collection of Voltaire's Essays*, Shanghai SDX Joint Company, 1990, p. 8.
53 Ludwig Feuerbach: *Selected Works of Feuerbach's Philosophy, Vol. 1*. PDX Joint Publishing Company, 1959, p. 545.
54 Chuang-tzu Zhile.
55 Ludwig Feuerbach: *Selected Works of Feuerbach's Philosophy, Vol. 2*. PDX Joint Publishing Company, 1959, p. 775.
56 Martin Heidegger: *Existence and Time*, PDX Joint Publishing Company, 1987, p. 288.
57 Jean-Paul Sartre: *Existentialism Is a Humanism*, Shanghai Translation Press, 1988, p. 22.
58 Chen Zhonggeng, Zhang Yuxin: *The Psychology of Personality*, Liaoning People's Publishing House, 1986, p. 62.

59 Fung Yulan: *Complete Works of Sansong Tang, Vol. 4*. Henan People's Publishing House, 1986, p. 442.
60 Ibid.
61 Mencius: *Gaozi*.
62 Nikolay Chernicheevsky: *What to Do?* People's Literature Press, 1996, p. 361.
63 Zu Desheng (ed.): *Russian Philosophy of the Eighteenth-Nineteenth Century*, Commercial Press, 1987, p. 365.
64 Immanuel Kant: *The Principles of Moral Metaphysics*, Shanghai People's Publishing House, 1986, p. 48.
65 Ibid., p. 57.
66 Xun Zi: *Fei Xiang*.
67 Fung Yulan: *A Brief History of Chinese Philosophy*, Peking University Press, 1985, p. 87.
68 Sigmund Freud: *Civilization and Its Discontents*, W. W. Norton & Company, New York, 1961, p. 87.
69 Edward O. Wilson: *On Human Nature*, Bantam Books, New York, 1982, p. 160.
70 Ignacio L. Gotz: *Conceptions of Happiness*, University Press of America, Inc. Lanham, New York, 1995, p. 287.
71 Friedrich Paulsen: *System of Ethics*, trans. Frank Thilly. Charles Scribner's Sons, New York, 1908, p. 393.
72 Li Zongwu: *The Continued Compilation of the Thick Black School*, United Press, 1990, p. 108.
73 Li Zongwu: *Compilation of the Thick Black School*, QiuShi Press, 1989, p. 132.
74 Abraham H. Maslow: *Motivation and Personality*, 2nd edn. Harper & Row, New York, 1954, p. 100.
75 Ibid., p. 62.
76 Ibid., p. 78.
77 Sigmund Freud: *New Introductory Lectures on Psycho-Analysis*, trans. W. J. H. Sprott. W. W. Norton, New York, 1933, p. 108.
78 Ibid.
79 Ibid., p. 104.
80 Sigmund Freud: *Introductory Lectures on Psycho-Analysis*, trans. James Strachey. W. W. Norton, New York, 1966, p. 353.
81 *The Analects of Confucius: Yong Ye*.
82 Edward O. Wilson: *On Human Nature*, Bantam Books, New York, 1998, p. 156.
83 Citing from other source: Liu Junning, ed.: *20 Lectures on Democracy*, China Youth Publishing House, 2008, p. 40.
84 Adam Smith: *An Inquiry into the Nature and Causes of the Wealth of Nations, Vol. 2*. Clarendon Press, Oxford, 1979, p. 688.
85 Ibid.
86 Ibid., p. 454.
87 Ibid., p. 421.

Part III
Moral value and moral norms
Excellent morality is the moral norms that conform to moral value

5 Good
General principles of morality

Meta-ethics shows that moral good and moral bad are the utility of the fact of ethical behavior to the goal of morality—especially the ultimate goal of morality or ultimate standard of morality—therefore it only emerges from, and can only be deduced from, the objective nature of the fact of ethical behavior through the goal of morality: moral good is the utility of the fact of ethical behavior which are consistent with the goal of morality; moral bad (evil) is the utility of the fact of ethical behavior which are inconsistent with the goal of morality. Fung Yulan put it correctly: "The so-called good is measured by only one standard, that is, with what accords with that standard ... the so-called bad is measured by only one standard, that is, with what contradicts that standard"[1] Unfortunately, he did not know that what he called the "standard" was the "goal of morality or the ultimate standard of morality."

This chapter studies "good" and "bad," namely the "moral good" and "moral bad," thus it ought to measure the good and bad of human nature (that is, the objective nature of the fact of human ethical behavior) with the goal of morality, and to deduce the general principle of morality "good" and the general principle of immorality "evil." Therefore this chapter is the evaluation of the goodness and evilness of the theory of human nature. Comparing it with the previous parts of the theory of human nature (namely the "conceptual analysis of human nature," the "qualitative analysis of human nature" and the "quantitative analysis of human nature"), we can term it "the analysis of the good and evil of human nature."

5.1 Good and evil

5.1.1 Good and evil of human nature: The moral value of 16 types of ethical behaviors

As mentioned above, all human nature in ethics can be summed up into 16 types as represented in Table 5.1.

It is not difficult to see that these 16 types of human nature, according to their utility in regard to whether they conform to or violate the goal of morality or ultimate standards of morality, can be summed up in four categories:

138 *Moral value and moral norms*

Table 5.1 Types of ethical behavior

Types of ends and means	Self-interest	Benefiting others	Self-harming	Harming others
Self-interest	1. completely self-interest	5. self-interest for benefiting others	9. self-interest for self-harming	13. self-interest for harming others
Benefiting others	2. benefiting others for self-interest	6. completely benefiting others	10. benefiting others for self-harming	14. benefiting others for harming others
Self-harming	3. self-harming for self-interest	7. self-sacrifice	11. completely self-harming	15. self-harming for harming others
Harming others	4. harming others for self-interest	8. harming others for benefiting others	12. harming others for self-harming	16. completely harming others

Actions that are *purely altruistic* and *purely self-interested* fall under the first category of human nature, including the four types of *completely benefiting others*, *completely self-interest*, *benefiting others for self-interest*, and *self-interest for benefiting others*. These types of actions, simply and clearly, undoubtedly conform to the ultimate moral standard of "promoting everyone's quantum of interests" or the ultimate moral sub-standard of "increasing quantum of interests without negatively affecting anyone," so they are all moral, good, and are what *ought* to be.

Actions that are *purely harming others* and *purely self-harming* fall under the second category of human nature, including the four types of actions of *harming others as an end* and the four types of actions of *self-harming as an end*. These eight types of actions are more complicated. At first glance these actions belong to the category of *harming others and self-harming*, and therefore are immoral and evil because they violate the goal of morality or the ultimate standard of morality. In fact they are not. For those actions of vengeance, such as the actions of *harming others as an end* for the purpose of an eye for eye (an exchange of equal harm), and the actions of *self-harming as an end* for self-punishment out of a sense of guilt (also an exchange of equal harm), are all in accordance with the principle of justice: the exchange of equal interests (harms).

These actions, which belong to the category of justice, have such an obvious effect: if one harms others, one will suffer from the same harms, thus does not dare harm rashly. Therefore, these actions provide security, and are beneficial to the development of society and interpersonal communications;

they conform to the ultimate standard of morality of "increasing everyone's quantum of interests" and thus are moral, good, and *ought to be*.

Therefore, the Bible says: "If any mischief follow, then thou shalt give life for life, eye for eye, tooth for tooth, hand for hand, foot for foot, burning for burning, stripe for stripe."[2] Except these, other actions of *harming others as an end* and *self-harming as an end* obviously violate the ultimate moral standard of "increasing everyone's quantum of interests" and the ultimate sub-standard of morality of "increasing quantum of interests without negatively affecting anyone," therefore they are immoral and *ought not to be*.

The third category of human nature is comprised of the mixed actions of the internal advantage and disadvantage in terms of the self and others, including the two types of actions of *self-harming for self-interest* and *harming others for benefiting others*. Most of these actions belong to actions which conflict between internal advantage and disadvantage of self-interest or benefiting others, thence certainly self-harming while self-interest, harming others while benefiting others. The activities of smoking and drinking are examples of self-benefiting and self-harming: one gains the benefits and pleasures of satisfying one's needs for tobacco and alcohol but harms one's own health. Disciplining one's own children to study hard in terms of their education both harms them and benefits them: the means of harsh discipline may benefit them with an outstanding career in the future.

It is clear that, in such cases, whether it is *self-harming for self-interest* or *harming others for benefiting others*, if the balance of advantage is over disadvantage, then its difference is advantage and conforms to the ultimate substandard of "the net balance of maximum interests," thus it is moral, ought to be, and good. On the contrary, if the balance of disadvantage is over advantage then its difference is disadvantage, violating "the net balance of maximum interests," thence it is immoral, ought not to be, and evil. For instance:

Taking medicine which has side effects is *self-harming for self-interest* in that it has an advantage over disadvantage, conforming to the standard of "the net balance of maximum interests," so it is good; on the contrary, drug taking is *self-harming for self-interest* in that the disadvantage outweighs the advantage, and violates the standard of "the net balance of maximum interests," thus it is evil. Severely criticizing children so as to educate them is *harming others for benefiting others* in that it has an advantage over the disadvantage, conforming to the standard of "the net balance of maximum interests," thus it is good; on the contrary, beating children to death to discipline them is *harming others for benefiting others*: the disadvantage far outweighs the advantage, violating the standard of "the net balance of maximum interests," thus it is evil.

The forth category of human nature is the mixed actions of both the internal and external advantage and disadvantage of the self and others, including the two types of actions of self-sacrifice and *harming others for self-interest*. It goes without saying that self-sacrifice is good and that *harming others for self-interest* is evil. *Harming others for self-interest* is not only evil but its evil is also absolute: under any circumstance—regardless of whether people's interests are consistent or conflict with one another—*harming others for self-interest violates* the goal of morality of "safeguarding the existence and development of society" and the ultimate standard of morality of "increasing everyone's quantum of interests." On the contrary, self-sacrifice as a goodness is relative: only when self-interest conflicts with the interests of others which cannot be compromised, self-sacrifice is moral good due to its conformity to the goal of morality and the principle of the "net balance of maximum interests." If self-interest does not conflict with the interests of others, or the conflicts can be compromised, then, no matter how self-sacrifice increases the net balance of interests, it is also immoral and *ought not to be* because it runs counter to the ultimate moral sub-standard of "increasing quantum of interests without negatively affecting anyone" under the circumstance when people's interests can be compromised.

Synthesizing the four categories of human nature we can know that, on the one hand, the ends of harming others, and the hatred for others or vengeance that cause it, as well as the ends of self-harming and the self-hatred or the sense of guilt that cause it, as far as they themselves are concerned, are all evil because they violate the goal of morality or the ultimate standard of morality; in terms of their outcomes, they are the common source of good and evil: if they are realized in the form of punishing others or self-punishment as exchanges of equal harms, they conform to the goal of morality or the ultimate standard of morality, and are therefore a source of goodness; if they are realized in any other form they violate the goal of morality or ultimate standard of morality, and are therefore a source of evil. However, envy and an inferiority complex, and the ends of harming others and self-harming caused by them, are both evil because they violate the goal of morality or ultimate standard of morality whether in themselves or in terms of the outcome.

On the other hand, the ends of self-interest, and self-love, the desire to live and self-respect that cause it, as far as they themselves are concerned, are all good because they conform to the goal of morality or the ultimate standard of morality; as far as their outcomes are concerned, they are a common source of good and evil: self-love, the desire to live, self-respect, and the ends of self-interest caused by them, if they are realized by the means of either self-interest, benefiting others, or self-harming, and have advantage over disadvantage, all conform to the goal of morality or the ultimate standard of morality, thence are the source of goodness; if they are realized by the means of harming others or self-harming, and the disadvantage outweighs the advantage, they violate the goal of morality or the ultimate standard of morality, and are therefore sources of evilness. Likewise, the ends of benefiting others, and the love for others, compassion, and gratitude that cause it, in themselves conform to the goal of morality or the ultimate standard of morality, and are therefore sources of goodness; as far as the results are concerned, they are a common source of good and evil: if they are realized by the means of harming others in which case the disadvantage outweighs the advantage, or realized by the means of self-harming under the circumstance where the interests are consistent, they are sources of evilness; if they are realized by the means of self-interest, benefiting others or the means of harming others, in which case they have an advantage over disadvantage, or by the means of self-harming under the circumstance of interests conflicts, they are sources of goodness.

Generally speaking, there are nine main types of human's evil actions: four types of "harming others as an end" (except the actions of punishing others out of vengeance for the exchange of equal harm) and four types of "self-harming as an end" (except the self-punishment out of a sense of guilt for the exchange of equal harm) and one type of "harming others for self-interest." Besides these there are two other relatively minor types of actions of evil: "harming others for benefiting others" and "self-harming for self-interest," of which the disadvantage is over advantage. On the contrary, there are mainly seven types of good actions of human: four types of actions of "benefiting others as an end" (except *harming others for benefiting others* in which the disadvantage is greater than the advantage), one type of "benefiting others for self-interest," one type of "complete self-interest," and one type of "self-harming for self-interest" (except self-harming for self-interest in which the disadvantage is greater than the advantage). Besides these, there are also two relatively minor types of good actions: the actions of punishing others as an end out of vengeance for the exchange of equal harm and the actions of self-punishment as an end out of a sense of guilt for the exchange of equal harm. These are the good and evil of 16 types of ethical behavior of human beings—namely all the ethical behavior of human beings—which are the good and evil of all human nature that ethics studies.

5.1.2 *The establishment of six principles of good and evil*

By understanding the good and evil of all human ethical behaviors, we can now establish the moral principles of good and evil that regulate all human ethical behaviors. Because the principles of moral good and evil are kinds of moral norms belonging to the category of ethical behavior, in the final analysis, they are types of good and evil of ethical behavior. Therefore, as long as all human ethical behavior are classified according to their natures of good and evil, the principles of moral good and evil can be established: the types of good and evil in the category of ethical behavior are the same as the principles of moral good and moral evil. According to the nature of good and evil of the 16 kinds of ethical behaviors—that is, all human ethical behaviors—it is not difficult to see that all moral behaviors can be summed up into three types of behaviors, three moral realms, three moral principles, and three principles of good:

The first type of actions includes four kinds of *benefiting others as an end* (excluding *harming others for benefiting others* in case the disadvantage outweighs the advantage), which can be called "selflessly benefiting others."

The second type of actions includes *benefiting others for self-interest* and two kinds of exchange of equal harm which include *harming others as an end* to punish others and *self-harming as an end* to punish the self, which also can be termed as "benefiting others for self-interest"; because the basic realm of *benefiting others for self-interest* obviously is the exchange of equal interests, it is generally equal to the moral value of exchange of equal harm. The third type of actions includes *complete self-interest* and *self-harming for self-interest* (excluding self-harming for self-interest where the disadvantage is greater than the advantage), which can be called "mere self-interest." Thus all human's moral behavior has three categories: *selflessly benefiting others*, *benefiting others for self-interest*, and *mere self-interest*. Morality is a kind of social contract and because the direct goal of morality is entirely for the safeguarding of the existence and development of society, the moral value of benefiting others (which is beneficial to society), as Darwin said, is higher than the moral value of self-interest:

> Man can generally and readily distinguish between the higher and lower moral rules. The higher are founded on the social instincts, and relate to the welfare of others. They are supported by the approbation of our fellowmen and by reason. The lower rules, though some of them when implying self-sacrifice hardly deserve to be called lower, relate chiefly to self.[3]

Therefore, the positive moral value of *selflessly benefiting others* is the highest: it is the highest principle of morality, the highest principle of good and the ultimate good, and the highest realm of the ethical behavior that *ought to be*. The moral value of *mere self-interest* is the lowest moral principle, the lowest principle of good, and the lowest good, and the lowest realm of ethical behavior that ought to be. *Benefiting others for self-interest*, however, as a point between the two, is in a realm that mixes benefiting others with self-interest. Therefore, its moral value lies somewhere between *selflessly benefiting others* and *mere self-interest*, and because of this is the basic realm of ethical behavior: it is the basic principle of morality, the basic principle of good or the basic good, and the basic realm of ethical behavior that *ought to be*.

On the contrary, all unethical or bad actions of human beings that ought not to be, can also be summed up as three large types of actions: that is, as three immoral realms, three immoral principles, and three bad principles. The first large type consists of four kinds of actions of *harming others as an end* (excluding the act of punishing others out of vengeance for the equal exchange of harm) and *harming others for benefiting others* where the disadvantage outweighs the advantage, which can be termed as "purely harming others." The second large type is "harming others for self-interest." The third large type includes four kinds of actions of *self-harming as an end* (excluding the action of self-punishment out of a sense of guilt for the equal exchange of harm) and self-harming out of self-interest where the disadvantage outweighs the advantage, all which can be termed as "pure self-harming." Thus all human bad actions can also be divided into three types: *purely harming others*, *harming others for self-interest*, and *pure self-harming*. The negative moral value of harming others is undoubtedly higher than the negative moral value of self-harming. Therefore, the negative moral value of *purely harming others* is the highest: it is the highest principle of immorality, the highest principle of bad and the ultimate bad, and the highest realm of ethical behavior that ought not to be; the negative moral value of pure self harm is the lowest: it is the lowest principle of immorality, the lowest principle of bad and the lowest bad, and the lowest realm of ethical behavior that ought not to be; the negative moral value of harming others for self-interest lies somewhere between *purely harming others* and *pure self-harming*: it is the basic principle of immorality, the basic principle of bad and the basic bad, and is the basic realm of ethical behavior that ought not to be.

The crux of the matter, however, is that selflessly benefiting others is only the highest good but not the greatest good; *purely harming others* is only the highest evil but not the greatest evil. This is because the law of human nature of the *degrees of love* shows that the constant actions of everyone either *benefiting others for self-interest* or *harming others for self-interest*, while *selflessly benefiting others, purely harming others, mere self-interest*, and *pure self-harming* can only be occasional, which implies:

On the one hand, that, in all evil actions, only "harming others for self-interest" can be constant, while "purely harming others" can only be occasional. In this way, the harms to others caused by the actions of "harming others for self-interest" certainly is the greatest of all, certainly greater than that of "purely harming others." Therefore, though "harming others for self-interest" is not the highest evil, it is the basic and constant evil, the greatest evil, the most important evil, the basic and constant principle of evil, the most important principle of immorality. Conversely, though *purely harming others* is the highest evil, it is an occasional evil, the highest but only occasional evil, the highest but only occasional principle of evil, the highest but only occasional principle of immorality, but not the greatest evil, not the most important evil, not the most important principle of evil, and not the most important principle of immorality.

On the other hand, in all good actions, only "benefiting others for self-interest" can be constant, while "selflessly benefiting others" can only be occasional. Thus the interests that "benefit others for self-interest" brings to others certainly is the greatest, certainly far more than that of "selflessly benefiting others": this is the great truth of "being universally applicable and can be carried out generation to generation"! No one will ever make great achievements if they do so intermittently or occasionally; great achievements can only be made with perseverance: only the constant activities (benefiting others for self-interest) can produce great achievements, occasional activities (selflessly benefiting others) cannot.

144   *Moral value and moral norms*

This is the reason why all the great figures in all walks of life who promote the progress of history embrace the strong pursuit of seeking self-interests, while those moral models who selflessly benefiting others, except for their noble virtues, most are as ordinary as others. Thus the interests the people who selflessly benefit others bring to others are often nothing more than a drop in the ocean, while the strong pursuit of seeking self-interests is the driving force to promote public interests: *benefiting others for self-interest* is the greatest and most important good for the development of society! This secret was long ago discovered by Smith: "Nor is it always the worse for the society, that is was no part of it. By pursuing his own interest he frequently promotes that of the society more effectively than when he really intends to promote it."[4] Sidgwick fully agreed with Smith's point of view: "The general happiness will be more satisfactory attained if men frequently act from other motives than pure universal philanthropy."[5]

Therefore, though *benefiting others for self-interest* is not the highest good, it is a basic and constant good, the greatest good, the most important good, the basic and constant principle of good, the most important principle of good, and the most important principle of morality. On the contrary, though *selflessly benefiting others* is the highest good, the highest but only occasional good, the highest but only occasional principle of good, the highest but only occasional principle of morality; but not the greatest good, not the most important good, not the most important principle of good, and not the most important principle of morality.

Thence, in view of this, in terms of what the ancient Chinese appreciated as "three immortalities," *the greatest and most important moral models* are not those who "set up virtue" but those who "set up great theories" or "have meritorious deeds"; they are not the noblest of people, not those who altruistically self-sacrifice their lives and shout "give up one's life for benevolence." Rather, they are those who *benefit others for self-interest*, that is through their own success or lived experience, that make greatest contributions to society. To name a handful: Newton, Leibniz, Beethoven, Goethe, and Hegel, in short, the pioneers in various fields who dreamed of being famous for hundreds and thousands of years in history.

Thence, in view of this, in terms of what the ancient Chinese appreciated as "three immortalities," *the greatest and most important moral models* are not those who "set up virtue" but those who "set up great theories" or "have meritorious deeds"; they are not the noblest of people, not those who altruistically self-sacrifice their lives and shout "give up one's life for benevolence." Rather, they are those who *benefit others for self-interest*, that is through their own success or lived experience, that make greatest contributions to society. To name a handful: Newton, Leibniz, Beethoven, Goethe, and Hegel, in short, the pioneers in various fields who dreamed of being famous for hundreds and thousands of years in the history.

Therefore, generally speaking, through the goal of morality or the ultimate standard of morality, from the objective nature of all the facts of human

Good: General principles of morality   145

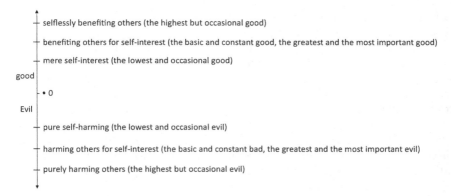

Figure 5.1 The six principles of good and evil

ethical behaviors, on the one hand, we have deduced three principles of good: that of *selflessly benefiting others, benefiting others for self-interest*, and *mere self-interest*, as well as their mutual relations; on the other hand, we have deduced three principles of evil: that of *pure self-harming, harming others for self-interest*, and *purely harming others*, as well as their mutual relations. The six principles of good and evil and their relationships can be expressed in a single axis (as shown in Figure 5.1).

5.1.3 The scope of application of six principles of good and evil

It is not difficult to see that the scope of application of the three principles of evil is absolute: under no circumstances should anyone *purely self-harm, harm others for self-interest*, and *purely harm others*. However, the scope of application of the three principles of good is relative. The scope of application of *mere self-interest* obviously mainly are ethical behavior which have no direct relation of advantage or disadvantage to society or others—but only have a direct relation of advantage or disadvantage to oneself, such as running, swimming, sightseeing, appreciating the beauty of flowers or the moon, and so on. These kinds of action all belong to the category of *mere self-interest*, and all conform to the moral principle of *mere self-interest*.

However, some ethical behavior which have a relation of advantage or disadvantage to society or others, such as one's unwillingness to donate one's kidney to uremic patients who need them, also seem to fall into the category of actions of *mere self-interest* which are neither beneficial nor harmful to others. But is it the case that such actions might conform to the moral principle of *mere self-interest*? Actually, it is not. Human beings are social animals, everything one owned is given by others, thence, as long as one lives in society one ought to help others when they have difficulties: one may not donate one's kidney but ought to do what one can to help uremic patients. If one stand by and do not give any help, it would be a kind of unjust action of ingratitude, and it would never be the action of mere self-interest which are neither beneficial nor harmful to others.

The actions of "selflessly benefiting others" and "benefiting others for self-interest," contrary to "mere self-interest," obviously are the moral principles that guide everyone's actions which are an advantage or a disadvantage directly related to society or others. These kinds of actions can be divided into two types: the first is the constant major actions done under the circumstance that interests are in no conflict or conflicts can be compromised; the second is the occasional minor actions done under the circumstance that interests are in conflict and no compromise can be achieved. Society is a system of cooperation in which everyone benefits others and others benefit everyone else, which means that in most cases people's interests are in no conflict or conflicts can be compromised; and that it is uncommon that people's interests are in conflict and no compromise can be achieved, otherwise a society certainly will collapse and no longer exist.

It goes without saying that *benefiting others for self-interest* only applies to actions that interests are in no conflict or conflicts can be compromised, but not to the actions in which conflicts of interests that cannot be compromised. When interests conflict and cannot be compromised, it is obviously impossible to benefit others for self-interest such that it is an advantage to both sides: *benefiting others for self-interest* only can exist under the circumstance that the interests are consistent and can be compromised. For example, business is beneficial to both buyer and seller, it is a kind of actions that are consistent in their interests and which can be compromised. It is therefore applicable to the principle of *benefiting others for self-interest*: business that benefits others for self-interest is moral; business that harms others for self-interest is immoral. On the contrary, take the example of war. If one is caught by the enemy, one may have to betray one's comrades if one hopes to survive; if one does not betray one's comrades one may be shot dead. Thus, one's self-interest conflicts with the interests of the comrades and cannot be compromised. Under such a circumstance it is clear that *benefiting others for self-interest* is impossible; *benefiting others for self-interest* cannot apply to the interest conflicts that cannot be compromised.

Then, what are the moral principles that can be applied to interest conflicts that cannot be compromised? No doubt it can only be *selflessly benefiting others* or self-sacrifice, because under such circumstance, if one does not sacrifice oneself, one will have no other choice but to harm others out of self-interest. Therefore, under the circumstance of interest conflict that cannot be compromised, only self-sacrifice or selflessly benefiting others is moral: self-sacrifice or *selflessly benefiting others* is the only moral principle to settle the conflict between self-interest and the interests of society or others. Then, is *selflessly benefiting others* also applicable to the action where interests are consistent and do not conflict—or to where the conflict can be compromised? No!

This is because *selflessly benefiting others* is the same concept as self-sacrifice: selflessly benefiting others must at least suppress and sacrifice certain desires of one's own and certainly may also consume a great amount of time and energy. Therefore, under the circumstance that the interests are consistent or conflicts can be compromised, *selflessly benefiting others* is *ought not to be* and immoral since it suppresses and sacrifices the self's desires and the self-interest, violating the ultimate standard of morality of "increasing the quantum of interests without negatively affecting anyone." Moreover, under such a circumstance, *benefiting others for self-interest* increases the quantum of interests of society and everyone more than selflessly benefiting others. This can be examined in two ways:

On the one hand, *selflessly benefiting others* seems not increase the total amount of social interests. Because *selflessly benefiting others* is not a "win-win" principle, though it increases others' quantum of interests, it does not increase the total amount of self-interest, it instead even reduces the total amount of self-interest: at least it suppresses and sacrifices certain desire and freedom of oneself and certainly may also consume a great amount of time and energy. On the contrary, *benefiting others for self-interest* obviously increases the total amount of interests of society. Because *benefiting others for self-interest* is a "win–win" principle, it not only increases the total interests of others but also increases the total amount of self-interest.

On the other hand, even if *selflessly benefiting others* increases the total amount of interests of society, it is certainly far less than the total amount of interests of society given by *benefiting others for self-interest*. For only *benefiting others for self-interest* is the most powerful ultimate motivation for promoting the interests of society. *Selflessly benefiting others* does not have such an ultimate motivation since it suppresses the pursuit of the personal interests. As Sidgwick said:

> It would clearly not promote the universal happiness for each one practically to concern himself with the happiness of others as much as with his own. For in the first place, generally speaking, each man is far better able to provide for his own happiness than for that of any other person, from his more intimate knowledge of his own desires and needs, and his greater opportunities of gratifying them. And besides, it is under the stimulus of self-interest that the active energies of most men are most easily and thoroughly drawn out.[6]

Therefore, under the circumstance that the interests are consistent or conflicts can be compromised, *benefiting others for self-interest* instead of *selflessly benefiting others* greatly increases the total interests of society, perfectly conforming to the ultimate standard of morality of "increasing everyone's quantum of interests" and is therefore perfectly moral and ought to be; on the contrary, *selflessly benefiting others* instead of *benefiting others for self-interest* greatly reduces the total amount of interests of society, seriously violating the

148 *Moral value and moral norms*

ultimate standards of morality, and is therefore entirely immoral and ought not to be.

Thence it can be seen that *selflessly benefiting others* is the highest but occasional principle of good which is only applicable to exceptional or occasional behaviors, that is, the interest conflict that cannot be compromised; *benefiting others for self-interest* is a basic and constant principle of good that only applies to the normal or constant actions, that is, the actions in which the interests are consistent or conflicts can be compromised. Unfortunately, for many years in China we did not understand this truth but strongly advocated that one "ought to be something and somebody for the sake of the motherland but not for oneself." Such advocacy is extremely immoral. Let's ask, what kind of people can benefit everyone the most? Are they not scientists such as Newton and Einstein? Are they not poets like Li Bai (李白), Dufu (杜甫), and Shakespeare? Are they not men of letters such as Cao Xueqin (曹雪芹) and Tolstoy? In a nutshell, they are famous persons. Thus, to be something and somebody not only benefits oneself the most, in a much broader perspective it is even more beneficial to others, belonging to "the actions where the interests are in harmony and is advantage to both sides."

Therefore, the requirement of "being something and somebody for the motherland but not for oneself" suppresses and sacrifices the self's desires; therefore, it violates the ultimate standard of morality of "increasing the quantum of interests without negatively affecting anyone" under the circumstance that the interests are consistent. Moreover, "being something and somebody for oneself" increases the total amount of interests of society more than "being something and somebody for the motherland": only the former but not the latter possesses the most powerful ultimate motivation for promoting the interests of society, namely the pursuit of the personal interests. Therefore, the teaching that "one ought to be something and somebody only for the motherland but not for oneself" entirely violates the ultimate general standard of morality of "increasing everyone's quantum of interests" for it greatly reduces everyone's quantum of interests. The traditional altruistic morality which advocates that "one ought to be something and somebody only for the motherland but not for oneself" is then an extremely inferior morality!

5.1.4 General principles of morality: Two principles of good and evil, as well as six principles of good and evil

To sum up, first of all, *selflessly benefiting others* is the highest and occasionally principle of good, the highest and occasional principle of morality, and it ought to and can only guide everyone's occasional actions; under the circumstance that self-interest conflicts with the interests of others, its function is to enable everyone to *selflessly benefit others* and self-sacrifice without *harming others for self-interest*. On the contrary, *purely harming others* is the highest but occasional principle of evil, the highest but occasional principle

Good: General principles of morality   149

of immorality, and therefore ought to and can guides everyone's occasional actions. Its function is to prohibit everyone's actions that purely harm others and reduce them to zero.

Secondly, *benefiting others for self-interest* is the basic and constant principle of good, the basic and constant principle of morality. It *ought to and can* guide everyone's constant behavior; its function is to enable everyone to benefit others not to harm others under the circumstance when self-interests are consistent with others' interests or conflicts can be compromised. On the contrary, *harming others for self-interest* is the basic and constant principle of evil, the basic and constant principle of immorality. It *ought to and can* guide everyone's constant actions; its function is to prevent everyone from harming others when one's acts affect others.

Finally, *mere self-interest* is the lowest and occasional principle of good, the lowest and occasional principle of morality, and it also ought to and can only guide everyone's occasional actions, its function is to enable everyone to benefit the self, not to harm the self under the circumstance when self-interests are consistent with others' interests or conflicts can be compromised. On the contrary, *pure self-harming* is the lowest and occasional principle of evil, the lowest and occasional principle of immorality, it ought to and can guide everyone's occasional actions; its function is to prohibit the acts of *pure self-harming* when one's acts neither benefit nor harm others, and continuously reduce them to zero.

This is the definition and scope of application of six principles of good and evil, determined by the law of human nature of the *degrees of love* and the ultimate standard of morality, the significance of which lies in showing that it is impossible for us and we ought not to regard selflessly benefiting others as the sole standard for judging whether or not all actions are moral: because selflessly benefiting others only should guide the actions under the circumstance that the interest conflicts cannot be compromised; and because everyone's ends certainly are constantly self-interested and occasionally benefit others. Therefore, no matter how noble, pure, and perfect the actions of selflessly benefiting others are, it ought to and can only be regarded as occasional principle of good, and ought to, and can only be used to guide the occasional actions of human; only benefiting others for self-interest, though this principle is not so noble and perfect as selflessly benefiting others and has been reprimanded by Kant and Fung Yulan as the principle of calculating, ought to and can be regarded as the constant principle of good, and ought to and can be used to guide the constant actions of human; only the combination of *selflessly benefiting others*, *benefiting others for self-interest*, and *mere self-interest* is a comprehensive moral principle, which can and ought to guide the all human actions to enable everyone to selflessly benefit others under the circumstance that the conflict of interests cannot be compromised, to benefit both the self and others under the circumstance when the interests are consistent and conflicts can be compromised, to benefit the self when one's actions have nothing to do with others, and not to do immoral actions under

150 *Moral value and moral norms*

any circumstances, such as *pure self-harming, harming others for self-interest*, and *purely harming others*. This is the limit of the noblest moral model! This is the limit of all functions of the best morality! Whoever wants to go beyond this limit regarding *selflessly benefiting others* as the sole moral standard for guiding all human actions, trying to create a moral model who constantly or even completely *benefiting others*, is destined to fail!

The six principles of good and evil are the principles of morality regulating all human ethical behaviors, so they can be termed as the general principles of morality. More precisely, as the general principle of morality, on the one hand, the so-called good, that is, the moral good, is all the ethical behavior that conforms to the goal of morality or the ultimate standard of morality, and thus is the ethical behavior that "increases the interests of society, others, oneself, and non-humans," namely "selflessly benefiting others," "benefiting others for self-interest," and "mere self-interest," which, in the final analysis, are the ethical behavior of "benefiting others" and "self-interest." On the other hand, as the general principles of morality, the so-called evil, that is, the moral bad, is all ethical behavior that violates the goal of morality or the ultimate standard of morality, and thus is the ethical behavior that "decreases the interests of society, others, oneself, and non-humans," namely "purely harming others," "harming others for self-interest," and "pure self-harming," which, in the final analysis, is the ethical behavior of "harming others" and "self-harming."

In this way, the general principle of morality consists of two aspects: one is "the general principle of good and evil" or "two principles of good and evil," which, in the final analysis, is "the good is benefiting others and self-interest" and "the evil is harming others and self-harming"; the other is "the sub-principles of good and evil" or the six principles of good and evil, namely "the good is *selflessly benefiting others, benefiting others for self-interest*, and *mere self-interest*," and "the evil is *purely harming others, harming others for self-interest*, and *pure self- harming*."

The general principle of good and evil is so broad that it does not distinguish between ends and means, and therefore cannot accurately measure the good and evil of all actions. Let's take two kinds of ethical behavior of *harming others for self-interest* and *self-harming for benefiting others* as an example. According to the general principle of good and evil that "the good is benefiting others and self-interest, evil is harming others and self-harming," it seems that *harming others for self-interest* and *self-harming for benefiting others* are both good and evil: that both *benefiting others* and *self-interest* seem to be good, and *self-harming* and *harming others* both seem to be evil. It seems difficult to explain why the moral value of *harming others for self-interest* is fundamentally different from that of *self-harming for benefiting others*: *self-harming for benefiting others* is good, while *harming others for self-interest* is evil.

To explain it clearly, to accurately evaluate the good and evil of everyone's specific and actual actions, the general principle of good and evil that "the good is benefiting others and self-interest; the evil is harming others and self-harming" should be specified and differentiated between ends and means, where they evolve into the six different principles of good and evil: "selflessly benefiting others," "benefiting others for self-interest," "mere self-interest," as well as "purely harming others," "harming others for self-interest," and "purely self-harming." Therefore, only the six principles of good and evil can accurately measure the good and evil of all actions, the general principle of good and evil cannot: the six principles of good and evil are precise general principles of morality, while the general principles of good and evil are imprecise general principles of morality.

5.2 Theories on the good and evil of human nature

The general principle of morality (the six principles of good and evil or the two principles of good and evil) is the outcome of the analysis of the good and evil of human nature. The good and evil of human nature is the basic problem of the theory of the general principle of morality, thus is also the important problem of human thought. People from all walks of life have been debating it since ancient times. However, the arguments that have the formed various systematic theories of the good and evil of human nature, lasting well over two thousands of years, are not to be found in the West; they are unique to Chinese philosophy. The theories that constitute one of the major characteristics of Chinese philosophy can be summed up as four kinds: a theory of human nature without good or evil, a theory of the good of human nature, a theory of the evil of human nature, and a theory of human nature with both good and evil.

5.2.1 The theory of human nature without good or evil

The theory of human nature without good or evil holds that human nature has no distinction between moral and immoral, good and evil. Gaozi (告子) is well known as the representative figure of the theory of human nature without good or evil. In Gaozi's view, human nature is nothing more than "Appetite and sexual desire": "Appetite and sexual desire are human nature."[7] Obviously appetite and sexual desire are inherent nature and need not be learned. Therefore, Gaozi also said: "what is inherent is nature."[8] Since human nature is inherent (or natural, inborn, unlearned, and instinctive), like all natural objects no distinction can be made between good and evil, moral and immoral:

> Nature is similar to the torrent of a stream, if the dike bursts in the east it runs to the east, if the dike bursts in the west it runs to the west. Human nature is similar to the stream that has no distinction of running to the east or west, and has no distinction of whether it is good or not.[9]

It is true that appetite and sexual desire are similar to feelings of compassion, envy, love, hatred, etc., all which are the inherent nature of human beings. Such feelings are also natural, inborn, unlearned, and instinctive. However, taken together, these do not all belong to the category of natural objects but to the category of human actions: they all belong to the category of behavioral psychology, which is the internal motivation and internal factor of actions. The internal motivation and internal factor of actions, in terms of their quantity, can be controlled at will by everyone: they can be suppressed or sublimated (becoming weaker and lesser in extent), or can be developed or indulged (becoming stronger and greater in extent).

Therefore, the human nature of appetite, sexual desire, feelings of compassion, envy, love, and hatred, etc. is different from the natural objects on his body that he cannot control himself—such as bigness or smallness of eyes, the sharpness or narrowness of nose—can be distinguished between good and evil: love and compassion obviously are beneficial to the existence and development of society and everyone, conforming to the goal of morality or the ultimate standard of morality, thence is good; hatred and envy are obviously harmful to the existence and development of society, violating the goal of morality or the ultimate standard of morality, thence is evil. The error of Gaozi's theory of human nature without good or evil lies in his regarding inborn human nature as the objects in nature, from that the objects of the nature have no distinction between good and evil; consequently drew the wrong conclusion that human nature that is inherent and natural has no distinction between good and evil.

5.2.2 The theory of the good of human nature

The theory of the good of human nature regards human nature as good not evil. Mencius, as is well known, established the theory and was the principal advocator of it. Like the Gaozi, Mencius also insisted that human nature is inherent: "It is not who teaches me but my inherent nature."[10] However, in Mencius' view, not all the inherent nature of human beings is human nature: human nature is rather the inherent characteristic that distinguishes human beings from non-human beings. Therefore Zhang Dainian (张岱年) wrote: "The so-called nature Mencius termed refers to the special characteristics that human beings are different from animals. The human characteristics that are the same as animals cannot be termed human nature."[11]

However, why is human nature the characteristic that defines human beings as human beings? It is because human nature is different, for instance, from dog nature and cattle nature:

> Mencius asks: "is not the nature that is inherent the same as white as white?" One answers: "Yes." He asks: "Is the whiteness of feather the same as the whiteness of snow, is the whiteness of snow the same as the whiteness of white jade?" One answers: "Yes." He asks: "But, is dog nature the same as cattle nature, and cattle nature the same as human nature?"[12]

Good: General principles of morality 153

This means that human nature is different from dog nature and cattle nature: that human nature is the characteristic of human beings that differentiates humans from dogs and cattles.

Then, what is the human characteristic that make human beings as human beings? Mencius replied:

> They are the mind of compassion, the mind of shame, the mind of modesty and yielding, the mind of rightness and wrongness ... If a person has no mind of compassion, he is not a human being, if no mind of shame, he is not a human being, if no mind of modesty and yielding, he is not a human being, if no mind of rightness and wrongness, he is not a human being.[13]

If one lacks one of the four "minds," one is not a human being, therefore, the four "minds" are what makes a human being a human being and are the unique characteristic of human nature. However, is human nature, considering its four "minds," good or evil? As an advocator of deontology, Mencius regarded the perfection of everyone's moral character and the realization of making a human being a human being—namely selflessly benefiting others—as the ultimate standard of morality for measuring the good and evil of all ethical behaviors. According to his view, because human nature (or four "minds") are precisely what makes a human being a human being, they fully conform to the ultimate standard of morality and are completely good:

> The mind of compassion is the starting point of benevolence, the mind of shame is the starting point of justice, the mind of modesty and yielding is the starting point of courtesy, the mind of rightness and wrongness is the starting point of wisdom.[14]

The argument that human nature is good not evil, held by the theory of the good of human nature, is obviously not based on Mencius' deontology but on Mencius' definition of human nature: human nature is what differentiates human beings from animals and defines human beings as human beings. If human nature is what defines human beings as human beings (namely the so-called "four minds"), then whether it is measured by the ultimate standard of deontology (perfecting everyone's moral character) or the ultimate standard of utilitarianism (promoting everyone's interests), human nature obviously conforms to it, and thence is good not evil.

The definition that human nature is what makes a human beings a human beings, at first glance seems tenable because human nature is obviously different from dog nature and cattle nature. Nevertheless, when we look into it, it is a fallacy for nothing is completely different. Human nature cannot be completely different from dog nature and cattle nature. Human nature may have different aspects from dog nature and cattle nature that make the human

154 *Moral value and moral norms*

being a human being, but it also shares aspects, namely the animal nature of human beings. Human animality, like human characteristics, is something embodied in human body. How can it not be human nature? The error of the theory of the good of human nature is that it only perceives the different aspects of human nature from dog nature and cattle nature, obliterating the shared animal aspects and thus only equating human nature with a part of human nature—namely the characteristic of human beings—asserting lopsidedly that human nature is the only characteristic that differentiates human beings from dog nature and cattle nature and makes a human being a human being.

5.2.3 The theory of the evil of human nature

The representative figure of the theory of the evilness of human nature, as is well known, is Xunzi (荀子) who writes: "Man's nature is evil, his good is learned."[15] But why is human nature evil? It is widely believed that this is because Xunzi and Mencius defined the concept of human nature differently: "Xunzi's so-called nature and Mencius's so-called nature actually are two different things."[16] In fact, Mencius and Xunzi's definition of human nature are basically the same in that both see human nature as the inherent nature of human beings. Xunzi said: "The thing that is innate is called nature," while Mencius also held that the human nature of the mind of compassion etc., "is not what who teach me but my inherent nature."[17]

It was only when further identifying what inherent things in human beings are human nature that Mencius and Xunzi parted ways. Mencius believed that the "four minds" are inherent; that the "four minds" are human nature and human nature is the "four minds," thus human nature is good. On the contrary, Xunzi believed that Mencius' "four-minds" are not human nature but are acquired. Since the "four minds" are only four beginnings, and only bud a little bit, they must expand before the bloom, so they are not inborn or inherent, but "are acquired."[18] Then, in Xunzi's view, what is the inherent nature of human beings? They are the mind of self-interest, envy, pursuits for beautiful things and melody, sexual desires, seeking pleasure, and comforts.[19]

Proceeding from the concrete content of human nature, that is, self-love and self-interest, Xunzi further drew the conclusion that human nature is evil:

> human nature is inherently greedy in terms of self-interest, thus when people fight for interests, modesty and yielding disappear; born with envy and hatred robbery and killing happen, thus honesty and loyalty disappear; born with sexual desire thus pursuing the attractive women and enjoy lechery, therefore are licentious, consequently courtesy, justice, culture and reason are destroyed. If we let mankind have their own way and follow their feelings, they will naturally fight for everything and disregard everyone, then society will fall into a violent state of disorder. Therefore people must be educated by masters and regulated by rules and laws.

Judging from this, it is obvious that human nature is evil, and its good is acquired.[20]

It is not difficult to see that the theory of evil of human nature is untenable, for no matter how evil a person might be, no matter how weak his love for others, compassion, and gratitude, it is impossible to completely lose the love for others, compassion, and gratitude: does not he love and sympathize with his children, his wife, and his parents? Everyone has an innate love for others, compassion, and gratitude, it's just that some people have more and some have less. Therefore the love for others, compassion, and gratitude are same as the hatred for others, envy, and vengeance; all are human nature. The error of the theory of evil of human nature obviously is to obliterate the aspects of loving others and benefiting others of human nature, equating human nature only with self-love and self-interest. This is just one aspect of the theory of evil of human nature that is wrong. The other aspect, yielding to the human nature of inherent greed for self-interest might cause either a behavior of fighting for interests, or the behaviors of modesty: the pursuit of personal interests might be harmful to society or others, thus is the source of evil; it also might be beneficial to society or others and thus is the source of good. The error of the theory of evil of human nature obviously exaggerates the aspects of self-love and self-interest which is harmful to others, obliterating their aspects of benefiting others, thus drawing the conclusion that human nature—namely self-love and self-interest—is evil. This is the double error of the theory of evil of human nature.

5.2.4 *The theory of the good and evil of human nature*

The theory of the good of human nature seems to be opposite to the theory of evil of human nature, but its error is the same. For, on the one hand, human nature is pluralistic: it has the inherent mind of compassion so it can benefit others, but also the inherent mind of self-love so it certainly will be self-interested. However, the definition of human nature in both theories is equally one-sided: the theory of the good of human nature thinks that human nature is only compassion and benefiting others while the theory of the evil of human nature holds that human nature is only self-love and self-interest. On the other hand, the ultimate standard of morality is to "increase everyone's quantum of interests." However, both the theories of the good of human nature and the evil of human nature are different sects within the Confucian school.

In terms of their mainstream thoughts they both adhere to deontology and regard the perfect realm of moral character "selflessly benefiting others," namely so-called benevolence of Confucianism, as the ultimate standard of morality for the measurement of the good and evil of human nature. The advocators of the theory of the evil of human nature use the ultimate standard to measure their so-called human nature and naturally declare that human nature is evil because self-love and self-interest are not the perfect realm of moral character and do not conform to the ultimate standard of morality as understood by deontology; on the other hand, the advocators of the theory of the good of human nature also use the ultimate standard to measure their so-called human nature and naturally come to the conclusion that human nature is good because compassion and benefiting others are the perfect realm of moral character in conformity with the ultimate moral standard as understood by deontology.

Both theories of the good of human nature and the evil of human nature are one-sided and also wrong, since human nature is neither pure good nor pure evil, but has both good and evil: The theory of the good and evil of human nature is the truth. However, the representative figures of the theory of the good and evil of human nature are still Confucians: Shi Shuo (世硕), Dong Zhongshu (董仲舒), and Yang Xiong (杨雄). The theory of the good and evil of human nature was started by the Confucian Shi Shuo in the Warring States period:

> Shi Shuo, who lived in the state of Zhou, thought that there is both good and evil in human nature: choosing the good in human nature, cultivating and fostering it then good grows. Cultivating and fostering the evil then evil grows.[21]

Dong Zhongshu, on the other hand, demonstrated in great detail the theory that there is both good and evil in human nature, and through those expositions he concluded:

> Man who is ordered by Nature, has the nature of loving good and hating evil, which can be cultivated but cannot be changed, can be increased or decreased but cannot be removed. It is similar to the shape of the human body, which can become fat and thin but the shape of the body cannot be transformed.[22]

Yang Xiong went further, putting forward the famous argument "nature is a mixture of good and evil": "Human nature is a mixture of good and evil, cultivating one's good one will be a good person, cultivating one's evil one will be an evil person."[23]

Both theories of the good of human nature and the evil of human nature are one-sided and also wrong, since human nature is neither pure good nor pure evil, but has both good and evil: the theory of the good and evil of human nature is the truth. However, the representative figures of the theory of the good and evil of human nature are still Confucians: Shi Shuo (世硕), Dong Zhongshu (董仲舒), and Yang Xiong (杨雄). The theory of the good and evil of human nature was started by the Confucian Shi Shuo in the Warring States period:

Shi Shuo, who lived in the state of Zhou, thought that there is both good
and evil in human nature: choosing the good in human nature, cultivating
and fostering it then good grows. Cultivating and fostering the evil then
evil grows.[24]

Dong Zhongshu, on the other hand, demonstrated in great detail the
theory that there is both good and evil in human nature, and through those
expositions he concluded:

> Man who is ordered by Nature, has the nature of loving good and hating
> evil, which can be cultivated but cannot be changed, can be increased or
> decreased but cannot be removed. It is similar to the shape of the human
> body, which can become fat and thin but the shape of the body cannot
> be transformed.[25]

Yang Xiong went further, putting forward the famous argument "nature is a
mixture of good and evil": "Human nature is a mixture of good and evil, cultivating one's good one will be a good person, cultivating one's evil one will
be an evil person."[26]

The theory of the good and evil of human nature, as Zhang Dainian said,
is a compromise between the theories of the good of human nature and of
the evil of human nature. However, besides the theory of the good and evil of
human nature, the theory of the three degrees of human nature also makes a
compromise between the theories of the good of human nature and of the evil
of human nature, which holds that human nature can be divided into three
different degrees: the human nature of one kind of people is good; the human
nature of another kind of people is evil; and the human nature of the third
kind of people lies between these two kinds of people in they are both good
and evil. In short, the so-called "theory of three degrees of human nature"
holds that everyone's human nature is not the same. The three different degrees
of human nature just outlined are respectively superior, inferior, and mediocre forms. *The theory of three degrees of human nature* is the extreme form
of *the theory of the good and evil of human nature*. Therefore, Dong Zhongshu
believed that human nature has the nature of the saint, the nature of lower
people, and the nature of mediocre people: "The nature of the saint cannot be
called human nature, the nature of lower people also cannot be called human
nature. The nature of mediocre people is human nature."[27] However, the
true representatives of *the theory of three degrees of human nature*, as is well
known, are Wang Chong (王充), Xunyue (荀悦), and Han Yu (韩愈). Han Yu
put it most clearly: "There are three degrees of human nature: the upper, the
lower and the mediocre. The upper is pure good; the mediocre can be guided
to the upper or to the lower; and the lower is pure evil."[28]

The theory of three degrees of human natures undoubtedly is a fallacy. This
is because, as mentioned before, the so-called human nature is the universal

nature inherent with the birth of every human being: in terms of the existence or absence of its quality, it is inherent in all human beings and is completely the same; only in terms of its quantity, within a certain limit, it is later acquired by learning and becomes different. That is to say, everyone's human nature, apart from the difference of quantity, is exactly the same. In other words, the human nature that anyone possesses can only be different in terms of quantity, but it is exactly the same in terms of quality: there can only be one kind of human nature, it is never possible for there to be three kinds of human nature. There can never be such human nature as that of a saint who is all good without evil, or such human nature as that of lower people who are all evil without good: everyone is both good and evil. No matter how noble a saint is, it is impossible for him not to have the slightest evil such as envy, vengeance, and hatred; no matter how evil a lowest person is, it is impossible for him not to have the slightest good, such as love for others, compassion, and gratitude. The only difference is that the saint's good human nature is much greater and the evil human nature in them is much smaller, while the lower person's evil human nature is much greater and the good human nature in them is much smaller. The error of *the theory of three degrees of human nature* obviously is that it exaggerates the difference aspects of the quantity of the human nature of three kinds of people, and obliterates the commonality of the existence or absence of the quality of human nature among them, consequently drawing the wrong conclusion that the human nature of three kinds of people is completely different, that there exist three different human natures.

Then, is the Confucian theory that human nature is both good and evil the truth? From a rough analysis it is no doubt the truth. Nevertheless, getting to the bottom of the matter, it's not quite the case. The evaluation of good and evil, on the one hand, depends on the definition of human nature, on what human nature refers to; on the other hand, it depends on what is the standard of the good and evil of human nature, on what is the ultimate standard of morality. If one of these two aspects is viewed differently, then the point of view as to whether human nature is good or evil is different: if the understanding of both these two aspects is the truth, then the theory of good and evil of human nature is the truth; as long as one of them is wrong, then the theory of good and evil of human nature contains errors. As to the definition of human nature, the Confucian theory of the good and evil of human nature holds that human nature has an inherent mind of compassion or an inherent altruism as well as an inherent self-love thus certainly self-interest, which is quite comprehensive and avoids the one-sidedness of the theory of the good and evil of human nature. But, with regard to the ultimate standard of morality, this Confucian theory makes the same mistake as the theories of the good of human nature and the evil of human nature: which all unilaterally regard "benevolence" or "selflessly benefiting others" as the standard for the measurement of human nature. In this way, like the theories of the good of human nature and the evil of human nature, it mistakenly thinks that self-love and self-interest are evil while compassion and benefiting others are good but takes both as human nature.

From above we know that what can be called truth is such a "new theory of the good and evil of human nature": on the one hand, like the Confucian theory of the good and evil of human nature, it holds that the inherent universal nature in all human beings—whether it is compassion and benefiting others, or self-love and self-interest—are human nature; on the other hand, different from the Confucian theory of the good and evil of human nature, it takes "increasing everyone's quantum of interests" instead of "increasing the perfection of everyone's moral character" or "selflessly benefiting others" as the measurement of good and bad of human nature. Thence, not only is the human nature of compassion and benefiting others good, the human nature of self-love and self-interest is also good, and only the forms of human nature such as envy and harming others are evil.

This "new theory of the good and evil of human nature," which originates from and transcends the former theories of good and evil of human nature, is the truth, but if it stops at this point it will not overcome the fundamental shortcoming of the former theories of human nature. In the classical theories of human nature of the Hundred Schools of Thought, whether theories of the good of human nature or the evil of human nature, or the theory of the good and evil of human nature, as Zhang Dainian put it, none studied the actual content of human nature:

> The features of Chinese theories on human nature are that they only discuss the good and evil, the nature of the good and evil of human nature, the main controversy being the problem of the good or evil of human nature. Even those who oppose discussing human nature simply in terms of its good and evil only stop at the point that human nature is neither good nor evil but never examine the actual content of human nature.[29]

It is undoubtedly the most fundamental shortcoming of the classical theories of human nature, which makes it impossible to establish a comprehensive and scientific moral norm. In order to overcome this shortcoming, my theory of human nature discusses in detail the actual contents of human nature such as 16 kinds of human nature and four laws of human nature: my theory of human nature is a "new theory of the good and evil of human nature" characterized by "16 kinds of human nature and four laws of human nature."

The general principles of morality, whether the general principles of good or evil, or six principles of good and evil, are the result of the analysis of the good and evil of human nature; therefore the theory of the good and evil of human nature originally belongs to the theory of general principle of morality. However, it is not the whole theory of the general principle of morality, but only part of its content because the theory of the general principle of morality also includes at least the theory of the goal of morality and the

160 *Moral value and moral norms*

ultimate standard of morality, as well as the theory of the principle of good and evil. Although the theory of the good and evil of human nature is only a part of the theory of general principle of morality, it is so fundamental and important that it is separated from the whole of the theory of general principle of morality and becomes a relatively independent theory. Therefore, the theory of the general principle of morality and the theory of the good and evil of human nature are the relationship between the whole and the part; thus, on the one hand, no matter how important and fundamental the theory of human nature is, it is far less complex and important than the theory of the general principle of morality; on the other hand, the analysis of the theory of good and evil of human nature is the basis and premise of analyzing the theory of the general principle of morality: starting from it then it is not difficult to analyze the theory of general principle of morality. Then, how many schools are there in the theories of the general principle of morality at all times and all over the world? What is their basic content and what are their pros and cons?

5.3 Theories on general moral principle

Theories on the general principle of morality are undoubtedly the most complicated and abstruse theories in ethics because meta-ethics shows that excellent moral principles are not made arbitrary but can only be derived from the facts of ethical behavior through the goal of morality or the ultimate standard. Thence theories on the general principle of morality includes three large contents of normative ethics: the first one is the theory of moral nature (namely the goal of morality and the ultimate standard of morality); the second is about the theory of human nature (namely the nature of the fact of human ethical behavior); and the third is about the principle of the good of human behavioral ought. Therefore, theories on the general principle of morality are general theories covering the whole system of normative ethics, and these problems have been the objects for both Chinese and Western ethicists with constant debates ever since.

These arguments mainly can be summed up as altruism, egoism (rational egoism and individualism, as well as psychological egoism and ethical egoism) and the doctrine of benefiting *both self-and-others*.

5.3.1 Altruism

The word "altruism," as Paulsen said, is created by the altruist Comte: "Comte, who coined the term, inclines to altruism."[30] Comte used the word to express the ethical theory advocated by thinkers such as Francis Hutcheson. The basic features of this doctrine are summed up by Hutcheson as "The pursuit of morality is neither motivated by the interests of the pursuer or by self-love, nor by any motive of his own interests."[31] That is to say, altruism is a theory

Good: General principles of morality 161

that, in its view, only *selflessly benefiting others* is good and moral, and as long as the end is for self-interest, it is evil and immoral: altruism is the theory regarding selflessly benefiting others as the general principle of morality for evaluating the good and evil of actions. Thus, in defining altruism, Paulsen wrote: "Acts have moral worth in so far as they are determined by purely altruistic motives."[32] However, if altruism were only the theory of Comte and Hutcheson, it would not make much sense. Comte is but the person who coined the word altruism, but the true representative of altruism is new and old Confucian theory of "benevolence," and new and old Christian ethics. Therefore, altruism matured in ancient times, occupied an absolute dominant position in the Middle Ages and still has had great influence in modern and contemporary times. Its main representatives are Confucius, Mozi, Jesus, and Kant.

First, from the view of the theory of human nature, they unanimously agree that everyone's purpose of action can reach the realm of selflessly benefiting others. Benevolence, which is the general moral principle of Confucianism, is altruism, because Confucians in every generation have defined benevolence as "loving others": loving others is obviously the psychological motivation of selflessly benefiting others, and selflessly benefiting others is the expression of the behavior of loving others. Therefore, Guo Moruo (郭沫若) said: "The meaning of benevolence is a kind of altruistic action which restrains one's selfishness … it wants people to get rid of all motives of selfishness and to self-sacrifice to the people."[33] The general moral principle of Mohism is also selflessly benefiting others:

> King Wen's universal love of the world is so broad and profound that it is the same as the sun and the moon, which is for the people of the whole world without self-interest. This is the universal love of King Wen. Mozi's so-called universal love is learned from the King Wen.[34]

"Love," which is the general moral principle of Christianity, is even more altruistic: as Paul said, seeking not the interests of oneself but that of others: "And though I bestow all my goods to feed the poor, and though I give my body to the burned, and have not charity, it profited me nothing."[35] Then, is the general moral principle of Kant's ethics "duty" also selflessly benefiting others? Yes, because on the one hand Kant said: "duty is the necessity of action due to the respect for the morality."[36] On the other hand, he said, "respect is the sense of value that makes egoism shameful."[37] Therefore Arsen Gliuga points out that Kant's "formula of duty is to seek the interests for others."[38]

Secondly, from the view of the nature of morality, both Kant and Christianity think that the origin and goal of morality is completely autonomous, and all lies in the perfection of everyone's moral character, actualizing what makes human beings different from animals and human beings as human beings. The Bible says over and over again that God made a covenant to make a man morally perfect:

> When Abram was ninety-nine years old, the LORD appeared to Abram, and said unto him, I am the Almighty God; walk before me, and be thou perfect. And I will make my covenant between me and thee, and will multiply thee exceedingly.[39]

Kant also wrote:

> Moral law ... begins with my invisible self, my personality ... With my personality, my value as a spiritual thing has been raised infinitely. In this personality, the moral law gives me a life that is independent of animal nature, even beyond the whole perceptual world.[40]

On the contrary, the Mohism thought that the origin and goal of morality are completely heteronomy, all for the safeguarding of the existence and development of society.

> When the world is in universal love it will be administered, and when it comes to the mutual evil it will be in the state of chaos. Therefore Mozi said, "it is the reason that you must not dissuade those who love others."[41]

Confucianism, on the one hand, acknowledges that the origin and goal of morality is to safeguard the existence and development of society, but, on the other hand, thinks that this is not the main origin and goal of morality; that the main origin and goal of morality is autonomous: morality originates from morality itself and from the needs of the perfection of everyone's moral character; that the goal of morality lies in morality itself, in perfecting everyone's moral character, actualizing what makes human beings different from animals and human beings as human beings. Mencius spoke very clearly about this point:

> Human beings as human beings, if having enough food and enough clothes, living comfortably without being educated, are similar to animals. The saints worried about this and sent Qi (契) to teach them human ethical relations—the blood relations between father and sons, the righteousness between monarchy and subjects, the difference between husband and wife, the superiority and inferiority between the elder and young, the honesty among friends.[42]

Finally, from the point of view of the principles of good and evil, Confucianism, Mohism, Christianity, and Kant all agree that all actions of benefiting oneself as an end are harmful to others and the perfection of one's own moral character, violating the goal of morality, therefore are immoral, evil, and are the actions of base persons; and that only the actions of selflessly benefiting others are beneficial to others and the perfection of the moral character of the self, conforming to the goal of morality, thence are moral and good, and the actions of the noble men. Therefore, Confucius said: "What virtuous man knows is righteousness; the base person keeps his mind only on his own interests."[43] The Mohist school said, "virtue is: what you do is not for your own fame and benefits; if what you do is for your own fame and benefits then it is deceit, like a theft."[44] The Bible says: "Let no man seeks his own, but every man another's wealth."[45] Kant also wrote: "This completely unrestricted legislator ... judges the actions of rational things only in the light of their selflessness, and only in terms of the idea of giving them dignity."[46] In a word, selflessly benefiting others is the only standard for the measurement of the good and evil of actions.

It can be seen that theories on the general principle of morality advocated by Confucianism, Mohism, Christianity, and Kant are almost completely consistent with the basic view of altruism advocated by Comte and Hutcheson, so it is no more appropriate to term their theories altruism: altruism is the theory of general principle of morality regarding *selflessly benefiting others* as the only standard for evaluating the good and evil of actions. The differences among Confucianism, Mohism, Christianity, and Kant are the internal differences of altruism, which can be attributed to a difference between whether love has degrees: Confucianism is the altruism which advocates that *love has degrees*, the closer one is to me the more I love, thus I ought to love my parents more than loving the parents of others; while Mohism and Christianity are the altruism which advocate that love has no degrees and all people should be loved equally, regardless of alienation or closeness, and therefore one's own parents and others' parents should be loved equally.

5.3.2 *Egoism: Rational egoism and individualism*

The so-called rational egoism, as is well known, is the theory of the general principle of morality which regards "benefiting others for self-interest" as the sole standard for evaluating the good and evil of actions. It matured in the eighteenth century and its acknowledged representatives are Helvetius, Holbach, Feuerbach, and Chernishevsky. However, Hobbes, Locke, and Bernard Mandeville and China's Laozi, Han Fei, Li Zhi, Gong Zizhen, Liang Qichao, and Chen Duxiu are undoubtedly also rational egoists.

First of all, from the point of view of the theory of human nature, rational egoism holds that everyone acts for the sake of self-interest: "every man works in his own way for his own happiness ... Admitting this, there is no one who can be selfless."[47]

Secondly, from the point of view of moral nature, rational egoism holds that the origin and goal of morality are completely heteronomous, and all for safeguarding the existence and development of society. Holbach said, "The public welfare is the end of virtue."[48] Liang Qichao also said: "The establishment of morality is for the people's interests."[49]

Finally, from the principle of good and evil, since the goal of morality is only to safeguard the existence and development of society, only the actions that are beneficial to others conform to the goal of morality, are moral and good; while only the actions that harm others are immoral and evil. So, Claude Helvetius said, "The public welfare is the standard of the good of human actions."[50] And Liang Qichao said: "The actions that are beneficial to people are good, while the actions that are not beneficial to people are bad, this standard can be applied all over the world and be followed generation to generation."[51]

In this way, rational egoism not only negates the principle of "selflessly benefiting others" or "purely benefiting others" but also the principle of "mere self-interest," regarding "benefiting others for self-interest" as the only standard for evaluating the good and evil of actions. Holbach concluded this standard as: "Virtue is but the art of making yourself happy with the welfare of others."[52] Therefore, the so-called rational egoism, in the final analysis, is a theory on the general principle of morality which regards benefiting others for self-interest as the sole standard for evaluating the good and evil of behaviors.

In contrast to rational egoism, individualism is a theory on the general principle of morality which is confusing, bizarre, and contrary to common sense, and perhaps as a result, individualists are far fewer than rational egoists. The well-known representatives of the theory of this general principle of morality are ancient Chinese philosophers Yang Zhu and Chuang-tzu, as well as modern Western philosophers Nietzsche, Heidegger, and Sartre.

Firstly, from the point of view of human nature, individualism also believes that the ends of everyone's actions can only be for the self. Yang Zhu said, "the self is the end of one's life, while everything else in the world is the means for the self."[53] And Nietzsche said, "there is no selfless actions."[54] Then, by what means can a person achieve his ends for himself? Individualism holds that society, collectivity, and others cannot be relied upon. Why? In the view of Yang Zhu, what society, the collectivity, and others have given me is nothing but the external fame and things, for which I take a "risk of being harmed and being killed," which is similar to "being beheaded in exchange for a hat and being killed in exchange for a piece of clothes"?[55] Nietzsche, Heidegger, and Sartre have the same view, except that the argument is not so vivid and intuitive, but rather a famous theory of alienation: as long as one lives in society, one cannot but lose his freedom and be at the mercy of others. Thus, what is created is the self chosen by others, that is, the self that has no unique personality; but not the self that is self-selected, not the self with unique personality: others and society are the root of self-alienation.[56]

Secondly, in terms of moral nature, individualism holds that the origin and goal of morality are completely heteronomous, all for the promotion of self-interest, which Chuang Tzu made it very clear: "The true goal of morality is to protect oneself."[57] Nietzsche also wrote: "I have never met such a person who seems to believe in morality in this light, that is, to take morality as a problem which is his own personal need, distress, happiness, and passion."[58]

Finally, from the point of view of the principle of good and evil, individualism holds that any action by means of relying on others—whether it is harmful or beneficial to others—is really harmful to oneself, violating goal of morality and therefore is evil; only by relying on the self as a means, that is, neither giving nor taking, neither benefiting others nor harming others but purely self-interested, can be really beneficial to oneself and conform to the goal of morality and thus is good: "mere self-interest" is the only standard for evaluating the good and evil of actions. This standard is summed up by Yang Zhu as a famous saying: "Never lose a piece of hair for the welfare of the world." Chuang Tzu extended that as: "Those who benefit others for their fame will bring harm to themselves, and those who harm others will be punished. One ought neither benefit others nor harm others. Only mere self-interest can protect oneself."[59] By the twentieth century, Nietzsche also said: "I live in my own light, and I absorb the flames from me."[60] The protagonist Logentine, who Sartre represented to show the moral principles he stands for in his novel *La nausea* is such a kind of person: "I live lonely and completely lonely, never talk with any others, receiving nothing and giving nothing."[61] In short, individualism is a theory on the general principle of morality that denies "selflessly benefiting others" and "benefiting others for self-interests" and regards "mere self-interest" as the sole standard of evaluating the good and bad of actions.

The similarities and differences between rational egoism and individualism show that, although they are opposed to each other, they are fundamentally identical, both being opposite to altruism, taking the action of self-interest as the sole purpose, starting point and ultimate destination, therefore both belonging to egoism: egoism is a theory on the general principle of morality holding that the ends of human actions can only be self-interested, thus negates *selflessly benefiting others* and takes *self-interest without harming others* as the sole standard for evaluating the good and evil of actions. Thus Paulson said, "Pure altruism asserts: It is not only allowable, but morally necessary to make individual welfare the sole end of action."[62] Therefore, the difference between rational egoism and individualism is the internal divergence of egoism, which, in the final analysis, lies only in asserting with what means to actualize the end of self-interest.

Rational egoism advocates benefiting others for self-interest, which obviously is in line with the social nature of human beings, and thus is reasonable, rational, and logical, and therefore can be termed as rational egoism. On the contrary, individualism advocates *mere self-interest* which neither benefits others nor harms others, which is obviously against the social nature of human beings, so is unreasonable, irrational, and not logical, and thus is irrational egoism. In the view of Brian Medlin, a modern Western ethicist, both of them are actually two contradictory lower concepts belonging to the category of egoism, thus forming the whole extension of egoism. However, he called individualism "individual egoism" and rational egoism "universal egoism," as he puts it:

> Universal egoism maintains that everyone ought to look after his own interests and to disregard those of other people except in so far as their interests contribute towards his own. Individual egoism is the attitude that the egoist is going to look after himself and no one else.[63]

5.3.3 Egoism: Psychological egoism and ethical egoism

Individualism and rational egoism are the external classification of egoism; on the contrary, psychological egoism, and ethical egoism (i.e., normative egoism) are the internal structure of egoism. The so-called psychological egoism is the theory considering that everyone's ends of action can only be self-interested while ethical egoism or normative egoism is the theory considering that people ought morally to pursue only their self-interest, as Joel Feinberg puts it:

> egoism takes either a psychological or a normative form. Psychological egoism is the view that people are by nature egoistic, that is, they are by nature motivated to pursue only their self-interest ... Normative egoism ... the view that people ought morally to pursue only their self-interest.[64]

It is obvious that psychological egoism and ethical egoism are only the internal structure of the ideological system of egoism: psychological egoism is a theory about the objective nature of the facts of human actions—it takes a behavioral view, while ethical egoism is based on psychological egoism but is a theory about the moral principles of human actions that ought to be—it takes a moral view. Because the establishment of ethical egoism depends entirely on whether psychological egoism can be established, the assertion can be made that if everyone's ends of action are not only self-interest, then everyone's ends of action no doubt should not only be self-interest.

Psychological egoism is untenable. Its error is to equate "the ends is to meet one's own needs" with "the ends is to benefit oneself" and to equate "the outcome of action" with "ends of action," which, in the view of contemporary Western ethicists, is the main basis for psychological egoism:

> Psychological egoism has seemed plausible to many people for a variety of reasons, of which the following are typical: a. "every action of mine is prompted by motives or desires or impulse which are *my* motives and not somebody else's." This fact might be expressed by saying that whenever I act I always pursuing my own ends or trying to satisfy my own desires. And from this we might pass on to—"I am always pursuing something for myself or seeking my own satisfaction." b. when a person gets what

he wants he characteristically feels pleasure. This has suggested to many people that what we really want in every case is our own pleasure.[65]

Indeed, everyone's ends of action are to satisfy his needs and desires. However, one's own needs (desires) include one's needs (desires) of self-love and self-interest, as well as one's needs (desires) of loving others and benefiting others. Thus, "satisfying one's own needs" is divided into "satisfying one's own needs of self-interest" and "satisfying one's needs of benefiting others." Obviously, "satisfying one's own needs of self-interest" is self-interested and belongs to the category of the action of ends of self-interest, while "satisfying one's own needs of benefiting others" is for the sake of others and belongs to the category of action of selflessly benefiting others. Therefore, "the ends are to meet one's own needs" is fundamentally different from "the ends are to benefit oneself." The sophistry of psychological egoism is to equate these two seemingly externally similar but internally different concepts and to thus draw the wrong conclusion from the correct premise that "everyone's ends of action is to satisfy his own needs": that everyone's ends of action are for oneself, for one's own pleasure, for avoiding pain, and all for self-interest.

It is true that one will be happy if one actualizes one's satisfaction of the needs and desires in selflessly benefiting others, and will feel pain if one fails to do so. But his ends of action are not to get his own pleasure and to avoid his own pain: his pleasure and pain are only the outcome of his actions, while the ends of his actions are to make others happy and avoid pain. For example, a virtuous person who hears people cry out for help in a house which is on fire would be very anxious. If he rushes into the fire and saves people one would be very happy; if he ignores the suffering cries of the victims and does nothing he would feel great pain. This pleasure or pain is clearly the outcome of his action, not the ends of the action, for it is absurd to say that the purpose of risking one's life to save the life of others is for one's pleasure and avoid any feeling of pain afterwards such as guilt or self-blame! The mistake of psychological egoism is to equate the result of the action with the ends of action, from the right premise that the outcomes of the action of selflessly benefiting others is to make oneself happy, it draws the wrong conclusion: that all ends of action are for one's own pleasure and self-interest.

5.3.4 The doctrine of benefiting self-other interests: The unity of altruism and egoism

The antagonism between egoism and altruism shows their respectively one-sidedness and error. Therefore, a theory on general principles of morality which overcomes the one-sidedness and errors of the two and unifies them came into being, which might be called "*the doctrine of benefiting self-other interests*," taking both *selflessly benefiting others* and *self-interest without harming others* (*benefiting others for self-interest* and *mere self-interest*) as the general principles of morality of evaluating the good and evil of actions. The doctrine of *benefiting self-other interests* has greatly matured as a system of thought with a huge camp of scholars behind it. Its representative figures are Spinoza, Diderot, Hume, Rousseau, Third Earl of Shaftesbury, Bentham, Mill, Sidgwick, Godwin, Marx, and Engels. But the creators of *the doctrine of benefiting self-other interests* as a mature system of thought which can compete with altruism and egoism are Freud and Freudians such as Fromm, as well as Darwin and Darwinians such as Hixly, Haeckle, Dawkins, and Wilson.

First of all, as far as a theory of human nature is concerned, the doctrine of *benefiting self-other interests* is contrary to egoism and consistent with altruism, holding that the ends of everyone's actions may selflessly benefit others. However, the doctrine of *benefiting self-other interests* overcomes altruism's mistake of believing that one may be constantly and completely selfless and further reveals that most ends of everyone's actions certainly is self-love and self-interest: "We may ask whether in the operation of our mental apparatus a main purpose can be detected, and we may reply as a first approximation that that purpose is directed to obtaining pleasure."[66]

Secondly, from the point of view of the theory of moral nature, the doctrine of *benefiting self-other interests* is opposite to the altruism's theory of the autonomy of the goal of morality, and consistent with that of egoism, holding that the goal of morality is heteronomous. However, egoism is a one-sided theory of the heteronomy of the goal of morality: rational egoism holds that the goal of morality is only for the existence and development of society, while individualism thinks that the goal of morality is only to promote self-interest. On the contrary, the doctrine of *benefiting self-other interests* is a comprehensive theory of the heteronomy of the goal of morality which is to safeguard the existence and development of society and promote everyone's interests. In summing up Darwin's theory of the heteronomy of the origin and goal of morality, Huxley wrote:

> Laws and moral precepts are directed to the end of curbing the cosmic process and reminding the individual of his duty to the community, to the protection and influence of which he owes, if not existence itself, at least the life of something better than a brutal savage.[67]

Finally, in terms of the theory of the principle of good and evil, the doctrine of *benefiting self-other interests* points out that both self-interest and benefiting others are good for they conform to the goal of morality—safeguarding the existence and development of society and promoting everyone's interests, while self-harming and harming others are evil for they violate the goal of morality: "'good' is what is good for man and 'evil' is what is detrimental to man; the sole criterion of ethical value being man's welfare."[68] Altruism denies self-love and self-interest and egoism denies *love for others*, which exaggerate their one-sided truth and slide to the two extremes of fallacy: the truth lies in the unity of the two which is the general principle of morality that

Good: General principles of morality   169

regards both "selflessly benefiting others" and "self-interest without harming others" as an evaluation of the good or evil of actions. So, Fromm said:

> The logical fallacy in the notion that love for others and love for oneself are mutually exclusive should be stressed. If it is a virtue to love my neighbor as a human being, it must be a virtue—and not a vice—to love myself since I am a human being.[69]

5.3.5 The comparison of truth and falsehood as well as the excellence and inferiority of altruism, egoism, and the doctrine of benefiting self-other interests

Truth and falsehood, as well as the excellence and inferiority of altruism, egoism, and the doctrine of *benefiting self-other interests*, in the final analysis, obviously depends on the degree of conformity of the three with their research objects—namely "the behavioral fact," "the goal of morality," and "the behavioral ought." Let's again consider what my previous analysis of these objects have revealed.

First of all, as far as human nature is concerned, on the one hand, all ethical behavior consists of six large types: *selflessly benefiting others, benefiting others for self-interest, mere self-interest, pure self-harm, harming others for self-interest,* and *purely harming others*; on the other hand, everyone certainly constantly benefits others out of self-interest or harms others out of self-interest, but only occasionally selflessly benefits others, occasionally acts out of *mere self-interest*, occasionally purely harms others and occasionally purely self-harms. Secondly, from the point of view of moral nature, morality is a necessary bad, so its origin and goal are heteronomous: the direct goal of morality is to safeguard the existence and development of society and the interest community; the ultimate goal of morality is to promote the interests of everyone. Finally, in terms of the principle of good or evil of action, selflessly benefiting others, benefiting others for self-interest, and *mere self-interest* are all good for they conform to the goal of morality: *selflessly benefiting others* is the highest principle of good, and is only occasional, *benefiting others out of self-interest* is the most fundamental principle of good, and is constant, and *mere self-interest* is the lowest principle of good, and is only occasional.

My theory can be called "new doctrine of *benefiting self-other interests*," namely the doctrine of *benefiting self-other interests* featured with "16 kinds and four laws of behavior and six principles of good and bad." My theory can be called the new doctrine of *benefiting self-other interests*, namely the doctrine of *benefiting self-other interests* featured with "16 kinds and four laws of behavior and six principles of good and evil." In putting forward this analysis, one can declare that the doctrine of *benefiting self-other interests* undoubtedly is the truth, since altruism and egoism both fall into two extremes of error as exaggerated one-sided truths.

The error of altruism is revealed in three ways. First, judging from a theory of human nature, it is mainly "a theory that exaggerates selflessly benefiting others": it is an exaggeration of the fact that one's end of actions can occasionally selflessly benefit others in its attempt to obliterate the fact that constant ends can only be self-interest, thence mistakes that the ends of human action as being ideally constantly selfless or even completely selfless. Second, judging from the theory of moral nature, it is mainly "a theory of the autonomy of the origin and goal of morality," which mistakenly thinks that the origin and goal of morality are for morality itself, aiming at the perfection of everyone's moral character. Thirdly, judging from the theory of principle of good and evil, it mainly exaggerates the ends of self-interest as being the source of all evil, obliterating that aspect of the ends of self-interest which is a source of good, thence regarding the purpose of self-interest, which is good in itself, as evil and the source of all evils. Inevitably, it is one-sided when it comes to the problem of the principle of good and evil: denying that benefiting others out of self-interest and mere self-interest mistakenly takes selflessly benefiting others as the sole standard for the evaluation of whether actions are moral.

The error of egoism is also revealed in three ways. First, as far as the theory of human nature is concerned, it exaggerates that the constant ends of each individual's action can only be self-interest, obliterating any possibility of selflessly benefiting others as ends of individual action, thus mistakenly thinking that the ends of each individual's action can only be selfish. Second, in terms of the theory of moral nature, egoism, which holds that the goal of morality is heteronomous, is a truth. But rational egoism exaggerates the social goal of morality, mistakenly holding that the goal of morality is only to safeguard the existence and development of society, while individualism exaggerates the individual goal of morality, mistakenly holding that the goal of morality is only to promote self-interest. Third, in regard to the theory of the principle of good and evil the error of egoism is mainly its denial of "selflessly benefiting others" and its mistaking "self-interest without harming others" as the sole standard for the evaluation of whether an action is moral; rational egoism mistakes "benefiting others out of self-interest" as the sole standard, while individualism mistakes "mere self-interest" as the sole standard.

It can be seen that altruism and egoism separately exaggerate the one-sided truth of the "two large types of ends of actions of benefiting others and self-interest" and three principles of the good of "selflessly benefiting others," "benefiting others out of self-interest," and "mere self-interest." Altruism exaggerates the occasional ends of action (for others) and the occasional and non-fundamental principle of good (selflessly benefiting others), obliterating the constant ends (for oneself), and the constant and fundamental principle of good (benefiting others out of self-interest); thus it is a truth in regard to the occasional and non-fundamental aspect, it is a fallacy that this is a constant and fundamental aspect. On the contrary, egoism exaggerates the constant ends (for oneself) and the constant and fundamental principle of the good (benefiting others for self-interest), obliterating the occasional ends of

Good: General principles of morality 171

action (for others) and the occasional and non-fundamental principle of the good (selflessly benefiting others); thus while it is a truth in regard to the constant and fundamental aspect, it is a fallacy in regard to the occasional and non-fundamental aspect. Therefore, though egoism and altruism are both fallacies, their degrees are different: the error of the former is slight and the latter is serious.

On the one hand, the error of altruism is serious because it violates everyone's desires and freedom the most: it violates or denies all ends of self-interest and attempts in vain to make all human actions achieve selflessly benefiting others. On the other hand, altruism promotes society and everyone's interests the least, for it denies *self-interest as an end* and is against all pursuit of personal interests, thus blocking the most powerful source for the promotion of the interests of society and others. Therefore, in sum, as a morality that gives the greatest ratio of disadvantage to advantage, the morality of altruism extremely violates the ultimate standard of morality of "promoting everyone's quantum of interests" and hence is the worst morality.

Although the morality of egoism denies selflessly benefiting others so that under the circumstance of the conflict of interests it certainly will decrease self-sacrifice and increase the harming others for self-interest, its error is slight in comparison to the altruism; on the one hand, of the two moralities, it violates everyone's desires and freedom the least in that it merely denies everyone's desires and freedom for harming others; on the other hand, it rapidly promotes the interest of everyone and the whole of society. In that it advocates the principle of *benefiting others out of self-interest* and encourages the pursuit of all personal interests that are beneficial to others and society, it opens up the most powerful source of promoting the interests of society so that everyone's potential creativity can be fully realized. Therefore, in sum, the morality of egoism is the morality that gives everyone the greater ratio of advantage to disadvantage, and basically conforms to the ultimate standard of morality of "promoting everyone's quantum of interests." In view of this it is a relatively excellent morality.

The doctrine of *benefiting self-other interests* is the truth, which obviously means that the morality of the doctrine of *benefiting self-other interests* is an excellent morality. Indeed, on the one hand, the restriction of the morality of the doctrine of *benefiting self-other interests* on everyone's desires and freedom is completely correct and minimized: it only denies everyone's desires and freedom of harming others, and requires selflessly benefiting others only when no compromise is possible in the circumstance of conflicting interest. On the other hand, it is the most rapid means of promoting everyone's interests and the interests of society, because it not only advocates selflessly benefiting others but also encourages people's enthusiasm for self-sacrifice when no compromise is possible in the conflict of interests, thus minimizing harming others for self-interest. Furthermore, it advocates *benefiting others out of self-interest*, personal freedom, and the realization of the potential creativity of the self, affirming all actions of self-interest without harming others

172 *Moral value and moral norms*

and encouraging all pursuits of personal interests that are beneficial to society and others—as a result, it maximizes the opening of the source that promotes everyone's interests and the interests of society. Therefore, in sum, the morality of doctrine of *benefiting self-other interests* is the morality which gives everyone the greatest ratio of advantage to disadvantage, and completely conforms to the ultimate standard of morality of "increasing everyone's quantum of interests," thus is the best morality.

Notes

1 Fung Yulan: *Complete Works of Sansong Tang, Vol. 4*. Henan People's Publishing House, 1986, p. 98.
2 Exodus 21: 23–24, The Holy Bible, King James Version.
3 Charles Darwin: *Descent of Man and Selection in Relation to Sex*, John Murray, London, 1922, p. 187.
4 Adam Smith: *An Inquiry into the Nature and Causes of the Wealth of Nations, Vol. 2*. Clarendon Press, Oxford, 1979, p. 421.
5 Henry Sidgwick: *The Methods of Ethics*, Macmillan and Co., London, 1922, p. 413.
6 Ibid., p. 431.
7 Mencius: *Gaozi*.
8 Ibid.
9 Ibid.
10 Ibid.
11 Zhang Dainian: *The Outline of Chinese Philosophy*, China Social Sciences Press, 1982, p. 5.
12 Mencius: *Gaozi*.
13 Mencius: *Gongsun Chou*.
14 Mencius: *Gaozi*.
15 Xunzi: *The Evil of Human Nature*.
16 Zhang Dainian: *The Outline of Chinese Philosophy*, China Social Sciences Press, 1982, p. 5.
17 Mencius: *Gaozi*.
18 Xunzi: *Zhengming*.
19 Ibid.
20 Xunzi: *The Evil of Human Nature*.
21 Wang Chong: *On the Nature of Balance: Human Nature*.
22 Dong Zhongshu: *Spring and Autumn Propagation: Jade Cup*.
23 Yang Xiong: *On Law and Self-Cultivation*.
24 Wang Chong: *On the Nature of Balance: Human Nature*.
25 Dong Zhongshu: *Spring and Autumn Propagation: Jade Cup*.
26 Yang Xiong: *On Law and Self-Cultivation*.
27 Dong Zhongshu: *Spring and Autumn Propagation. Jade Cup*.
28 Han Yu: *The Inherent Human Nature*.
29 Zhang Dainian: *The Outline of Chinese Philosophy*, China Social Sciences Press, 1997, p. 87.
30 Friedrich Paulsen: *System of Ethics*, trans. Frank Thilly. Charles Scribner's Sons, New York, 1899, p. 379.

Good: General principles of morality 173

31 Zhou Fucheng (ed.): *Selected Works on Western Ethics, Vol. 1*. Commercial Press, Beijing, 1954, p. 792.
32 Friedrich Paulsen: *System of Ethics*, trans. Frank Thilly. Charles Scribner's Sons, New York, 1899, p. 379.
33 Guo Moruo: *Ten Thesis on Criticism*, People's Publishing House, 1959, p. 213.
34 Mozi: *Universal Love.*
35 Corinthians: XIII.
36 Kant: *The Principle of Moral Metaphysics*, Shanghai People's Publishing House, 1986, p. 50.
37 Ibid., p. 51
38 Gliuga: *Biography of Kant*, China Social Sciences Press, 1981, p. 300.
39 Genesis 17:1.
40 Immanuel Kant: *Critique of Practical Rationality*, Commercial Press, Beijing, 1960, p. 87.
41 Mozi: *Universal Love.*
42 Mencius: *Tengwen Gong.*
43 *The Analects of Confucius: Liren.*
44 Tan Qifu: *Classification of the Mohist Classic*, p. 196.
45 Corinthians, X.
46 Immanuel Kant: *The Principle of Moral Metaphysics*, Shanghai People's Publishing House, 1986, p. 56.
47 Paul Anly Holbach: *The System of Nature, Vol. 1.* Commercial Press, 1964, p. 271.
48 Compiled by Peking University: *French Philosophy in the 18th Century*, Commercial Press, Beijing, 1957, p. 465.
49 Liang Qichao: *The Ice Chamber Album, Vol. 3.* p. 11.
50 Zhou Fucheng, ed.: *Selected Works on Western Ethics*, Commercial Press, 1954, p. 54.
51 Liang Qichao: *The Ice Chamber Album, Vol. 3.* p. 15.
52 Paul Anly Holbach: *The System of Nature, Vol. 1.* Commercial Press, 1964, p. 287.
53 *Lu's Spring and Autumn.*
54 Zhou Fucheng, ed.: *Selected Works on Western Ethics*, Commercial Press, 1954, p. 815.
55 *Lu's Spring and Autumn.*
56 See Friedrich Nietzsche: *Morning Glow*, Section 491; Martin Heidegger: *Existence and Time*, 1987, p. 155; Liu Mingjiu: *Sartre Research*, China Social Sciences Press, 1981, p. 303.
57 Chuang Tzu: *Cherishing-life.*
58 Friedrich Nietzsche: *Science of Happiness*, China Peace Press, 1987, p. 260.
59 Chuang Tzu: *Cherishing-life.*
60 Friedrich Nietzsche: *Charastura Says So*, Culture and Art Press, 1987, p. 29.
61 Jean-Paul Sartre: *Aversion and Others*, Shanghai Translation Publishing House, 1987, p. 36.
62 Friedrich Paulsen: *System of Ethics*, trans. Frank Thilly, Charles Scribner's Sons New York, 1899, p. 379.
63 Louis P. Pojman: *Ethical Theory: Classical and Contemporary Readings*, Wadsworth, Belmont, CA, 1995, p. 74.
64 Lawrence C. Becker: *Encyclopedia of Ethics, Vol. II.* Garland Publishing, New York, 1992, p. 296.

174 *Moral value and moral norms*

65 Stevn M. Cahn and Peter Markie: *Ethics: History, Theory, and Contemporary Issues*, Oxford University Press, New York, Oxford, 1998, p. 558.
66 Sigmund Freud: *Introductory Lectures on Psycho-Analysis*, trans. James Strachey, W. W. Norton, New York, 1966, p. 443.
67 Thomas Henry Huxley: *Evolution and Ethics*, Cambridge University Press, digitally printed version, 2009, pp. 33–34.
68 Frich Fromm: *Man for Himself*, Routledge & Kegan Paul, 1948, p. 13.
69 Ibid., p. 128.

6 Justice and equality
Fundamental value standard of state institutions

Justice is not only a topical issue in the contemporary world, but also an interdisciplinary problem in ethics, politics, jurisprudence, and economics. The problem is so difficult that "When we look deeply into this face, trying to unravel the secrets behind its outward appearance, bewilderment is apt to befall us."[1] However, tracing back the theory of justice through the various accounts we can see that it is originally constituted by the following four aspects: "the general principle of justice," "the fundamental principle of justice," "the fundamental principle of social justice," and "the principle of equality." Clearly, a good starting point for solving the perplexities surrounding the theory of justice is a definitive explanation of the term.

6.1 The exchange of equal interests or harms: The general principle of justice

6.1.1 The definition of justice: The exchange of equal interests or harms

What is justice? Aristotle replied, "Justice is the sum of all virtues,"[2] which, when cited, is often equated with all that is "good," "ought," and "right." André Comte-Sponville wrote: "Justice, though not a substitute for any virtue, may include all other virtues."[3] These views simply are not tenable. Can justice include the two extremely important virtues advocated by Confucianism and Christianity—"benevolence" and "forgiveness"? Obviously it cannot. If a person gives a roadside beggar 1,000 yuan, the action itself is not a matter of justice but benevolence, which is beyond justice; similarly, not to retaliate against one's enemies on regaining power is not justice but forgiveness, which is higher than justice. This is why Smith's *The Theory of Moral Sentiments* and Hume's *A Treatise of Human Nature* both see justice not only as just one principle of morality, but also as opposed to benevolence, which "is less essential to the existence of society than justice." Smith writes, "Benevolence ... is less essential to the existence of society than justice."[4] According to Hume, "If every man had a tender regard for another, or if nature supplied abundantly all our wants and desires ... you render justice useless, by supplying its place with much nobler virtues, and more valuable blessings."[5]

We can, therefore, take it that justice is not "the sum of all virtues," not all *good*, all *ought*, and all *right*. Frankena is right in saying:

> Not everything that is right is just, and not everything that is wrong is unjust. Incest, even if it is wrong, can hardly be called unjust ... giving another person pleasure may be right, without its being properly just at all.[6]

Then, what kind of *good* is justice? What kind of *ought* is justice? What kind of *right* is justice? Plato answered: "Justice is the right reward for every man."[7] The Roman jurist Domitius Ulpianus also said: "Justice is the eternal will to give every man what he deserves."[8]

Both assertions were recognized by later thinkers as the classical definition of justice. Accordingly, justice is one's due, which is to give people what they deserve but not what they do not deserve: "It is universally considered just that each person should obtain that (whether good or evil) which he deserve; and unjust that he should obtain a good, or be made to undergo an evil, which he does not deserve."[9] For example, while it is just for the wicked to receive retribution for evildoing and for the good to be rewarded for good deeds; it is unjust if the wicked are rewarded and the good receive retribution. Elaborating on "the proper reward of justice," Plato wrote: "Justice is 'giving good to friends and evil to enemies.'"[10]

Obviously, the classic definition of justice in giving people what they deserve is right, but it is not clear enough for "deserve" is not a simple and straightforward concept: one may ask, what is "giving people their due"? Is it doing what ought to be done to people? Plato's answer was yes: "Justice is doing what should be done."[11] While this definition appears to equate *justice* with *ought*, *right*, and *good*, "doing what one should do to others" and "giving one's due," however, are by no means the same concept. Consider the statements "What John did for Jim is what Jim deserved" and "What John did for Jim is what he should have done for Jim." At a rough glance, there seems to be no difference. But when you examine it carefully they are very different. "John did for Jim what Jim deserved" must be related to Jim's previous actions: what John did for Jim is in return or exchange for what Jim had done before, so Jim deserved it. On the contrary, "what John did for Jim is what he should have done for Jim" does not have to be related to Jim's previous actions, it does not have to be in return for Jim's previous actions, so it does not have to be what Jim deserves, but just what John should do. For example, if Jim is taken ill in bed and John helps him with money, can we say, "what John did for Jim is what Jim deserved"? This depends on Jim's previous actions. If Jim had helped John before, we can say that "what John did for Jim is what Jim deserved," otherwise, it can only be said that "what John did for Jim is what he should have done for Jim."

Obviously, the word "deserves" certainly relates to previous good or bad actions of a person or persons: as a kind of return or exchange it is synonymous with the understanding of "justice is due." As Nietzsche had observed: "Exchange is the original characteristic of justice."[12] However, "returning small favors with big ones" or "returning big favors with small ones" are both a kind of return or exchange. But are these actions just? Do they "give people their due"? Clearly not. Then, what kind of actions of requiting or exchange does justice or giving people their due belong to? Aristotle has repeatedly said that justice is a kind of requiting or an exchange of things that are fair, equal or proportional in nature:

> Justice is the mean of gain and loss in involuntary communication, which is equal before and after intercourse.[13]
>
> In this respect, when justice is considered it is in fact based on equality "but not for all, only for those who are equal to each other." And when inequality is considered it is in fact based on what is just, "not for all, but for those who are unequal."[14]
>
> Since justice is equality, the equality based on proportion should be just, this ratio implies at least four terms ... "such as A:B, then C:D." For example, the more properties one has, the more tax one pays, and the less properties one has the less tax one pays; the more one works, the more one gains, the less one works, the less one gains.[15]
>
> Injustice lies in inequality ... where victimization and actions are distributed unequally [such as where one beats or kills a person or where one is beaten or killed by a person] a judge's efforts at justice are made by means of punishment, taking something from the perpetrator and restoring equality.[16]

All in all, Aquinas concludes,

> Justice is all about having an equal proportion between one internal activity and another.[17]

From these concise and profound discussions, it is not difficult to see that justice is an act of "good" for it is an exchange of equal interests or harms; and that injustice is an act of "evil" for it is an exchange of unequal interests or harms. For instance, the act of saving someone's life or the act of killing someone is not itself a matter of justice or injustice. If, however, A saves the life of B, and B happens to have once saved the life A, then it can be seen as an act of justice (an exchange of equal interests), because, at some level, the act can be attributed to A's gratitude for B; on the contrary, if A does nothing to save B it can be regarded as an act of injustice (an exchange of unequal interests). In this case, not only does A exhibit no gratitude for B saving his life in the past, B's unwillingness to save A's life can also be deemed an act of evil. Take another example. If A avenges the death of his father by killing B who had killed his father, it is an act of justice (an exchange of equal harms); if, however, A kills B because B insulted him, it is an act of injustice (an exchange of unequal harms), hence also an act of evil.

178 *Moral value and moral norms*

The definition that justice is the exchange of equal interests or harms can be confirmed by Hume's far-reaching theory on the origins of justice origins:

> Justice takes its rise from human conventions; and ... these are intended as a remedy to some inconveniences, which proceed from the concurrence of certain *qualities* of the human mind with the *situation* of external objects. The qualities of the mind are *selfishness* and *limited* generosity: And the situation of external objects is their *easy change*, join'd to their *scarcity* in comparison of the wants and desires of men.[18]

Why does Hume allude to a "lack of something" as the origin and premise of justice? Isn't it because the essence of justice is the exchange of equal interests and that lacking something such as wealth necessarily requires the equal exchange of interest? If wealth is not something wanted or desired because there is a great abundance of everything that one needs, there would be no need for petty exchanges of equal interests, and hence no need for justice. Why is it that selfishness and limited generosity are the origin and premise of justice? Isn't this because justice is both an exchange of equal interests and an exchange of equal harms, and that selfishness and limited generosity necessarily require an exchange of petty equal interests and an exchange of petty equal harms? If everyone loves others more than themselves, and acts in the interests of others more than for themselves, there is no need for the equal exchange of either interests or harms, and thus no need for the principle of justice. Therefore, to quote him in full, Hume went on to write:

> If every man had a tender regard for another, or if nature supplied abundantly all our wants and desires, that the envy of interest, which justice supposes, could no longer have place; nor would there be any occasion for these distinctions and limits of property and possession, which at present are in use among mankind. Increase to a sufficient degree the benevolence of man, or the bounty of nature, and you render justice useless, by supplying its place with much nobler virtues, and more valuable blessings.[19]

6.1.2 Justice, fairness and evenhandedness: The same concept

The definition that justice is an exchange of either equal interests or equal harms shows that justice, fairness, and evenhandedness are the same concepts given they all by definition stand for the exchange of either equal interests or equal harms. If the exchange of equal interests in which *good returns good* is justice, is not the exchange also one of fairness and impartiality? And if the exchange of equal harms in which *evil returns evil* is justice, is not the exchange also one of fairness and evenhandedness? On the matter of retributive justice, the Bible says: "If there any mischief follow, then thou shaft give life for life, eye for eye, tooth for tooth, hand for hand, foot for foot, burning for burning, stripe for stripe."[20] This kind of vengeance is just, but isn't it also fair and evenhanded?

Borrowing money then returning the money is just, but isn't it also fair and evenhanded? Borrowing money but not returning it is unjust, but isn't it also unfair? Trading in exchange for equal value is fair, but isn't it also just and evenhanded? Trading in exchange for unequal value is an unfair, but isn't it also one-sided and an unjust?

Not only that! If justice, fairness, and evenhandedness are not the same concepts, the serial of principles of justice are not the principles of fairness and the principles of evenhandedness: do they have a different set of principles?

- Exchange of either equal interests or equal harms.
- Rights and duties ought to be equal.
- Rights that society distributes to a person ought to be proportional to his contribution and equal to his duties.
- Basic rights ought to be fully equal and non-basic rights ought to be proportionately equal.
- Political liberty ought to be fully equal and political office ought to be proportionately equal.
- Distribution according to factors of production.
- Equality of opportunity.

Let's consider the above principles of justice: are they not also principles of fairness and impartiality? Does fairness and evenhandedness have a set of principles that are different from these? Not possible. This is not even the case with one of them! Can we think of a principle that can be called justice but is not regarded as fair and impartial? Not so! Even if justice, fairness, and evenhandedness are not exactly the same concepts, at least they are inseparable from each other. If each of them has a different set of principles, wouldn't they be in a mess and in stark contrast to the adage that "The greatest truths are the simplest"?

Although the concepts of justice, fairness, and evenhandedness are fundamentally the same they do differ in their applications as terms. The term justice is generally associated with dignified, important occasions, such as where the phrase "a just war" is a commonly evoked reference to a certain battle. One never hears the phrase "a fair war" or "an evenhanded war." The concepts of fairness and evenhandedness by contrast are mostly used in daily life. For example, we use fairness in business in reference to trading fairly and also in terms of the "fair trade" movement and its codes of practice. And more generally we use fairness in everyday life in reference to treating others fairly. Terms such as trading justly or just trade, and treating others justly, are seldom used, even though the expressions obviously have the same meaning. The term fairness is somewhere between justice and evenhandedness but given it can often have a more dignified tone than evenhandedness, we can say fairness is closer to justice. Nevertheless, where justice is limited in

180 *Moral value and moral norms*

its application, fairness can be applied to any situation and to any field. Yu Keping (俞可平) articulates the difference well. In his masterpiece *Rethinking Equality, Fairness and Justice*, a work which has the philosophical depth of Hegel and Marx, Keping writes:

> There is a division between a broad sense and narrow sense of "fairness." The broad sense of "fairness" is the abbreviation of fairness and justice, usually corresponding to justice in English; in a narrow sense, then, "fairness" is roughly equivalent to "justice," it means "fairness and integrity, without prejudice," or "fairness and decency, without selfishness," which usually corresponds to fairness and impartiality.[21]

However, Yu Keping does not think that concepts of justice, fairness, and evenhandedness are the same: it is only

> [s]ince Rawls first published *Justice as Fairness* in 1985, and especially since the publication of his work *A Theory of Justice*, [that] the concepts of "fairness" and "justice" have been inextricably linked in the western world and started to gain currency in the academic community.[22]

As a matter of fact, Rawls' so-called "justice as fairness" does not imply that fairness and justice have been treated as two different concepts nor does it suggest that there exists justice that is not fairness. To reiterate my earlier point, where is there justice that is not fairness? Let's consider, then, exactly Rawls means by "justice as fairness."

It turns out that Rawls inherited the tradition of moral contract theory believing that justice and other moral principles are just contracts, while the correct moral principle of justice and other principles can only be the contract that is agreed to in an equal, fair, original position. He therefore called the principle of justice agreed upon in the original position of fairness "justice as fairness," and the principle of rightness agreed upon in the original position of fairness "rightness as fairness":

> The original position is, one might say, the appropriate initial status quo, and thus the fundamental agreements reached in it are fair. This explains the propriety of the name "justice as fairness": it conveys the idea that the principles of justice are agreed to in an initial situation that is fair.
> [23] Obviously if justice as fairness succeeds reasonably well, a next step would be to study the more general view suggested by the name "rightness as fairness."[24]

Clearly, what Rawls calls "justice as fairness" is not "fair justice"—so that fairness and justice are two different concepts—but rather an abridgment of the "principle of justice agreed to in the initial state of fairness"; similarly what he called "rightness as justice" is not "fair rightness" but the abridgment of "principle of rightness agreed to in the initial state of fairness."

In short, the concepts of justice, fairness, and evenhandedness are the same but are applicable to different fields concerning the exchanges of either equal interests and equal harms. The applied field of justice, fairness and evenhandedness that we have studied is mainly the value standard of the goodness or badness of state institutions, which Rawls calls "the first virtue of social institutes."[25] As an extremely important area of philosophical inquiry, the term "justice" most appropriately encapsulates the essence of the Rawls' work: hence the title *A Theory of Justice*, not *A Theory of Fairness* or *A Theory of Impartiality*.

6.1.3 Types of justice: Distributive justice and retributive justice

Justice is the exchange of either equal interests or equal harms, which obviously means that justice has both positive and negative sides: adopting the justice terms of Hugo Grotius and Schopenhauer, the exchange of equal interests is "positive justice" and the exchange of equal harms is "negative justice."[26] Negative justice is also so-called retributive justice. Mill writes: "evil for evil, is not only included within the idea of Justice ... but is a proper object of that intensity of sentiment which places the human estimation above the simply expedient."[27]

No doubt any justice is a kind of good, and belongs to the category of moral good. But the exchange of equal harms has an end which belongs to states of action of vengeances, retaliation, and harming others: how can it be a moral good? Indeed, an exchange of equal harms alone is not good but evil. As Mill said regarding retaliation, "sentiment, in itself, has nothing moral in it."[28] However, in terms of its results, an exchange of equal harms is a greater good, for although a person who harms others will suffer equal harm, which is evil-in-itself, such penalties prevent people from harming each other; thus, it conforms to the goal of morality and benefits society through the promotion of equal interests. Therefore, the exchange of equal harms, in terms of the net balance of good-in-result over evil-in-itself, is undoubtedly good and moral, not vicious and immoral. So, writes Mill:

> There goes to the composition of sentiment, not a rational only but also an animal element, the thirst for retaliation; and this thirst derives its intensity, as well as its moral justification, from the extraordinarily important and impressive kind of utility which is concerned. The interest involved is that of security, to everyone's feelings the most vital of all interests.[29]

If an exchange of equal harms is an extremely important moral good, is it more important and more fundamental than another type of justice—an exchange of equal interests? The value and significance of exchanges of equal harms are to avoid harming each other, while the value and significance of exchanges of equal interests are to achieve mutual interests. In this way, the question of which of the two—the principle of the exchange of equal harms and the exchange of equal interests—is more fundamental and important, in the final analysis, lies in the question of which of the two—avoiding mutual harm and achieving mutual benefit—is more fundamental and important. Gilbert Harman believes that the former is more fundamental and more important. As he put: "in our morality avoiding harm to others is taken to be more important than helping those who need help."[30]

Harman's view is untenable because, on the one hand, qualitatively speaking, the so-called society, as Rawls put it, is just "a system of cooperation designed to advance the good of those taking part in it."[31] People make connections and establish societies for mutual interests but not for avoiding harms: harming one another is a kind of side effect of social cooperation and interpersonal connections. On the other hand, from a quantitative point of view, the actions of harming each other in the total actions of the whole society surely are less than that of mutual interests. Otherwise, harms arising from social cooperation and interpersonal relations would be greater than the interests they obtain, tearing away at the fabric of society. Therefore, the principle of justice of the "exchange of equal interests" aimed at achieving mutual interests is more fundamental and important than the principle of justice of the "exchange of equal harms" aimed at avoiding harming each other. Thus, can we say that all exchanges of equal interests are the most fundamental and the most important justice?

No! This is because many exchanges of equal interests such as "if you give me a peach I'll give you a plum" or "if you give me a pair of boots I'll give you a pair of gloves" and so on, obviously count for little. Exchanges of equal interests are only more fundamental and important than the exchanges of equal harms because the most fundamental and most important kinds of justice are kinds of exchanges of equal interests, not kinds of exchanges of equal harms: exchanges of equal harms belong to the category of justice which is less important and fundamental than equal interests. Then, what kind of exchange of equal interests is the most fundamental and most important justice? Mill's answer is: "the essence of the idea of justice, [is] that of a right residing in an individual."[32] And according to Rawls: "The primary subject of justice is the basic structure of society, or more exactly, the ways in which the major social institutes distribute fundamental rights and duties."[33]

Both views are so right! The most fundamental exchanges of interests worldwide undoubtedly are the exchanges of rights and duties: these are the core issues of justice; the exchange of non-rights and non-duties is a non-fundamental issue of justice. More precisely, non-fundamental justice is not concerned with the exchange of rights and duties. For example, one has rights as a child to be nurtured by parents but in later life one has a duty to support their ageing parents. As a reversal of rights and duties, this type of exchange is fundamental justice. On the other hand, if one gives money to help a former benefactor who is in trouble, it cannot be said that this is fulfilling one's duties. It is rather a kind of exchange of equal interests which has nothing to do with rights and duties. This type of exchange is non-fundamental justice.

Exchanges of equal interests and exchanges of equal harms, as well as fundamental justice and non-fundamental justice, are obviously classified according to the nature of the actions of justice itself. If it is not based on the nature of the action of justice—but on the nature of the agent of justice— then justice can be divided into individual justice and social justice: individual justice is the justice where the subject of the action is an individual; it is the action of exchange of equal interests or harms by an individual, such as John reciprocating good for a good, or exacting an eye for an eye, and so on; social justice is the justice where the subject of action is society; it is the exchanges of equal interests or harms of society, such as a borrower paying off money to a creditor or sentencing a killer to pay with his life. As for this classification of justice, Adler makes it quite clear:

> The domain of justice is divided into two main spheres of interests. One is concerned with the justice of the individual in relation to other human beings and to the organized community itself—the state. The other is concerned with the justice of the state—its form of government and its laws, its political institutions and economic arrangements—in relation to the human beings that constitute its population.[34]

If we link social justice with individual justice, as well as the fundamental justice with non-fundamental justice, we can see that the fundamental principle of justice is social justice instead of individual justice. This is because fundamental justice is built on exchanges of rights and duties distributed by society, not an exchanges between individuals. Thus, so-called fundamental justice belongs to the "justice of social distribution." Since society is usually represented by special individuals who represent the will of society, such as the leaders, administrators, or rulers of society (i.e., kings, presidents, various executive, and judicial officers, and so on), so-called social justice, in fact, is the justice of governance.

However, a square and a circle cannot be made without a ruler and compass. Social governance (or the types of management associated with it) is the realization of behavioral norms—power norms (law) and non-power norms (morality). Therefore, social justice, in the final analysis, concerns the norms of social behaviors, that is, the justice of institutions. This is because so-called institutions, according to the likes of Rawls, Douglas C. North, and Commons, are none other than systems of norms of conduct established or recognized by society, namely its laws and moral systems:

Rawls asserts, "by an institute I shall understand a public system of rules."[35] In North's view, an "[i]nstitution is a set of regulations that governs individual behavior in the pursuit of maximum wealth or personal utility, following procedural and ethical codes of conduct."[36] And Commons says, "It seems that the institution can be likened to a building, a structure of laws and regulations in which individuals, like the occupants of a house, operate."[37]

Thence social justice can be summed up as the "justice of governance" and as the "justice of institutions." It is not difficult to see that the justice of institutions determine the justice of governance; that the justice of governance expresses the justice of institutions. The justice of institutions is the major part of social justice since it is decisive, fundamental, and as comprehensive; the justice of governance is the minor part of social justice since it is determined, non-fundamental, and not as comprehensive. As Deng Xiaoping said:

> Good institutions can prevent evil people from doing anything evil at will, and bad institutions can inhibit good people from doing enough good, or even vice versa. Even a great man like Comrade Mao Zedong was so badly affected by some bad institutions that he had caused great misfortunes to the Party and to the state, including to himself—this by no means is to say that he himself is not responsible for that, but rather to say that the system of leadership, the system of the organization are more fundamental and long-term.[38]

Therefore, justice, fundamentally speaking, is mainly social justice, a justice of governance rather than individual justice; but, in the final analysis, it is the justice of institutions rather than the justice of governance, namely, the justice concerned with the distributive institutions of rights and duties. Thus, Rawls repeatedly stressed:

> The principle of social justice is the basic structure of society, the arrangement of major social institutions into one scheme of cooperation. We have seen that these principles are to govern the assignment of rights and duties in these institutions and they are to determine the appropriate distributions of the benefits and burdens of social life.[39]

In summary, we can see that though the problem of justice is very complicated, at core, it is nothing but the justice in which rights and duties are exchanged, after all, it is the justice of distributive institutions for everyone's rights and duties: the justice of distributive institutions is the most fundamental and most important justice. Since Aristotle, justice had been simply summed up as two main types: distributive justice and retributive justice. However, in the 1960s scholars began to pay attention to the process or the means of the realization of all justice, especially to the relationship between the justice of means of actions and the justice of ends of actions, respectively referred to as procedural justice and substantive justice. These are complex and intractable types of justice which classical thinkers since Aristotle had failed to enquire about.

6.1.4 Types of justice: Procedural justice and substantive justice

The relationship between "procedural justice" and "substantive justice," otherwise called "the justice of outcome," is that of the relationship between the "justice of means and the justice of ends" What is procedure? According to Ji Weidong, "from a legal point of view, the word *procedure* mainly reflects the process of making legal decisions in a certain order, manner and step."[40] That is to say, legal procedure belongs to the category of the behavioral process. Indeed, procedure, as its name implies, is a sequence of process, a process of action with certain order. On the contrary, without a certain order of process of actions, it is only a process of action and not called a procedure. For example, my sports activities every morning are running and swimming, but it is not certain whether I will swim or run as my first sporting activity. My sporting activities are not so much a procedure as they are a mere process of actions without a certain order. However, if every morning I run first and then swim, my morning exercises would be a sequence of actions called my "morning exercise procedure": running first and then swimming.

A behavioral process has a certain order, not only a time order, but also a spatial order or arrangement. For example, a trial process can only be conducted by the court, which cannot be interfered with by any other institutes. This is one of the so-called just legal procedures of a trial. It is not time order, but the spatial correlation of the subjects of legal acts and the spatial order or arrangement of a trial process. The spatial order or arrangement of the behavioral process of a trial can also be expressed as the choice of various specific behavioral forms. For example, what form of a trial process takes, whether it is a public or secret trial, also has a kind of legal procedure. Therefore, in a word, procedure is a behavioral process with a certain time and spatial sequence: "We can preliminarily generalize 'legal proceedings' as the legal temporal and spatial steps and methods that people must follow or perform in carrying out legal acts."[41]

While so-called procedural justice is a justice concerning behavioral process, a behavioral process with a certain sequence of time and space, the justice concerning the outcome of the action caused by the behavioral process is often literally referred to as the justice of outcome or as substantive justice. For example, acknowledgments such as "No one ought to be a judge in his own case" and "one ought to hear the views of both parties" are the principles of justice in the trial process and thus belong to the category of procedural justice. Such processes of a trial may lead to the just outcome of the "conviction of the guilty person and the immunity of the innocent person from criminal prosecution," which is the justice of the outcome of the trial and belongs to the category of the justice of outcome or substantive justice. As Anpei Taniguchi wrote:

> When we say, "justice has no social distinction between the rich and the poor" we are talking about substantive justice. Here we focus on the final

outcome, not the process of achieving it. Conversely, if we talk about the process, it leads to procedural justice.[42]

But why do we call the justice of outcome substantive justice? What is the relationship between procedural justice and the justice of outcome or substantive justice?

First of all, any procedure or process of actions intended to achieve a certain outcome of action, is undoubtedly the means and method to achieve the expected outcome of action: the procedure or the process of action is the means, while the expected outcome of action is the ends. Therefore, procedural justice is a justice of means, and the justice of outcome is a kind of justice of ends. For example, "no one ought to be a judge in his own case" falls under the procedural justice of the trial, and "the conviction of the guilty and the immunity of the innocent from criminal prosecution" is the justice of outcome of the trial: the former is clearly a justice of means while the latter is a justice of ends.

Secondly, the means or methods are undoubtedly derived from and attached to the ends in that they are produced and determined by the ends: the ends are the source and the substance, while the means or methods are a product of the ends. In this way, the relationship between a procedure or a process of action and the outcome of action it aims at is a relationship of *dependence* and substance. Thus, the justice of outcome is a kind of substantive justice, while procedural justice is a kind of dependent justice, which is why Bentham called procedural law "subsidiary law" as opposed to "substantive law" in its pursuit of the justice of outcome, and why we now call the justice of outcome substantive justice.

Finally, the means of action are external and visible, belonging to the category of forms and phenomena; the ends of action are internal, invisible and belong to the category of content and essence. Therefore, procedural justice, as a justice of means, is a formal justice concerned with the visibility or transparency of its procedures, while the justice of outcome, as the justice of ends, is a justice concerned with content and essence. The relationship between procedural justice and the justice of outcome, as is well known, is summed up in an old legal maxim: "Justice must not only be done, but must be seen to be done." What is expressed in the first part of this maxim is the justice of outcome or ends which is an "invisible" kind of justice, whereas the latter part of the maxim is procedural justice, which is a "visible" kind of formal justice.

In sum, the relationship between procedural justice and the justice of outcome is that of the relationship between a "justice of means and justice of ends" (or that between subordinate justice and substantive justice, formal justice, and justice concerned with content). However, it must not be said that procedural justice and the justice of outcome are a relationship between *means* and *ends*. To be sure, procedures are a means that serves outcomes but is not a means to serve the justice of outcome. Take, for example, "the prohibition against the invasion of privacy." This principle of procedural justice is

Justice and equality 187

clearly not a means of achieving a justice of outcome. For, as is well known, the prohibition of the invasion of privacy can in many cases be an obstacle to the truth and achieving a justice of outcome. Then, why is procedural justice not a means of the justice of outcome?

Procedural justice is not the means of the justice of outcome: the internal value of procedural justice

Any procedure has both internal and external values: it has the "value of means and external value" which can achieve a certain outcome and end, and has "end value and intrinsic value," which in itself is able to meet human needs and itself is the end that people desire. For example, "the prohibition against the invasion of privacy" may be a bad procedure because criminals can exploit it, contrariwise leading to the "injustice of outcome": this is its value of means and external value. However, the procedure, on its own, protects the right of privacy of individuals, so it is still a just procedure. Indeed, procedural justice, which is independent of the outcome, can satisfy the needs of individuals by itself, which is the end that people desire: this is its end value and intrinsic value. It was Robert Summers, an American jurist, who first perceived the end value and intrinsic value of procedure and called the intrinsic value of procedure "procedural value": "Procedural value is the value standard by which we judge whether a legal procedure is a good procedure, independent of any 'good outcome effectiveness' that the process may have."[43]

Is, then, all procedural justice intrinsic value and end value of procedure? The answer is yes. It is clear that whether a procedure is just has nothing to do with whether the outcome is just. This is because a procedure such as the invasion of privacy is an unjust procedure no matter how just its outcome is, whereas the prohibition against the invasion of privacy is a just procedure, no matter how unjust the result is. Therefore, procedural justice is a value independent of the outcome of the procedure: it is not the utility of the procedure to the outcome, nor the value of the means and the external value which the procedure possesses for achieving a certain outcome; it is the intrinsic value of a procedure that itself can satisfy the moral needs of human beings, and is the end value the procedure possesses, which, in itself, is the end that people demand. As Anpei Taniguchi and Berles wrote: "procedural justice must be seen as an independent value."[44] "Even if the values of justice, dignity and participation do not improve the accuracy of the judgment, the legal procedure must uphold these values. We can call this method a consistent analysis method of the 'intrinsic value of procedure'."[45]

Thus, the evaluation of the goodness or badness of a procedure has double standards of value: if it can achieve the justice of outcome or substantive justice, it has good value of means and external value; if it is itself just, it has a good end value and intrinsic value. Obviously, a procedure is a really good procedure only if it can achieve the justice of outcome so as to have good value of means, and can itself be justice so as to have good intrinsic value. In

188   *Moral value and moral norms*

other words, only the procedural justice that can achieve the justice of outcome is a really good procedure; procedural justice that fails to achieve the justice of outcome is not a really good procedure. Therefore, we might ask, is procedural justice certain to achieve the justice of outcome? What is the relationship between procedural justice and the justice of outcome?

Procedural justice, as described above, is not the value of means or external value the procedure possesses that is capable of achieving a certain outcome; instead, it is the end value and intrinsic value the procedure possesses, which, in itself, is the end that people desire. Therefore, although procedure is a means that serves an outcome, procedural justice is not a means of serving the justice of outcome. Procedural justice is not a means to serve the justice of outcome, but is a moral restriction of the means or procedure which serves the justice of outcome: a procedure or means that serves the justice of outcome ought to be just, moral, and good instead of unjust, immoral, and bad. Since the essence of procedural justice is to achieve outcomes and ends that are just, good, and moral, we should adopt just, good, and moral means and procedures instead of unjust, bad, and immoral means or procedures. That is to say, though procedural justice is not the means of the justice of outcome, it can achieve a justice of outcome. But to what extent can procedural justice achieve a justice of outcome? Is it inevitable or accidental? Can it be achieved in most cases or in all cases?

Procedural justice, in most cases, certainly leads to justice of outcome

Rawls believes that some procedural justice, such as the one who cuts the cake is the last to get a share, certainly leads to a justice of outcome that is independent of the standard of procedural justice. He called it "perfect procedural justice." Other procedural justice does not necessarily lead to a justice of outcome that is independent of the standard of procedural justice, such as procedural justice in criminal trials, which he called "imperfect procedural justice." There are also some other types procedural justice, such as gambling procedural justice, that certainly lead to a justice of outcome that is not independent of the standard of procedural justice, which he calls "pure procedural justice."[46] However, Rawls' classification is unscientific because these three categories of procedural justice are based on two natures or standards, namely whether it must lead to the justice of outcome and whether the justice of outcome is independent of the standard of procedural justice, which obviously violates the principle that classifications can only be made based on the same nature or standard.

Furthermore, on closer inspection, the biggest drawback of Rawls' classification is that it fails to grasp the essential features of procedural justice. In terms of the relationship between procedural justice and the justice of outcome, the essential feature of procedural justice is statistical: procedural justices certainly lead to the justice of outcome *in most cases*. This is because in most cases, just processes and means undoubtedly are more likely to lead to just ends and outcomes than unjust processes and means. This obviously means that procedural justices are more likely to lead to the justice of outcome than procedural injustice. Let's again take the two most fundamental principles of procedural justice in criminal trials for example "no one can be a judge in his own case" and "the opinions of both parties ought to be heard." The procedural justice that follows these principles is more likely than procedural injustice which violates these principles to lead to the justice of outcome that is "the conviction of the guilty or the immunity of the innocent from criminal prosecution." From a different perspective, however, it is true that procedural justice prohibiting the invasion of privacy is less likely to lead to the justice of outcome than procedural injustice invading privacy. But this is a very exceptional, local, special phenomenon. Therefore, as Taylor said, "In general, a just procedure produces a more just outcome than an unjust procedure."[47]

In most cases, procedural justice and justice of outcome must be consistent; in other words, procedural justice, on the whole, certainly leads to the justice of outcome; in the final analysis, because, in most cases, just procedures lead to the justice of outcome they are truly good procedures. Even if under the circumstance that procedural injustice leads to the justice of outcome more than procedural justice, procedural justice and justice of outcome can be consistent and both can be achieved. Because most of the procedures used to achieve the justice of outcome are diverse, if one kind of just procedure cannot achieve the justice of outcome it does not prevent other just procedures from achieving the justice of outcome. For example, procedural justice that prohibits violations of privacy may not achieve the justice of outcome of putting criminals in jail. However, this does not hinder other procedural justice which can achieve the justice of outcome of putting criminals in jail, such as "no one can be a judge in his own case" and "the opinions of both parties ought to be heard." Therefore, the irreconcilable conflict between procedural justice and the justice of outcome is a very rare exception.

When there is no conflict between procedural justice and the justice of outcome, and both can be achieved, both procedural justice and the justice of outcome should of course be taken into account. But what should we do when there is a conflict between the two with no possible compromise? Undoubtedly the one with less value should be sacrificed to preserve the one with greater value. Consequently, when no compromise can be reached, generally speaking, we should preserve procedural justice and sacrifice the justice of outcome, because, as mentioned above, procedural justice, in general, certainly leads to the justice of outcome, which means that if procedural justice is preserved, generally it can preserve procedural justice as well as realize the justice of outcome. On the contrary, if procedural justice is sacrificed, generally speaking, both procedural justice and the justice of outcome would be sacrificed. In a word, procedural justice, in general, implies a justice of outcome, thus its value is greater than the value of the justice of outcome: procedural justice then overall has priority over the justice of outcome. This is the

190 *Moral value and moral norms*

true meaning of the legal maxims of "process before rights," "justice before truth" and "procedure is the heart of law."

Robert H. Jackson, a former Associate Justice of the Supreme Court of the United States, once said:

> The fairness and stabilities of procedure are indispensable elements of liberty. As long as the procedure is fair and impartial, tough substantive law can also be tolerated. In fact, people would rather live under a Soviet substantive law system that faithfully applies our Anglo-American legal procedures than our substantive law system ... is implemented by the Soviet process, if the choice is to be made.[48]

Another former associate justice William Douglas also wrote:

> Most of the provisions of the Bill of Rights are procedural, and this is not meaningless. It is procedure that determines most of the differences between the rule of law and arbitrary or capricious rule of man. Firm adherence to strict legal procedures is our primary guarantee of equal access to justice before the law.[49]

Procedural instrumentalism and procedural departmentalism

The relationship between procedural justice and the justice of outcome or substantive justice, as mentioned above, is very abstract and difficult, and thus constitutes a major problem in the theory of justice. Around this problem the two major schools of procedural instrumentalism and procedural orientation were formed. In the view of procedural instrumentalism, procedure does not have intrinsic value and end value independent of outcome, but only the means that serves outcomes, and only the value of means and external value used to achieve a certain outcome or end. Thence procedural law and procedural justice—both belonging to the category of procedural norms—are only means that serve substantive law and the justice of outcome, and thus have only the value of means and external values used to realize substantive law or the justice of outcome. On this point, Bentham, the representative figure of procedural instrumentalism explained very clearly: "The only legitimate purpose of procedural law is to maximize the realization of substantive law."[50]

Bentham is wrong however. Although procedure is a means that serves substantive law and substantive justice or the justice of outcome, procedural law and procedural justice, as mentioned previously, are not the means of serving the justice of outcome and substantive law. Procedural law and procedural justice are not a means of serving justice of outcome and substantive law, but a legal and moral restriction on means or procedure that serve the justice of outcome and substantive law: the procedure or means that serve the justice of outcome and substantive law should be lawful, just and moral, not illegal, unjust, and immoral. Therefore, to reiterate, the essence of procedural law and procedural justice is: in order to achieve just, moral outcomes and ends, legal, just, and a moral means and procedure should be adopted instead of illegal, unjust, and immoral means or procedure. The obvious mistake of procedural instrumentalism is to equate "procedural law" or "procedural justice" with "procedure," thus drawing the wrong conclusion that *procedural justice and procedural law are the means serving the justice of outcome and substantive law* from the correct view that *procedure is the means serving the justice of outcome and substantive law.*

Procedural departmentalism correctly sees that the procedure has not only the value of means and external value that can be used to achieve a certain outcome, but also possesses the end value and internal value which is the end that people desire, thus correcting the error of procedural instrumentalism. However, procedural departmentalism then holds that the intrinsic value of procedure and procedural justice are decisive and standard, while the external value of the procedure and the justice of outcome are determined and derived. As one of the representatives of procedural departmentalism explains, "The justice of the referee is intrinsically related to the justice of the procedure in which it was produced."[51] In other words, it holds that procedural justice certainly leads to the justice of outcome and that procedural injustice certainly leads to the outcome of injustice.

This view is also incorrect. Indeed, if procedural justice certainly leads to the justice of outcome, then procedural justice determines the justice of outcome, thus is decisive and standard, while the justice of outcome is decided and derived. However, as mentioned above, procedural justice does not necessarily lead to the justice of outcome; procedural justice only generally speaking can lead to the justice of outcome. Therefore, generally speaking, procedural justice can be decisive and standard, while the justice of outcome can be determined and derived. The error of procedural departmentalism lies in exaggerating "most cases" to "all cases": it exaggerates that "procedural justice is bound to lead to the justice of outcome in most cases" with the fallacy that "procedural justice certainly leads to the justice of outcome"; it exaggerates that "procedural injustice, in most cases, certainly leads to unjust outcomes" with the fallacy that "procedural injustice certainly leads to the outcome of injustice"; and it exaggerates that "procedural justice, in most cases, is decisive and standard" with the fallacy that "procedural justice is decisive and standard."

6.1.5 *The principle of justice: The fundamental value standard of state institutions*

The definition and types of justice indicate that, in terms of the highness and lowness of moral values, justice is much lower than benevolence or *unselfishly benefiting others*; however, in terms of importance of moral value, it is far greater and more important than benevolence or *unselfishly benefiting others*, and far greater and more important than all other morality: justice is the most important and most fundamental morality because the value of moral principles such as justice and benevolence is the utility of these principles to the goal of morality, which, as we have mentioned, is to safeguard the existence and development of society and the interest of the community, and finally promote everyone's interests.

To achieve the goal of morality, on the one hand, people must avoid harming each other. As Smith put it:

> society, however, cannot subsist among those who are at all times ready to hurt and injure one another. The moment that injure begins, the moment that mutual resentment and animosity take place, all the bands of it are broken asunder.[52]

On the other hand, everyone must strive to promote the interests of others and society because so-called society, after all, is a form of cooperation in the interest of "I am for all and everyone is for me." If everyone does not work hard to advance the interests of others and society then society will collapse, as Hume put it: "without justice, society must immediately dissolve, and everyone must fall into that savage and solitary condition, which is infinitely worse than the worst situation that can possibly be supposed in society."[53]

It is not difficult to see that the most important and effective principle of avoiding harming one another is undoubtedly the principle of justice of exchange of equal harms. For exchange of equal harms means that if you harm others you harm yourself; you harm yourself as much as you harm others. In this way, the inverse proposition is also true.

Conversely, the most important and effective principle of promoting the interests of others and society is undoubtedly the principle of justice of exchange of equal interests, for the exchange of equal interests means that if you promote the interests of others you equally promote your own interests; how much interests you promote for others is equal to how much you promote yourself. In this way, if people want to promote and maximize their own interests, they must also promote and maximize the interests of others.

Justice, therefore, though it is not sublime, is the greatest good, the most important and the most fundamental good, and the most important and the most fundamental moral principle. So Aristotle said, "Of all virtues, justice is considered the most important."[54] Smith put it another way:

> Beneficence, therefore, is less essential to the existence of society than justice. Society may subsist, though not in the most comfortable state, without beneficence; but the prevalence of injustice must utterly destroy it ... Beneficence ... is the ornament which embellishes, not the foundation which supports the building, and which it was, therefore, sufficient to recommend, but by no means necessary to impose. Justice, on the contrary, is the main pillar that upholds the whole edifice. If it is removed, the great, the immense fabric of human society ... must in a moment crumble into atoms.[55]

Rawls put it in a nutshell: "One may think of a public concept of justice as constituting the fundamental charter of a well-ordered human association."[56]

However, if we only see that justice is the most critical morality, we cannot discern the fundamental difference between justice and moral principles such as benevolence and altruism. To reiterate, the main principle of justice is social justice, a justice of governance, which, in the final analysis, is institutional justice, namely the justice of distributive institution concerning the rights and duties of everyone: the justice of distributive institution is the most critical justice. It is this that makes justice so fundamentally different from moral principles such as benevolence: benevolence is the moral principle that restricts all human beings and ought to be followed by everyone's behavior. Justice, by contrast, is the morality that restricts the rulers or leaders of the state apparatus: it is the fundamental value standard to evaluate the goodness and badness of the governance of a society, and its state institutions, and, in the final analysis, is the fundamental value standard of the goodness or badness of all state institutions.

It was Plato who first discovered this great truth: "When we founded the city-state, we had established a universal principle from the very beginning. I think this principle, or some form of this principle, is justice."[57] Aristotle greatly promoted Plato's discovery entrenching the term in his own writings: "The city-states are guided by the principle of justice. The law of propriety derived from justice can be relied upon to judge the merits of the world. Justice is exactly the basis for the establishment of social order."[58] Rawls summed up the great tradition of Plato and Aristotle with a majestic declaration:

> Justice is the first virtue of social institutions, as truth is of systems of thoughts. A theory however elegant and economical must be rejected or revised if it is untrue; likewise laws and institutions no matter how efficient and well-arranged must be reformed or abolished if they are unjust.[59]

Justice, as a fundamental value standard of state institutions, is certainly quite complicated, thus is not a single principle but a system of principles consisting of a series of sub-principles and a general principle: the exchange of either equal interests or equal harms is only the general principle of justice. From this general principle of justice it is not difficult to deduce a series of principles of justice, and the most fundamental principle of justice is undoubtedly that the rights and duties distributed to everyone by society should be equal: the equality of rights and duties is the fundamental principle of justice.

6.2 Equality between rights and duties: Fundamental principle of justice

The fundamental problem of justice is the exchange or distribution of rights and duties. Thence, how should rights and duties be exchanged or distributed so as to achieve justice? Or, what is the principle of justice in the exchange of rights and duties? After all, what is the fundamental principle of justice?

194 *Moral value and moral norms*

This is an extremely complicated problem. The starting point for studying this problem clearly is: what are rights and duties?

6.2.1 Definitions of right and duty

Land, population, and power (and its governing organizations or organs) are undoubtedly the three elements that make up all societies, and thus the three elements of a state; the power and its constituent elements that constitute the state are the supreme power and its organization or government. But why the need for such power?

In fact, for any society to exist and develop there must be rulers, and the rulers must have a coercive force that is generally recognized, accepted, and agreed upon by the members of society to compel the ruled to obey. Only in this way it is possible to ensure that people's activities abide by a certain social order so that society can exist and develop, otherwise, social activities are bound to conflict with each other leading to chaos, thus making the existence and development of society impossible. Therefore, the coercive force that rulers possess and is generally agreed upon by the members of society is the fundamental condition for the existence and development of any society. This coercive force is called power.

> The existence of a power means that a collective cultural system establishes formal inequality, endows some people with the power to rule others, and forces the ruled to submit to the latter.[60]

The fundamental characteristic and nature of power differentiated from other coercive forces lies in the recognition, acceptance or common agreement of society, otherwise, it is not power but a so-called "force to bind pigs." Since Rousseau, power that is sanctioned by society, has been referred to as "legitimacy": legitimacy, of course, means that something must be enforced in accordance with the law, but not limited to compliance with the law; it refers generally to the nature of the coercive forces that are generally recognized, accepted, and agreed upon by the members of that society:

> The legitimacy of power is simply because it is recognized as power by its members, or at least by a majority. If there is common agreement on the legitimacy of power, such power is legitimate. Unlawful power is no longer a power, but a force.[61]

Thence power is the coercive force with legitimacy possessed by rulers, and thus has internal opposition between *legitimacy and coercion, necessity and oughtness*. As a coercive force, power is a necessity, it is a force that people must obey, otherwise they will be punished; as the legitimate force recognized by society or agreed upon by most, power is also an "ought," it is a force that people ought to obey. In short, power is a coercive force possessed by rulers and recognized by society to force the ruled to obey: as something that the rulers possess and the ruled ought to and must obey, this force is the fundamental means to safeguard the existence and development of society.

Not only that! Because society is a community in which two or more people are bound by certain interpersonal relationships, it is after all, as Rawls put it, just "a system of cooperation designed to advance the good of those taking part in it."[62] This kind of interest cooperation, on the one hand, is *I'm for everyone: I seek the benefit for others*, that is, I "give" to others or make a so-called "contribution" to others; on the other hand, *everyone is for me: I benefit from others*, that is, I make a so-called "claim" or "demand" on others.

Therefore, the so-called power, after all, is also the fundamental means to safeguard people's interest cooperation, their mutual contributions and claims, what they give and demand. The interests, claims, or demands which ought to be protected by power are the so-called rights. Is it not that my interests, claims, or demands on society which ought to be safeguarded by power are my rights? On the contrary, services and contributions which ought to be protected by power are so-called duties: is it not that my service and contributions to others and society which ought to be protected by the power are my duties? However, power clearly does not protect all of the above. Examined in detail, everyone's claims or demands, and interests obtained from others fall under following three types:

The first has only a necessity rather than an "oughtness." It is the interest that others *must but not ought to* give me, and is my demands and claims that others *must but not ought to* satisfy: it is necessary, otherwise others will be punished by coercive force; but it is not what ought to be because it violates morality. For example, when I robbed a bank with a gun, the bank clerk knew that he should not give me the money but still had to give it to me, otherwise he would be punished by my coercive force: a gunshot. It is clear that these kinds of interests, claims, or demands ought not be protected by power and therefore are not my right: I have no right to rob a bank.

The second type, which has only an "oughtness" rather than a necessity, is the interests that others *ought to but not must* give me. That is, it is my demands and claims that others *ought to but not must* satisfy. It conforms to morality, and thus *ought to be*, but it is not necessary because it has no important social utility, and hence others will not be punished by coercive force if not obeyed. For example, when I am in trouble a friend will help me through the difficulties, or someone might simply give me a gift out of love. These kinds of interests, claims, or demands are moral and therefore ought to be. But they are not necessary because my friends and others will not be punished with violence or administrative punishment if they do not help me in some way or other. It is clear that these kinds of interests, claims, or demands ought not to be protected by power and therefore are not my right: I don't have the rights to ask for gifts and help from friends.

The third type has both a necessity and an "oughtness." It is the interests that others *must and ought to* give me, that is, it is my demands and claims that others *must and ought to* satisfy: it conforms to morality therefore it ought to be; at the same time, it is also of important social utility and therefore it is necessary, and hence others will be punished by coercive force if it is not obeyed.

That my parents raised me when I was a child, that my company paid me wages when I worked for it, and that my children will support me when I am old, are all examples of the satisfaction of my interests, claims or demands. These types of interests, claims, or demands are moral and therefore ought to be; at the same time, they are also necessary, otherwise others will be punished by coercive force. It is clear that these kinds of interests, claims, and demands ought to be protected by power and therefore are my right: as a child it was my right that my parents nurtured me; when I work I have the right to ask for payment from my company; and when I am old I have the right to request the support of my children.

It can be seen that rights are interests, claims, or demands that have significant social utility; these interests, claims, or demands are conditional on both necessity and oughtness, meaning that rights must and ought to be obtained. Thus rights are the interests, claims, or demands that ought to be protected by power (law and politics). The key word here is "ought," for while rights are the interests, claims, or demands that *ought to be* protected by power they are not necessarily the interests, claims, or demands that are *actually* protected by power. Beauchamp did not understand this and was caught in an inextricable contradiction: on the one hand, he admitted that the right without protection of power is not a real right; on the other hand, he said that real rights may not be protected by power. He wrote:

> If there is no actual power behind a legitimate demand, however, it would seem that we have only hollow rhetoric about rights, and no real right at all ... Rights without powers thus seems insufficient, for we can have rights in the complete absence of powers; innocent persons have a right not to be punished for crimes they did not commit, yet they may have no power to prevent the punishment. Rights, then, seem not to entail powers at all.[63]

Indeed, some rights, such as the right that innocents are free from being punished, though not actually safeguarded by power, remain rights because, although these rights are not actually safeguarded by power, they ought to be safeguarded by power: rights are interests that ought to be safeguarded by power. This definition also contains more profound and important implications. This is because, as mentioned above, politics is the administration or management of power while laws are the norms of power. Therefore, rights are the interests that ought to be safeguarded by power, which implies: rights are the interests that ought to be safeguarded by politics and law. Thus, Rudolph Von Jhering said:

> Right is the interest safeguarded by law. Not all interests are rights, only those recognized and safeguarded by law are rights.[64]

Justice and equality 197

The definition of the concept of right settles the definition of the concept of duties, for duties are nothing but a reversal of rights. Like rights, duties are interests that have important social utility and a necessity and an oughtness. However, the interests are such that one *must and ought to* give to others. The interests therefore are services or contributions which, like rights, ought to be safeguarded by power (law and politics) and ought to be obeyed to avert punishment such as for breach of duty of care. So Bentham said:

> That is my *duty* to do, which I am liable to be punished, according to law, if I do not do: this is the original, ordinary, and proper sense of the word *duty*.[65]

6.2.2 Types of rights and duties: Moral rights and duties, statutory rights and duties and natural rights and duties

Rights and duties, based on the nature of their existence, are divided into actual rights and duties and due rights and duties. The so-called "actual rights and duties" are the rights and duties that actually exist, that is, the rights and duties recognized and conferred by society, which, after all, are the rights and duties recognized and conferred by the various norms of society: the actual rights and duties completely exist in all kinds of norms systems of society. These social norms are only two types: law and morality.

The provisions of the law on rights and duties, that is, the rights and duties conferred by the law, are called statutory rights and legal duties. The moral stipulation of rights and duties, that is, the rights and duties recognized and conferred by morality, are called moral rights and moral duties. But why are rights and duties recognized and conferred by law, and at the same time by morality? The definition of rights and duties (rights are the interests with significant social utility that *must and ought to* be obtained and duties are interests with important social utility that *must and ought to* give to others) means that rights and duties are not only a moral code, but also a legal code, because what morality regulates and protects are the actions with social utility, but what the law regulates and protects are the actions with important social utility. Thus, actions with important social utility such as rights and duties, which, because of their being an important social utility, are stipulated by both law and morality, and obtain the double protection of law and morality.

Thence, any kind of right or duty, by its very nature, should be statutory rights and duties as well as moral rights and duties. However, some rights and duties, such as human rights, have been recognized only by morality and not by law in certain periods in history; therefore they are only moral rights and duties but not statutory legal rights and duties. On the contrary, some other rights and duties, such as those established or recognized by despots and tyrants (thus not recognized by morality but only by law), are only statutory rights and duties not moral rights and duties. Obviously, then, the kinds of rights and duties, which are either statutory rights or moral rights, are imperfect forms of rights and duties, lacking complete protection, and therefore are difficult to realize: if moral rights and duties are to be realized, they must be recognized by law and become statutory rights and duties at the same time; if statuary rights and duties are to be realized, they must be recognized by morality and become moral rights and duties at the same time.

Then, besides statutory rights and duties and moral rights and duties, are there other rights and duties recognized by society? No, there are no others, because the extension of statuary rights and duties is much greater than the extension of legal rights and duties. Law, as we know, includes statute and policy. So, statutory rights and duties are different from legal rights and duties: statutory rights and duties include rights and duties conferred by statute and policy while legal rights and duties are only the rights and duties conferred by the statute. Thus, statutory rights and duties, as well as moral rights and duties clearly include all the rights and duties recognized by society. The so-called political rights and duties, economic rights and duties, religious rights and duties, are only the rights and duties of political activities, economic activities, and religious activities that are stipulated and conferred by law and morality. The so-called customary rights and duties are only the customary unwritten statutory rights and duties, as well as moral rights and duties.

Statutory rights and duties and moral rights and duties, although including all rights and duties recognized and conferred by society, are not all rights and duties. This is because some rights and duties, although not recognized by society's laws and morality, are still rights and duties: only they are not actual rights and duties but are the due rights and duties. For example, in slave society the human rights of slaves were not recognized by the social norms, whether by laws or morality, thus slaves had actually no human rights. But since slaves were also human beings, their human rights, although not recognized by society, ought to have been recognized by society; and, subsequently, although not recognized by law and morality, ought to have been recognized by laws and morality. The kind of human rights that slaves did not actually possess but ought to have we call "due rights." Therefore, so-called due rights and duties are the rights and duties which are not recognized and conferred by society but which ought to be recognized and conferred by society, are the rights and duties that are not recognized and conferred by social norms—morality and law—but ought to be recognized and conferred, for, in the final analysis, these are rights and duties that people do not actually have but ought to have.

However, all rights and duties are recognized and conferred by certain rules. If the due rights and duties are not recognized and conferred by society, by law and morality, then by what are they recognized and conferred? The theory of natural law answers this question: due rights and duties are recognized and conferred by "natural law." What is the natural law? Hobbes, the master of natural law theory, replied: "The definition of natural law is the instruction of right reason."[66] In the note to this sentence, Hobbes gave a further explanation of so-called "right reason":

In terms of the right reason of man in the state of nature, much of what is desired refers to a gift that is never negligent; but what I mean is the act of rational thinking, that is, the right rational thinking that people think about their actions ... I use the term "right rational thinking" and I mean, rational thinking draws a conclusion from the principle of truth that is correctly expressed, for all transgressions of natural law lie in wrong rational thinking or in folly.[67]

It can be seen that so-called "right reason" is in fact the "correct" rational thinking about *the nature of* human behavior, that it is the rational thinking that conforms to *the nature of* human behavior, and is thereby the rational thinking that *conforms to human nature*; therefore the so-called "instruction of right reason" is the correct behavioral principle that accords with excellent human nature, and, so-called natural law concerns the excellent norms of behavior conforming to human nature: *natural law* shares the same concept with *excellent norms of behavior*. But why are the excellent norms of behavior called "natural law"?

It is because the excellent (correct) norms of behavior that conform to human nature parallel the laws operating in the natural world as objective, inevitable, and independent of human will. Conversely, bad (wrong) norms of behavior that violate human nature are subjective, accidental, and dependent on human will.

Thus, due rights and duties are conferred by right reason and the excellent principles of behavior in conformity with human nature, and, in the final analysis, are conferred by natural law and therefore called "natural rights and duties": natural rights and duties are the same concepts as due rights and duties. Accordingly, actual rights and duties (statutory rights and duties and moral rights and duties) are those given by two kinds of contract or convention law—the law and morality of a society—thus are called "contractual rights and duties": in other words, "natural right or law [is] contracted with conventional right or law."[68] Therefore, the statutory rights and duties and moral rights and duties can be either just or unjust while natural rights and duties certainly are just. So Rawls said:

> This fact can be used to interpret the concept of natural rights. For one thing, it explains why it is appropriate to call by this name the rights that justice protects. These claims depend solely on certain natural attributes ... the existence of these attributes and claims based upon them is established independently from social conventions and legal norms. The propriety of the term "natural" is that it suggests the contract between the rights identified by the theory of justice and the rights defined by law and custom.[69]

Therefore, if a society is just, it should be based on natural rights and duties to establish or recognize moral rights and duties and statutory rights and duties, namely to transform natural rights and duties into moral rights and duties and the statutory rights and duties, thus finally make moral rights and duties, statutory rights and duties and natural rights and duties completely consistent. This process of transition, formulation, approval, or consistency generally follows the law of the development of *natural rights and duties—moral rights and duties—legal rights and duties*:

Natural rights and duties are rights and duties that are not recognized and conferred by society, but should be recognized and conferred, and are rights and duties that are not recognized and conferred by social norms—morality and law—but should be recognized and conferred, therefore they are pure due rights and duties; although moral rights and duties are recognized and conferred by society, they are only recognized and conferred by the moral norms of society but not by the law, and are protected only by public opinion but not by power, thence are incomplete actual rights and duties; statutory rights and duties, generally speaking, are recognized and conferred both by law and morality, protected both by power and public opinion, thence are complete actual rights and duties.

Therefore, the process of realization of rights and duties from due to actual is the evolutionary process from pure natural rights and duties to complete actual statutory rights and duties. In this evolutionary process, it often passes through the intermediary stage of incomplete actual moral rights and duties. Let's take human rights as an example. Until the eighteenth century human rights were a natural right. After the Declaration of Independence of the United States in 1776 and the Declaration of Human Rights in France in 1789, human rights were gradually recognized by morality and became a contractual moral right. Since the middle of the twentieth century, human rights have finally become part of the constitutions of many countries, so in these countries it is not only a moral right but also a statutory right. Therefore, the realization of human rights from natural rights to statutory rights has transitioned through 200 years of the intermediary moral rights.

6.2.3 Types of rights and duties: rights and duties between human and non-human beings

The rise of contemporary western ecological ethics shows that there is an increasingly more important type of rights and duties, namely, rights and duties between human beings and non-human beings. However, traditional ethics tells us that rights and duties only exist among human beings, not between human beings and non-human animals and plants. The most representative theory of this traditional view, as Tom Regan, a contemporary animal rights theorist put it, is Kant's theory of "indirect duty." Kant stated that:

> So far as animals are concerned, we have no direct duties. Animals are not self-conscious ... *Our duties towards animals are merely indirect duties toward humanity.* Animal nature has analogies to human nature, and by

> doing our duties to animals in respect of manifestations of human nature, we indirectly do our duty towards humanity. Thus, if a dog has served his master long and faithfully, his service, on the analogy of human service, deserves reward, and when the dog has grown too old to serve, his master ought to keep him until he dies. Such action helps to support us in our duties toward human beings, where they are bounden duties. If then any acts of animals are analogous to human acts and spring from the same principles, we have duties towards animals because thus we cultivate the corresponding duties towards human beings. If a man shoots his dog because the animal is no longer capable of service, he does not fail in his duty to the dog, for the dog can not judge, but his *act is inhuman and damages in himself that humanity which it is his duty to show towards mankind.* If he is not to stifle his human feelings, he must practice kindness towards animals, for he who is cruel to animals becomes hard also in his dealing with men.[70]

It can be seen that the so-called "the theory of indirect duty" is a theory which holds that the so-called duty of a person to a non-human being is only an indirect duty to another human being, and that human beings do not have duties to non-human beings so that non-human beings do not have rights over human beings: the theory of indirect duty is a theory which denies the rights of non-human beings. According to this theory, we do not have a relationship of rights and duties with animals. Our so-called duties to animals, such as the protection of pandas under the law, are in fact only our protection of human interests, and therefore our indirect duties to mankind, just as our duty not to pollute the river, is actually not our duty to the river but only our indirect duty to human beings. We have no duty to animals, which clearly means that animals do not have rights over us: animals have no rights.

This "theory of indirect duty" which denies the rights of animals is untenable. Take the example that Kant gave about the dog. It has long served its master faithfully, so ought the master to keep it until it dies given that it is too old to continue its service? The answer is yes. Why, however, ought the master do so? Why does a conscientious master feel guilty and uneasy if he does not do this but shoots it? Is it, as Kant put it, that by being cruel to dogs one can be cruel to human beings, and thus indirectly fail in one's duties to human beings?

Of course that makes sense. Kant's view is similar to that of Mencius who famously said in relation to man's benevolence to animals that "virtuous men should keep away from the kitchen." But this is not the main reason. A conscientious master who shoots the dog would feel guilty and uneasy, mainly because shooting the dog is unjust to the dog and fails in his duties to the dog; but not—or mainly not—because being cruel to dogs one can be cruel to human beings, thereby indirectly failing in his duties to human beings.

According to the principle of justice—the exchange of equal interests—the dog has given the master a great benefit, so the master's returning with the huge benefits is what the dog deserves. Only when the master returns such a great benefit does he conform to the principle of justice of exchange of equal interests and thus is just, fulfilling his due duties, and at peace with his conscience. Otherwise, if he shoots his dog, he violates the principle of justice of exchange of equal interests, which is unjust for the reason that he does not fulfill his duties to the dog; thence, when the master does so he feels guilty and uneasy. So, says Feinberg:

> We [not only] ought to treat animals humanely but also that we should do so for the animal's own sake, that such treatment is something that we owe animals as their due, something that can be claimed for them, something the withholding of which would be an injustice and a wrong, and not merely a harm.[71]

The master's duties to the dog to keep it until it dies implies that the dog has the right to be provided for by the master until its death. Then, is it the dog's right to be provided with such a great benefit from the master? No doubt, the dog deserves it even if it had not saved the master's life, for the dog gave him another kind of great benefit which was loyal service. But is the benefit that the dog ought to obtain from the owner the right of the dog? If the dog's benefit is something that it not only ought to have, but also must have, thus ought to be protected by law, then the dog's benefit would become the dog's right: rights are interests that ought to be protected by law.

In fact, as early as 1641, the Code of Freedom in the British colonies had such laws that protected the interests of animals: "No man shall exercise any Tirranny or Cruetie towards any bruite Creature which are usually kept for man's use. A 'rite' obliged persons who 'leade or drive Cattle' to rest and refresh them periodically."[72] In 1822, the British House passed the famous Martin Act: The Prohibition of the Abuse of Livestock Act. In the twentieth century, the theory of animal rights and the animal liberation movement gained momentum in western ideological circles, particularly in the United States: the Marine Mammal Protection Act and the Endangered Species Act were adopted in 1972 and 1973 respectively, both which, as Joseph Petulla said, "[Embody] the legal idea that a listed nonhuman resident of the United States is guaranteed, in a special sense, life and liberty."[73] Thus, the interests of animals, such as dogs and livestock, not only ought to be protected but are actually protected by law: with interests protected by law dogs and livestock thus have rights. Then, do all animals and even all non-human beings have rights?

On this issue, Nash believes that Feinberg's paper written in 1971 on *The Rights of Animals and Unborn Generations of Human Beings* is a "milestone in the subsequent philosophical study of the legitimacy of the extension of rights." In this paper, Joel Feinberg asked the essential question: "What sort of beings or things could be said to possess rights? His formula for answering it depended on 'the interest principle'."[74] What is the "interest principle"? In a nutshell, Feinberg said: "a being without interests has no 'benefits' to act in."[75]

It is so right! Any kind of non-human being may have rights only if it has the *evaluative competence to distinguish goodness or badness and advantage or disadvantage* and the *abilities to choose advantage and avoid disadvantage*: the *evaluative competence to distinguish goodness or badness and advantage or disadvantage* and the *abilities to choose advantage and avoid disadvantage* are the premise of possessing rights. It is obviously impossible for things without these potentials to possess rights.

Consequently, something, such as the sun and the earth, the air and the rain, the stones and the mountains and rivers and so on, no matter how great the benefits they give us, do not have any rights. Because they have no *evaluative competence to distinguish goodness or badness and advantage or disadvantage* and the *abilities to choose advantage and avoid disadvantage*, they clearly do not have interests to begin with. Who can say that the sun and the earth, the air and rain, stones and rivers etc., have interests? Therefore, Singer wrote: "It is meaningless to say that it is against the interest of a stone for a schoolboy to kick a stone along the road. The stone has no interests."[76] Indeed, the stone has no interests, because it does not have the *evaluative competence to distinguish goodness or badness and advantage or disadvantage* and the *abilities to choose advantage and avoid disadvantage*.

Then, do only animals such as dogs and livestock have the *evaluative competence to distinguish goodness or badness and advantage or disadvantage* and the *abilities to choose advantage and avoid disadvantage*? No, the *evaluative competence to distinguish goodness or badness and advantage or disadvantage* and the *abilities to choose advantage and avoid disadvantage* are the inherent attributes of all living creatures—humans and animals, plants and microbes. It is only that they are at different levels of evolutions that they have different *evaluative competence to distinguish goodness or badness and advantage or disadvantage and abilities to choose advantage and avoid disadvantage*. As Taylor said: "All organisms, whether conscious or not, are teleological centers of life in the sense that each is a unified, coherently ordered system of goal-oriented activities that has a constant tendency to protect and maintain the organism's existence."[77]

Thence, is it possible to conclude that all living creatures have rights? The answer from many ecological ethicists is yes. John Lawrence argued that "life, intelligence, and feeling necessarily imply rights."[78] Brigid Brophy said that "once we acknowledge life and sentiency in the other animals, we are bound to acknowledge ... the right to life, liberty and the pursuit of happiness."[79] Bill Devall said that "all things in the biosphere have an equal right to live and blossom and to reach their own individual forms of ... self-realization."[80] Tom Regan also wrote: "for animal rights ... we do know that many of these animals are the subjects of a life ... and with this, their equal right to be treated with respect."[81] As a result, some eco-ethicists have further concluded that the living creatures which cause great disaster to humans, such as cholera, plague, syphilis, hepatitis B, AIDS, and other viruses and bacteria, as well as lice, fleas, are also living creatures, so they have rights just as other living creatures. These eco-ethicists have even advocated the construction of hospitals for lice and fleas. Is there anything more ridiculous than this?

However, *the evaluative competence to distinguish goodness or badness and advantage or disadvantage and the abilities to choose advantage and avoid disadvantage*, are only a sufficient condition of interests, not a sufficient condition of rights. The condition for non-human beings to have rights, not only should have *the evaluative competence to distinguish goodness or badness and advantage or disadvantage and the abilities to choose advantage and avoid disadvantage* to have their interests, but should also be beneficial to human beings in that they bring interests, and are thereby able to form an interest community with human beings that is mutually beneficial in general.

Similarly, not all human beings should have rights. If a person deprives others of rights by killing and arson, he has no corresponding rights. Even if one is a good man and a war hero, he maybe an enemy we are fighting against, and so has no right to life in an actual confrontation on the battle field. Therefore, in killing the enemy we do not violate their rights and are not immoral. On the contrary, the more enemies we kill the more heroic we are and the more virtue we have.

If even human beings behave savagely like this, let alone non-human beings, then why does an old work dog have the right to be provided for by its master until it dies? We know that it is because it has served its master faithfully and brought great benefits to its master. But if the dog turns on his master and bites or attacks him for no reason, can it still have this right? Only those non-human beings which have *the abilities to choose advantage and avoid disadvantage*, and are beneficial to human beings, have rights; if they are harmful to human beings, as Feinberg put it, they have no rights.

Therefore, living things that are beneficial to human beings can form a kind of reciprocal interest community with humans, which is the basis for non-human beings' rights. Such interests, contributions or services of non-human beings to humans, undoubtedly are of great social utility and are necessary and due services or contributions, thus should be protected by law: it is due because they get corresponding interests and rights from humans, and it is necessary otherwise they will lose the interests and rights obtained from humans.

Just think of the dog that serves its master faithfully. It brings interests to its master, which is the basis of its right to be looked after by its master until it dies. The interests, contributions, or services the dog gives to his master are necessary and what ought to be since the dog receives corresponding interests and rights from the master, and so should be protected by law. But if the dog attacks his master it will lose its interests and rights from its master, and if it attacks a stranger for no reason, it may even be sentenced to death by a court. Nash tells us: "from time to time, in the Middle Ages, courts of law conducted criminal trials of animals that, for instance, killed humans."[82] In October 2004, a British court sentenced a dog to death after it bit a passerby on the arm.

It can be seen that interests brought by non-human beings that enjoy rights are kinds of services or contributions with important social utility that *must be and ought to be*, and also are kinds of services and contributions that ought to be protected by law, which, in the final analysis, are the duties of non-human beings to human beings. Thus, being beneficial to human beings and forming an interest community with humans are the basis of their rights.

However, John Passmore and other advocates of anthropocentrism, like Kant, believed that only self-conscious human beings can be responsible for their own actions, thus have duties and rights; conversely, they held that non-human beings without self-consciousness cannot be responsible for their actions and therefore have no duties and rights.[83] This is not tenable. As animal rights advocators point out, persons who are not responsible for their actions, such as infants, mentally ill persons and persons with dementia, still have the same rights and duties or responsibilities; only their rights and duties are exercised and performed with the help of their agents.

Mental patients, for example, cannot be responsible for their actions, but have the same rights to liberty and life, as well as the same duty as normal people to not deprive the liberty and life of others. Regardless of whether a mentally ill person is found by law to have been of unsound mind at the time of physically harming or even killing someone, he is "punished" as a normal person, in the sense that he is deprived of his rights to liberty and incarcerated in an institution for the mentally ill who commit such offences. Therefore, it is untenable to assert that non-human beings, which are not self-conscious and cannot be responsible for their own actions, cannot have duties and rights. They do have rights and duties, but their rights and duties are exercised and fulfilled by their "human being" agents.

From the above, we can see that *the evaluative competence to distinguish goodness or badness and advantage or disadvantage and the abilities to choose advantage and avoid disadvantage* possessed by living beings but not by non-living things is the premise for non-human beings having rights; and that being beneficial to humans are the duties of non-humans to humans being's duty to human beings and thus the basis for non-human rights.

Therefore, there is no relationship of rights and duties between human beings and non-living things, or living things that are harmful to human beings; humans only have relationships of rights and duties among themselves and with living things that are beneficial to them: the right of a non-human being is a necessary and due interest from human, that is, the interest it receives from human beings that ought to be protected by law, which, after all, is the duty of human beings to non-human beings; the duty of a non-human being is the interest that it ought to and must give human beings, and is the interest that it gives human beings and ought to be protected by law, which, in the final analysis, the right that human beings enjoy over non-human beings.

6.2.4 The relationship between rights and duties: The fundamental principle of justice

The definition of rights and duties (rights are the interests, claims or demands that ought to be protected by the law; duties are the services or contributions that ought to be protected by law) indicates that a "right" and a "duty" belong to the category of "claim" and "contribution" respectively, so they are just different terms for the same kind of interests for different objects: a right to the recipient and a duty to the giver. For example, the rights of employees and the duties of employers are in fact the same interests in regard to the "wages of employees": wages are a right to an employee and a duty to an employer. As Hobhouse said: "Right is a due seen from the point of view of the party to whom it is owned, and duty is the same thing from the point of view of the party owning it."[84]

It can be seen that an individual's rights must be the duty of others, and vice versa. Thus, the norms of rights can be transformed into norms of duties, and vice versa. This is the necessary, objective and factual relationship between an individual's rights and the duties of others, which is often referred to as the logical correlation of rights and duties. For this principle of correlation, Beauchamp and Feinberg had a very good generalization of it: "Rights and duties are logically correlative. One person's right entails someone else's obligation to refrain from interfering or to provide some benefit, and all obligations similarly entails rights."[85] "This is the doctrine that (1) all duties entails other people's right and (2) all rights entails other people's duty."[86] However, some people, such as Mill, denied this logical correlativity between rights and duties. In his view, the principle that "all obligations confer rights on others" is inconsistent with the fact that "imperfect obligations do not confer rights" and he wrote:

> Now it is known that ethical writers divided moral duties into two classes, denoted by the ill-chosen expressions, duties of perfect and of imperfect obligations; the latter being those in which, though the act is obligatory, the particular occasions of performing it are left to our choice; as in the case of charity of beneficence, which we are indeed bound to practice, but not toward any definite person, nor at any prescribed time. In the more precise language of philosophic jurists, duties of perfect obligation are those duties in virtue of which a correlative *right* resides in some person or persons; duties of imperfect obligation are those moral obligations which do not give birth to any right.[87]

Indeed, the so-called duties of imperfect obligation or imperfect duties do not confer rights on others. However, these so-called duties of imperfect obligation or imperfect duties such as charity or benevolence, are not actually duties, for charity, benevolence and so forth are clearly not compelled by power or law, but only interests that one *ought to but are not compelled to* give to others; duties are the interests that one *must and ought to* give others and should be enforced and guaranteed by power or law. Thus the so-called imperfect duties such as charity or benevolence, as Rawls put it, are not duties but supererogatory actions: "among permissions is the interesting class of supererogatory actions. These are acts of benevolence and mercy of heroism and self-sacrifice. It is good to do this but it is not one's duty or obligations."[88] Therefore Mill's denial of the principle of correlativity of "all duties should confer rights on others" by the fact that imperfect duties do not confer rights on others, is untenable.

What rights a person enjoys, is what corresponding duties the other party assumes; what the duties a person assumes, is what right the other party enjoys. This is a fact, a necessity but not oughtness. Then why should a person enjoy rights that make the other party assume duties? Obviously, it is only because he has a duty to the other party so that the other party enjoy rights. Thus, a person's rights ought only to be in exchange for his own duties to the other party; in other words, the rights he gets from the other party should only be exchanged for the duty he undertakes from the other party. In turn, why is it that a person ought to assume duties so that the other side can enjoy rights? Obviously, he only enjoys rights because the other party undertakes duties to him. Therefore, the duties of a person ought only to be in exchange for his rights: one's duties for the other side ought only to be exchanged for the rights one receives from the other side.

It can be seen that the rights enjoyed by a person and his duties ought only to be a kind of exchange relationship, which is completely based on and derived from the principle of logical correlativity between rights and duties. Otherwise, if rights and duties are not logically relevant, if a person enjoys a right that does not compel others to assume duties, the right he enjoys is not the reason that he ought to assume the duties so that others enjoy rights, thus his rights and his duties ought not to be an exchange relationship. Thus, only the necessary and the factual correlativity that "one's rights must be the duty of others" can produce and determine the due and moral correlativity that "the relationship between the rights one enjoys and the duties one assumes ought to be a kind of exchange relationship."

Thus the relationship between rights and duties can be summed up as two types of correlativity: one is the necessary and factual correlativity that "one's rights must be the duties of others" which is called "the logical correlativity of rights and duties"; the other is the due correlativity that "one's rights ought to be the exchange of his duties," thus can be called "the moral correlativity of rights and duties." The ethicist who clearly distinguishes between the two seems to be Feinberg. He wrote:

> It is often said that there can be no rights without obligations, and that the prerequisite for acquiring and owning rights is the abilities and willingness to assume obligations and responsibilities. Acceptance of an obligation is the price that anyone must pay in order to acquire rights. This

theory is called the moral theory of rights and duties, which is absolutely different from the theory of logical correlativity of rights and duties that asserting the conference of rights to a person logically requires the existence of at least one other person who has an obligation to him.[89]

Then, what is the specific content of the moral correlativity between rights and duties? In other words, what kind of exchange relationship ought one's rights and one's own duties be? Ought there to be more rights than duties or more duties than rights, or equal rights and duties? This is a rather complicated question, for one's rights and duties, examined in detail, have a dual relationship: on the one hand, there is a relationship between the rights one enjoys and the duties one assumes; on the other hand, there is a relationship between the rights one exercises and the duties one performs.

The rights one enjoys and the duties one assumes are clearly not freely chosen but are distributed to him by society. Therefore, "the rights one enjoys and the duties one assumes" and "the rights and duties distributed to one by society" are the same concept. So how ought society to distribute them? Hegel replied: "by how much obligations a person has, how much rights he has; how much rights he has, how much obligations he has."[90] Indeed, it is just only when the rights distributed to a person by society equals his duties; if not, it is unjust, regardless of whether rights outweigh duties or duties outweigh rights.

The logical correlativity of rights and duties shows that a person's rights are the other party's duties; that a person's duties are the other party's rights. Thus, if society distributes more rights to a person than his duties, then the rights conferred upon him by the other party's duties are more than the rights conferred by his duties on the other party, that is, the rights he obtains from the other side are more than the rights he gives to the other party, thus he encroaches on the other party's rights and is therefore unjust. Conversely, if society distributes more duties to a person than his rights, then the rights conferred by his duties on the other party are more than the rights conferred upon him by the other party's duties, that is, the rights he confers to the other party are more than the rights conferred to him by the other party, thus his rights are encroached by other party and is therefore also unjust. So, only when one's duties distributed by society equals his rights distributed by society, the rights conferred by his duties on the other party are equal to the rights conferred upon him by the other party's duties, and the rights he confers to other party are equal to the rights conferred to him by the other party, thus are just: justice is the exchange of equal interests (or harms).

Therefore, the rights everyone enjoys are equal to the duties they assume, that is, the rights that a society distributes to everyone equal their duties, which is a just principle that a society distributes equal rights and duties to everyone. On the contrary, the rights everyone enjoys that are not equal to their duties is an unjust principle such that a society distributes unequal rights and duties to everyone. The distribution of rights and duties in society, as mentioned above, is a fundamental issue of social justice, therefore, the rights everyone enjoys are equal to the duties they assume (i.e., the rights that a society distributes to everyone equal their duties) is not only a kind of social justice but also a fundamental social justice and a fundamental principle of social justice. Conversely, the rights everyone enjoys that are not equal to their duties are not only a kind of social injustice but also a fundamental social injustice and a fundamental principle of social injustice.

On the contrary, the rights exercised by a person and the duties he performs can be chosen by himself: he may give up some of his rights and thus exercise less rights than he enjoys, or he may not perform some of his obligations and thus perform less obligations than he assumes. It goes without saying that the rights exercised by a person should be at most equal to the duties he performs. In other words, the rights a person exercises ought to be less than or equal to the duties he performs. It is obviously unjust that a person exercise more rights than the duties he performs; it is undoubtedly just that the rights he exercises is equal to the duties he fulfills; if the rights he exercises is less than the duties he performs, there is no issue of being just or unjust but supererogatory actions beyond justice. The exercise of rights and the fulfillment of duties by everyone, as mentioned above, are fundamental issues of personal justice. Thus the right exercised by a person equal to the duties he performs is not only a kind of personal justice but also a fundamental personal justice and the fundamental principle of personal justice; on the contrary, if the rights exercised by a person are greater than the duties he performs, it is not only a kind of personal injustice, but also a fundamental personal injustice and a fundamental principle of personal injustice.

On the whole, rights and duties (whether it is the rights and duties between human beings, or the rights and duties between human beings and non-human beings, as well as whether it is statutory rights and statutory duties or moral rights and moral duties) have a double relationship. On the one hand, it is the relationship of fact and inevitability, that is, a person's rights are necessarily related to the duties of others or non-human beings and vice versa: a person's rights are the duties of others or non-human beings; on the other hand, it is the relationship of ought to be, that is, the rights one enjoys should be equal to the duties he assumes, and the rights he exercises ought to be at most equal to the duties he performs: that the rights one enjoys are equal to the duties one assumes (i.e., the rights society distributes to everyone are equal to their duties) is the fundamental principle of social justice; that the rights a person exercises are equal to the duties he fulfills is the fundamental principle of personal justice; and that rights are equal to duties is the fundamental principle of justice.

6.3 Principle of contribution: Fundamental principle of social justice

It is not difficult to see that the fundamental principle of social justice—that "the rights and duties society distributes to everyone ought to be equal"—is imperfect: it obviously is a direct deduction of the fundamental principle of justice that "the right and the duty ought to be equal" without anything new or different added. Therefore, it is not so much a fundamental principle of social justice as it is a fundamental principle of justice; if we regard it as a fundamental principle of social justice, it is simplistic, deficient, imperfect, and unpractical. Imagine if society was to distribute to everyone exactly the same rights and duties, though it would conform to this fundamental principle of social justice, it no doubt is not what ought to be: everyone's duties and rights must and should be different to some extent.

Thus, the flaw of this fundamental principle of social justice is that it just tells us that the rights and duties distributed to everyone ought to be equal, without telling us how many rights and duties ought to be distributed to everyone, and on what basis different rights and duties ought to be distributed, and on what basis some people ought to be distributed with more important rights and duties, while some others are distributed with less important rights and duties.

These are the problems concerning source and basis of the distribution of rights and duties. Thus, the shortcoming of the fundamental principle of social justice (the rights and duties society distributes to everyone ought to be equal) then lies in that the source and basis of the distribution of rights and duties do not defined. What, then, is the source and basis of social distribution of everyone's rights and duties? It is contribution! Contribution is the source and basis of rights; in other words, society ought to distribute rights according to contributions and duties according to rights; in the final analysis, the rights that society distributes to everyone ought to be proportional to their contribution and equal to their duties. This is the perfect fundamental principle of social justice, known as the "principle of contribution."

6.3.1 Distribution of rights according to contribution: Actual principle of contribution

Saint-Simon once summed up the principle of contribution in one sentence: "to enable each member of society to receive the greatest wealth and welfare of his own according to his contribution."[91] Adler also wrote about this principle: "To each in proportion to his contribution to the total wealth that all engaged cooperatively in producing."[92] Both are so true! The so-called principle of contribution is the distribution of rights according to contributions and duties according to rights. It is almost a self-evident axiom that the principle of contribution is the principle of social justice, for, despite so many different theories of social justice in academia, almost no one refutes this principle; on the contrary, as Arthur Okun said, "They all paid tribute to the initial assumption that income should be based on contributions to output."[93] But why is the principle of contribution the fundamental principle of social justice?

It is because rights and duties respectively belong to the concepts of "claim" and "contribution" and to the category of "interests": rights are interests, claims, or demands that ought to be protected by power or law; duties are interests, contributions, or services that ought to be regulated by power or law. It is very clear that the contribution is the first and the claim is the second: contribution is the source of the claim because so-called society, as Rawls put it, is "a system of cooperation designed to advance the good of those taking part in it."[94] In this way, everyone contributes interests to society first (contribution), then society distributes the interests to everyone (claim): the interests that society distributes to everyone are nothing more than the interests that everyone contributes and the exchange of interests that everyone contributes. Therefore, how much interest society distributes to everyone should be based only on how much interest everyone contributes: contribution being the basis for claims. So Hayek said: "People should enjoy advantages in proportion to the benefits which their fellows derive from their activities."[95]

Contribution is the source and basis of the claims, thus the source and basis of rights. Because rights belong to the category of claim, right is a special kind of claim, and is the necessary and due claim protected by power or law. That contribution is the source and basis of rights it undoubtedly means that rights ought to be distributed according to contribution. The distribution of rights according to contributions means that the rights ought to be proportional to the contributions: the less the contributions, the less the rights; the more the contributions, the more the rights. On the one hand, however, no matter how many the rights, they ought not to be more than or equal to, but ought to be less than contributions; on the other hand, no matter how few the rights are, they ought not to be less than but equal to the contributions regulated by law ("contribution regulated by law" and "duty" are the same concept): rights ought not to be less than, but ought to be equal to duties.

It is obviously unjust for one to enjoy more rights than his contributions, for one's rights are the interests he gets from others which are protected by law. Therefore, if one enjoys more rights than his contribution, it would be same as forcing others to give him the extra portion of interests freely and is a kind of forcible deprivation of the interests of others and is therefore unjust. This injustice was the fundamental characteristic of the state institutions in ancient China: the rights of the official class were far more than their contributions. Since the Five Emperors Period, especially during the Xia, Shang and Zhou dynasties to the Qing Dynasty, the autocrats and their official classes had been in full power in China controlling everything in every field—political power, economic power, social power such as association and assembly, as well as cultural power such as speech and publication. As a result, they almost monopolized all rights. *The civilian population class, who were slaves, serfs and servants subordinated or attached to the official class, suffered from the four compulsions of monopoly of the official class's* full power. *Although they had interests, there was almost no power to protect them, therefore they had almost no rights at all: rights are the interests protected by power.*

It is also unjust that rights are equal to contributions. Because, on the one hand, contributions are not equal to duty, contributions certainly are

212 *Moral value and moral norms*

more than duties: duties are only a special contribution and only a contribution stipulated by law. Therefore, if the rights given to a person are equal to his contributions, his rights would be more than his duties, then his claim protected by law would be more than his contributions stipulated by law, and his rights obtained from others would be more than the rights he gives to others, and he would invade the rights of others, which is unjust. On the other hand, claims are not equal to rights, and certainly are more than rights: rights are only special kinds of claims which are protected by power. Therefore, if the rights given to a person are equal to his contributions, then his claims certainly outweigh his rights and thus outweigh his contributions, and that would be the same as forcing others to freely contribute to him the extra part of interests. As a kind of forcible deprivation of others interests it is thus unjust. These two aspects can be summed up in two columns:

Contributions certainly are more than duties Claims certainly are more than rights
if rights are equal to contributions if rights are equal to contributions
Rights are more than duties. Claims are more than contributions

So, if the rights are equal to the contributions, claims are more than contributions and the rights are more than duties, which is therefore unjust. Though it is just if a person's claims are equal to his contribution, it is unjust that his claims that are protected by power—rights—are equal to his contributions. Clearly, his claims that are protected by power are just only if they are equal to his contributions protected by the power (duties): it is just only when rights are equal to duties, but it is unjust when rights are equal to contributions. Then, what is the relationship between rights and contributions?

Rights ought neither to be more than, nor equal to contributions, which clearly means that rights ought to be less than contributions. Indeed, a person's rights ought to be less than his contributions, or, his contribution only ought to be more than his rights. Because in terms of social distribution, rights and duties ought to be equal, claims and contributions ought to be equal. Duty is a special contribution, which is a necessary and due contribution protected by power: contributions certainly are more than duties. On the contrary, right is a special kind of claim, which is a necessary and due claim protected by power: claims are certainly more than rights. Thus, taken together it can be concluded that contributions ought to be more than rights:

Contributions certainly are more than duties Claims certainly are more than rights duties and rights ought to be equal Contributions and claims ought to be equal Contributions ought to be more than rights Contributions ought to be more than rights.

It can be seen that everyone's rights only ought to be less than his contributions, not equal to or more than his contributions. However, in

Justice and equality 213

terms of social distribution, it is just that a person's rights are less than his contributions only within a certain limit, while beyond this limit, it is unjust. This limit is the duty which is a kind of contribution stipulated by law: no matter how little the right a person has, it ought not to be less than but only ought to be equal to his contributions that are stipulated by law, that is to say, it ought not be less than but only ought to be equal to his duties, for it is just only when a person's rights are equal to his duties. If a person's rights are less than his duties or his contributions stipulated by law, then the rights his duties give to the other party are more than the rights the other party's duties give him. In the final analysis, the rights he gives the other party are more than the rights other party gives him, thus his rights are encroached upon by the other party, and it is therefore unjust.

Thus, the distribution of rights according to contributions neither implies that rights and contributions ought to be equal, nor implies that rights ought to be more than or less than contributions, and thus only refers to that rights ought to be proportional to contributions: the more one contributes, the more rights one ought to enjoy; the less one contributes, the less rights one ought to enjoy. But no matter how many the rights are, they ought not to be more than or equal to contributions; no matter how little the rights are, they ought not to be less than but only ought to be equal to the contributions stipulated by law (i.e., duties): the rights society distributes to everyone ought to be proportional to his contributions and equal to his duties. The principle is shown in Figure 6.1.

Generally speaking, contribution is the source and basis of rights; in other words, society ought to distribute rights according to the contributions, and duties according to rights; in the final analysis, *the rights that society distributes to everyone ought to be proportional to his contributions and equal to his duties.* This is the veritable fundamental principle of social justice, known as the "principle of contribution," which, however, on closer examination, is

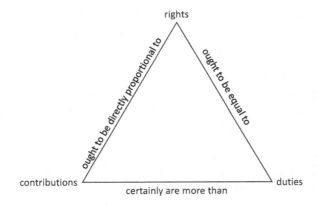

Figure 6.1 The principle of contribution

not the whole of the principle of contribution but only one aspect of it: the actual principle of contribution. The principle of contribution has another aspect: the potential principle of contribution.

6.3.2 Distribution of rights according to virtue and talents: The potential principle of contribution

Contribution as the source and basis of rights implies that contribution comes first, right follows later. In practice, however, many of the most important rights such as position, status and power, and so on, usually ought to be distributed before contributions. Historically, many people have been promoted to important positions first and then made great contributions, so doesn't this negate the principle of the distribution of rights by contribution? Well, no, it doesn't. There are actual contributions and potential contributions. The distribution of rights, such as position, status and power, in fact, is also based on contributions: the contribution comes first then right follows later but the contribution is potential rather than actual.

The so-called potential contribution in this respect rests on internal contribution factors such as "talents and virtue" and on external contribution factors such as "luck and birth." In other words, these factors or reasons can lead to contribution. They are in this sense the possible state of contribution. That is, as contributions yet to be made. On the contrary, the actual contribution is the product of the combination of the contribution factors such as virtue, talents, luck, and birth. It is a contribution in a real state, that is, a contribution that has been made. The distribution of rights, such as position, status, and power, usually ought to be based on everyone's potential contribution; however, it ought not to be based on any potential contribution, which is to say that it ought not to be based on external contribution factors such as luck and birth, it ought to be based on virtue and talents which are the two internal contribution factors.

It is true that external factors such as luck and birth are important factors to determine the contribution: better luck and birth may lead to greater contribution, and worse luck and birth may lead to a smaller contribution. However, it is accidental and possible, but not inevitable, and destined because we can see everywhere that people with good luck and birth often overlook opportunities and fail in life because they take life for granted, while many people with bad luck and birth are very successful and often make meritorious contributions because of their hard work. Therefore, we might say, external contribution factors such as luck and family background are a potential contribution with occasionality; the potential contribution may or may not become actual since accidental factors of contribution make for unpredictable contributions. Thence, the distribution of rights according to accidental external factors of contribution such as luck and birth may lead to the possession of rights without contribution and thus deviate from the principle of distribution of rights according to contribution. No distribution of rights therefore should be based on external factors alone.

On the contrary, virtue and talent are everyone's internal contribution factors and the combination of the two is a sufficient condition for determining the contribution: those who have higher virtue and talent will make greater contributions while those who have lower virtue and talent will contribute less. Therefore, virtue and talent are potential contributions with necessity, the potential contributions are bound to be actual, for virtue and talent can be accurately predicted as the inevitable factor of contribution. Consequently, the "distribution of rights according to virtue and talent" is the distribution of rights according to contributions that are bound to be made, thus it is only a special and a potential form of "distribution of rights according to contribution": virtue and talent are the potential basis for the distribution of rights while contribution (that is realized) is the actual basis for the distribution of rights.

However, the distribution of rights according to virtue and talent does not mean that the distribution of rights based on either virtue or talent but on both virtue and talent. This is because only the combination of "virtue" and "talent" can become the sufficient condition of contribution, that is, the factor that inevitably leads to contribution; if the two are separated, they are no longer sufficient conditions for contribution and are no longer inevitable factors leading to contribution. If one has virtue but no talent, though one may have a good motive to contribute and benefit others, it is no certainty that one's contribution does much to benefits others—one could even harm others with their good intention. As Marx said: "The road to hell is paved with good intentions."[96] On the other hand, if one has talent without virtue, there is no telling whether he'd be the maker of great contributions or great calamities:

> Ever since ancient times, the able ministers of the states and the prodigal sons in families usually ruin the country and families, for they have talents but no virtues.[97]

It is obvious that any individual, no matter whether he has virtue without talent or talent without virtue, is able to make or fails to make contributions. Therefore, if "virtue" and "talent" are separated, they are merely accidental factors leading to contributions, like luck or birth are. Thus, the separation of "virtue" from "talent" as a separate basis for the distribution of rights may lead to the possession of rights without contribution, deviating from the principle of justice which distributes rights according to contributions. Therefore, in terms of its administration, a fundamental principle of social justice is neither "appointing people by talent" (distributing rights merely according to one's talent); nor "appointing people by virtue" (distributing rights merely according to one's virtue), but "appointing people by both virtue and talent" (distributing rights according to both virtue and talent). This is why the principles of "distributing rights according to contribution" and "distributing rights according to virtue and talent" are just, but the principles of "distributing rights according to virtue" and "distributing rights according to talent" are unjust.

However, there are many kinds of talents and there is absolutely no individual with all talents. Similarly, the moral character of human beings vary greatly and no individual is morally perfect. Furthermore, so-called intelligent and able persons certainly only are capable in some fields but not in all; while so-called virtuous persons certainly are virtuous in some respects but not in all. Indeed, we could create a whole list: for instance, one might be brave, but not circumspect, very diligent but not abstemious, have self-respect but not modesty, be very kind but not be fair, or be professional but not take good care of oneself. Therefore, so-called appointments by a combination of virtue and talent are not fault-finding and demanding perfection but by "appointing people in like manner to utilizing tools and making the best use of the advantages by overlooking the disadvantages": just as we use different tools for different purposes, or, as the saying goes, the right tool for the job, individuals ought to be assigned corresponding positions according to the type of character and talents they possess. Take, for example, the appointment of a military commander in ancient China:

If the position of a military commander-in-chief is distributed as a right according to the principles of *appointing people in like manner to utilizing tools* and of *making the best use of the advantages by overlooking the disadvantages*, then, the person appointed to the position of a military commander-in-chief, on the one hand, judging from his talent, may be lacking literary skills and eloquence and be without the art of governing the country, but certainly must have a good command of the military arts and knowledge of wars. On the other hand, the person appointed, from a moral point of view, might be unkind to others, not filial to his parents, greedy, or self-interested, but certainly must have never been reckless or cowardly, or one to betray the country and monarch that cherishes his abilities. The principle of appointing people not by talent or virtue alone is attributed to Cao Cao (曹操), the ancient minister in charge of military talent in ancient China, who said: "Every gentleman has his shortcomings, but we should make good use of his strong point."[98]

What he called "recommending all the persons who have good talents" is not that he did not pay attention to virtue, but only did not care much for the generally dispensable orthodox virtues of benevolence, filial piety, and probity. Instead, he stressed the qualities that are essential for being generals and ministers of state, such as loyalty: otherwise, he would not have killed Lv Bu who was talented but capricious and virtueless. Wu Qi (吴起), Chen Ping (陈平), and Han Xin (韩信), the greatest generals in Chinese history who he cited as examples to promote his principle of "recommending all the persons who have good abilities," simply lacked the conventional virtues:

> Before rising in ranks to general and as generals, both Han Xin and Chen Ping were often taunted for their eccentricities, and Wu Qi was greedy,

he had killed his wife for the king's trust, squandered money to obtain the position of a military commander and did not return home when his mother died.

However, all three had the moral characters necessary for being great generals and ministers of the state; in particular they demonstrated a certain loyalty to their monarchs. Wu Qi, for example, had forsaken the state of Lu for the state of Wei, then left Wei for the state of Chu, not because he was capricious or out of ingratitude but because the monarch of the states of Lu and Wei became "suspicious of him and did not trust him."[99] Han Xin was loyal to Liu Bang, who thought highly of him, so when Xiang Yu sent Wu She (武涉) to persuade Han Xin to betray Liu Bang and make himself the King and divide China into three states, Han Xin refused him:

> When I served King Xiang I was a low rank officer as a guard ... King Xiang never listened to my opinions or adopted my suggestions, therefore I left him for the State of Han. The King of Han appointed me as the commander-in-chief and put tens of thousands of solders under my command ... gave me his own food and clothes, listened to and accepted ... my opinions ... It is inauspicious to betray the man who truly trusts me, and I will not betray him even if I die.[100]

Chen Ping had affairs with his sister-in-law and accepted bribery, but he was not disloyal to his master, otherwise, no matter how capable he was, Liu Bang would not promote him. When the other two important ministers, Zhou Bo (周勃) and Guan Ying (灌婴), slandered Chen Ping as "a capricious and disloyal official who betrayed his monarch," Liu Bang became very suspicious of him and

> reproached him: "You at first served the State of Wei, then left for the State of Chu, so now that you are following me, how many masters are you going to serve?" Chen Ping replied: "When I served King of Wei he did not accept my suggestions, thus I left him for King Xiang, but King Xiang did not trust people except his own relatives and clan members and did not like to use people of great capacity if they had no personal relations with him, that's why I left him. Since I heard that your majesty makes good use of people I came to you. I came here without a penny and have to accept money for personal expenses. If your majesty thinks that there are some things in my suggestions that are useful, your majesty may use it; if your majesty thinks that my suggestions are useless, all the money I accepted is still here, please seal the money for official use and I will return to my home country and die there." The king of Han apologized and bequeathed him with a great sum of money, then appointed him as a high ranking general.[101]

218 *Moral value and moral norms*

It can be seen that the distribution of rights concerning general appointments for official positions ought to be based on both virtues and talents, while with the rights concerning special positions of office, certain non-essential qualities of virtue and talents can be disregarded. This is what is meant by the principles of *making the best use of the advantages by overlooking the disadvantages* and *appointing people in like manner to utilizing tools*.

In a word, "virtue" and "talent" are the potential source and basis of rights such as appointments to official positions; in other words, society should appoint people based both on their virtues and talents, distributing duties and other rights according to everyone's "virtue" and "talent"; in the final analysis, society should *make best use of the advantages by overlooking the disadvantages and thereby appoint people in like manner to utilizing tools*, distributing to everyone corresponding duties according to the nature of their moral character and talents. This "principle of virtue and talents" is fundamental social justice and is the "potential principle of contribution" deduced from the "actual principle of contribution"—the rights that society distributes to everyone should be proportional to everyone's contribution and equal to everyone's duties.

The principle of contribution (taking into account both the actual principle of contribution and the potential principle of contribution) is the principle that society distributes the rights and duties to everyone, thus is a fundamental principle of social justice: the distribution of rights and duties are the fundamental issue of social justice. However, when we specifically distribute the basic and non-basic rights of everyone on the basis of this principle of contribution, we find that the most important fundamental principle of social justice is equality: on the one hand, the basic rights enjoyed by everyone should be fully equal; on the other hand, the non-basic rights enjoyed by everyone should be equal in proportion.

6.4 Equality: The most important justice

6.4.1 *The concept of equality*

What is equality? Giovanni Sartori said: "Equality conveys the idea of *sameness* ... Two or more persons or objects can be declared equal in the sense of being—in some or all respects—identical, of being the same, alike."[102] Indeed, equality is the sameness among people. But the sameness among people is not necessarily equality. If one has a black nevus on his hand which is the same as someone else's black nevus, we cannot say they have an "equal" black nevi. They might also have the same surname, but it cannot be said the surname is equal. Then, what kind of sameness is equality among people?

Equality is the sameness among people related to the obtaining of interests. This sameness means either the interests they get are the same or the source of the interests they get are the same: either this or that. For example, people's

Justice and equality 219

talent and gender are not directly benefits, but can bring benefits, thus are the source of benefits. As a result, if two persons are the same in talent and gender, they thus have the same source of interests. Correspondingly, people's salaries and ranks are direct benefits, therefore if two persons have the same salary and rank, they have the same interests. The sameness among people can be called equality only if it concerns either the interests or the sources of interests. So, then, in the above example, why can we say that the two persons have the same (but not "an equal") nevus or have the same (but not "an equal") surname? why can we say that the two persons have equal sex, talent, and position. Isn't it because the nevus and the surname are not related to interests while the gender and position are?

It can be seen that the sameness or difference among people is not necessarily related to interests, while equality or inequality between people is certainly related to interests: equality is the sameness between people in relation to the acquisition of interests while inequality is the difference among people in relation to the acquisition of interests.

However, the causes of equality and inequality, as seen by Rousseau, can be divided into two categories: natural and artificial (what Rousseau calls spiritual or political):

> I discern two sorts of inequality in the human species: the first I call natural or physical because it is established by nature, and consists of differences in age, health, strength of the body and qualities of the mind or soul; the second we might call moral or political inequality because it derives from a sort of convention, and is established, or at least authorized, by the consent of men.[103]

To be more precise, equality and inequality, on the one hand, originate from nature and are caused by nature, and therefore neither can be chosen nor can be evaluated morally, and neither has issues of being good or evil, ought to be or ought not to be, such as gender, color, race, appearance, figure, or talent. This is natural equality and inequality. Equality and inequality, on the other hand, arise or result from the free activities of mankind, and therefore can be chosen and morally evaluated, having issues of being good or evil, ought to be or ought not to be, such as the gap between the poor and the rich, the distribution of wealth in society, or equalization of income. This is artificial equality and inequality.

Thus, though natural equality and artificial equality are both related to the interests, and are matters concerning the interests among people, natural equality is only a matter of interests, not a matter of rights with oughtness. On the contrary, artificial equality is not only a matter of interests, but also, in essence, a matter of rights with oughtness, artificial equality, as countless philosophers have said, is actually the equality of rights. That's why we can say that we have the right to acquire a certain kind of salary, position, status, but no right to acquire a certain kind of color, gender, and talent.

Since only artificial equality—rather than natural equality—has a connection with what ought to or ought not to be, equality, as a moral principle or value standard of *ought*, can only be artificial, not natural equality. Artificial equality is essentially equality of rights. Therefore, the principle of equality is the principle of equality of rights. The French *Declaration of Human Rights* writes: "Equality means that all men have the same rights." In China, *Cihai* (《辞海》) also said: "Equality means that people are equal in society and have equal rights in politics, economy, culture, etc."

Does this imply, then, that all human rights ought to be fully equal? Should all the rights enjoyed by the president and by civilian population be fully equal? Obviously not. It is neither possible nor *ought to be* that all the rights enjoyed by the president and by civilians are fully equal. Does this mean, then, what the *Declaration of Human Rights* advocates is wrong and that everyone should not enjoy equal rights? It does not. However, since it is right that everyone should enjoy equal rights, and it is also true that the president and the civilian population should not enjoy equal rights, is this not a paradox? It's not a paradox at all. This is because the principle of equality of rights has two meanings: on the one hand, the basic rights everyone enjoys ought to be fully equal; on the other hand, the non-basic rights everyone enjoys ought to be proportionately equal. Full equality is the principle of distribution of basic rights while proportional equality is the principle of distribution of non-basic rights.

6.4.2 The principle of full equality

The so-called basic rights are the necessary, minimum, and the lowest rights for human survival and development; they are the rights to meet the basic, minimum, and the lowest needs of people in the fields of politics, economy, and thought, etc.; non-basic rights are higher rights for human survival and development, the rights that satisfy the higher needs in the fields of politics, economy, and thought, etc. For example, in terms of politics, whether a person enjoys the right to vote and the right to be elected is a question of whether a person enjoys the lowest, minimum, and basic political rights, while, if a person is elected or appointed as an official the issue is then whether that person enjoys the higher level and non-basic political rights. In terms of economic rights, the rights of food and clothing are the minimum and basic rights; good food and beautiful clothes are higher and non-basic economic rights. In terms of thought, freedom of speech is a minimum and fundamental right of thought, but whether it is possible to speak at certain academic conference, or to publish a book in certain publishing houses, or to be paid a high or low remuneration for it are higher and non-basic rights of thought.

The classification of basic rights and non-basic rights is very simple. However, the question of the source and basis of these two kinds of rights is so extremely complex and difficult to understand that for more than two

Justice and equality 221

thousand years, from Aristotle to Rawls, thinkers have been trying to find out why everyone ought to be entitled to both basic and non-basic rights? What is the source and basis for everyone to have both basic and non-basic rights? This difficult problem has not been answered with satisfactory explanations. The difficulty in solving this problem lies in the fact that all rights should be distributed merely according to contribution; thus everyone's basic rights ought to be distributed merely according to their contributions to society. However, if the distribution of basic rights ought to be fully equal, doesn't it mean that, no matter how many contributions one makes, the basic rights one enjoys ought to be totally equal? Isn't that contradictory?

This is not the case. Everyone ought to enjoy basic rights on a fully equal footing because everyone is a member of society. That is, we are all shareholders in the creation and establishment of society. As countless philosophers have argued, human beings are essentially social animals and so without society no human beings could survive. Thus, without a doubt, society has the greatest value or utility for everyone; thereupon a just society is in everyone's interests. Society, we know, is a community of two or more people connected in one way or other. In other words, a community is created or established by the basic human need to unite with others. Therefore, through the unions that are formed by making contributions to others within community, one is already beyond community participating in and contributing to the creation and establishment of the greater or more diversified society. Whatever the contribution one makes it is based on this! Without community or society, no one could survive, or, at least not in the long term: there would be nothing to contribute to. Without society, would Beethoven have written *Symphony No. 5*, Cao Xueqin (曹雪芹) written *The Dream of the Red Chamber*, or Watts invented the steam engine?

Therefore, the creation of society is most basic and most important contribution of all the contributions everyone makes. In other words, to society, one makes their most basic and greatest contribution. Not only that, but everyone's contribution comes at the expense of their own loss, for there are gains and losses in forming any community. For example, getting married one will lose the freedom of being single, but may make a happy partner and parent, enjoying all sorts of benefits of family life. Although human society is also a community formed by individuals, the difference is that it is not formed voluntarily; it cannot be chosen freely because it is what one is born into. This is to say, historically, human beings have never had the natural state of being separated from society first before forming society by contract. But, as social contract theorists like Rawls point out, what does not exist in history may as well exist logically. Logically, everyone who forms a society out of the natural state has his share of gains and losses, such as the loss of one's natural freedom, which the social contract theorists have made clear. Then, what does everyone get in society? Obviously, everyone, whatever their contributions are, at least ought to get what they deserve as a shareholder in human society. But what does a shareholder of human society deserve? There is no doubt at least the necessary, minimum, and lowest right for their survival and development, that is, the so-called basic rights.

Everyone ought to not only enjoy basic rights but also enjoy basic rights on a completely equal footing, for although people's talents, virtue, and contributions are different, everyone's most basic and most important contribution to the creation of society and the losses suffered as a result is the same. We do not participate in the creation or establishment of society in the sense that once we reach adulthood only then do we make valuable contributions i.e., whether that be as a president or a writer, or as just an ordinary civilian or illiterate person; we have rather no option at all but to participate in and contribute to the creation and formation of society as soon as we are born. The reason why everyone, no matter how much they contribute, should enjoy basic rights on a completely equal footing is because, and only because, the most basic, the most important contribution everyone makes in their participation in the creation of society, including the losses as a result of the contribution, is completely the same. Therefore, it is not a gift but a debt that the common people are distributed the same basic rights as that of a great president. Paine put it well: "Society has not given him anything in vain. Everyone is a shareholder of society and thus has the right to draw on equity."[104]

It can be seen that the equal distribution of basic rights is not contrary to but consistent with the principle of "distribution of rights according to contributions": basic rights are the rights that everyone ought to enjoy on a fully equal footing because everyone is as the same as others as a shareholder in the creation of society; that is to say, basic rights are the rights that everyone ought to enjoy on a completely equal footing because everyone forms society. The crux of the problem is that as long as one is born, he naturally and non-optionally participates in the creation of society and becomes a shareholder of human society. Therefore, human rights or basic rights are innate and endowed by nature: NATURAL RIGHTS. In a word, *basic rights*, *human rights* and *natural rights* are the same concepts. Beauchamp said: "The expression 'human rights' is a recent label for what has traditionally been referred as 'natural right' or, in an old vernacular, the 'rights of man.' Such rights are often touted as inalienable and possessed equally by all persons."[105]

So-called natural rights only mean that human rights are an inherent entitlement concerning the innate contribution of everyone in the creation of society. Unfortunately, however, almost all human rights theorists believe that human rights are an inherent entitlement regarding common human nature: "Human rights are equal rights for all people because they are human beings."[106] "How does our humanity justify our right to these equalities? The answer is that, by being human, we are all equal."[107] This type of theory is a fallacy, for in this way, a person, as long as he is alive and as long as he is a human being, should enjoy human rights: that human rights are absolutely inalienable for everyone under all circumstances. Thus, no matter how evil a person may be, no matter how much harm he causes to others, he ought not to be deprived of human rights—he ought to enjoy the same human rights as a good person—both a good person and an evil person have the same human nature.

However, faced with the reality, these human rights theorists have to admit that not everyone should enjoy human rights; for example, concede that a murderer violates the most basic human right and so should be deprived of his right to life, which is an argument akin to French *Declaration of Human Rights* that says: "Every human being shall exercise his natural rights to the extent that he must let others to freely exercise the same rights."

This is correct. However, in a way, these human rights theorists are paradoxical: they advocate that all people should enjoy human rights, but also that bad people should not enjoy human rights. The only way for this to be a reasonable argument is to deny one of the propositions: for instance, if they cannot deny that all people should enjoy human rights, they then have to deny that evil people are not human beings. Chiu Ben wrote: "Evil people cannot be deprived of their human rights until they are evil enough to the extent that they no longer are human beings."[108] Can evil people be evil enough to the extent that they no longer are human beings? No matter how evil the evil people are, aren't they still evil people? Or do they have the same human nature the same as anyone else?

Strictly speaking, no one should be entitled to human rights so as long as the harm done to others is greater than or equal to his contribution, or in such a way that the net balance is harm or zero, so, in answer to the above question, one ought to be treated humanely at best, having the interests of being a human but not the rights. On the latter point, let's suppose, for instance, that an infant abandoned in a deep forest subsist thereafter—say raised by wolves—completely isolated from the world. If we should come across him in the forest as a grown child or adult, does he have rights such that we then assume duties, as one human to another, so that he enjoys the basic rights or human rights, e.g., so-called economic rights, political rights, and so on? Obviously, no, for this person has not made any contribution to society, and thus has no so-called rights. What we *should* rather than *must* assume or extend to him is humane care. That is, we ought to establish a fraternity that seek benefits or interests for him, because, as humans, what we ought to all enjoy is not so much rights as interests; so, if, as part of the fraternity, this person brings equal interests, he contributes to human society, and like everyone else, he not only enjoys interests but also enjoys human rights.

Therefore, although human rights are natural rights and ought to be enjoyed by everyone on a completely equal footing, the enjoyment of human rights, just like the enjoyment of other rights, are premised on the basis of certain duties everyone assumes. Duties, on the one hand, are positive, that is, everyone must make the contribution of forming a society together with others, which is the source and basis for the equal enjoyment of human rights by all; on the other hand, duties can also be of a kind that are negative, that is, it is everyone's duty to not infringe on the rights of others, which is the guarantee and condition of the equal enjoyment of human rights by all. Of course, an exception to the former duties are hermits who on completely opting out of society shirk such responsibilities concerning their fellow humans, while those who commit some kind of atrocity violate the latter duties, which, because it outweighs or nullifies their contributions, means they should not enjoy human rights.

In a word, since everyone's most basic contribution—as a shareholder in the construction of a society—is fully equal, that is, everyone ought to enjoy basic rights or human rights on a fully equal footing. This is the principle of the full equality of basic rights or human rights, and is also the so-called "principle of human rights."

6.4.3 The principle of proportional equality

Everyone should enjoy human rights or basic rights on a completely equal footing seems to mean that everyone ought to enjoy unequal non-human rights, non-basic rights or higher rights. Actually, this is not the case because the equality as the principle of distribution of rights implies that any unequal distribution of rights is immoral, ought not to be, and has negative value. How, then, should non-basic rights be distributed? It should be according to proportional equality! Equality of proportion was first created by Aristotle. Let's revisit Aristotle's illustration of proportional equality:

> Since justice is equality, equality based on proportion should be just. This ratio implies at least four terms, "such as A:B, then C:D." For example, the more properties one has, the more tax one pays, and the less properties one has the less tax one pays; the more one works, the more one gains, the less one works, the less one gains, it is also the proportion.[109]

From this we can see that the so-called proportional equality of non-basic rights only means that those who make a greater contribution ought to enjoy more non-basic rights and those who contribute less ought to enjoy less non-basic rights: as a result of their unequal contributions, everyone ought to enjoy the corresponding unequal non-basic rights. In this way, although the non-basic rights people enjoy are not equal, the unequal proportion of non-basic rights they enjoy ought to be fully equal with the unequal proportion of their contributions. In other words, the proportion of everyone's rights to their contributions ought to be fully equal. This is the principle of proportional equality of non-basic rights.

For instance, John ought to enjoy "one portion of rights" if he made "one portion of contributions," and Jim ought to enjoy "three portions of rights" if he made "three portions of contributions." In this way, John's rights are not equal to Jim's rights. However, the unequal proportion of the rights John and Jim enjoy is completely equal to the unequal proportion of their contributions. In other words, the proportion of their rights to their contributions ought to be completely equal:

John's one portion of rights	John's one portion of contributions	one portion of rights	three portions of rights
equal to		or John	equal to Jim
Jim's three portions of rights	Jim's three portions of contributions	one portion of contributions	three portions of contributions

The principle of proportional equality of non-basic rights indicates that society should distribute non-basic rights to everyone unequally. But the unequal distribution of such rights should be based solely on the unequal contributions, so that the unequal proportion of non-basic rights people enjoy can be fully equal with the unequal proportion of their contributions. In order to do so, in the unequal distribution of rights, as Rawls's principle of compensation argues, the person who is more advantaged ought to also grant a corresponding right of compensation to the one who is less advantaged:

> Social and economic inequalities, for example inequalities of wealth and authority, are just only if they result in compensation benefits for everyone, and particular for the least advantaged members of society.[110]

It turns out, as mentioned above, "society" and the "system of social cooperation," as Rawls put it, are in fact the same concept; for society is just "a system of cooperation designed to advance the good of those take part in it."[111] It is the resource created by everyone on a completely equal footing, and therefore should be used by everyone on a completely equal footing: complete equal access to the resources of social cooperation is the right of everyone. This means that whoever makes more use of resources of social cooperation will encroach on the rights of those who use less, and therefore must give them compensation rights that "are equal to the rights they encroach upon"; otherwise it is unjust.

The crux of the problem is: according to the principle of proportional equality, those who enjoy more rights make greater contributions and have stronger abilities, are bound to make more use of the resources of the social cooperation, while those who enjoy less rights contribute less and have weaker abilities, are bound to make less use of resources of the social cooperation: this is why the more advantaged members must give the less advantaged members compensation rights. According to this view, the less advantaged members make less use of the common resources of "social cooperation"; therefore, those who are the least advantaged members should enjoy the most compensation rights since they usually make the least use of "social cooperation." For example:

Those who are more advantaged, such as singing stars, entrepreneurs, and great writers, obviously made more use of the common resource of "social cooperation" more than those who are less advantaged, such as workers and farmers. Without "social cooperation," all these singing stars, entrepreneurs, and great writers would achieve nothing; they wouldn't have made great contributions if they had not made more use of the common resource of "social cooperation." Since the contributions of the more advantaged contain more use of common resources, the contributions indirectly contain the contributions of the less advantaged. Thus, the rights the more advantaged enjoy as a result of their tremendous contributions contain the rights of the less advantaged. Therefore, as compensation, we ought to take out the corresponding part of rights from the more advantaged and return them to the less advantaged through individual income tax and other ways. Otherwise the more advantaged would encroach on the rights of the less advantaged, which is unjust. Nozick, however, opposed the principle of compensation, believing that it violated individual rights. He gave the example:

> Now suppose that Wilt Chamberlain is greatly in demand by baseball teams, being a great gate attraction. He signs the following sort of contract with a team: In each home game, twenty-five cents from the price of each ticket of admission goes to him. The season starts, and people cheerfully attended his team's game; they buy their tickets, each time dropping a separate twenty-five cents of their admission price into a special box with Chamberlain's name on it. They are excited about seeing him play; it is worth the total admission price to them. Let us suppose that in one season one million persons attend his home games, and Wilt Chamberlain winds up with $250,000, a much larger sum than the average income and larger ever than anyone else has. Is he entitled to this income?[112]

Nozick's answer is yes. In his view, since Chamberlain is entitled to the $250,000, would it not violate Chamberlain's right to redistribute a portion of his $250,000 income through individual income tax? Nozick's view is untenable, because individual income tax, which embodies the principle of compensation, does not infringe Chamberlain's rights. Chamberlain's huge individual income of $250,000 is, of course, the result of his enormous contribution to sports entertainment. But what would Chamberlain do without social cooperation (e.g., no crowd, no competition, no income, no contracts, no team, and so on)? If he had not much talent for anything else, his living conditions, I'm afraid, would likely not even be as good as that of a common farmer. As a talented baseballer, Chamberlain was able to make a huge contribution to the sport not just because the conditions of society enabled him to pursue his interests, that is, in the same way that farmers or other ordinary civilians pursued theirs, but because he made more use of the common resource of "social cooperation" than farmers or others. Thus, the contributions of farmers and others are indirectly contained in Chamberlain's huge contributions as sporting talent, just as the incomes of farmers and others are also indirectly contained in his huge income of $250,000. Therefore, taking out the corresponding part of Chamberlain's income through his income tax so as to indirectly compensate the farmers and all others in society does not violate Chamberlain's rights. In fact, letting

Chamberlain own all of the $250,000 without taxation would be a violation of the rights of everyone in society.

However, Rawls' account of social cooperation and compensation neglects the fact that the more advantaged make more use of "social cooperation" than the less advantaged and that this is the fundamental reasons why the more advantaged ought to compensate the less advantaged. Instead, Rawls only holds that the more advantaged should transfer part of their income to the less advantaged because the income of the more advantaged relies on the cooperation of the less advantaged.[113] This is not a sufficient reason, because the income of the less advantaged obviously depends entirely on the social cooperation of the more advantaged. If the more advantaged ought to transfer part of their income to the less advantaged because they rely on social cooperation, then oughtn't the less advantaged also transfer part of the income to the more advantaged because of social cooperation? This is why Nozick refutes Rawls' principle of differential compensation:

> No doubt, the difference principle presents terms on the basis of which those less well endowed would be willing to cooperate. But is this a fair agreement on the basis of which those *worse* endowed could expect the *willing* cooperation of others? With regard to the existence of gains from social cooperation, the situation is symmetrical. The better endowed gain by cooperating with worse endowed, *and* the worse endowed gain by cooperating with the better endowed. Yet the difference principle is not neutral between the better and the worse endowed. Whence the asymmetry?[114]

The true reason for this asymmetry (that the better endowed or the more advantaged compensate the worse endowed or the less advantaged and the less advantaged do not compensate the more advantaged) obviously is not that the more advantaged *make use* of social cooperation, but that the more advantaged *make more use* of social cooperation. Nozick believes that the principle of compensation infringes on individual rights, which, in the final analysis, is also because he does not perceive that the more advantaged make more use of social cooperation, thus mistakenly believing that the more advantaged and the less advantaged equally make use of social cooperation.

In summary, as a result of people's unequal contributions, they ought to enjoy the corresponding unequal non-basic rights, *that is*, the unequal proportion of non-basic rights people enjoy ought to be fully equal with the unequal proportion of their contributions, which maintains that those who enjoy more rights should return corresponding compensation rights to those who enjoy less rights because the former make more use of the common resources of "social cooperation" which ought to be used equally. This is the principle of proportional equality to distribute non-basic rights.

6.4.4 The relationship between full equality and proportional equality: The general principle of equality

It is not difficult to see that "the principle of full equality of basic rights" takes precedence over "the principle of proportional equality of non-basic rights": when the two conflict, the latter should be sacrificed to preserve the former. For example, when the material wealth of a society is extremely scarce, if everyone is satisfied and thus enjoy equal basic rights, then almost no one will have good food and enjoy non-basic rights. In this way everyone enjoys economic rights on an almost fully equal footing, thus violating the principle of proportional equality and the non-basic rights of those who made a greater contribution. On the contrary, if those who made greater contributions have good food and enjoy non-basic rights, then others would not enjoy basic rights and some people would starve to death. In this way, basic rights are not enjoyed equally by everyone, thus violating the principle of full equality and the basic rights of some people.

What should we do under such circumstances? It is clear that we should violate the principle of proportional equality and the non-basic rights of those who made greater contributions to "have good food" in order to follow the principle of full equality and guarantee the basic rights of everyone to "have enough food": human rights are sacred, of first order, inviolable, and inalienable. So, in any society, if it is just, as long as there is one person who can't enjoy human rights to have enough food, then anyone, no matter how much he contributes, ought not to enjoy non-human rights to have good food; as long as one person is too poor to enjoy human rights to have a pair of trousers, then anyone, even the president, ought not to enjoy non-human rights to wear good trousers.

But why does a person's human rights, no matter how insignificant he is, take precedence over the non-basic rights of another man—no matter how exalted the other man is? That's because, as Rawls put it, society is "a system of cooperation designed to advance the good of those taking part in it."[115] Everyone is a shareholder in this system of cooperation in which there is no doubt that those who contribute more ought to enjoy more rights and those who contribute less ought to enjoy less rights. But no matter how little a person's contributions are, he is also a shareholder of a society just like the one who contributes the most, and therefore ought at least to enjoy the lowest, minimum, and fundamental rights, namely, human rights. On the contrary, the contributions of those who make great contributions, no matter how great, are based on the premise of the existence of society, and therefore are completely based on the premise of the most basic contribution that everyone participates in the creation of society. Therefore, whether those who make great contributions ought to enjoy non-basic rights ought to be completely based on the premise whether everyone enjoy basic rights. In a word, the priority and inviolability of human rights or basic rights of everyone lies in that the basic contribution of everyone's participation in the formation of a society has priority over, and is more important than, any other contributions.

However, the sanctity, priority, inviolability, and inalienability of human rights are not absolute and unconditional but relative and conditional because, as mentioned earlier, if a person, such as a hermit, completely shirks society or violates the human rights of others, then he should not enjoy the corresponding human rights. The human rights of everyone are priority, sacred, inviolable, and inalienable only when they are in conflict with the non-human rights of others.

However, in the final analysis, "the full equality of basic rights" and "the proportional equality of non-basic rights" obviously are two sides of "the principle of equality of rights."

Thus, taken together, it can be concluded that, on the one hand, because everyone is fully equal in their most basic contributions—everyone is the same as others as a shareholder in the creation of society—everyone ought to enjoy basic rights or human rights on an entirely equal footing. This is the principle of full equality, the so-called principle of human rights, the distribution principle of human rights or basic rights. On the other hand, as a result of *their* unequal contributions, *everyone* ought to enjoy the corresponding unequal non-basic rights; that is to say, the unequal proportion of non-basic rights people enjoy ought to be fully equal with the unequal proportion of their contributions, which maintains that those who enjoy more rights should return corresponding compensation rights to those who enjoy less rights because the former make more use of the common resources of "social cooperation" which ought to be used equally. This is the principle of proportional equality, the distribution principles of non-basic rights or non-human rights.

These are the two aspects of the general principle of equality of rights, the general principle of equality as well as the general standard of equality for the evaluation of state institutions and state governance. The reason why it is called the general principle or the general standard of equality is that a series of more specific principles of equality, such as political equality, economic equality, and equal opportunity, can be deduced from it. Nevertheless, before the deduction of these principles of equality, obviously, it is necessary to analyze the theories on the general principle of equality over the past two thousand years.

6.4.5 Theories on general principle of equality: The contribution and imperfections of Rawls' A Theory of Justice

The discovery and establishment of the general principle of equality

For the general principle of equality, thinkers have been searching and arguing for more than two thousand years. It was Aristotle who first revealed this principle on which he wrote:

> There are two kinds of equalities: equality in amount and equality in terms of value or virtue. By equality of amount I mean same or equal in amount or size; equality on the basis of value or virtue refers to equality in proportion ... Equality in amount should be applied in some respects and equality on the basis of value or merit in others.[116]
>
> Justice is considered to be, and in fact, is equal, however, it is not for all but for those who are equal to each other. Inequality is considered to be, and in fact, is just, and also not for all ... but for those who are not equal to each other.[117]

Feinberg called this principle "the principle of equality in form" and summed it up as follows:

> Our formal principle (which derives from Aristotle) would have us (1) treat alike (equally) those who are the same (equal) in relevant respects, and (2) treat unalike (unequally) those who are unalike (unequal) on relevant respects, in direct proportion to the differences (inequalities) between them.[118]

Sartori also wrote: "Criteria of equality: (1) *the same to all*, i.e., equal shares (benefits or burdens) to all; (2) *the same to sames*, i.e., equal shares (benefits or burden) to equal and therefore unequal shares to unequal."[119]

It is not difficult to see that Aristotle and his followers' great achievements lie in the two levels of discovery and establishment of the general principle of equality: one is absolute and complete equality, the other is relative and proportional equality. However, they failed to settle the following questions: (1) what are the things that should be distributed equally or unequally? In further examination, what kinds of rights that should be distributed on an entirely equal footing or on a proportionally equal footing? And (2) what are the same or different aspects of the people on which equal distribution or unequal distribution are based? These are two more difficult problems of the general principle of equality. What Rawls' masterpiece, *A Theory of Justice*, aims to solve, in the final analysis, are these two problems.

Rawls' contribution and imperfections of A Theory of Justice

If the mission of ancient thinkers was mainly to put forward ideas and theories, then the mission of modern thinkers is to prove and revise these views and theories, reconstructing the ancient views and theories which are not systematic into a system of rational knowledge. Undoubtedly, Rawls' main contribution is that, for the first time, from the viewpoints and theories on the two principles of equality since Aristotle, he constructed a system of rational knowledge, that is, a rational knowledge system to prove the justice of the two equal principles, which, in the final analysis, is a scientific system to prove the justice of the two equal principles: with this, he turned the unsystematic arguments since Aristotle into a science. In a word, what is called science, as Wartofski put it, is a system of rational knowledge about the universality of what actually exists: "Science is an organized or systematic body of knowledge, using general laws or principles."[120]

Rawls himself made this clear in the preface to *A Theory of Justice*:

> Indeed, I must disclaim any originality for the views I put forward. The leading ideas are classical and well known. My intention has been to organize them into a general framework by using certain simplifying devices so that their full force can be appreciated.[121]

Not only that, generally speaking, Rawls also solved the first difficult problem of the general principle of equality: that what ought to be distributed on an entirely equal footing is everyone's basic rights; and that what ought to be distributed on a proportionally equal footing is everyone's non-basic rights. But Rawls' statement of the two principles is inaccurate. Let's examine his final and most comprehensive statement of these two principles:

> First principle: each person is to have an equal right to the most extensive total system of equal basic liberties compatible with a similar system of liberty for all. Second principle: social and economic inequalities are to be arranged so that they are both: (a) to the greatest benefits of the least advantaged, consistent with the just savings principle; and (b) attached to offices and positions open to all under conditions of fair equality of opportunity.[122]

The second principle has often been called "proportional equality" since Aristotle. In Rawls' work, however, it is described as the principle of "inequality," which is a major setback in the theory of equality for the greatest achievement in the theory of equality before Rawls' was not so much to put forward the very simple principle of full equality, but to put forward the principle of proportional equality in the unequal distribution of rights: its phenomenon is inequality while its essence is a special kind of equality, namely proportional equality. Rawls, however, retreated from the insights of proportional equality to the superficial inequality so that the "two principles of equality" since Aristotle degenerated into "the principle of equality and the principle of inequality." This might be the reason that Rawls deviates from the tradition of "two principles of equality" and calls them "two principles of justice" instead.

Rawls' misrepresentation of the two principles of equality also lies in his failure to make it clear: what are the things that should be distributed equally (i.e., on an entirely equal footing) or unequally (i.e., on a proportionally equal footing)? His first principle is about what should be distributed equally; the second is about what should be distributed unequally. But, in his view, what should be distributed equally is merely liberty, which is too narrow. For what should be equally distributed are all basic rights or human rights and liberty is undoubtedly only one of the basic rights or human rights. Shouldn't other basic rights or human rights be equally distributed?

Rawls' misrepresentation also lies in that, in his view, what should be distributed unequally are social and economic rights, which is both too wide and too narrow. It is too wide because not all social and economic rights should be unequally distributed. What should be distributed unequally are merely non-basic social and economic rights; basic social and economic rights should be equally distributed. It is too narrow because not only social and economic rights should be unequally distributed. Non-basic rights in politics, culture, speech, publishing, and so on should be unequally distributed. Shouldn't the president and common people enjoy unequal non-basic political rights?

In particular, Rawls deviates from the long tradition of calling the two principles—the full equality of basic rights and the proportional equality of non-basic rights—"the principle of equality," but called them "the principles of justice" instead, which is incorrect. It is true that these two principles are just, but they cannot be called principles of justice because they are just. For example, the principle of humanitarianism that "treats human beings as human beings" is just, but should be called a "principle of humanity" not a "principle of justice." And the principle that "the legitimate power of government derives from the consent of the governed" in the *Declaration of Independence* is just, however it should not be called the "principle of justice" but rather only the "principle of political liberty." By the same token, the principles of "the full equality of basic rights and of the proportional equality of non-basic rights" are also just; however, they should not be called the "principles of justice" but the "principles of equality." Why should all the principles of humanity, political liberty, and equality not be called "principles of justice" although they are just? This is because justice is the common denominator of these principles while "humanity," "political liberty" and "equality" are their distinguishing features. Our terming of any principle should obviously be based only on its features, not on its commonalities. Otherwise, these principles would only have one term, all of which are called the "principles of justice" without distinctions among them.

Another problem of the general principle of equality is: what is the relevant difference among people on which the completely equal distribution and the proportionally equal distribution are based? Or what is the basis to distribute rights on a completely footing or on a proportionally equal footing? This issue, as Sartori put it, is the most difficult to deal with: "The most intractable issue is, in the longer run, why *these* and not *other* differences (of the same kind) should be deemed *relevant*?"[123] The issue is so intractable that Western academia has not yet solved it. The key to the failure to solve this problem is, I am afraid, that they do not understand that the basis on which everyone should enjoy human rights on an entirely equal footing is that everyone is completely equal in their most fundamental contribution of being a shareholder in the creation of society.

They do not understand this truth, believing that everyone has equal rights based on human nature. Adler made this clear: "How does our humanity justify our right to these equalities? The answer is that, by being human we are equal ... all have the same species-specific properties."[124] Although this is the mainstream view in Western academia, it is simply not true. Because, according to this view, as long as a person is alive and as long as he is a human being, he should enjoy human rights: human rights are absolutely inalienable for everyone under all circumstances. Thus, no matter how evil a person might be, no matter how much harm he causes to others and society, no matter how many people he kills, his human rights should not be denied, nor should he be deprived of his right to life, he should enjoy human rights like good people. For no matter how evil he is, he is a human being like the best kind of person, possessing the universal and the same human nature. This is obviously absurd.

Rawls' main fallacy: The proof method of the justness of the principle of justice with contract theory

Rawls is unique in believing that the basis for the justness of the two principles of justice is the agreement of everyone, which is what the main content of his *A Theory of Justice* tries to prove. His proof, in short, is a proof of the contract theory. Because, in his view, the two principles are just not because they are based on the contribution of everyone but because they are a social contract: the agreement of everyone is the proof of the justness of the principle of justice.

Of course, Rawls points out that these two principles of justice concern the distribution of everyone's rights and duties. But in real society, people's status and abilities are different, thus it is impossible to reach the social contract that everyone agrees on in terms of the distribution of rights and duties which is vital to everyone's life. Thus Rawls made a major revision to the traditional contract theory: the object of traditional contract theory is a true, realistic and historical society while the object of Rawls' contract theory is an ideal and hypothetical society used to establish and demonstrate the principle of justice. He called this hypothetical society "original position."

> This original position is not, of course, thought as an actual historical state of affairs, much less as a primitive condition of culture. It is understood as a purely hypothetical situation characterized so as to lead to a certain conception of justice. Among the essential features of this situation is that no one knows his place in society, his class position or social status, nor does anyone know his fortune in the distribution of natural assets and abilities, his intelligence, strength, and the like.[125]

234 *Moral value and moral norms*

Since everyone is obscured by this "veil of ignorance" without knowing their own positions and abilities, the principle of the distribution of rights and duties that they agree upon must be just:

> The principles of justice are chosen behind a veil of ignorance. This ensures that no one is advantaged or disadvantaged in the choice of principles by the outcome of natural chance or the contingency of social circumstances. Since all are similarly situated and no one is able to design principles to favor his particular condition, the principles of justice are the result of a fair agreement or bargain.[126]

In short, "principles of justice are justified because they would be agreed to in an initial situation of equality."[127]

On closer examination, this proof method of the *justness* of the principle of justice simply is not tenable: it confuses the *freedom property* of the principle of justice with the *justness* of the principle of justice. The *freedom property* of a principle refers to whether the principle is a free principle while the *justness* of a principle refers to whether it is a just principle. Then how to prove whether a principle is a free principle? Only by the agreement of everyone: the principle that is agreed by everyone is a free principle, while the principle that is not agreed by everyone is not a free principle.

For so-called freedom, as it is known, is autonomy, an activity that can be carried out according to one's own will, therefore if a principle, if directly or indirectly agreed on by all members of society, becomes a manifestation of "public will," then everyone's obedience to it is the obedience to the will of others as well as their own, thus it is free: a true free principle is the principle that everyone agrees on directly or indirectly. On the contrary, a principle that cannot be directly or indirectly agreed on by everyone in a society is not an expression of public will, then the dissenters' obedience to it is only to the will of others but not to their own, and thus is not free: an unfree principle is the principle that cannot be agreed on by everyone directly or indirectly.

Whether a principle is free depends on whether or not everyone agrees, which means the *freedom property* of a principle does not relate to the principle itself, but depends only on the opinion of the people involved in the formulation of the principle, thus it is completely random, arbitrary, subjective, accidental, depending on human will. This kind of subjective arbitrariness is manifested in the following aspects: the same principle, such as "even out wealth," if it does not get the unanimous consent of everyone today, then it is not a free principle today, while tomorrow, if everyone agrees, it is a free principle from tomorrow.

It is not difficult to see that whether a principle is free is fundamentally different from whether a principle is just: a free principle might be either just and good or unjust and bad. For any principle, no matter how unjust or bad, is a free principle as long as everyone agrees and it is an unfree principle if it is not agreed by everyone, no matter how good or just it might be. Suppose there is a society in which everyone agrees on the principle that the appointment of all officials is determined by wealth. This is a free principle but not a just principle, for it violates the principle of social justice of "appointing people by both virtue and talents."

It can be seen that the proof method of the contract theory of agreement by everyone can only prove the *freedom property* of a principle, but cannot prove the *justness* of a principle. Whether a principle is a free principle, is really the result of a contract, and an issue of contract theory as to whether everyone agrees with it. Conversely, whether a principle is a just principle is neither the result of a contract, nor an issue of contract theory as to whether everyone agrees with it.

To be sure, any moral norm or moral principle—the principle of justice is no exception—is a human agreement and a kind of contract: "Morality is sometimes, *defined* as an instrument of society as a whole."[128] However, moral norms and moral principles, or the *"justness"* of principles of justice, "justice itself" and "justice" are not recognized and not a contract, because the *"justness"* of the principle of justice is a kind of *ought* and a kind of *value*, belonging to the category of *moral value*: who can say that value is an agreement or a contract?

Any value—whether moral value or non-moral value—is clearly not agreed upon and not a contract. In what way can the nutritional value of pork be agreed upon? How can it be a contract? The fact is that the nutritional value of pork is not agreed upon and not a contract; only the behavioral norm of how to eat pork is agreed upon and thus is a contract.

Obviously, only the "principle of justice" is a contract, but the *justness* of principle of justice, "justice itself" or "justice" is not agreed upon and not a contract. The error of Rawls' proof method of the *justness* of the principle of justice with contract theory, in short, is that it confuses the *"freedom properties"* of the principle of justice with the *"justness"* of the principle of justice, which, in the final analysis, undoubtedly lies in that the tradition of contract theory he follows equates "justice" with the "principle of justice," mistaking justice as a contract, and as the result of a contract, such that it "is an expedient contract to prevent people from hurting each other"[129] and "establishes itself by a kind of convention or agreement."[130]

The proof method of the justness of principle of justice with the value theory

Since the *justness* of the principle of justice is a kind of moral value, the proof of the *justness* of a kind of principle of justice should be a kind of axiological proof, which, in the final analysis, should be a proof method of moral value, that is, the deductive method of moral value.

This method is discussed in detail in *Meta-ethics*, which can be summed up as follows: the moral value of the ought of ethical behavior is the utility of the fact of ethical behavior to the goal of morality—to safeguard the existence and development of society. Therefore, the moral value of the ought of ethical behavior emerges and is deduced from the fact of ethical behavior through the goal of morality: the moral value of the ought of ethical behavior is equal to the conformity of the fact of ethical behavior with the goal of morality; the moral value of the *ought-not* of ethical behavior is equal to the nonconformity of the fact of ethical behavior with the goal of morality. The formula:

> Premise 1: The fact of ethical behavior (substance of moral value)
> Premise 2: The goal of morality (standard of moral value)
> Conclusion: The ought of the ethical behavior (moral value)

According to this view, although the principle of justice is made by human beings, only false principles of justice are arbitrary; the true principle of justice can only be derived from the facts of a certain type of ethical behavior (the value substance of justice) through the goal of morality (the value standard of justice): the *justness* of the principle of justice is the utility of a certain type of ethical behavior that conforms to the goal of morality—safeguarding the existence and development of society; the true principle of justice must be consistent with this kind of *justness*, and therefore is a certain type of ethical behavior that conforms to the goal of morality. Then, what kind of ethical behavior is it?

The so-called ethical behavior are the actions dominated by the consciousness of interests, and thus can be divided into two categories: exchange of equal interests (or harms) and exchange of unequal interests (or harms). The exchange of equal interests (harms) undoubtedly conforms to the goal of morality and is an action of moral good. The exchange of unequal interests can be divided into two types: one conforms to the goal of morality, for example, benevolence and forgiveness, such as "returning small favors with big ones" and "returning hatred with virtue," which can be called the moral good of the exchange of unequal interests (or harms); the other does not conform to the goal of morality, and can be called the evil of the exchange of unequal interests (or harms). The principle of true justice is a kinds of actions of moral good and therefore must be among the three kinds of an action of moral good, that is, the exchange of equal interests (harms), benevolence and forgiveness. It goes without saying that benevolence and forgiveness do not have the issue of being just or unjust, but are supererogatory actions beyond justice. Therefore, the principle of true justice can only be the action of the exchange of equal interests (harms), and the principle of true injustice can only be the action of the exchange of unequal interests (harms)—with the exception of benevolence and forgiveness, that is, the exchange of unequal interests (harms) that does not conform to the goal of morality, which, in the final analysis, is the evil of the exchange of unequal interests (harms). It is illustrated in Figure 6.2.

This is the proof that the "exchange of equal interests (harms)" is a principle of true justice, namely the proof of the justness of the principle

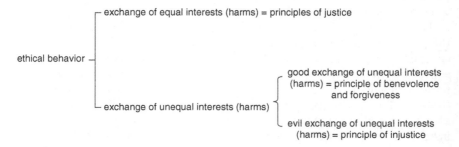

Figure 6.2 The proof of the justness of the principle of justice

of justice. Therefore, as a principle of true justice the "exchange of equal interests (harms)" does not relate to whether people agree with it or not, but is deduced from the objective nature of the facts of certain types of ethical behavior only through the goal of morality, which is independent of human will—safeguarding the existence and development of society—thus, it is objective, inevitable, and independent of human will.

The principle of justice is a system consisting of a number of principles. The "exchange of equal interests (harms)" is the most general principle of justice, therefore it dominates other principles of justice which are deduced from it. Indeed, as mentioned earlier, by using the general principle of justice of the "exchange of equal interests (harms)" to measure the distribution of rights and duties we can deduce the fundamental principle of social justice of "distributing rights according to contribution," and using the principle of the "distribution of rights according to contribution" to measure the distribution of basic and non-basic rights, we can deduce the two principles of equality, that is, "full equality of basic rights" and "proportional equality of non-basic rights":

(1) Everyone should enjoy basic rights on a completely equal footing because of their completely equal basic contributions (everyone is a shareholder in the creation of society); (2) everyone should enjoy unequal non-basic rights because of their specific unequal contributions; in the final analysis, the unequal proportion of everyone's non-basic rights should be completely equal to the unequal proportion of their specific contribution.

This is the scientific expression of "two principles of equality"—especially Rawls' "two principles of justice"—since Aristotle. Therefore, the reason that Rawls' so-called two principles of justice are just, and that even all the principles of justice are just, is because they are deduced from the general principle of justice; in the final analysis, they are derived from the objective nature of the facts of certain types of ethical behavior through the goal of morality, thus are objective, inevitable, and independent of human will.

From above we know that the justness of a principle is fundamentally different from the freedom property of a principle. The freedom property of a principle, that is, whether a free principle is a true free principle, depends on whether people agree to it, thus is subjective, casual, accidental, and dependent on human will: it is a question of contract theory, not of axiology. Therefore, the proof of whether a principle is a free principle should be a proof of contract theory instead of a proof of axiology. On the contrary, the justness of a principle, that is, whether a just principle is a true just principle, has nothing to do with whether people agree, but is derived from the objective nature of the facts of a certain type of ethical behavior through goal of morality, thus is objective, inevitable, and independent of human will: it is a matter of axiology instead of contract theory. Therefore, the scientific proof of whether a just principle is a true just principle should be a proof of axiology, not a proof of contract theory.

Rawls' error is to equate the two, and thus draw the wrong conclusion that the proof of the justness of the principle of justice is the agreement of everyone from the correct premise that "the proof of the freedom property of the principle of justice is the agreement of everyone." In this way, the justness of the principle of justice is subjective, casual, accidental, and dependent on human will. Rawls clearly acknowledges that the original position may not reflect the agreement of everyone in real society, but this does not change its subjectivity, contingency, and arbitrariness because the justness of the principle of justice, whether it depends on the agreement of everyone in real society or in the original position, after all, depends on the agreement of everyone: since it depends on everyone's agreement, how can it not be subjective, accidental and arbitrary? Isn't it contradictory to say that "agreement" is independent of human will?

Through the study of the general principle of equality and its theories, we finally established the general principle of equality: basic rights should be completely equal and non-basic rights should be proportionately equal. Then, is this principle sufficient to settle the problem of equality that we encounter in real life? The answer is no. As Sartori put it, equality is a "Gordian knot": "The extent to which the intricate—I called it the labyrinth—of equality are greater than the complex of liberty is now apparent."[131] "I can think of nothing as complicated as equality."[132] Thus, in order to truly settle the problem of equality, the general principle of equality alone is not enough; it is necessary to take the general principle of equality as a guide, and according to the specific types of equality, deduce the corresponding specific principles of equality: the principle of political equality, the principle of economic equality and the principle of the equality of opportunities.

6.5 Specific principles of equality

6.5.1 The principle of political equality

The conceptual analysis of equality shows that equality is not all equality of rights, but that the *principles of equality* are all the principles of equality of rights. Therefore, the so-called *principle of political equality* is the principle of equality of political rights. Political rights obviously are the rights for political domination with political power. These kinds of rights can be divided into two types: the right of political liberty and the right of political position. Political liberty is the freedom of all citizens to carry out the politics of the country according to their own will, which only can be actualized by controlling the supreme power of the country: the right of political liberty is the right of running the supreme power of the country.

From this point of view, isn't political liberty the highest political rights? No! Political liberty is not the supreme power of a person but the supreme power shared by all citizens. As Ma Qihua said, the size of power is inversely proportional to the number of holders of the same power:

> In terms of the number of persons exercising the same power, the smaller the number, the greater the power per person; the greater number the less power per person. So the power of a single head is greater than that of a collegial head.[133]

It is therefore true that though all citizens who enjoy political liberty share the highest and greatest power: what is distributed to every citizen is not the highest power but the lowest and least power which is less powerful than the power the lowest officials possess: it is the power of one of the hundreds of millions of votes. Therefore, the rights of political liberty everyone enjoys, which are minimum, are basic rights or human rights; on the contrary, a person's rights to hold political office, which are higher rights, are non-basic rights but not human rights. Therefore, Marx said:

> Part of human rights is political rights which can be exercised only with others. The content of this right is to join the community, and to join the political community and the state. These rights fall within the realm of political liberty.[134]

Political liberty is a human right. Therefore, according to the principle that human rights should be completely equal, everyone should enjoy political liberty on a completely equal footing. In other words, everyone should decide the political fate of the country together on a completely equal footing. In the final analysis, everyone should jointly hold the supreme power of the country in complete equality: "There is only one for everyone, but no one for a few."[135] This is the principle of complete equality of political rights, the principle of human rights in politics, the so-called principle of people's sovereignty, and thus is also one of the fundamental bases of democratic politics.

It is not difficult to see that, on the one hand, equality or democracy stipulated by this principle is the fundamental guarantee for the realization of all equality among people. For, if democracy is practiced so that everyone, in full equality, exercises the supreme power of the state, the realization of other equality of every human being, such as economic equality and equality of opportunity, depends entirely on their own will, and is therefore guaranteed. Conversely, if democracy is not achieved and the supreme power of the state is not fully equal in the hands of everyone, but only in the hands of one or some persons, then, whether other equalities of everyone can be achieved depends entirely on the will of the person or persons who hold the supreme power instead of their own will, and is therefore insecure. Thus, democracy or the equality of supreme power determines all other equalities and is the fundamental guarantee for realization of all other equalities.

On the other hand, the equality or democracy stipulated by this principle is undoubtedly the most important and fundamental equality among people. Putting democracy into practice in accordance with this principle everyone shall jointly hold the supreme power of the country in full equality, everyone shall be the holder of the supreme power of the country in full equality, everyone shall be the supreme ruler of the country in full equality, and everyone is the master of a country who holds the highest power in full equality. In this way, people are truly equal to each other, and even though they are quite unequal in wealth and social position, there are no distinctions of master and slave among them; all are the masters of the country who possess the highest power, and thus are fully equal. Conversely, in contrast to this principle, without democracy, so that the supreme power of the country is in the hands of one or some people, only the persons in charge of the supreme power are the masters; hence all others are slaves to supreme authority—a master–slave relationship that is extremely unequal.

When it comes to countries that have achieved real democracy—so that everyone holds the supreme power of their country in full equality—how different is the leader from a professor? Teaching on the democracy in the USA, I used to ask my students the following questions: can anyone tell the president apart from any other civilian? Clinton is nothing, how much power does he really have? That Bush bounces about like a tennis player! What's the actual difference between American presidents and civilians? Do the ordinary civilians seem to be afraid of their presidents? Even the most revered presidents such as Washington, Jefferson, Madison, Lincoln, etc., were truly not much different from ordinary people. The inequality between these men and the common people, no doubt, would have been far less than the inequality between a small county official and common people in a despotic society! Why are people so fully equal in a democratic society? After all, isn't it because everyone in a democratic society is a master of a country who holds the supreme power on a completely equal footing? Therefore, full equality in holding the supreme power, determines equalities among people, is the fundamental guarantee for the realization of equalities, and is the most important, the most fundamental and the most decisive equality.

Compared with political liberty, one's political position concerns non-basic rights or non-human rights. Therefore, according to the principle of proportional equality of non-basic rights, people should enjoy rights to hold political position on a proportionally equal footing according to their political contributions. That is to say, whoever has the greater political contribution should hold a higher political position and whoever has the smaller political contribution should hold a lower political position: everyone should hold the corresponding unequal political office because of their unequal political contributions. Thence, though the right to hold political position is unequal, the proportion of each person's right to hold political office to his political contribution is equal. As shown below:

    higher political positon   lower political positon

John -------------------------------   equal to   Jim -----------------------------

    greater political contributions   less political contributions

From this, we can see that, on the one hand, political position should not be distributed solely according to political talents. For if a person has talents without virtue, that is, has higher political talents without official virtue, rather than make political contributions, he may cause serious harms to society. On the other hand, political positions should not be distributed solely according to official virtue, that is, by appointing positions on this basis alone, because if a person has virtue without talent, or only official virtue and low political talent, he may not only lack the political acumen necessary to make the right decisions and thus great political contributions but may end up causing more harm than good given that often "The road to hell is paved with good intentions."[136] As a result, political posts should be distributed merely according to both virtue and talents: a person can make greater political contributions only if he has both official virtue and higher political talents.

In a nutshell, everyone should hold corresponding unequal political positions because of the inequality of their political contributions (political talents plus official virtue). In other words, the proportion of inequality in everyone's political position should be fully equal with the proportion of inequality in their political contributions (political talents plus official virtue). This is the principle of the proportional equality of political rights to distribute political positions. Aristotle was the first who established this principle, as he put: "A just distribution of office shall take into account the abilities, morality or merits of each incumbent."[137]

In view of the principle of equality of political rights, it can be concluded that on the one hand, everyone, no matter how much specific political contribution he makes, should enjoy political rights on a completely equal footing, that is, hold the supreme power of the country together on a completely equal footing, so as to determine the political destiny of the country on a completely equal footing; on the other hand, everyone should hold the corresponding unequal political position because of the inequality of everyone's specific political contributions (political talents plus official virtue), so as to make the proportion of inequality in political positions held by everyone fully equal with the proportion of inequality in their political contributions (political talents plus official virtue). This is the general principle of political equality, which is the value standard of political equality of state institutions and state governance.

6.5.2 *The principle of economic equality*

It is not difficult to see that everyone's economic rights and economic contributions or duties are the same thing, that is, the products provided by everyone: my economic contributions are the products I give to others and society, and my economic rights are the products others and society give to me. Therefore, the process of social distribution of economic rights for everyone is nothing more than the process of exchange of products provided by everyone. Consequently, according to the principle of justice of the exchange of equal interests, products or economic rights that contain equal exchange value should be distributed to everyone according to the exchange value of the products contributed: distribution of equal value is the principle of equality of economic rights.

The study of economics shows that the three factors of production (labor, capital, and land) which are condensed and consumed in products—are the ultimate sources and substance of creating and determining the exchange value of products. The marginal utility theory finds that the exchange value share created by these factors of production is the value of their marginal products: the magnitude of value created by unit labor is equal to the magnitude of value of the marginal product of labor; the magnitude of value created by unit capital is equal to the magnitude of value of the marginal product of capital; the magnitude of value created by the unit land is equal to the magnitude of value of the marginal product of the land. In this way, according to the principle of the justice of exchange of equal interests, it is obvious that the product or economic right containing equal exchange value should be distributed according to the marginal product value of the factors of production provided by each person. This is the so-called distribution according to factors of production: distribution according to labor and distribution according to capital.

Distribution according to factors of production clearly belongs to the category of the principle of the proportional equality of economic rights. Although the economic rights enjoyed by each person are unequal due to their unequal capital, land and labor, the proportion of economic rights enjoyed by each person to the capital, land and labor contributed is completely equal. As illustrated below:

Three portions of economic right	One portion of economic right
John ------------------------------ equal to	Jim ------------------------------
Three portions of capital or land, or labor	One portion of capital or land, or labor

However, proportional equality is only the principle to distribute non-basic rights or non-human rights. Therefore, distribution according to factors of production is also only the principle to distribute non-basic economic rights or non-human rights in economics. Then, what are the principle to distribute basic economic rights or human rights in economics? It is the distribution according to needs: to distribute basic economic rights on a fully equal basis according to the material needs of human beings. For it can be inferred from the general principle of equality that "basic rights should be fully equal": everyone should enjoy basic economic rights on a fully equal basis no matter how much contribution each person makes; to distribute basic economic rights on a fully equal basis is to distribute basic economic rights according to the basic material needs of human beings, that is, to distribute basic economic rights according to needs. This is because, on the one hand, the basic economic right is the right to satisfy the basic material needs of human beings, but it is impossible for it to satisfy the non-basic material needs of human beings; on the other hand, the differences or inequalities in people's material needs exist only in non-basic and more advanced areas, while basic, minimum, and the lowest needs are the same and equal: "The natural needs that are common to all human beings."[138]

In short, distribution according to need is the distribution principle of the full equality of basic economic rights or human rights in economics, while distribution according to factors of production (i.e., distribution according to labor and distribution according to capital) is the distribution principle of the proportional equality of non-basic economic rights or non-human rights in economics. Thus, according to the principle of priority of human rights, distribution according to need takes precedence over distribution according to factors of production: in the circumstance of conflict, the latter should be sacrificed to preserve the former.

For example, a primitive society with low productivity and lack of material wealth is faced with two scenarios. First, whether to distribute according to need. That is, to distribute equally according to the basic material needs of everyone so that everyone enjoys basic economic rights equally. In this way, those who work more will not get more and thus cannot enjoy non-basic economic rights, which violates the principle of distribution according to labor and other factors of production. Second, whether to distribute according to labor. In this way, those who work more will get more and thus enjoy non-basic economic rights. However, not everyone will enjoy non-basic economic rights and some will even starve to death, which violates the principle of distribution according to need. So, what should the primitive society do? Obviously, it should sacrifice distribution according to labor and implement distribution according to need, which is just and right.

It can be seen that distribution according to need takes precedence over distribution according to labor and other factors of production. However, the premise of distribution according to labor and other factors of production is corresponds distribution according to need. Although distribution according

244 *Moral value and moral norms*

to labor and other factors of production means those who work or invest more ought to get more and those who work or invest less ought to get less, no matter how little some people work and invest, what they get should be no less than what can satisfy their basic material needs; while no matter how much some people work and invest, what they get ought not to be so much as to deprive others of their basic material needs. On these matters, Adler stated very clearly:

> Distribution according to labor takes precedence over distribution according to need.[139]
>
> Those who have made a greater contribution are justly entitled to more wealth than those who contribute less. Two qualifications must be immediately attached to this rule. First, all, in one way or another, must be equal on the economic base line that is determined by that minimal measure of sufficient wealth to satisfy man's economic needs. To this much everyone has a natural right. Second, since the amount of wealth available for distribution is limited, no one should be in the position to earn by his productive contribution—to earn, not to steal or seize—so much wealth that not enough remains for distribution, in one way or another, to put all individuals or families on the base line of economic sufficiency. In short, should be rendered destitute by the distribution of wealth in unequal amounts, even if that distribution can be justified by the inequality of individual contributions.[140]

In summary, on the one hand, in any society, no matter how much one works or how much one contributes, everyone should be distributed the basic economic rights on a completely equal footing with the basic material needs of human beings (i.e., distribution according to need). On the other hand, the non-basic economic rights with equal exchange value should be distributed according to the marginal product value of the factors of production provided by everyone so that the proportion of inequality in non-basic economic rights enjoyed by everyone is fully equal with the proportion of inequality in the marginal product value of the factors of production provided by everyone (i.e., distribution according to factors of production, distribution according to labor and distribution according to capital). This is the general principle of economic equality, which is the value standard of economic equality of state institutions and the state governance.

6.5.3 Principle of equality of opportunity

Like the principle of political and economic equality, the principle of equality of opportunity is also a principle of equality of rights. However, on the one hand, such rights, are not political or economic rights but opportunities to obtain them; on the other hand, the opportunity for the rights involved in the principle is merely an opportunity to compete for non-basic rights—primarily position, status, power, and wealth—rather than the opportunity to compete for basic rights, because basic rights should be enjoyed by everyone on a fully equal basis: it requires neither competition nor opportunity to obtain basic rights.

However, on closer examination, the equality of opportunity competing for non-basic rights is only the formal and superficial equality of opportunity, while the essential and deep-level equality of opportunity is the equality of opportunity for the development of talents and virtue and making contributions. Clearly, those who have lower talents and virtue and make less contributions enjoy less non-basic rights usually because they lack opportunities to develop their talents and virtue; on the contrary, those who have higher talents and virtue and make greater contributions enjoy more non-basic rights is usually because they fully enjoy the opportunities to develop their talents and virtue and to make contributions. These two types of equality of opportunity have been well illustrated by the example cited by Douglas Rae:

> Suppose that in a certain society great prestige is attached to membership of a warrior class, the duties of which require great physical strength. The class has in the past been recruited from certain wealthy families only; but egalitarian reformers achieve a change in the rules by which warrior are recruited from all sections of society, on the results of a suitable competition. The effect of this, however, is that the wealthy families still provide virtually all the warriors, because the rest of the populace is so undernourished by reason of poverty that their physical strength is inferior to that of the wealthy and well-nourished.[141]

This example vividly shows that the egalitarian reforms only achieve the formal and superficial equality of opportunity: where the warrior profession is open to all everyone has the same opportunity to serve as a warrior, so this belongs to the category of the equality of opportunity for competing for the non-basic rights but it does not achieve the substantive and deep-level equality of opportunity: where everyone is well-nourished and thus have the same opportunity to develop their physical strength, this belongs to the equality of opportunity to develop talents and virtue and to make contributions. Douglas Rae referred to these two types of equality of opportunity as the "equality of opportunity on the future" and "equality of opportunity on means":

> 1 *Prospect-regarding equal opportunity*. Two persons, J and K, have equal opportunities for X if each has the same probability of attaining X. 2 *Means regarding equal opportunity*. Two persons, J and K, have equal opportunities for X if each has same instruments for attaining X.[142]

Sartori's analysis of equality of opportunity also took this classification as a premise: "I propose to subdivide 'equality of opportunity' into equal access and equal start."[143] "*Equal access* amount, in essence, to non-discrimination in entry or promotion; the access is made equal to equal abilities ... the notion of equal start addresses an entirely different and preliminary problem, namely, how equally to develop individual potentialities."[144]

Thus, equality of opportunity can be divided into two categories. One is called "equality of opportunity for competing for rights," which is the equality of opportunity for the ends of competing for non-basic rights, mainly the equality of opportunity to get position, status, power, and wealth. This equality of opportunity can be summed up as "position and status which is based on talents and virtue and is open to all," which is basically what Rawls said: "position and office open to all," "career open to talents," and "the equality of opening career to talents."[145] It is the formal and superficial equality of opportunity. The other is called "the equality of opportunity for developing potentialities," which is the equality of opportunity for the means of competing for non-basic rights, mainly the equality of opportunity in education, but best summed up as "everyone has equal opportunity to develop their talents and virtue," which is the essential and deep-level equality of opportunity.

This classification of equality of opportunity is undoubtedly of great importance: to establish the principle of equality of opportunity, we ought not only to concern the equality of opportunity for the ends of competing for non-basic rights—office, position, power, wealth, etc., but to pay more attention to equality of opportunities for the means of competing for non-basic rights such as good education, developmental potential, etc. However, this classification, at best can only indicate the depth of equality of opportunity but not the moral value of equality of opportunity, that is, it can't indicate whether the equality of opportunity *ought to be* or not. Should all opportunities then be equal or should only certain opportunities be equal?

It does not depend on whether equality of opportunity is formal or essential. The moral value of equality of opportunity does not really depend on the nature of equality of opportunity itself but entirely on who the provider of opportunity is. According to the situation of their providers, opportunities can also be divided into two categories: opportunities offered by society and those provided by non-society. The opportunities offered by non-society are more complex, mainly including the opportunities offered by family, opportunities offered by natural endowment and opportunities offered by luck.

Rawls believes that inequality of opportunity provided by factors such as family, natural endowment, or luck, that one cannot be responsible for is undeserved and unfair: "We do not deserve our place in distribution of native endowments, any more than we deserve our initial starting place in society."[146] Why is it that such factors are undeserved and unfair? In Rawls's view,

> "The fair opportunity principle," says that no person should be granted social benefits through properties for which he is not responsible; and that

Justice and equality 247

no person should be denied social benefits on the basis of properties for which he is not responsible.[147]

This means that everyone should be entitled only by free choices and efforts that they can be responsible for, and not by factors that they cannot be responsible for, such as family, natural endowment, luck, etc. This is what Rawls calls "fair opportunity principle." This is obviously a view that opportunity should be completely equal, which undoubtedly is ideal, beautiful, and perfect, yet it is unrealistic and unfair. In reality, it is not only impossible for opportunity to be completely equal, but the unequal opportunities offered by family, natural endowment, luck and other factors that one cannot be responsible for is also deserved and fair, while making them equal is unfair.

First of all, for different families, the opportunity to compete for non-basic rights is unequal. Paul Anthony Samuelson wrote on this:

> By the time they reach the age of one, children from wealthy families and carefully cared for by their parents have gained a slight advantage in the competition for economic and career status. By first grade, six-year-old children in urban suburbs had a greater lead than their slum or rural peers. Over the next 12 to 20 years, people who are already ahead are getting ahead.[148]

The inequality of opportunity offered by the family, not only Rawls, but also many others, such as Okun, considered unfair, because "When some people face obstacles, other competitors have already taken the lead. The differences in social and economic status of various families make the race unfair."[149]

Okun and others do not understand that the race in life is a never-ending relay race from generation to generation. It is not unfair that everyone's starting point is not at the same starting line because their original ancestors started on the same starting line. Rather, more exactly, the opportunity provided by families to compete for non-basic rights is nothing more than a transfer of rights between family members. The opportunities enjoyed by the children are transferred by the parents and thus transformed into the rights of the children themselves. This is what Nozick's "the principle of justice in transfer" says: "A person who acquires a holding in accordance with the principle of justice in transfer, from someone else entitled to the holding, is entitled to the holding."[150] Since the opportunities provided by the family are the rights of those who enjoy them, then these unequal opportunities are deserving and fair, while making it equal infringes the rights of opportunity owners and is unfair and ought not to be. To demonstrate the inequality of opportunity, let's use Nozick's example in which a child from an affluent family enjoys the opportunity to swim in his family pool, while a child from a poor family does not share the same opportunity. Is it unfair, asks Nozick, that the child from the affluent family has a pool to swim in and that the child from the poor family doesn't? No, says Nozick. This is because the inequality of opportunity is merely a transference of rights from one family generation to the next; that is, the father of the child with the swimming pool had inherited the house and pool from his own father. The inequality of opportunity as transference of rights from one family generation to the next is fair. What would be unfair, however, and no doubt absurd, is if the father of the child from the poor household asked the other father to stop his child from swimming in pool, or asked the father to buy his child a pool so that both children could enjoy the equal opportunity to swim. Clearly, such requests would infringe on the rights of the affluent family to enjoy their pool.

Secondly, for people with different gifts, the starting point and chances of winning in the competition for non-basic rights such as position, power and wealth are obviously unequal. This inequality of opportunity is also deserved and fair because society, in the final analysis, is, at core, a form of cooperation for everyone's interests. Everyone's gifts, efforts, and so on are their equity in the community. Thus, as Nozick puts it, everyone has the right to their equity of "talent and effort" and their benefits of "office, position, opportunity, and wealth" for people "are entitled to natural assets, and to what flows from them."[151] Thus one's unequal opportunities caused by his unequal talent is the right to which he is entitled, making them equal would violate his rights and thus is unjust and ought not to be.

Finally, the inequality of opportunities to compete for non-basic rights are often the result of individual luck. Buchanan made a very vivid exposition of this comparing the good luck of farmer who struck oil to farmers to the bad luck of others whose properties are destroyed by floods, fires, or epidemics. "My argument is that luck is, to some extent, a well-established contingent factor that provides everyone with the chance to play."[152] But is the inequality of opportunity offered by luck fair? Buchanan's answer is that "Luck does not undermine the basic principles of justice."[153] He is quite right because the fundamental principle of social justice is to distribute rights according to contributions, and anyone's contributions and achievements, as Zeng Guofan (曾国藩) said, which contain luck factors, is the result of a combination of talents, effort, luck, and other factors.[154] Therefore, luck, like natural endowment and effort, can bring rights by making contributions, and the benefits brought by luck, like those brought by talent and effort, are the rights of the gainer. Is it not that a farmer has the same rights to farm if a harvest brings him luck one year and disaster the next? Therefore, the benefits and inequality of opportunities offered by luck are indeed the rights of the fortunate; if the fortunate are deprived of opportunities, so as to make opportunities equal, their rights are violated, which is unfair and unjust.

Opportunities not offered by society, such as those offered by one's family background, talent, and luck, are, in short, the individual rights of the fortune and therefore no matter how unequal they are, neither society nor others have the right to interfere. However, by taking advantage of more opportunities, which results in greater contribution and attainment of rights, the fortunate surely use more of the resources that are co-created with the less fortune.

Therefore, because fortunate persons have more opportunities to make greater use of common resources, including and as a result of the social cooperation, their contributions not only reflect the greater proportion of the common resources but also indirectly contain the contributions of the less fortunate. Consequently, the rights that the fortunate acquire also contain the rights of the less fortunate who have fewer opportunities to make contributions and gain rights.

Therefore, the corresponding part of rights should be taken out from those who have more opportunities to compensate those with fewer opportunities through high progressive tax, estate tax, social welfare measures, etc. Only in this way are the rights of those who have more opportunities equal to their duties, and thus fair; otherwise, those who have more opportunities would encroach on the rights of those with fewer opportunities, which is unfair.

The opportunities offered by society, which are mainly by various management organizations such as government, are fundamentally different from those offered by family, natural endowment, and luck, which are the private rights or individual rights of those who enjoy them. On the contrary, the opportunities offered by society, government, and various management organizations belong to public rights; these are the rights of everyone in society or, more precisely, as Jefferson pointed out, the basic rights or human rights of everyone.[155] What the principle of equality of opportunity calls "opportunity" is clearly not the opportunity to compete for basic rights—basic rights should be enjoyed by everyone on a fully equal footing without competition—but the opportunity to compete for non-basic rights. The opportunity provided by society to compete for non-basic rights are obviously not non-basic rights but basic rights or human rights. Thus, in accordance with the principle that basic rights or human rights should be fully equal, the opportunities provided by society to compete for non-basic rights should be enjoyed by all on a fully equal basis: everyone should enjoy the educational opportunities provided by society to develop their potential talents on a fully equal basis; everyone should enjoy the opportunities provided by society to contribute on a fully equal basis; and everyone should enjoy the opportunities provided by society to compete for non-basic rights such as power, wealth, position, and status. Therefore Hayek said, "It is neither possible nor desirable to make all start with the same chance."[156] However, "Justice does require that those conditions of people's lives that are determined by government be provided equally for all."[157]

Rawls, by contrast, argues that the opportunities provided by society and government should not be equal but "unequal":

> Since inequalities of birth and natural endowment are undeserved, these inequalities are to be somehow compensated for. Thus the principle holds that in order to treat all persons equally, to provide genuine equality of opportunity, society must give more attention to those with fewer native assets and to those born into the less favorable social positions. The idea

is to redress the bias of contingencies in the direction of equality. In pursuit of this principle greater resource might be spent on the education of the less rather than the more intelligent, at least over a certain time of life, say the earlier years of school.[158]

This view of Rawls is wrong because the opportunities offered by family background and natural endowment are in themselves the individual rights of the fortunate, and do not in any way involve or infringe upon the rights of the persons with less opportunities, thus they should not compensate those with less opportunities. On the contrary, the fortunate do take advantage of more opportunities to get rights and in so doing do surely make more use of the resources of "social cooperation" created with those with less opportunity, so what they should compensate is the corresponding rights. Therefore, what ought to be compensated is the utilization of opportunities rather than the possession of opportunities, that is, to compensate the right of taking advantage of the opportunity but not for taking the opportunity itself. Rawls, however, equated the use of opportunities with the possession of opportunities, the compensation of rights with the compensation of opportunities, and therefore argues that those who have more opportunities should compensate by "giving back" opportunities to those with fewer opportunities, thus society should compensate for the inequality of opportunities gifted by family background and natural endowment by providing unequal opportunities (i.e., more to the less fortunate) as a means of redressing or righting undeserved opportunities. However, the opportunities provided by society are the basic rights or human rights of everyone in society, so if the distribution is not equal, giving more opportunities to those with bad family backgrounds and lower natural endowment, wouldn't it infringe on the human rights of those with good family background and higher natural endowment?

Thus, Rawls makes two mistakes: on the one hand, he mistakes that the unequal opportunities provided by family background, natural endowment and luck, as well as other factors which one cannot not be responsible for, are unfair and not ought to be, thus on the other hand, he mistakenly holds that the opportunities provided by society should conversely be unequal in order to compensate for the unequal opportunities created by factors such as family background etc., so that everyone's opportunity is "truly" and completely equal but the beautiful ideal of full equality of opportunity is the root cause of his mistakes

From what we discussed above, it can be concluded that the opportunities provided by society for the development of potential talents, the making of contribution, the competition for non-basic rights such as position, status, power, and wealth, are the basic rights or human rights of everyone in society, which should be enjoyed by everyone on a completely equal footing. On the other hand, the opportunities not provided by society, such as family background, natural endowment, and luck are the individual rights of the fortunate; others have no right to interfere with these rights no matter how unequal they are. But those who take more advantage of opportunities and thereby gain more rights should compensate those with less opportunity with corresponding rights for the "social cooperation," which enables them to do so and which they make more use of, is shared by everyone. This is the principle of the equality of opportunity, which is the value standard of the equality of opportunity of state institutions and state governance.

6.6 Theories on social justice

In summary, though justice is divided into individual justice and social justice, it mainly is the social justice, namely the distributive justice, which essentially can be attributed to *the principle of contribution*: the rights distributed to everyone by society should be directly proportional to their contribution and equal to their duties. In the end, however, the principle of contribution can be attributed to *the principle of equality*: that is, to the general principle of equality—the complete equality of basic rights and the proportional equality of non-basic rights—as well as to principles of political equality, economic equality, and equality of opportunity. Though derived from the principle of contribution, these principles of equality are undoubtedly far more important than the principle of contribution and far more important than all other principles of justice, and thus are the most important and most essential justice: equality is the most important justice.

Indeed, as Aristotle often stressed in one way or other, "Justice, its true meaning, lies primarily in equality."[159] Likewise, Mill wrote: "Maxims of equality and impartiality ... are included among the precepts of justice."[160] Thence, in the final analysis, justice is the fundamental value standard of state institutions, which means that equality—the general principle of equality and the principle of political equality, as well as the principle of economic equality and equality of opportunity—are the most important and most fundamental value standard of state institutions.

However, how to achieve justice, how to distribute the rights and duties of everyone, is not only the fundamental problem of social justice, it is also the core challenge of the interdisciplinary fields of ethics, political philosophy, legal philosophy, and economic philosophy, as has been debated in great detail in the works of Plato, Aristotle, Rawls, and Nozic. All the arguments, as seen by the likes of Feinberg, Beauchamp, and Frankena, can be summed up as four theories: the theory of contribution (including the theory of talents and the theory of moral character), egalitarianism, the theory of need, and the theory of liberty-justice.[161]

6.6.1 *The theory of contribution*

The so-called theory of contribution, as its name implies, is the theory of social justice which regards contribution as the basis for the distribution of rights, that is, the theory of "distributing rights according to contribution" as the principle of social justice. However, as mentioned earlier, there are potential contributions and actual contributions: potential contributions are talent, virtue, and other internal contribution factors, as well as luck, birth, and other external contribution factors, which lead to contributions, and are the contributions that have not been made but will made and the contributions in potential, while actual contributions are the combination of virtue, talent, luck, and birth, which are the contribution that have been made and the contributions in reality. Therefore, "the theory of talents" which advocates the distribution of rights according to talents and the "theory of virtue" that distributes rights according to virtue belong to the category of "theory of contribution," but they are all a one-sided "theory of contribution."

The founder of the *theory of contribution* was Aristotle, for through a great deal of argumentation, he concluded that:

> The just distribution is to pay something of proper value to the person who has the corresponding income. I've already talked about this in *Ethics*, and according to it a just distribution of functions ("political rights") should take into account the talents or merits of each incumbent ("civil duty").[162]

Therefore, "the distribution of political rights must be based on the extent to which people contribute to the factors that make up the city-state."[163] For more than two thousand years since Aristotle, the *theory of contribution* has been close to a self-evident axiom, which not only has been regarded by wise rulers as the golden rule for the state governance, but also advocated by many liberalist and socialist.

Our study of the fundamental issues of social justice shows that the distribution of rights according to contribution is the fundamental principle of social justice: virtue and talents are potential contributions and the potential basis for the distribution of rights, while contribution is the actual result of virtue and talents, which is the actual basis of distribution of rights. Therefore, the principle of virtue and talents is nothing more than the principle of potential contribution which is the potential principle of fundamental social justice, while the principle of contribution is the actual principle of social justice.

According to this view, the *theory of contribution* and the *theory of virtue and talent* are the truths, while the *theory of talents* and the *theory of virtue* are one-sided truths. Only the combination of virtue and talent is the necessary factor and sufficient condition to determine the contribution. On the other hand, the separation of virtue and talent, like luck and birth, would be a factor and a necessary condition for accidental contributions: a person, whether he has virtue or talent, is likely to make or fail to make contributions. Thus, if virtue and talent are separated and either of them is regarded as the basis for the distribution of rights, it might lead to the enjoyment of rights without contribution, and thus deviate from the principle of justice which distributes rights according to contributions. Therefore, the fundamental principle of social justice is to distribute rights neither according to talents nor according to virtue, but according to both virtue and talents.

6.6.2 *The theory of need*

The so-called "theory of need" is a theory which consider "distribution according to need" as the fundamental principle of social justice. The advocates of this theory are numerous, but they mainly are thinkers of socialism and communism, such as Thomas More, Tommas Campanella, Gerrard Winstanley, William Godwin, Morelly, Mabley, Owen, Theoddre Dezamy, Brown, Marx, and Engels. At present, there are still many thinkers in the West, such as Michael Walzer, David Miller, and Bernard Williams, who regard "distribution according to need" as the fundamental principle of social justice.

However, the principle of distribution according to need is not actually a principle of justice, but is either a principle of benevolence, which is higher than justice, or a principle of injustice (or rather an unjust principle). In other words, what kind of principle it is depends entirely on the kind of society it is practiced in. If, for example, the basic relationship of all members of a society is based on their own interests rather than mutual love for one another, then the members of that society would likely take account of benefits in terms of gains and losses for themselves. Thus, "those who contribute more but need less rights" (which according to the principle of justice they should enjoy) would not voluntarily transfer and give their rights to "those who contribute less but need more rights" (which is unjust). Conversely, however, if the distribution is carried out according to need, this would be a forcible deprivation of the rights of "those who contribute more but need less rights," thus is unjust because it violates the rights of "those who contribute more but need less rights." Thus, distribution according to need is an unjust principle if applied in an interest-based society run by a state.

If, by contrast, the basic relationship of all members of a society, is based on mutual love rather than individual interests, then the members of that society would not care about benefits in terms of the gains and losses for themselves, but would willingly agree with the distribution according to needs. In this case, it is not unjust that "those who contribute more but need less rights" are distributed less rights while "those who contribute less but need more rights" are distributed more rights. Thus, out of the love for those "who contribute less but need more rights," those "who contribute more but need less rights" fully agree with the distribution according to needs, that is, they voluntarily transfer or give their rights (which according to the principle of justice they deserved) to "those who contribute less but need more rights." Conversely, "those who contribute less but need more rights" merely accept rather than violate the rights given by "those who contribute more but need less rights." In this way, if distribution according to need was implemented in a love-based society (i.e., we could say a nuclear or extended family is such a society), it is a principle of benevolence, which is beyond justice and thereby has no issue of being just or unjust. So, says Feinberg:

> "From each according to his ability, to each according to his needs" ... The famous socialist slogan ... was not intended, in any case, to express a principle of distributive justice. It was understood to be a rejection of all considerations of "mere" justice for an ethic of human brotherhood. The early socialist thought it unfair, in a way, to give the great contributors to our wealth a disproportionately small share of the product. But in the new socialist society, love of neighbor, community spirit, and absence of avarice would overwhelm such bourgeois notions and put them in their proper (subordinate) place.[164]

6.6.3 The theory of liberty-justice

"Liberty-justice," as we know, is a basic concept of Hayek's theory of justice. However, no one seems to have noticed that this concept is the fundamental feature of the libertarian theories of social justice not only of Hayek, but of Nozick and Rawls as well. Therefore, we call it the "the theory of liberty-justice" because it is the theory of social justice advocated by all three thinkers. The typical feature of this theory is to equate liberty with justice, and thus regard the principle of liberty in the distribution of rights as the principle of social justice. While its representatives are Nozick, Rawls, and Hayek, it is not, however, a theory of social justice peculiar to liberalism because, on the one hand, not all libertarians advocate this theory of social justice, but also because, on the other hand, some non-liberalists, such as Michael Walzer, a communalism thinker, also advocate the theory of liberty-justice.

Slow at first to advocate something close to theory of liberty-justice, Nozick eventually did criticize almost all principles of social justice put forward by mankind. According to Nozick, the principles of distributive justice are all narrow and incorrect because they are all patterned: "Almost every suggested principle of distributive justice is patterned: to each according to his moral merits, or needs, or marginal product, or how hard he tries, or the weighted sum of the foregoing, and so on."[165] "To think that the task of a theory of distributive justice is to fill in the blank in 'to each according to his____' is to be supposed to search for a pattern."[166]

But, in Nozick's view, the actual holdings of justice or facts of justice, which are regulated by the patterned principles of justice, are not actually patterned at all. As he went on to say:

> The set of holdings that results when some persons receive their marginal products, others win at gambling, others receive a share of their mate's income, others receive gifts from foundations, others receive returns on investment, others make for themselves much of what they have, others find things, and so on, will not be patterned.[167]

Justice and equality 255

Thence Nozick concluded that any patterned principle of justice does not fit or conform to the actual holdings of justice or facts of justice, and is therefore incorrect.

This is Nozick's argument for criticizing the principles of social justice such as the distribution of rights according to contribution patterns. At first glance, it seems that Nozick is right: "it is true that some people get income from their spouses and some get gifts from worshippers [but] which kind of patterned principles of social justice do these actual holdings of justice or facts of justice fit?" Do they fit the principle of contribution, or the principle of virtue and talent, or the two principles of equality? Clearly none of them, as Nozick put it:

> The likelihood is small that any actual freely-arrived-at set of holdings fits a given pattern; and the likelihood is nil that it will continue to fit the pattern as people exchange and give.[168]

On closer examination, however, Nozick's critiques are untenable: it confuses individual justice with social justice, because, as mentioned earlier, individual justice is the justice of individual actors, the fundamental principle of which is "the rights exercised by a person are equal to the duties performed." Social justice is the justice of social actors, the fundamental principle of which is that "the rights distributed to everyone by society should be directly proportional to their contributions and equal to their duties."

According to his view, Nozick's facts of justice are both the facts of social justice (get interests from loans or investments, etc.) and the facts of individual justice (get income from one's spouses, get a gift, win a gamble, etc.) However, the principle of distribution according to contributions, the two principles of equality and so on, which he opposes, are only the principles of social justice. Obviously, any principle of social justice can only fit the facts of social justice but not the facts of individual justice, just as the principle of individual justice can only fit the facts of individual justice but not the facts of social justice. Therefore, the principles of social justice such as distribution according to contributions are demolished only because they do not fit the fact of social justice not because they are unfit for the facts of individual justice. Thus, Nozick doesn't make a distinction between the facts of social justice and the facts of individual justice, basing his argument wholly on the reason that distribution according to contributions does not fit all the facts of justice (that is, not fit the facts of individual justice), and then asserting that all the principles of justice are untenable. However, if, in Nozick's view, almost all the principles of social justice are incorrect, then, then what are the comprehensive (and basically correct) principles of social justice? Nozick claims:

> So entrenched are maxims of the usual form that perhaps we should present the entitlement conception as a competitor. Ignoring acquisition and rectification, we might say:

From each according to what he choose to do, to each according to what he makes for himself (perhaps with the contracted aid of others) and what others choose to do for him and choose to give him of what they've been given previously (under this maxim) and haven't yet expended or transferred.

This, the discerning reader will have noticed, has its defects as a slogan. So as a summary and great simplification (and not as a maxim with any independent meaning) we have:

From each as they choose, to each as they are chosen.[169]

Clearly, Nozick's principle is nothing more than to say that giving and getting should be voluntary and free, that is, free exchange is the fundamental principle of social justice. Nozick, however, only proves the so-called non-patterned principle of social justice. Walzer also advocates free exchange, but unlike Nozick who regards it as the sole principle of social justice, Walzer sees it as one of the principles of social justice:

I should ignore any claim to the sole distribution criterion, for none of them may be commensurate with the diversity of social goods. However, three criteria seem to meet the requirements of this never-concluded principle and are often argued as the origin and purpose of distributive justice. Therefore, I must discuss each criterion a little bit, which are free exchange, deserved and need. All three standards have true power, but no one is able to transcend all areas of distribution. All of them are only part of the story but not the whole.[170]

It is easy to see that Nozick and Walzer's "free exchange" is the so-called economic freedom. It is true that if economic freedom or free exchange was a principle of social justice, it would be a non-patterned principle, but is it a principle of social justice? The answer is no. For even Walzer himself admits that "free exchange puts distribution totally in the hands of individuals."[171] This means that the actors of free exchange or economic freedom are individuals not societies. Thus, free exchange or economic freedom belongs to the category of individual behavior but not to social behavior (such as the distribution of society), so it can only be the principle of individual justice, not the principle of social justice. Hayek, who also advocates the free exchange principle, seems to see this; rejecting it as a principle of social justice, he calls it the principle of "liberty-justice."

However, it is also incorrect for Hayek to call this principle the principle of liberty-justice, because economic freedom or free exchange are not necessarily just or moreover a principle of justice. The exchanges of labor for wages, freedom for bread, sex for money, and money for power, and so on are voluntary and free, and hence belong to the category of free exchange. But none of them in themselves are just. Thus, freedom of exchange or economic freedom as a moral principle, should be based on the premise of not violating justice, which is even the opinion of Smith, the founder of this principle:

> All systems either of preference or of restraint, therefore, being thus completely taken away, the obvious and simple system of natural liberty establishes itself of its own accords. Every man, as long as he does not violate the laws of justice, is left perfectly free to pursue his own interest his own way, and to bring both his industry and capital into competition with those of any other man, or order of men.[172]

This is to say that free exchange that violates justice is immoral, therefore, conceptually, free exchange is nothing other than "economic freedom" (or vice versa), meaning that it is not bound by the principle of economic freedom, that is, not bound by the moral principle of economic freedom; put another way, only the economic freedom which does not violate justice can be regarded as a moral principle and can be called the principle of economic freedom. But even then, it would be only the principle of economic freedom, not the principle of economic justice. Therefore, it is not only wrong for Nozick and Walzer to regard free exchange or economic freedom as a (or the) principle of social justice, but also untenable for Hayek to call it the principle of "liberty-justice."

Taking a closer analysis, the reason why Hayek takes "free exchange" or "economic freedom" as the principle of liberty-justice is that he equates "liberty" with "justice" at the outset and further equates the "principle of liberty" with the "principle of justice." As the basic category of Hayek's theory of justice, the term "liberty-justice" in a nutshell connotes that liberty and justice are the same concepts. It is true that this liberty, which does share the same concept with justice, is a special freedom in Hayek's view, which he calls "freedom under the law," i.e., the principle of freedom under the law, in the final analysis, is the principle of liberty: the principle of liberty is the principle of justice, and is the principle of liberty-justice.[173] On the basis of this theory of liberty-justice (i.e., the principle of freedom is the principle of justice, the principle of non-freedom is the principle of injustice). Hayek, however, further deduces that any social justice is virtually impossible because so-called social justice is the justice of social distribution, and any kind of social distribution is undoubtedly a certain destruction of free exchange or economic freedom, which is unjust: a free principle is a just principle and an unfree principle is an unjust principle. This, for Hayek, is the "illusion of social justice." He writes: "the ubiquitous dependence on other people's power, which the enforcement of any image of 'social justice' creates, inevitably destroys that freedom of personal decisions on which all morals must rest."[174] But, is not this denial of the existence of any social justice a fallacy? Thus, according to *reductio ad absurdum*, its premise (the equivalence of the principle of freedom with the principle of justice) must surely be wrong.

However, Rawls also equated "a free principle" with "a just principle." In Rawls' view, as we raised earlier, the two principles of justice he put forward are just, not because they are based on the contribution of everyone but because they are a social contract, and the justification of their justness is the agreement of everyone: "Certain principles of justice are justified because they would be agreed to in an initial situation of equality."[175] Thus Rawls, like Hayek, equated the principle of liberty with the principle of justice, but he based it on the fundamental characteristic of the principle of liberty that everyone agrees. Rawls thus concluded that the justness of the principle of justice is the agreement of all and, from that, the freedom property of the principle of justice is the agreement of all. The basic content of his *A Theory of Justice* is the proof of how his two principles of justice are agreed upon by all in their initial situations: the contract theory is completely based on the equation of the principle of liberty with the principle of justice.

It is true that from the wrong premise that liberty is equal to justice, Rawls nevertheless draws a correct conclusion that the two principles he established are the principles of social justice. Hayek also equated justice with liberty, but came to the extremely absurd conclusion that social justice is a subjective illusion, so it does not actually exist: as the principle of social distribution, any principle of social justice quashes freedom and is surely doomed to destroy liberty, thus is an unjust principle. Nozick also equated justice with liberty and also wrongly concluded that all principles of social justice, with the exception of free exchange, violate the principle of freedom because they are patterned, which is narrow and incorrect.

6.6.4 Egalitarianism

So-called egalitarianism, as we all know, is a theory about how the interests and burdens and the rights and duties of everyone should be distributed, the fundamental feature of which is that only equal distribution is just: the theory regards the principle of the equal distribution of the interests of everyone and the principle of the equal distribution of rights as the principles of social justice, which, in the final analysis, is the theory that takes the principle of equality as the principle of social justice. I am afraid that egalitarianism is the most popular school in the history of human thought.

Not only are all socialists and democrats, as is well known, more or less egalitarians, but also almost all libertarians are, in different degrees, egalitarians. Therefore, representatives of egalitarians are numerous, such as Plato, Aristotle, stoic, Locke, Voltaire, Rousseau, Jefferson, Paine, Kant, Bentham, Mill, Marx, Engels, Babeuf, Blanchi, Theoddre Dezamy, Alexis Tocqueville, Rawls, Dworkin, Hayek, Nelson, Adler, Satori, Feinberg, and so on.

Socialism, democracy and liberalism has various types respectively, which makes the types of egalitarianism they advocate more complicated. However, we may divide egalitarianism into two main types: extreme or absolute egalitarianism and relative egalitarianism. Extreme egalitarianism is a theory that regards the completely equal distribution of all rights as a principle of social justice; its representative figures include Moore, Muntzer, Mabley, Tommas Campanella, Godwin, Diderot, Babeuf, as well as the old welfare economist Pigou. Some of the views of Confucius and Laozi are very similar to extreme egalitarianism, for example, "Inequality rather than poverty is the cause of trouble,"[176] and "The natural law takes up surplus to make up for insufficiency."[177] This thought later developed into an egalitarian program for Chinese peasant uprisings: "Even out the distribution of wealth; eliminate the difference between the noble and humble."

But extreme egalitarianism is wrong for it violates the fundamental principle of social justice, that is, the distribution of rights according to contributions. Egalitarians who hold this view are very small in number in the huge camp of egalitarians. Most egalitarians oppose the complete equality of all rights, and regard the relative equality of rights, such as the *full equality of basic rights* and the *proportional equality of non-basic rights*, as the principle of social justice. This kind of relative egalitarianism, based on the related items or properties of the distribution of rights, is divided into four specific types: "egalitarianism of the theory of need," "egalitarianism of the theory of human nature," "egalitarianism of the theory of liberty-justice," and "egalitarianism of the theory of contribution."

"The egalitarianism of the theory of need" is advocated by social justice theorists who believe in distribution according to need. In the final analysis, it is mainly advocated by socialists and communists. This egalitarianism is clearly a combination of the theory of need and egalitarianism, which is the egalitarianism that is based on the need of everyone as the basis for the distribution of rights, and is the egalitarianism that advocates distribution according to need so that everyone's needs can be met equally—thus achieving "de facto true equality," and, after all, is the egalitarianism that regards "the de facto equality" (or true equality) of distributing rights according to need as the principle of social justice.

It goes without saying that this kind of egalitarianism, like distribution according to need, if it is implemented in a society based on love, such as a family or some kind of brotherhood, is a principle of benevolence which is beyond justice and has no issue of being just or unjust; if it is implemented in a society based on interests, such as the state, it is an unjust principle because the rights of those who contribute more and need less rights are forcibly deprived of their rights, thus violating their rights.

The "egalitarianism of the theory of human nature"—the mainstream ideology of western society since the seventeenth century—is the egalitarianism which regards the human nature of everyone as the same and therefore as the basis for the distribution of rights. This egalitarianism is untenable for according to it, a person, no matter how evil he is, ought to enjoy the same rights as a good person for both a good person and an evil person are the same as a human being.

260 Moral value and moral norms

The "egalitarianism of the theory of liberty-justice" mainly represented by Rawls, is nothing more than a combination of the theory of liberty-justice and egalitarianism, which takes liberty as the basis of the justness of the distribution of rights. In other words, it is an egalitarianism that takes the agreement of all as the basis of the justness of the distribution of rights, and, which, in the final analysis, is an egalitarianism that takes the agreement of all as the basis of the justness of the principle of equality of rights. Its fundamental shortcoming is to equate a free principle with a just principle.

The "egalitarianism of the theory of contribution" mainly represented by Aristotle, is the combination of the theories of contribution and egalitarianism which takes the principle of the equality of distribution of rights according to contribution—the full equality of basic rights and the proportional equality of non-basic rights—as the principle of social justice: only this kind of egalitarianism can be regarded as the truth of the theory of social justice because it conforms to the general principle of the "exchange of either equal interests or equal harms."

Notes

1 Edgar Bodenheimer: *Jurisprudence: The Philosophy and Method of the Law*, Harvard University Press, Cambridge, MA, 1978.
2 Aristotle: *Complete Works of Aristotle, Vol. 8*. Renmin University of China Press, 1992, p. 96.
3 Andre Conte Sponville: *Small Love with Great Virtue*. Central Compilation Bureau Press, 2001, p. 58
4 Adam Smith: *The Theory of Moral Sentiments*, China Sciences Publishing House, Chengcheng Books Ltd, Beijing, 1979, p. 86.
5 David Hume: *A Treatise of Human Nature*, Clarendon Press, Oxford, 1949, p. 199.
6 William K. Frankena: *Ethics*, Prentice-Hall, Englewood Cliffs, NJ, 1973, p. 46.
7 Plato: *The Republic*, The Commercial Press, Beijing, 1994, p. 7.
8 Edgar Bodenheimer: *Philosophy of Jurisprudence and Its Methods*, Huaxia Press, 1987, p. 253.
9 Robert Maynard Hutchins, ed.: *Great Books of the Western World, Vol. 43. Utilitarianism, by John Stuart Mill*. Encyclopedia Britannica, Inc., 1980, p. 466.
10 Plato: *The Republic*, The Commercial Press, Beijing, 1994, pp. 8, 13.
11 Cited from Burn Weides: *Jurisprudence*, Law Press, 2003, p. 159.
12 Quoted from Ci Jiwei: *The Two Faces of Justice*, SDX Joint Publishing Company, 2014, p. 151.
13 Aristotle: *Complete Works of Aristotle, Vol. 8*. Renmin University of China Press, 1992, p. 103.
14 Ibid., p. 89.
15 Ibid., p. 279.
16 Ibid., p. 101.
17 Mortimer J. Adler: *Treasures of Western Thought*, Jilin People's Publishing House, 1988, p. 951.
18 David Hume: *A Treatise of Human Nature*, Clarendon Press, Oxford, 1949, p. 199.
19 Ibid.

Justice and equality 261

20 Exodus 21: 23–24, The Holy Bible, King James Version.
21 *Academic Monthly*, No. 4, 2017, p. 3.
22 Ibid., p. 4.
23 John Rawls: *A Theory of Justice, Revised Edition*, The Belknap Press of Harvard University Press, Cambridge, MA, 2000, p. 11.
24 Ibid., p. 15.
25 Ibid., p. 3.
26 Arthur Schopenhauer: *Two Basic Questions of Ethics*, Commercial Press, 1996, p. 243–224.
27 Robert Maynard Hutchins, ed.: *Great Books of the Western World, Vol. 43. Utilitarianism by John Stuart Mill*, Encyclopedia Britannica, Inc., 1980, p. 472.
28 Ibid., p. 470.
29 Ibid., p. 471.
30 Louis P. Pojman: *Ethical Theory: Classical and Contemporary Readings*, Wadsworth, Belmont, CA, 1995, p. 43.
31 John Rawls: *A Theory of Justice, Revised Edition*, The Belknap Press of Harvard University Press, Cambridge, MA, 2000, p. 4.
32 Robert Maynard Hutchins, ed.: *Great Books of the Western World, Vol. 43. Utilitarianism by John Stuart Mill*, Encyclopedia Britannica, Inc., 1980, p. 471.
33 John Rawls: *A Theory of Justice, Revised Edition*, The Belknap Press of Harvard University Press, Cambridge, MA, 2000, p. 6.
34 Mortimer J. Adler: *Six Great Ideas*, A Touchstone Book, Simon & Schuster, New York, 1997, p. 186.
35 John Rawls: *A Theory of Justice, Revised Edition*, The Belknap Press of Harvard University Press, Cambridge, MA, 2000, p. 47.
36 Douglas C. North: *Structure and Change in Economic History*, Commercial Press, Beijing, 1992, p. 195.
37 John Commons: *Institutional Economics*, Commercial Press, 1997, p. 86.
38 Deng Xiaoping: *Selected Works of Deng Xiaoping, Vol. 2*. People's Press, 1994, p. 333.
39 John Rawls: *A Theory of Justice, (Revised Edition*, The Belknap Press of Harvard University Press, Cambridge, Ma, 2000, p. 47.
40 Ji Weidong: "The Significance of Legal Procedure," *Chinese Social Sciences*, No. 1, 1993, p. 85.
41 Sun Xiaoxia: "An Analysis of Legal Procedure," *Legal Science*, No. 6, 1993, p. 3.
42 Song Bing: *Procedure, Justice and Modernization*, China University of Political Science and Law Press, 1998, p. 356.
43 Chen Ruihua: "The realization of procedural justice through law," *Beijing University Law Review, Vol. 1*. Law Press, 1998, p. 184.
44 Song Bing: *Procedure, Justice and Modernization*, China University of Political Science and Law Press, p. 376.
45 Michael D. Berles: *Principles of Law*, China Encyclopedia Press, 1996, p. 32.
46 John Rawls: *A Theory of Justice, Revised Edition*, The Belknap Press of Harvard University Press, Cambridge, MA, 2000, p. 74.
47 Chen Ruihua: *The Theory of Criminal Trial*, Peking University Press.
48 Song Bing: *Procedure, Justice and Modernization*, China University of Political Science and Law Press, 1998, p. 375.
49 Chen Ruihua: *A Visible Justice*, China Legal Publishing House, 2000, p. 4.
50 Ibid., p. 28.

262 Moral value and moral norms

51 Ibid., p. 35.
52 Adam Smith: *The Theory of Moral Sentiments*, China Sciences Publishing House, Chengcheng Books Ltd, Beijing, 1979, p. 86.
53 David Hume: *A Treatise of Human Nature*, Clarendon Press, Oxford, 1949, pp. 199, 202.
54 Aristotle: *Complete Works of Aristotle, Vol. 8*. Renmin University of China Press, 1992, p. 96.
55 Adam Smith: *The Theory of Moral Sentiments*, China Sciences Publishing House, Chengcheng Books Ltd, Beijing, 1979, p. 86.
56 John Rawls: *A Theory of Justice, Revised Edition*, The Belknap Press of Harvard University Press, Cambridge, MA, 2000, p. 5.
57 Plato: *The Republic*, 433 AD. The Commercial Press, Beijing, 1998, p. 48.
58 Aristotle: *Politics*, Commercial Press, Beijing, 1996, p. 9.
59 John Rawls: *A Theory of Justice, Revised Edition*, The Belknap Press of Harvard University Press, Cambridge, MA, 2000, p. 3.
60 Morris Diverges: *Political Sociology*, China Press, 1987, p. 116.
61 Ibid., p. 117.
62 John Rawls: *A Theory of Justice, Revised Edition*, The Belknap Press of Harvard University Press, Cambridge, MA, 2000, p. 4.
63 Tom L. Beauchamp: *Philosophical Ethics*, McGraw-Hill, New York, 1982, p. 196.
64 Mei Roscow Ponde: *The Task of Adopting Legal Social Control/Law*, Commercial Press, 1984, p. 46.
65 Jeremy Bentham: *A Fragment on the Government*, Basil Blackwell, Oxford, 1960, p. 107.
66 Thomas Hobbes: *On the Citizen*, Guizhou People's Publishing House, 2003, p. 15.
67 Ibid., p. 27.
68 Tom L. Beauchamp: *Philosophical Ethics*, McGraw-Hill, New York, 1982, p. 206.
69 John Rawls: *A Theory of Justice, Revised Edition*, The Belknap Press of Harvard University Press, Cambridge, MA, 2000, p. 442.
70 Louis P. Pojman: *Environmental Ethical: Reading in Theory and Application*, 3rd edn. Wadsworth, Belmont, CA, 2001, p. 32.
71 James E. White: *Contemporary Moral Problems*, 4th edn. West Publishing Company, St. Paul, 1994, p. 428.
72 Roderick Frazier Nash: *The Rights of Nature: A History of Environmental Ethics*, The University of Wisconsin Press, London, 1989, p. 18.
73 Ibid., p. 161.
74 Ibid., p. 126.
75 James E. White: *Contemporary Moral Problems*, 4th edn. West Publishing Company, St. Paul, 1994, p. 428.
76 Peter Singer: *Animal Liberation*, Guangming Daily Press, 1999, p. 10.
77 Paul W. Taylor: *Respect For Nature: A Theory of Environmental Ethics*, Princeton University Press, Princeton, NJ, 1986, p. 122.
78 Roderick Frazier Nash: *The Rights of Nature: A History of Environmental Ethics*, The University of Wisconsin Press, London, 1989, p. 24.
79 Ibid., p. 142.
80 Ibid., p. 121.
81 Steven M. Cahn and Peter Markie: *Ethics: History, Theory, and Contemporary Issues*, Oxford University Press, New York, Oxford, 1998, p. 831.

Justice and equality 263

82   Roderick Frazier Nash: *The Rights of Nature: A History of Environmental Ethics*, The University of Wisconsin Press, London, 1989, p. 18.
83   John Passmore: *Man's Responsibility for Nature*, Duckworth Press, London, 1974, p. 29.
84   Leonard T. Hobhouse: *The Elements of Social Justice*, Routledge/Thoemmes Press, 1993, p. 37.
85   Tom L. Beauchamp: *Philosophical Ethics*, McGraw-Hill, New York, 1982, p. 202.
86   Ibid., p. 204.
87   Robert Maynard Hutchins, ed.: *Great Books of the Western World, Vol. 43. Utilitarianism by John Stuart Mill*, Encyclopedia Britannica, Inc., 1980, p. 468.
88   John Rawls: *A Theory of Justice, Revised Edition*, The Belknap Press of Harvard University Press, Cambridge, MA, 2000, p. 100.
89   Cited from other source: Joel Feinberg: *Freedom, Rights and Social Justice*, Guizhou People's Publishing House, 1998, p. 87.
90   Georg Wilhelm Hegel: *Principles of Philosophy of Law*, The Commercial Press, Beijing, 1962, p. 652.
91   Henri de Saint-Simon: *Selected Works of Saint-Simon, Vol. 2*. Commercial Press, 1982, p. 293.
92   Mortimer J. Adler: *Six Great Ideas*, A Touchstone Book, Simon & Schuster, New York, 1997, p. 178.
93   Arthur Okun: *Equality and Efficiency*, China Press, 1987, p. 37.
94   John Rawls: *A Theory of Justice, Revised Edition*, The Belknap Press of Harvard University Press, Cambridge, MA, 2000, p. 4
95   Friedrich A. Hayek: *The Constitution of Liberty*, The University of Chicago Press, 1978, p. 94.
96   Karl Marx: *Capital, Vol. 1*. China Social Sciences Press, 1983, p. 179.
97   Li Guoxiang and other editors: *Complete Translation of Zi Zhi Tong Jian, Vol. 1*. Guizhou People's Publishing House, 1990, p. 18.
98   Xia Chuancai: *Interpretation of the Works of Caocao*, Zhonghua Book Company, 1979, p. 160.
99   Shiji (Historical Records): *Biographies of Sun Tzu and Wu Qi*.
100 Shiji (Historical Records): *Biography of Marquis of Huaiyin*.
101 Shiji (Historical Records): *Prime Minister Chen's Family*.
102 Giovanni Sartori: *The Theory Democracy Revisited*, Chatham House, Chatham, NJ, 1987, p. 338.
103 Jean-Jacques Rousseau: *Discourse on the Origin and Foundation of Inequality among Men*, Maurice Cranston, 1984, p. 77.
104 Thomas Paine: *Selected Works of Paine*, Commercial Press, 1963, p. 143.
105 Tom L. Beauchamp: *Philosophical Ethics*, McGraw-Hill, New York, 1982, p. 206.
106 Shen Zongling, Huang Nansen, eds.: *Western Theory of Human Rights*, Sichuan People's Publishing House, 1994, p. 116.
107 Mortimer J. Adler: *Six Great Ideas*, A Touchstone Book, Simon & Schuster, New York, 1997, pp. 165–166.
108 Qiu Ben: "Human Rights without Compensation and Mortalism," *Philosophical Studies*, No. 2, 1997, p. 41.
109 Aristotle: *Complete Works of Aristotle, Vol. 8*. Renmin University of China Press, 1992, p. 279.
110 John Rawls: *A Theory of Justice, Revised Edition*, The Belknap Press of Harvard University Press, Cambridge, MA, 2000, p. 13.

264 *Moral value and moral norms*

111　Ibid., p. 4.
112　Robert Nozick: *Anarchy, State and Utopia*, China Sciences Publishing House Chengcheng Books Ltd, Beijing, 1999, p. 161.
113　John Rawls: *A Theory of Justice, Revised Edition*, The Belknap Press of Harvard University Press, Cambridge, MA, 2000, p. 88.
114　Robert Nozick: *Anarchy, State and Utopia*, China Sciences Publishing House, Chengcheng Books Ltd, Beijing, 1999, pp. 192—193.
115　John Rawls: *A Theory of Justice, Revised Edition*, The Belknap Press of Harvard University Press, Cambridge, MA, 2000, p. 4.
116　Aristotle: *Complete Works of Aristotle, Vol. 9*. Renmin University of China Press, 2012, p. 163.
117　Ibid.
118　Joel Feinberg: *Social Philosophy*, Prentice Hall, Englewood Cliffs, NJ, 1973, p. 100.
119　Giovanni Sartory: *The Theory of Democracy Revisited*, Chatham House, Chatham, NJ, 1987, p. 34.
120　Marx W. Wartofsky: *Conceptual Foundations of Scientific Thought*, Macmillan Company, New York; Collier-Macmillan, London, 1968, p. 23.
121　John Rawls: *A Theory of Justice, Revised Edition*, The Belknap Press of Harvard University Press, Cambridge, MA, 2000, p. xviii.
122　Ibid., p. 266.
123　Giovanni Sartori: *The Theory of Democracy Revisited*, Chatham House, Chatham, NJ, 1987, p. 350.
124　Mortimer J. Adler: *Six Great Ideas*, A Touchstone Book, Simon & Schuster, New York, 1997, pp. 165–166.
125　John Rawls: *A Theory of Justice, Revised Edition*, The Belknap Press of Harvard University Press, Cambridge, MA, 2000, p. 11.
126　Ibid.
127　Ibid., p. 19.
128　William K. Frankena: *Ethics*, Prentice-Hall, Inc., Englewood Cliffs, NJ, 1973, p. 6.
129　Mortimer J. Adler: *Treasures of Western Thought*, Jilin People's Publishing House, 1988, p. 944.
130　David Hume: *A Treatise of Human Nature*, Clarendon Press, Oxford, 1949, p. 494.
131　Giovanni Sartori: *The Theory Democracy Revisited*, Chatham House, Chatham, NJ, 1987, p. 352.
132　Ibid., p. 338.
133　Ma Qihua: *Political Theory, Vol. 2*. Taiwan Commercial Press, 1977, p. 163.
134　Karl Heinrich Marx and Friedrich Engels: *Complete Works of Marx and Engels, Vol. 1*. People's Publishing House, 1956, p. 437.
135　Thomas Paine: *Selected Works of Paine*, Commercial Press, 1963, p. 145.
136　Karl Marx: *Capital, Vol. 1*. China Social Sciences Press, 1983, p. 179.
137　Aristotle: *Politics*, Commercial Press, 1996, p. 136.
138　Mortimer J. Adler: *Six Great Ideas*, A Touchstone Book, Simon & Schuster, New York, 1997, p. 180.
139　Ibid., p. 178.
140　Ibid.
141　Douglas W. Rae: *Equalities*, Harvard University Press, Cambridge, MA, 1981, p. 74.

142 Ibid., pp. 65–66.
143 Giovanni Sartori: *The Theory Democracy Revisited*, Chatham House, Chatham, NJ, 1987, p. 344.
144 Ibid., pp. 346–347.
145 John Rawls: *A Theory of Justice*, Revised Edition, The Belknap Press of Harvard University Press, Cambridge, MA, 2000, pp. 53–57.
146 Ibid., p. 89.
147 Tom L. Beauchamp: *Philosophical Ethics*, McGraw-Hill, New York, 1982, p. 252.
148 Paul Anthony Samuelson: *Economics*, Commercial Press, 1982, p. 232.
149 Arthur Okun: *Equality and Efficiency*, China Press, 1987, p. 38.
150 Robert Nozick: *Anarchy, State and Utopia*, China Sciences Publishing House Chengcheng Books Ltd, Beijing, 1999, p. 151.
151 Ibid., p. 226.
152 James M. Buchanan: *Freedom, Markets and the State*, Beijing Institute of Economics Press, 1989, p. 130.
153 Ibid., p. 130.
154 See *Complete Works of Sansong Tang, Vol. 4*. Henan People's Publishing House, 1988, p. 681.
155 Mortimer J. Adler: *Treasures of Western Thought*, Jilin People's Publishing House, 1988, p. 1047.
156 Friedrich A. Hayek: *The Principles of Free Order*, SDX Joint Publishing Company, 1997, p. 172.
157 Ibid., p. 99.
158 John Rawls: *A Theory of Justice*, Revised Edition, The Belknap Press of Harvard University Press, Cambridge, MA, 2000, p. 86.
159 Aristotle: *Complete Works of Aristotle, Vol. 8*. Renmin University of China Press, 1992, p. 279.
160 Robert Maynard Hutchins, ed.: *Great Books of the Western World, Vol. 43. Utilitarianism by John Stuart Mill*, Encyclopedia Britannica, Inc., 1980, p. 467.
161 Joel Feinberg: *Social Philosophy*, Prentice Hall, Englewood Cliffs, NJ, 1973, p. 109; Tom L. Beauchamp: *Philosophical Ethics*, McGraw-Hill, New York, 1982, p. 229; William K. Frankena: *Ethics*, Prentice-Hall, Englewood Cliffs, NJ, 1973, p. 49.
162 Aristotle: *Politics*, Commercial Press, Beijing, 1996, p. 136.
163 Ibid., p. 150.
164 Joel Feinberg: *Social Philosophy*, Prentice Hall, Englewood Cliffs, NJ, 1973, p. 114.
165 Robert Nozick: *Anarchy, State and Utopia*, China Sciences Publishing House, Chengcheng Books Ltd, Beijing, 1999, p. 156.
166 Ibid., p. 159.
167 Ibid.
168 Ibid., p. 168.
169 Ibid., p. 160.
170 Michael Walzer: *The Realms of Justice*, Yilin Press, 2002, p. 25.
171 Ibid.
172 Adam Smith: *An Inquiry into the Nature and Causes of the Wealth of Nations, Vol. 2*. Clarendon Press, Oxford, 1976, p. 687.
173 Friedrich A. Hayek: *The Constitution of Liberty*, The University of Chicago Press, 1978, p. 153.

266 *Moral value and moral norms*

174 Friedrich A. Hayek: *Legislation and Liberty*, *Vol. 2*. China Social Sciences Publishing House, Chengcheng Books Ltd, Beijing, 1999, p. 99.
175 John Rawls: *A Theory of Justice, Revised Edition*, The Belknap Press of Harvard University Press, Cambridge, MA, 2000, p. 19.
176 *The Analects of Confucius*: Jishi, 16.
177 *Lao-tzu*, the 77th chapter.

Index

Note: Page numbers in **bold** and *italics* refer to tables and figures, respectively.

Abbey, Edward 33, 35
absolute egalitarianism 258–9
absolute morality 14–17, 20–4, 62
absoluteness 14–17, 21–3
action with moral value 88
activities with social utility 40–2
actualization of morality 47–9
actual principle of contribution 210–14, 218
Adler, Alfred 104, 183, 233, 244
Alpert 108
altruism 119, 160–3
Analects of Confucius, The 113
anger 94–6
Anpei Taniguchi 185–7
anthropocentrism 31, 54–6, 205
anti-anthropocentrism 31, 54–6
anti-humanism 35
Appetite and sexual desire 151
appointments by combination of virtue 216
approximate ultimate general standard 67
Aquinas, Thomas 26, 55, 177
Aristotle 26, 54, 64, 84, 98, 175, 177, 192–3, 224, 229–30, 252
arson 7, 39, 204
artificial equality 219–20
autonomy theory of origin and goal of morality 57
Ayer, M. J., 24

bads 54; *see also* good and evil
basic emotions: anger 94–5; fear 94–5; pleasure 94–5; sadness 94–5
basic rights 220, 222
Beauchamp, Tom L. 20, 65, 75, 196, 206

Beethoven, Ludwig van 144, 221
behavioral fact 10–12
behavioral norm 6
behavioral oughts 4–6, 11
behavioral process 185
behavior of benefiting others as an end 99
beneficence 15, 192
benefiting others 111, **138**; as an end 109; for harming others **91**, 93, **138**; for self-harming 92; for self-interest 18–19, 91, 94, 128–30, 138, 142, 144, 147–8, 169
benevolence 161, 175, 193, 216
benevolence of Confucianism 155
Bentham, Jeremy 50, 56, 67, 74, 76, 190, 197
Berkeley, George 74
Berles, Michael D. 187
Binkley, Luther J. 23
Blocker, H. Gene 20
Bolin 50
Bond, E. J. 26
boundary of moral community 31–3
Bradley, Francis Herbert 73
Brink, David O. 26
Buchanan, James M. 248

Cai Yuanpei 96, 98
Callicott's biocentrism 35
Campanella, Tommas 253
Cao Cao 216
Cao Xueqin 221
Chamberlain, Wilt 226–7
Chen Ping 216
Chernyshevsky, Nikolay 110, 163
Christian ethicists 57, 73

268 *Index*

Christianity 161, 163, 175
Chuang-tzu 107, 164
Cihai 220
claim 195
class struggle 39
Code of Freedom in the British colonies 202
coercion 194
coercive forces 194
cognition 38
Commons, John R., 183
community 37
compassion 46, 84, 87, 101
completely benefiting others **91**, 92, 138, **138**, 150
completely harming others 91, 93, **138**
completely self-harming 92
completely self-interest 91, 138, 141–2
compulsions 7
Comte, Auguste 160–1
Comte-Sponville, André 175
Confucianism 57, 73, 110–11, 161–3, 175
Confucians 156
Confucian school 3
Confucian Shi Shuo 156
Confucian theory on human nature 158
Confucius 47, 57, 99, 119
consciousness 88–9
continence 46
contractual rights and duties 199
contribution 251–3
corruption 39
criminal prosecution 186
criticism 39
Crusoe, Robinson 45–6
cultural activities 38
cultural ethical relativism 20
Cultural Revolution 83
culture 38
culturing 39

Darwin, Charles 44, 46, 74, 100, 142
Declaration of Human Rights in France 1789 200, 220
Declaration of Independence of the United States 1776 200
deductive formula of moral value 12
degrees of human natures 157
degrees of love 111–16, *112*, 118–19, 149
demand 195
democracy 258
Deng Xiaoping 184
denouncement 39

deontology 73–9, 156
dependence and substance 186
Descartes, René 55
desires to live 107–9
Devall, Bill 203
distribution of rights 213
doctrine of benefiting self-other interests 167–9
Dong Cunrui 119
Dong Zhongshu 73, 84, 156–7
Douglas, William 190
Dream of the Red Chamber, The (Cao Xueqin) 221
due rights and duties 198
Durkheim, Emil 20, 24
duties 197–200; to animals 201; of imperfect obligation 206; of person to non-human being 201

economic activities 37
economic equality 242–4
economic inequalities 225
economic man 119–21, 126
economic rights 223
edification 39
education 39
egalitarianism 258–60
egoism 110
Einstein, Albert 116
Ellwood, Charles A. 84, 114
Elvis 74
emotion 38, 94; basic 94; non-basic 94
Endangered Species Act 202
enemy 29
envy 102
Epicurus 6, 24
equality 41, 218–20, 230; general principles of equality 228–38; principle of economic equality 242–4; principle of equality of opportunity 244–51; principle of full equality 220–4; principle of political equality 238–42; principle of proportional equality 224–7; specific principles of equality 238
equality of opportunity 244–51; for competing for rights 245; on the future 245; on means 245
equalization of income 219
error of egoism 170
ethical absolutism 20, 22–4
ethical behavior 87–8, 90; benefiting others **91**; defined 88–89; harming

others **91**; means of 90; self-harming **91**; self-interest **91**; structure 89–90; types of 90–4, **91, 138**; ultimate motivation of 90
ethical behavior, relative quantity of means of 123; non-statistical law 123–4; statistical law 124–7
ethical egoism 166–7
ethical holism 35
ethical relativism 20–2
ethics: Chinese etymological meaning 3–4; and morality 4
evenhandedness 178–81
evolutionary process 200
excellent morality 17–20
excellent norms of behavior 199
experience 38

fairness 178–81
fair rightness 181
fair trade movement 178–81
fear 94–95
Feinberg, Joel 166, 202–3, 206–7, 230, 251, 254
Feuerbach, Ludwig 96 163
force to bind pigs 194
forgiveness 175
"four minds" 154
Frankena, William K. 6, 47, 75, 176
fraternal love 98
freedom of interpersonal activities 63
Freud, Sigmund 51, 89, 96, 102, 104, 114
Freudian psychology 117
Fromm, Erich 104
fundamental ends of action 90
fundamental justice 183
fundamental value standard of state institutions 191–3
Fung Yulan 57, 74, 84, 89–90, 94, 114, 137, 149

gambling procedural justice 188
Gaozi 84, 151–2
general principles of equality 228–38
generosity 46
goal of morality 10–11, 16, 18
Godwin, William 253
Goethe, Johann Wolfgang von 144
good and evil: establishment of six principles 141–45; moral value of ethical behaviors 137–41; principles of good and evil *145*; principles of morality 148–51; scope of application of six principles 145–8
good and evil, theories of: altruism 160–3; evil of human nature 154–5; good and evil of human nature 155–60; good of human nature 152–4; human nature without good or evil 151–2; psychological egoism and ethical egoism 166–7; rational egoism and individualism 163–6; truth and falsehood 169–72; unity of altruism and egoism 167–9
good-as-an-end 50, 52
good-in-itself 50, 52
gratitude 101
greatest happiness for the greatest number 67–9
greatest possible surplus of pleasure over pain 65
Grotius, Hugo 181
group of humans 37
Guo Moruo 161

Han Xin 216–17
Han Yu 84, 157
happiness 43
happiness is ends and aim of morality 74
Hare, R. M. 19, 26
Harman, Gilbert 6, 20, 24–5, 70, 182
harming others 111, 125, **138**; as an end 109, 138; for benefiting others **91**, 92, **138**, 139, 141–2; for self-harming 93; for self-interest 18, **91**, 92, 102, 126, 128–30, **138**, 139–40, 142–50, *145*, 169, 171
Hartland-Swann, John 5, 88
hating-others 85–6
hatred 96
Hegel, Georg Wilhelm Friedrich 144, 180
Helvetius, Claude 163
heteronomy of morality 52–4
higher-levels of human nature 87
Hobhouse, Leonard T. 206
Holbach, Paul Anly 74, 163
honesty 46
Horney, Karen 104, 106
Huang Jianzhong 87
Huang Jiguang 119
human activities 37
human animality 86–7
human association 193
human behavioral oughts 5

Index

human characteristics 86–87
human interests conflicts 33–7, 66, 68
human nature 19, 83–4, 155–7; defined 83–4, 153–4; quantitative analysis of 123–31; structure of 85–6; substance 86; substance and utility 85–6; types of 86–7; utility 86
human rights 223, 228–9
human's evil actions 141
human society 43
Hume, David 6, 24, 74, 96, 120–1, 175, 178
humility 106
Hutcheson, Francis 26, 160, 163
hypocrisy 119

"id" 117–18
imperfect duties 207
imperfect procedural justice 188
individual egoism 166
indoctrination of thought 39
inferior morality 17–20
intelligent persons 216
interest community 32, 53
interpersonal activities 38
interpersonal relationships 3; elderly and young 3–4; father and son 3–4; friends 3–4; husband and wife 3–4; monarch and his subjects 3–5
intransigence 117
intrinsic good 50
involuntary communication 177

Jackson, Robert H. 190
Jhering, Rudolph Von 196
Ji Weidong 185
Joan of Arc 119, 121
Jung 104
jurisprudence 42
justice 41, 46; definition of 175–8; distributive justice 181–4; fairness and evenhandedness 178–81; fundamental value standard of state institutions 191–3; procedural justice 185–91; retributive justice 181–4; substantive justice 185–91; types of 181–4
Justice As Fairness (Rawls) 180
justice of governance 184
justice of outcome 185–91
justice of social distribution 183

Kant, Immaneul 15, 22, 26, 47, 55, 57, 61–2, 73, 110–11, 149, 162–3, 200–1, 205; formula of duty 161; moral absolutism 23; theory of moral autonomy 57
knowledge 38
Kraut, Richard 42
Kropotkin, Peter 29

law of diminishing marginal utility 72
law of human nature of the degrees of love 118–19
law of relative quantity of types of ethical behavior 127; non-statistical law 127–9; statistical laws 129–31
laws 197
legal duties 197
legitimacy of power 7, 194
Leibniz, Gottfried Wilhelm 144
Leopold, Aldo 55
Liang Qichao 94, 164
liberalism 258
liberty 41
liberty-justice 254–8, 260
Liu Bang 217
Liu Yingjun 119
living beings 31–3
Li Zongwu 115
Locke, John 55, 96
love 48, 94, 96, 101
loving-others 85–6
lying 62

Mabley 253
Manheim, Carl 20, 24
Mao Dun 97
Mao Zedong 184
Ma Qihua 38, 239
Marine Mammal Protection Act 202
Martin Act 202
Marx, Karl 53, 180, 215, 239
Maslow, Abraham 116
Mencius 39, 84–5, 87, 101, 109, 152–4, 162, 201
mental patients 205
mere self-interest 145, 149, 169
meta-ethics 62, 137
Mill, Stuart 16, 43, 56, 74, 181, 206–7
Miller, David 253
mind of compassion 153
moderation 46
Mohism 163
Moore, David 26, 74
moral absolutism 22
moral agent 29–31

moral autonomy 56–9
moral bad 137; *see also* good and evil
moral bargaining 6
moral behaviors 30–1
moral community 29, 31, 33
moral conflict 61
moral consciousness 30–1
moral contract 34
moral duties 197
moral facts 26
moral good 137; *see also* good and evil
moral heteronomy 56–9
morality 197; absolute 14–17; basic structure 8–9; categories *15*; complete structure 9–10; deep structure 10–12; defined 3–8, 47; ethical absolutism 22–4; ethical relativism 20–2; and ethics 3–5; excellent 17–20; first principle 16; inferior 17–20; and law 6–8; moral norm and moral value 8–9; moral objectivism 26–7; moral realism 26–7; moral subjectivism 24–5; nihilism/skepticism 24–5; and ought 5–6; particular 12–14; person community 88; relative 14–17; in safeguarding 33–7; in self-regarding 46; social contract 45; social needs of 41; structure of 8–12, *11*; theories on concepts 20–7, 160; types of 12–20; universal 12–14
morality, origin and goal 10–11, 16, 18, 37–41; anthropocentrism 31, 54–6; anti-anthropocentrism 31, 54–6; boundary of moral community 31–3; heteronomy of 52–4; human interests 33–7; moral agent 29–31; moral autonomy 56–9; moral heteronomy 56–9; moral patient 29–31; personal moral needs 47–9; social moral needs 37–41; social nature 44–7; sources and goal 41–4; ultimate standard of 137; virtue and 49–52
morally perfect people 129
moral needs of society 42; development of culture 42; economic activities 42; excellent politics 42; interpersonal activities 42; making excellent laws 42
moral nihilism/skepticism 24–5
moral norms 8–9; suicides 13; for women 13
moral objectivism 20
moral patients 29–31
moral perfection, limit of 118–19

moral principles 13, 42
moral realism 20
moral rights and duties 197–200
moral rules 30
moral skepticism 20
moral standing 29–30
moral subjectivism 20, 24–5
moral value 8–9
moral value judgment 9–10, 19–20
More, Thomas 253
Morelly, Étienne-Gabriel 253
motherly love 96, 100
Mozi 113
multi-levels nature 87
murder 39
muscles, utility of 45

Nash, Roderick Frazier 35, 202
natural equality 219
natural law 198–9
natural rights 197–200, 222
nature 152
necessary bad 50
necessity 194
need 253–4
negative emotions 95
negative justice *see* retributive justice
net balance of interests 64
net balance of maximum interests 66–9
neurosis 51
Newton, Isaac 144
Newton's theory to psychology 116
Nietzsche, Friedrich 164, 176–7
non-basic economic rights 243
non-basic rights 220, 224, 240, 244
non-ends causes 90, 95
non-fundamental justice 183
non-human animals 34, 56
non-human interests 36
non-human rights 240
non-human-rights economic rights 65
non-living beings 31–3
non-moralism 23
non-power behavioral norm 7
non-power coercion 39
non-power force 38
non-power management 38
non-teleology 73
normative ethical relativism 20
North, Douglas C. 183
Norto, Bryan 54
Nozick, Robert 254–6

objectivism 26–7
Okun, Arthur 210
open-mindedness 46
origins of justice origins, Hume 178
ought and morality 5–6
oughtness 194–5, 219
Ou Yanggu 7

pain 94, 97
Paley, William 74
parental love 97
Pareto, Vilfredo 72
Pareto criterion 72
Pareto optimum 72
particular morality 12–14
Passmore, John 54, 204
Paulsen, Friedrich 6, 48, 74, 115–16, 161
personal justice 209
personal moral needs 47–9
Petulla, Joseph 202
Pigou, Arthur Cecil 72
Plato 26, 54, 176, 193
pleasure 46, 94–95, 97
Pojman, Louis P. 3, 22, 26
political equality 238–42
political liberty 239
political philosophy 42
political rights 223
politics 38–9
positive emotions 95
positive justice 181
potential principle of contribution 214–18
power 7, 38, 194–5
praise 39
principle of contribution 209–10, *213*, 251–3; actual principle of contribution 210–14; potential principle of contribution 214–18
principle of economic equality 242–4
principle of equality 229–30
principle of equality of opportunity 244–51
principle of full equality 220–4
principle of justice 33
principle of justice in transfer 247
principle of people's sovereignty 239
principle of political equality 238–42
principle of proportional equality 224–28
principle of social justice 253
Pritchard, H. A. 73
private ownership 121–3

problem of moral community 29
procedural departmentalism 190–1
procedural instrumentalism 190–1
procedural justice 185–91; internal value of 187–8; to justice of outcome 188–90
procedural value 187
Prohibition of the Abuse of Livestock Act 202
proportional equality 224–7, 231
proportional equality of non-basic rights 259
prudence 46
psychological egoism 166
psychology 87, 94
public comments 39
public ownership 121–3
punishing others 140
punishment 56
purely harming others 103, 128–30, 138, 142–3, 145, 148, 150–1, 169
purely harm others 145
purely self-harming 138, 143, 145, 149, 169

Qi 162
Qing dynasty 211
quantitative analysis of human nature: degrees of love 111–16; economic man 119–21; law of human nature of the degrees of love 118–23; law of relative quantity of the ends of ethical behavior 116–18; moral perfection, limits of 118–19; non-statistical law of relative quantity of means of ethical behavior 123–4; non-statistical law of relative quantity of types of ethical behavior 127–9; public ownership 121–3; significance of statistical law of relative quantity of means of ethical behavior 126–7; statistical laws of relative quantity of means of ethical behavior 124–6; statistical laws of relative quantity of types of ethical behavior 129–31
quantum of interests 61–4, 70, 76, 122, 139; increasing or decreasing 67; without negatively affecting anyone 69–73
Quotations from Gao Zhi, The (Mencius) 86

Rae, Douglas 245
rational egoism 163–6

Rawls, John 180, 183–4, 188, 193, 195, 199, 227–32, 246–50
realism 26–7
realization of rights 200
reciprocal relationship 32
Regan, Tom 55, 200
relative egalitarianism 259
relative morality 14–17
Rethinking Equality, Fairness and Justice (Yu Keping) 180
retributive justice 181–4
righteousness 4
rightness: as fairness 180; as justice 181
right reason 198–9
rights 195
rights and duties: definitions of 194–7; equality between 193–4; between human and non-human beings 200–5; relationship between 206–10; types of 197–200
rogue hypothesis 120
Rolston III, Holmes 55
Roosevelt, Theodore 253
Ross, W. D. 73
Rousseau, Jean-Jacques 194, 219
ruling of virtue 38, 49
Russell, Bertrand 24, 44–5

sadness 94–5
safeguarding interest community 33–7
Samuelson, Paul Anthony 247
Sartori, Giovanni 218, 230
Schopenhauer, Arthur 181
Schweitzer, Albert 55
science 38
self-abandonment 106
self-benefiting 139
self-confession 106
self-confidence 106
self-fulfillment 46
self-harming 90, 102, 106, 111, 124–5, **138**, 139, 141–3; as an end 104–5, 109, 138, 142; for harming others 93; for self-interest 91, 94, 104, 139, 141–2
self-hatred 105
self-interest 18, 48, 104, 111, 124–6, 128–31, **138**, 140, 142, 144, 155; as an end 104, 109; for benefiting others 92, 138; for harming others **91**, 93, **138**; physical desire 117–18; for self-harming 92
selfless 46
selflessly benefiting others 74, 94, 100–1, 119, 129, 141, 144, 147, 161, 169

self-love 107–9, 113, 140, 155
self-punishment 106, 138, 140
self-realization 203
self-respect 106–9, 140
self-sacrifice 1, 46, 51, 92, 94, 120, 140
self's desires 148
self-sufficiency 64
self-torture 51
sexual desires 89
sexual love 97–8
sexual partner 97–8
Shang dynasty 211
Sher, George 16
Shi Shuo 156
Sidgwick, Henry 7, 26, 65, 74, 76
Singer, Peter 55
Situation Ethics (Flatcher) 22–3
Slote, Michael 73
Smith, Adam 15, 122, 125, 144, 175, 191–2
social activities 37, 42
social behaviors 183
social cooperation 226
social inequalities 225
socialism 258
social justice, theories on 183–4, 209, 251–60; egalitarianism 258–60; theory of contribution 251–3; theory of liberty-justice 254–8; theory of need 253–4
social life 123
social moral needs 37–41
social nature 44–7
social needs of morality 41
social structure 41
social utility 5–7, 39–40
society 42, 124, 182, 191, 211; dynamic structure 40, *40*; social activities 40
Socrates 74, 99
soft-core altruism 120
specific principles of equality 238
Spencer, Herbert 74
standard of greatest interests for the greatest number 68
standard of moral ought 62
standard of net balance of maximum interests 65
statutory rights 197–200
statutory rights and duties 198
stealing 39
Stevenson, Charles L. 24
stubbornness 117
subjectivism 24–5
substance 86

substance of moral value 11
substantive justice 185–91
Su Dongpo 85
Suicides 13
Summers, Robert 187
Sumner, William Graham 20, 24
Sun Yat-sen 38
Symphony No.5 (Beethoven) 221

talents 214–18
Taylor, Paul 20, 30–31, 33, 55
theories on social justice 251–60
theory of contribution 251–3
theory of deontology 73
theory of indirect duty 201
Theory of Justice, A (Rawls) 180–1, 229–38
theory of liberty-justice 254–8
Theory of Moral Sentiments, The (Smith) 175
theory of need 253–4
theory of public choice 119–21
"Thick and black" (Li Zongwu) 115
Three Cardinal Guides 13–14
Three Obediences 13–14
Tilly 74
Tomkins 95
Treatise of Human Nature, A (Hume) 175
Trianosky, Gregory Velazco Y. 73
trolley dilemma 66
truth 159

Ulpianus, Domitius 176
ultimate motivation of ethical behavior 89–90, 94–6, 109–11; hating others, envy, and vengeance 102–4; love and hatred 96–9; loving others, compassion and gratitude 99–102; self-harming as an end 104–7; self-interest as an end 107–9
ultimate standard of morality 69; defined 63; deontology 73–9; net balance of maximum interests 64–9; quantum of interests 61–4; quantum of interests without negatively affecting anyone 69–73; utilitarianism 73–9
ultimate value standard for evaluation 64
universal morality 12–14
unselfishly benefiting others 191
utilitarianism 73–9, 110
utility 86

value 88
vengeance 103
virtue 38, 51, 214–18; and morality 49–52; ruling of 40
virtuous persons 216

Walzer, Michael 253–6
Wang Chong 157
Wang Jie 119
Warnock, G. J. 42, 62
Washington, George 121
wealth-creating management activities 38
Westermarck, Edward 20, 24
will 38
Williams, Bernard 253
Wilson, William Julius 114
Winstanley, Gerrard 253
Wittgenstein, Ludwig 24
Wu Mazi 113
Wundt, Wilhelm 29
Wu Qi 216–17
Wu She 217

Xia dynasty 211
Xiang Yu 217
Xunyue 157
Xunzi 154

Yang Xiong 156–7
Yang Zhu 45, 164–5
Yan Hui 119
Yu Keping 180

Zeng Guofan 248
Zhang Dainian 152, 157, 159
Zhou dynasty 211
Zhu Xi 49